Exploring
Criminology

MACMILLAN CRIMINAL JUSTICE SERIES

Allen/Simonsen: *Corrections in America*, 4th ed.
Bartollas/with Jaeger: *American Criminal Justice*
Binder/Geis/Bruce: *Juvenile Delinquency*
Bottom/Kostanoski: *Security and Loss Control*
Bowker: *Women and Crime in America*
Brantingham/Brantingham: *Patterns in Crime*
Chambliss: *Criminal Law in Action*
Chambliss: *Exploring Criminology*
Chambliss: Harry King: *A Professional Thief's Journey*
Conklin: *Criminology*, 2nd ed.
Hagan: *Research Methods in Criminal Justice and Criminology*
Hudzik/Cordner/Edwards: *Planning in Criminal Justice
    Organizations and Systems*
McCaghy: *Crime in America*, 2nd ed.
Pursley: *Introduction to Criminal Justice*, 4th ed.
Radelet: *Police and the Community*, 4th ed.
Simonsen/Gordon: *Juvenile Justice in America*, 2nd ed.
Smykla: *Community-based Corrections: Principles and Practices*
Smykla: *Probation and Parole*
Swanson/Territo/Taylor: Police Administration, 2nd ed.

Exploring Criminology

William J. Chambliss

The George Washington University

Macmillan Publishing Company
NEW YORK

Picture credits: page 3—Paul DeRienzo; page 27—Arthur Tress/Photo Researchers; page 57—Alon Reininger/Contact/W. Camp & Assoc.; page 93—David Burnett/Contact/W. Camp & Assoc.; page 131—Leslie Wong/Contact/W. Camp & Assoc.; page 151—Angel Franco/Woodfin Camp & Assoc.; page 171—David Burnett/Contact/W. Camp & Assoc.; page 209—Arthur Tress/Photo Researchers; page 231—Jim Anderson/Woodfin Camp & Assoc.; page 251—John Garrett/Woodfin Camp & Assoc.; page 273—Bettye Lane/Photo Researchers; page 299—Mike Maple/Woodfin Camp & Assoc.; page 327—courtesy of New York Public Library/Picture Collection

For Lisa
and the terror of tautologies

Macmillan Publishing Company
866 Third Avenue, New York, New York 10022

Picture research by Yvonne Freund

LIBRARY OF CONGRESS CATALOGING-IN-PUBLICATION DATA

Chambliss, William J.
    Exploring criminology / William J. Chambliss.
      p.   cm.
    Includes indexes.
    ISBN 0-02-320730-2
    1. Crime and criminals.   I. Title.
HV6025.C395   1988   87-16830
364—dc19   CIP

Printing: 3 4 5 6 7   Year: 9 0 1 2 3 4

Preface

When a sculptor creates a figure or a craftsman working in glass or clay creates a pot, the piece sometimes has a flaw in its materials that is indiscernible yet ultimately fatal. The flaw will grow until the piece eventually cracks or breaks apart. Artworks thus invisibly but irreparably flawed suffer, in the language of artists, from an "inherent vice." In the same way, the history of scientific, philosophical, and religious thought is punctuated with examples of theories flawed in such a way that they will inevitably—even if slowly—be disproved by scientific study. This process is important to our understanding of criminology, the scientific study of crime.

This text is a description and evaluation of criminology. To understand this science, we must recognize its problems as well as its achievements. We must become sensitive to any inherent vice in the theoretical and methodological works of criminologists. We will see that criminologists, like all scientists, must continually be alert to flawed beliefs—or theoretical assumptions—that might prevent them from achieving reliable knowledge through scientific inquiry. However, we must remember that reliable knowledge is never established once and for all; it is transitory. Current knowledge that seems immutable may possess an inherent vice, and scientific inquiry may reveal the flaw and thus revolutionize, but not necessarily destroy, current thinking.

For example, not all astronomical assumptions or religious beliefs were undermined by the discovery that the earth was not the center of the universe. Much of the work of astronomers, physicists, and religious thinkers to that time was salvaged even in the face of so fundamental a contradiction to previously held beliefs. So it is with criminology. As knowledge is accumulated, criminology shifts and changes to incorporate the new findings. At times the field even seems to backtrack, as criminologists rediscover ideas or previously established facts that overturn current beliefs.

The search for knowledge involves a series of confrontations and refutations. Science is a series of arguments over how to solve puzzles, and the discovery of facts throws into question previously held beliefs. Arguments then ensue among those who want to salvage the existing beliefs and those who want to replace them with new ones. The day-to-day work of science is an attempt to test established beliefs and to develop new theories that make more sense of the existing knowledge than do previous theories.

People impatient for truth find the ways of science frustrating. Politicians, for example, are rarely satisfied with the gradual accumulation of knowledge; they want a clear-cut, immediate solution to the "crime problem." Reliable knowledge, unfortunately, does not come neatly wrapped in packages. It grows slowly, moving forward by fits and starts. Today we know more than we did 50 or 100 years ago about crime, just as we know more about producing powerful bombs; however, we do not yet know how to solve the problems created by either. In seeking reliable knowledge, criminologists must carefully apply scientific methods of study.

Throughout this text we return to these issues. We analyze contemporary criminological thinking for any tendencies toward the retention of ideas or beliefs that produce inherent vice in the system of thought. We examine commonsense views about crime as well as scientific data and theories to see what needs to be abandoned or retained in our quest for reliable knowledge.

Part I provides the framework for the discussion. Chapter 1 is a collage, a brief consideration of examples of crimes that occur on the streets and in corporate boardrooms, government offices, and homes. By reading this chapter, you can get a feel for the varieties and shapes of criminality. Chapters 2 and 3 go beyond the impressions gleaned from newspaper clippings and sociological descriptions to a systematic evaluation of what data exist about crime; how these facts are gathered; and how politicians, social scientists, the media, and others use this information.

In Part II we explore a variety of theories and empirical facts about crime and the criminal law. Chapter 4 on the criminal law centers on the question, Why do some acts get defined in law as crimes whereas others do not? This chapter contains a discussion of various theories about why and how criminal laws are devised. In Chapter 5 we discuss how to evaluate the soundness, reliability, and usefulness of different theories. Chapters 6 to 10 utilize the principles of the scientific method, as described in Chapter 5, to evaluate the major theoretical traditions of criminology: the biological, psychiatric, social psychological, and sociological paradigms.

In Part III we attempt to move beyond the current paradigms to one that builds upon the strengths and reduces the weaknesses of previous efforts. We provide a general framework in Chapter 11, the specifics of the theory in Chapter 12, and in Chapter 13 an illustration of how the theory can be used to explain a particular type of criminality—that which is organized and perpetuated by government officials.

It is often difficult to study crime with an open mind; myths abound. Criminology, like all science, must debunk these myths. This text can help you view crime more clearly. If, as you read, you build on what you already know, change your mind when your preconceptions are wrong, and discover new ways of looking at crime, the writing of this book will have been worth it, and your foray into criminology will be of lasting value.

Acknowledgments _____

Writing a book is rather like swimming: you put strokes together and somehow stay afloat, but you never really understand exactly how it worked. One facet of writing, however, that every author fully understands is the debt owed to others. The entire manuscript was read and extensively commented on by some of my closest friends and colleagues: Roland Chilton, *University of Massachusetts at Amherst;* Phil Davis, *Georgia State University;* John Galliher, *University of Missouri at Columbia;* Philip Jenkins, *The Pennsylvania State University;* Janet Katz, *Old Dominion University, Norfolk, Virginia;* Raymond J. Michalowski, *University of North Carolina at Charlotte;* and Marjorie Zatz, *Arizona State University*. Their insights, criticisms, and evenhandedness were immensely helpful at every stage of the writing. I cannot possibly thank them enough. Frank Scarpitti read parts of the manuscript, as did Alan Block and Herman Schwendinger. Their observations and suggestions improved the work considerably. I am indebted as well to the students who have taught me so much.

Finally, Claire Blessing, Carole Andersen, Carole Tuchrello, Kathy Russell, Janet Shope, Cheryl Ripetti, and Nelson Kofie worked with support and good humor on the typing, footnoting, and other tedious tasks that accompany the final stages of manuscript preparation. I am forever grateful to them for their help.

W.J.C.

Contents

Chapter 1 Prologue to the Study of Crime   **3**

Matthew Washington Who Had Death in His Eyes   4
Varieties of Crime   6
Rebels in Eden   19
Conclusion   25

Chapter 2 Data on Crime: Part I   **27**

Bias in Official Statistics   29
Victim-Survey Data   32
Self-Report Surveys   43
Cross-Cultural Studies   53
Conclusion   54

Chapter 3 Data on Crime: Part II   **57**

Corruption   57
White-Collar Crime   62
State-Organized Crime   78
Political Crime   81
Organized Crime   86
Professional Theft   89
Conclusion   91

Chapter 4 Criminal Law   **93**

Definition of Behavior as Criminal   93
Criminal and Civil Law   96
Process of Law Creation   99
Crime in Early England   101
Consensus Theory   112

Societal-Needs Theory   113
Ruling-Class Theory   115
Pluralist Theory   120
Structural-Contradictions Theory   120
Racism and Sexism in American Criminal Law   124
Conclusion   129

Chapter 5   Explanation and Description of Criminality   131

Constructing Scientific Theory   132
Conclusion   148

Chapter 6   Criminological Theory: An Overview   151

Historical Sketch of Explanations of Crime   152
Recent Developments in Criminology   158
Conclusion   169

Chapter 7   Biological Paradigms   171
(by Janet Katz and W.J.C.)

Early Studies of Biology and Crime   172
Studies of Intelligence and Crime   192
Current Status of Biological Theory   197
Conclusion   206

Chapter 8   Psychiatric Paradigms   209

Freud and Crime   209
Criminal Mind   227
Conclusion   228

Chapter 9   Social-Psychological Theories   231

Theoretical Developments   234
Conclusion   250

Chapter 10   Sociological Tradition: Normative Paradigms   251

Sociological Paradigms   255
Conclusion   271

Chapter 11   Crime and Social Structure   273

Structural Theories   275
Conclusion   296

Chapter 12   Crime and Structural Contradictions   299

Contradictions and Conflicts   300
Crime in Capitalist Societies   306
Crime in Socialist Societies   321
Conclusion   325

Chapter 13   State-Organized Crime   327

Smuggling   332
State-Organized Assassinations   340
Conspiracies   343
Other Illegal Activities   344
Conclusion   345

Chapter 14   Conclusion   349
References   359
Index   392

Exploring
Criminology

1

Prologue to the Study of Crime

Whether in Los Angeles or Little Rock, Harlem or Amsterdam, Berlin or Boston, it is a familiar story—infinitely varied but always basically the same. Youths go looking for excitement and finally make the excitement they are unable to find. Living in a world that appears to have no place for them, they create a place for themselves that makes sense only to insiders. Resentful of the slights, rejections, and injustices—real and imaginary—to which they have been subjected, they band together to share their bitterness. Cut off from the mainstream of community life, they plunge into one of the eddies that goes against the current or one of the whirlpools that goes only in circles.[1]

Cool and defiant on the outside, they remain scared and uncertain on the inside. Intensely motivated, their purpose is obscure to outsiders. Fiercely independent, they cling to each other. Cursing their insignificance, they talk big. By feel, impulse, and whim, they react to the world as it strikes them. They cannot tell you why they behave as they do; they are as puzzled as anyone else. Pushed by a vague search for escape from desperation, pulled by the longing for something different, they have little comprehension of the forces that shape their own emotions and actions.

They do not revel in delinquency, even when they are getting their kicks. They are not even confident that this is what they want to be doing and sometimes they curse the hurt that it brings. But they go on unless something or someone steps in to stop them. Many wake up as adults with a regular job and a house in the suburbs. Others wake up in prison—wondering whatever happened to the kid who liked popcorn, played baseball, and dreamed about "when I grow up. . . ."

Matthew Washington, Who Had Death in His Eyes _____

A 16-year-old black youth, Matthew Washington, was not looking for excitement, but he found it nonetheless.[2] He had risen at 5:00 A.M. to deliver his papers. He looked forward to the time when he could stop delivering the papers and just go to school: "One more year of this jive and then its all Little Ricky's. And he can have it. So damn sleepy all the time."

Matthew returned home from the paper route at 6:45, gobbled down a breakfast of cold cereal, and left for the school bus that would take him and the other black kids from his neighborhood to a school across town, which was recently integrated in compliance with rulings by the U.S. Supreme Court.

The ride to school was noisy that morning. The driver spoke to no one in particular: "All right, let's knock it off back there or we'll have an accident." There was a moment of relative silence. Then one of the kids spat on a girl sitting across the aisle from his, his saliva "splattering on the side of her neck just under her jaw, sticking there for a moment and slowly draining downward." Matthew Washington was one of several boys who grabbed the assailant, Lester, and pulled him toward the rear of the bus.

Later that day, a crowd gathered in a small courtyard behind the swimming pool on the school's east side. The crowd of young and old, black and white, watched as Lester, "sinewy, defiant, flailing about in a world in which he could find no sense of control or order," attacked Matthew Washington.

> [Matthew] was able to call upon that special reservoir of strength only anger can yield . . . avenging the honor of women . . . in a brand of chivalry that only the young, perhaps, would dare preserve. [The onlookers] stood in a circle around the two combatants, both bloodied and with welts appearing on their faces. Their shirts were ripped open and Lester had a tear in the seat of his pants.

"Oh Jesus God, stop them." People all about were crying and begging the boys to stop. School employees and teachers were rushing out of the four doors that led into the grassy courtyard, where row upon row of tulips were about to open.

> Three young policemen and an older lieutenant literally blasted their way through the crowd, which now numbered almost a hundred persons. When they broke through the last group of teachers and referees—boys who ringed the fighters—Lester's eyes were almost totally closed. His cheeks were cut and his nose smashed up against the right side of his face, broken. Matthew had blood on his head and his clothes. His lower lip was ripped open and dried blood lined his nostrils. He was crying and appeared utterly crazed, a man gone beserk. 'You're dealing with Roscoe's only son,' he kept yelling at Lester, upon whom he now sat, slapping the beaten boy's face with the back of his hand, which was also dripping with blood: 'You're dealin' with Roscoe Washington's only son.'

The police separated the fighters:

> Lester had a cut that ran from behind his ear down the edge of his jaw and stopped somewhere near his chin. Through a hole in his face you could see a white tooth protruding. Matthew walked by

proud and tough. He offered no objections to the two white police-men who held his arms, half supporting him, half imprisoning him.

The audience lingered after the boys were taken away. One teacher commented "who really cares, let the blacks kill each other off," which prompted another teacher to curse and shove him. Matthew and Lester were taken to jail, booked, and released. Another statistic on the police blotter; another record to be called up at a later date if either were ever arrested again. Another fact to be used as evidence by social workers and court officials making a decision as to whether to jail, bail, or release on probation a boy arrested for assault, attempted robbery, or the possession of an illegal substance.

Varieties of Crime

In this chapter, we are going to describe a wide variety of different types of behaviors that share the fact that they are legally prohibited and may be punished by imprisonment. We are not going to put them into categories or analyze them at this point. The goal of this chapter is to give a sense of the types of acts that comprise the subject matter of criminology.

Big-city newspapers and magazines are a source of reports on different types of crime that can give us a picture of criminality in the modern world. On Tuesday, May 13, 1986, the *New York Times* reported that

- A Wall Street broker was charged with using confidential information illegally in several stock-trading schemes that netted him at least $12.5 million in profits.
- A physician was mortally wounded by a stranger who approached him while he was sunbathing on the grass in a park and stabbed him in the chest with a kitchen knife. The physician managed to write down the license-plate number of the assailant before he died. A 37-year-old man with a history of mental illness was arrested and accused of committing the crime.
- Borough President Stanley Simon of the Bronx was asked to testify before a grand jury investigating corruption and payoffs to city officials and politicians.
- A federal prosecutor outlined the way racketeering in local moving and storage industries forced companies to give pay-

offs to a teamsters local union to assure labor peace and enable companies to rig bids on contracts. These activities, it was alleged, were controlled by an organized-crime family headed by Joe Bonanno.

- A 19-year-old Brooklyn man was arrested for the murder of a Roman Catholic priest. The priest was found dead from two gunshot wounds to his chest, heart, and lungs. The defendant pleaded not guilty but told the police that the priest had approached him on the street and solicited him for a paid sexual encounter.

A resident of Georgia, Michael Hardwick, was arrested in his home for committing sodomy. A police officer found Mr. Hardwick and another man engaged in oral sex. This case will be discussed further in Chapter 2.

On January 19, 1985, an 83-year-old woman was released from jail in New York City. She was paroled after serving 1 year of a 3-year sentence for selling $25.00 worth of marijuana to a friend.

In 1983, over 40 birth-control and abortion clinics were bombed in the United States, with property losses of hundreds of thousands of dollars. That same year, Secretary of Labor Raymond J. Donovan took a leave of absence and later resigned from his cabinet post to defend himself against criminal charges filed in federal court alleging that Secretary Donovan committed larceny and fraud when he was an officer of the Chiavone Construction Company of Secaucus, New Jersey—a company allegedly affiliated with organized crime. Secretary Donovan was found not guilty of the charges.

Bernhard Hugo Goetz, a white commuter on the New York subway, was approached by four black youths who asked him if he had 5 dollars. Mr. Goetz pulled a revolver from his pocket and shot each of the youths, three of them in the back, as they tried to run away. Mr. Goetz was arrested and charged with attempted murder. A jury of his peers found Mr. Goetz not guilty of attempted murder. Earlier he was found guilty of illegally possessing a weapon.

When the news of the Goetz shooting appeared in newspapers, New York State Senator Alphonse D'Amato said that he was afraid to get into the subway system even with a body guard. Another subway rider, John Coleman, suggested that Senator D'Amato may have over-reacted:

In the month of January 1986 there were 38 felonies in the New York Transit System. There were millions of passengers carried every

Vigilantism. *(Jeffrey D. Smith/Woodfin Camp & Assoc.)*

day of the week. I ride that subway nearly every day of the year. I have yet to see a single bit of what he [D'Amato] is talking about.[3]

High schools in the United States are the scene of a great deal of crime. Youths hanging around together take drugs, buy and consume alcohol, steal, fight, vandalize property, avoid school, drive while under the influence of alcohol, and generally "raise hell." Observations conducted over a 2-year period in one high school provided a detailed description of two delinquent gangs in a middle-sized town. The boys in these gangs ranged in age from 15–19 years old. They engaged in a wide variety of delinquent acts ranging from petty theft to aggravated assault. The sociologist-observer named the gangs the Roughnecks and the Saints to underscore the way the gangs were viewed by teachers and members of the community. The Roughnecks were a lower-class gang who frequently engaged in petty theft, fighting, public intoxication, and verbal abuse. They were seen by school officials, police, and other members of the community as "boys heading for trouble" and "up to no good." The Saints were a middle-class gang engaged in delinquency and crime that was equally serious, but they were perceived as "good boys" who were only "sowing their wild oats." The Saints sowed their wild oats by being constantly truant from school, harassing shop owners and strangers (especially women), driving while intoxicated, vandalizing public and private property, and stealing gasoline. The Roughnecks were frequently arrested and booked, and some were sent to reform school. The Saints were rarely caught in their delinquencies; when they were, they were given a warning and sent home. As adults, several of the Roughnecks were sentenced to prison for felonies; most of the Saints went to college, and none was ever sentenced to jail or prison.[4]

An 18-year-old farm boy from Indiana was sentenced to prison for driving a car used in a robbery. He wrote the following letter to his friends Pat and John Liell:

Dear Pat:

Hi Pat and John. I hope you and the kids are all o.k. I'm OK, all except for the big walls around me. Pat, I should be coming back to Bloomington this week or next, so Reta and I can get married. I don't know if I ever told you this or not but right now she is seven months, two weeks pregnant and we are going to get married while I'm here so the baby can have my name. Pat, I miss my hunten most of all. Pat, I wish I could be standing under a big oak tree wateing for a squrel to come out in stead of wateing for these walls to move. Pat, I was laying here thinking about the last few days I had of freedom, they where in the woods that I love and around the people I love. Pat, I only got to 16 squerrls this year. But when I get out, I sure will make up for the ones that got away. I only have 9 more months before I go home. Pat, ask Johnny if he wants to be my best man when they bring me back to get married. Pat, sometimes I lay in my cell and I feel like crying when I think about the things I like and the people I love. I hope you all have a happy thanksgiving. Pat, there is a few of my friends up here that never gets interviews or litters and if you could, I would apursate it if you could get someone to write them. Course, I know what its like not to get any letters or visits. Pat, I can't think of anything else to write so I guess I will say good-bye for now. Write soon. Pat, I bet you thought I would forget you all, didn't you? But I never.

Your Lovin Friend,

Ricky

Allen Kearbey, a 14-year-old ninth grader in Goodard, Kansas, walked to school on January 20, 1985, carrying an automatic rifle and a .357-caliber revolver. When the principal of the high school asked him why he was carrying a rifle, the youth shot the principal in the chest. He shot three other people as he ran out of the school. The principal died. Allen Kearbey was described by acquaintances and teachers as a loner. He was considered quiet and inoffensive with no prior record of delinquency or crime.

Criminology seeks to explain why some people who engage in crime are arrested and sentenced to prison while others are not. Criminology also tries to explain why some people who engage in crime spend their lives as adults engaging in criminality while others do not. Very few young people, for example, whatever their social-class background or their involvement in delinquency, continue lives of crime when they grow up. Indeed, one of the facts discovered by criminologists is that youths who engage in crime and delinquency tend to grow out of these activities by the time they are in their mid-twenties.[5]

Please forgive me
Always running away
Taking my sweet time
Running with bad people
In trouble
Can't control myself
I snatch bags
Always starting fights

Sign in home for runaway girls, N.Y.C. *(Ed Lettau, Photo Researchers)*

Professional Thieves

Some few people, however, grow up to become professional thieves. There is a burgeoning literature on professional thieves that shows strikingly similar patterns in every society. Those few who join the society of professional crime spend their lives in a world of prisons, prostitutes, racketeers, corrupt policemen and judges, and lawyers who specialize in "the fix."[6]

Harry King was a professional thief. His specialty was opening safes; among professional thieves, safecrackers are known as "box-men." Harry was one of the best. He enjoyed his life of crime and accepted prison sentences when they came as "the price you pay." Harry would spend twenty thousand dollars on a weekend in Las Vegas; buy his current girlfriend a house, and pay cash for it; wear expensive suits; and lavish money on friends and strangers alike. The money came from grocery stores, banks, and restaurants. If he were arrested, he was well-enough known by attorneys and bail-bondsmen that they would get him out of jail. If he did not have any money at the time of his arrest, he would immediately go out and commit another "caper" to get the ten or twenty thousand dollars needed to pay the bondsman, his lawyer, and whatever bribes needed to be paid to judges and prosecutors to have the case "fixed."[7]

In 1975, a group of professional thieves broke into Milan's Gallery of Modern Art one morning and stole 28 paintings. The theft included well-known works by Cezanne, Gaugin, Renoir, Van Gogh, and other masters of the 19th and early 20th centuries. Experts estimated that the stolen paintings were worth over $5 million. Only 11 days before the Milan theft, three priceless Renaissance paintings—one by Raphael and two by Francesco—were stolen from the National Museum in Urbino in a similar night-time burglary.[8] These paintings were never recovered. Thieves capable of conducting such thefts are rarely art lovers who would risk long prison sentences for the pleasure of having the paintings hanging in their homes. Most often, thefts such as this are done on "commission." A wealthy person lets it be known that he or she wants to have the paintings; thieves are hired and deliver the paintings for a fee. The paintings then hang in locked basements or rooms in mansions of the rich where they are shown to only a select few.

Another type of theft is depicted in the following article from the *International Herald Tribune* of March 20, 1975:

> Three thieves, using a confidence trick, got away with more than
> $500,000 in jewels from Christie's, the London fine arts auctioneers,
> Scotland Yard said today.
>
> A police spokesman said the men went to Christie's March 23 for
> a sale of items listed as 'magnificent jewels.' The men all made bids
> and secured three lots of gems valued at $585,600.
>
> After the auction, the buyers presented forged Christie's receipts,
> collected the jewels and vanished.
>
> 'We have had only vague descriptions of these thieves,' a Scotland
> Yard spokesman said.[9]

The many faces of crime are so varied as to defy complete description. Trying to capture the varieties of crime is like trying to
draw a map of the world. If the map has all the details on it, it is
as large as the world and worthless as a map. If it leaves out all
the rivers and mountains, roads and alleys, it is compact but does
not tell us enough to give us a sense of where we are or where we
are going. So we settle in maps, and in our descriptions of crime,
for efforts that glean the varieties without overwhelming us with
endless descriptions.

State Crime

Sometimes crime involves the institutionalization of state policies. Such was the case in Norway in the 1940s, when a group of
bearded, shabby, somewhat sickly people were brought to a small
port in the northern part of the country. These people were citizens of Yugoslavia who had been captured by the Germans and
brought to Norway. When they arrived at the beach, German soldiers and Norwegian citizens beat them with sticks and stung them
with bayonets. Over 2,500 Yugoslavs were forced into trucks with
barbed-wire nets to keep them from escaping. They were then
transported to nearby camps, where they were held prisoner. One
year later, over 1,700 of these people were dead from hunger, disease, ill-treatment, and execution. Thirty years after the end of
World War II, 17 of the Norwegian citizens who worked as guards
or in other capacities in the camps were punished by Norwegian
courts for the crimes of manslaughter and ill-treatment of prisoners.[10]

Throughout Europe, similar acts of genocide, murder, and political persecution took place from 1930–1945. Over 6 million Jews
and over 12 million people of all religious, ethnic, and national
identities were killed in concentration camps run by German sol-

diers with the complicity and cooperation of people from other European countries. After the war, some soldiers and civilians were tried and punished.

Drugs

In most nations of the world, it is illegal to possess or use a wide variety of drugs: heroin, morphine, marijuana, cocaine, and a host of pharmaceuticals. Despite the legal restrictions on the distribution and use of drugs, their consumption is widespread. A heroin addict, Judy, describes her experiences and her drug habit like this:

> I think a girl's problems are always different from a guy's. Girls are brought up differently. They are taught to be ashamed of almost everything they do.
>
> I remember when I first made it with my boyfriend. I felt terrible. I didn't want anyone to know. It was the most secret part of my life. I was torn because to feel part of the group I had to have a boyfriend. But everything that went on with us had to be kept secret.
>
> I had to be dishonest to survive. I made my mother spend a lot of money on clothes. Everything had to be perfect on the outside. Inside I felt terrible. I was always scared and ashamed. That's what I liked about drugs. They made me feel like there was nothing wrong. Just like the other kids. By the time I was sixteen I was doing a lot of speed and LSD. A year later I started doing heroin.
>
> I was lucky that I didn't have to be a prostitute or anything like that. Mostly, I let people use my apartment to get off. In return they'd give me some drugs. Most girls are controlled by their addict boyfriends. They either become prostitutes or are used to cash bad checks. The guy usually keeps most of the money.
>
> No one can keep their respect living that way. Not knowing who you are going to wake up next to or anything. Everyone lying and stealing. One of my best friends even died in my apartment, and I was too stoned to realize it.
>
> You feel so bad that your appearance goes way down. All you care about is getting high. Controlled and manipulated not only by junk but by male junkies. You feel completely rotten. That was my life for two years.[11]

A young man, Michael, described the effects of heroin use this way:

> Yes, under its ecstatic influence, one is made oblivious to ugly realities. But there is a trick, a cruel monstrous trick, a deadly flim-

flam awaiting its naive, youthful victim, for as the illusionary beauty of the heroin-induced high begins to vanish, correspondingly, the temporary immunity from reality attained under its chemical trance vanishes. The reality that the pathetic victim sought so desperately to escape, once again descends upon and re-engulfs him. The rancid stench of urine-soaked tenement dungeons begins to assail his nostrils. Those black cries of anguish seem to blend with the wailing sirens of pig-police cars. He hears them now, very loud and very clear—in stereophonic sound. And that garbage that flows over into the streets from uncollected trash cans is felt underfoot. . . . Whatever he must do for a 'shot' he will do, he must do, for he is a slave to the plague.[12]

White-Collar Crime

Allen Dorfman, an official with the Teamsters union and a millionaire Chicago businessman, was shot and killed in a car park in Chicago in 1983. One of his business associates, Roy Williams, was later elected president of the Teamsters union. Mr. Williams was soon tried and found guilty of misusing Teamsters funds. The Chicago police believe that Mr. Dorfman was killed to keep him from giving information to the police. Another associate of Mr. Dorfman was the Chicago mobster and reputed Mafia boss, Sam Giancana. Giancana was a major figure in the organization of the rackets: illegal gambling, prostitution, drug smuggling, land frauds, and so forth. During the presidency of John F. Kennedy, Giancana, along with several other mobsters, worked with the CIA in a plot to assassinate Cuban President Fidel Castro. The plot to assassinate Castro failed, but someone else succeeded in murdering Giancana in his kitchen early one morning when he was opening his refrigerator. His death occurred only days before he was to testify before a Senate committee investigating the assassination of President John F. Kennedy. According to a night-club singer in Jack Ruby's Dallas bar, Sam Giancana refused to go along with a plan to assassinate President Kennedy that involved Jack Ruby and Lee Harvey Oswald.

R. Foster Winans was a successful journalist writing for one of America's most prestigious newspapers, the *Wall Street Journal*. Mr. Winans was arrested and prosecuted in 1986 for "insider trading." The Securities and Exchange Commission is responsible for enforcing regulations governing the exchange of stocks, securities, and bonds. Mr. Winans—along with a clerk at the *Wall Street Journal* and Kenneth P. Felix, a stockbroker with Kidder, Peabody and Company—was charged with conspiracy, securities fraud,

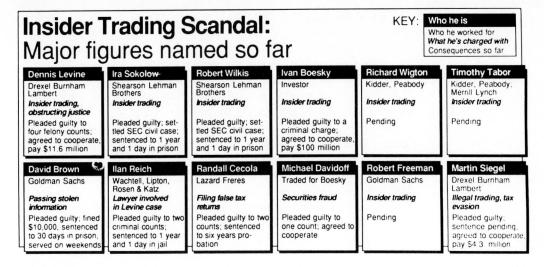

Insider Trading Scandal:
Major figures named so far

KEY:
Who he is
Who he worked for
What he's charged with
Consequences so far

Dennis Levine	Ira Sokolow	Robert Wilkis	Ivan Boesky	Richard Wigton	Timothy Tabor
Drexel Burnham Lambert	Shearson Lehman Brothers	Shearson Lehman Brothers	Investor	Kidder, Peabody	Kidder, Peabody; Merrill Lynch
Insider trading, obstructing justice	*Insider trading*	*Insider trading*	*Insider trading*	*Insider trading*	*Insider trading*
Pleaded guilty to four felony counts; agreed to cooperate, pay $11.6 million	Pleaded guilty; settled SEC civil case; sentenced to 1 year and 1 day in prison	Pleaded guilty; settled SEC civil case; sentenced to 1 year and 1 day in prison	Pleaded guilty to a criminal charge; agreed to cooperate, pay $100 million	Pending	Pending

David Brown	Ilan Reich	Randall Cecola	Michael Davidoff	Robert Freeman	Martin Siegel
Goldman Sachs	Wachtell, Lipton, Rosen & Katz	Lazard Freres	Traded for Boesky	Goldman Sachs	Drexel Burnham Lambert
Passing stolen information	*Lawyer involved in Levine case*	*Filing false tax returns*	*Securities fraud*	*Insider trading*	*Illegal trading, tax evasion*
Pleaded guilty; fined $10,000, sentenced to 30 days in prison, served on weekends	Pleaded guilty to two criminal counts; sentenced to 1 year and 1 day in jail	Pleaded guilty to two counts; sentenced to six years probation	Pleaded guilty to one count; agreed to cooperate	Pending	Pleaded guilty; sentence pending, agreed to cooperate, pay $4.3 million

White-collar crime. (AP/Pat Lyons)

and mail and wire fraud. It is a crime for anyone who, by virtue of his or her position in a company, takes advantage of knowledge gained because of that position to profit from stock transactions before the knowledge is made public. The prosecutor alleged that

> Mr. Winans knew the information would influence the stock market and was passing it on specifically so that others could trade on the knowledge and make a profit after the information appeared in the newspaper.[13]

John DeLorean, a former vice president of General Motors and founder of the DeLorean Car Company in Belfast, Northern Ireland, was arrested and charged with conspiracy to import $25 million worth of cocaine. His trial ended in his acquittal when the jury decided that the FBI had entrapped him.

On August 3, 1983, the trustees of Chemical Bank in Seattle, Washington, filed suit charging the Washington Public Power Supply System with fraud and negligence in issuing $2.25 billion in bonds to finance two cancelled nuclear-power plants.

Sometimes for profit, sometimes out of principle, people in highly respected professions commit criminal acts. Where abortions are illegal as determined by state law, medical doctors may find themselves making difficult decisions:

Dr. Kenneth Edelin convicted of manslaughter in the death of a fetus he aborted, was sentenced today to a year's probation. Judge James McGuire of Suffolk County Superior Court said that the sentence would be stayed pending appeal.

Dr. Edelin, 36, although calling the sentence "extremely fair," said that his appeal would be filed late today against the conviction handed down by a jury after a six-week trial.

His lawyer, William Homans, said that the appeal would be based in part on the due-process legal guarantee in the U.S. Constitution's 14th Amendment. The attorney said that he will question whether Dr. Edelin was convicted of an act which, prior to his indictment, had not been defined as a crime.

After the prosecutor failed to recommend a sentence, the defense counsel asked the judge for leniency because "Dr. Edelin is not an individual who has any violence in his heart.[14]

Even for the vast majority of people who escape serious involvement with the law (regardless of how much crime they may engage in their youth), adulthood may well hold a career in which criminality is part and parcel of the way of life. Those who go to a university and ultimately join the world of commerce and industry may escape the label "criminal" or the trauma of having the long arm of the law around their neck, but that does not guarantee their lives will be free from criminal acts. For some, committing criminal acts will become an integral part of their economic and personal lives.

For example, executives of Braniff and Texas International Airlines conspired in the 1970s to monopolize business among airports in Dallas–Fort Worth, Houston, and San Antonio, Texas.

A federal grand jury today indicted Braniff Airways and Texas International Airlines on charges of conspiring to monopolize business among the airports at Dallas–Fort Worth, Houston and San Antonio.

The indictment, returned in U.S. District Court in San Antonio and announced by the Justice Department, accused the two companies of attempting to exclude Southwest Airlines from operating at airports in the metropolitan areas.

Braniff and Texas International were accused of attempting to delay Southwest's entry into the market and increase its costs. The companies exchanged information, schedules and fares to step up the competitive pressures against Southwest and undertook a boycott of Southwest by preventing passengers from cancelled flights to switch to Southwest flights, the indictment said.[15]

Another example from an almost endless number of cases that could be cited comes from Washington, D.C.:

> Five Midwest meat-packing firms have been charged with using unfair business practices, including "commercial bribery," in promoting sales to several food distributors in Kansas, Texas, and California, the Agriculture Department announced yesterday.
>
> Officials said the firms have the right to a hearing on the complaints filed by the department's Packers & Stockyards Administration (PSA). If the charges are sustained in the hearings, the companies could be placed under a "cease-and-desist" order forbidding them to continue illegal practices, officials said.
>
> In addition to bribery, charges include an allegation that the Dold firm paid discriminatory advertising allowances and that several of the firms involved made illegal brokerage payments to induce employees of food buyers to place orders with the packers.
>
> Officials said the bribery charges involved payments made to several employees—and wives, in some cases—of three firms. They are the Fleming Co., a wholesale food dealer in Topeka, Kansas; Affiliated Food Stores of Dallas, Texas; and Market Basket of Los Angeles, a division of the Kroger Company of Cincinnati.[16]

Some college graduates who become business people will knowingly violate existing laws governing health and safety standards for workers. They thereby contribute to the severe health problems from work-related illness and injury experienced by 2.5 million people in the United States every year. They may even be responsible for some of the deaths of over 100,000 people killed each year by accidents or illnesses resulting from work.

Some children of the modern era will commit a wide variety of crimes, both while they are young and on into adulthood. Some will become regular users of illegal substances: marijuana, cocaine, and unprescribed amphetamines. A few will become addicted to heroin. Child molesting, child beating, wife beating, and assault will not be uncommon experiences for future generations.

Politics and Crime

If their lives lead them into politics or law enforcement, these people may join the endless list of politicians and law enforcers whose lives are riddled with the criminality of corruption, bribes, payoffs, and, for a few, even murder. In any given year, even a casual reading of the newspaper reveals an amazing number of exposés of bribery and corruption in government. Recent years bear witness to the ubiquitous nature of this phenomenon as we have seen the governors of Florida, Ohio, Oklahoma, Maryland, Illinois, and West Virginia, and even the Vice President of the United States, forced to resign because of bribery and corruption. Entire police forces are exposed as being involved with a wide range of criminal activities from organizing gambling and selling drugs to burglaries, murder, and illegal beating of citizens. Recently, Philadelphia joined a long line of city police departments wracked by scandals and deeply rooted, wide-ranging corruption.

In the early 1970s, the United States witnessed one of the most far-reaching political scandals in its history: the "Watergate affair," which began with the break-in of the Democratic Party election headquarters in the Watergate Hotel in Washington, D.C., and ended with the exposure of criminal acts by the highest-ranking people in the federal government:

> In the entire cast of Watergate characters, none had posed so serenely above the mess as Maurice Stans. Although he headed Richard Nixon's campaign-finance committee in 1972, Stans blithely professed no knowledge of the illegal Watergate activities that the money had financed, which led Chairman Sam Ervin of the Senate Watergate Committee to ask in frustration: 'Can you explain to a simple-minded man like me the mental processes by which you can determine how much money ought to be spent for a particular project unless you know what the project is?' Replied Stans coolly: 'Mr. Chairman, there is no yardstick by which you judge the necessities of a political campaign.'[17]

Stans admitted failing to report two contributions ($30,000 from Ernesto Lagdameo, former Philippine Ambassador to the United States, and $39,000 from former Montana Governor Tim Babcock) and the disbursement of $81,000 to Frederick C. LaRue, a Nixon re-election committee aide who arranged some of the payments to the arrested Watergate burglars, and having accepted two illegal corporate contributions ($40,000 from Goodyear Tire & Rubber Company and $30,000 from Minnesota Mining and Manufacturing Company). For each violation, Stans could have been sentenced to a maximum of 1 year in prison and a $1,000 fine.

At one point during the Watergate hearings, Stans pleaded with the Watergate Committee to "give me back my good name." Instead, Stans joined other Nixon cabinet members and political associates whose "good names" were tainted as they were convicted of crimes: former Attorney Generals John Mitchell and Richard Kleindienst; and oil heir Frederick LaRue, who admitted taking part in the payoffs to the burglars and, in so doing, implicated Nixon's staff members H. R. Haldeman, John Ehrlichman, and Robert Mardian. LaRue was sentenced to jail along with Ehrlichman, Mitchell, Haldeman, Kleindienst, Mardian, John Dean, and the burglars.[18]

A Florida senator, Edward J. Gurney, who was one of President Nixon's principal defenders during the Watergate hearings, was prosecuted in an alleged political-extortion racket. A 2-year investigation by the *Miami Herald* culminated in a Justice Department investigation and the convening of a Miami grand jury to hear charges that:

> a sometime associate, assertedly acting for Gurney, extracted kickbacks totaling at least $300,000 from builders seeking lucrative contracts from Gurney appointees to the Federal Housing Administration. . . . A Miami contractor, John J. Pirestes, has told investigators that Williams and FHA administrator William Peleski, appointed under Gurney's sponsorship, extracted $170,000 in cash from him in return for lucrative Federal contracts in South Miami. The *Herald* reported last week that payoffs from government contractors went into a secret 'Gurney Boosters Fund' set up in 1971 to pay the senator's office and travel expenses.[19]

Rebels in Eden _____

Not all criminality is the result of individuals seeking personal gain or acting violently toward others. Some criminality is politically motivated as an expression of discontent. Indeed, the history of the United States is replete with the criminality of disenfranchised peoples—including workers, minorities, women, and farmers—at different times in the nation's history. In the late 1960s and early 1970s, riots and rebellions broke out in ghettos and slums in most major American cities.

> Riot police were called to quell disorders in a Washington slum today after a white policeman shot two Negro women, one of whom reportedly had chased him with a butcher knife. Helmeted members of the city's Civil Disturbance Unit used tear gas to clear a 10-block section of 14th Street N.W. when crowds, angered by the shootings,

began stoning passing cars occupied by whites. Some of the whites were dragged from their cars and beaten, and three cars were burned at widely separated intersections. The heavily Negro neighborhood is the same one that was virtually destroyed as a commercial center during the riots that followed the assassination of the Reverend Dr. Martin Luther King, Jr., in April.

Just three weeks ago, on October 9, rioters set fire to one building and broke several windows after a white policeman shot and killed a man he had stopped for jaywalking.

The police said the officer who fired the shots today was driving down 14th Street when a woman ran up to his car and told him of a 'crazy woman' on a nearby street.

An eyewitness, who gave his name but asked that it not be used, said the woman was a middle-aged neighborhood figure. He said she was on a brick porch at the corner of 14th and Euclid, shouting and waving a butcher knife.

A young woman, described by onlookers as the woman's daughter, met the policeman near a set of steps leading to the porch, the witness said, and told him not to bother the woman—that she had never hurt anyone.

The policeman headed up the stairs, the witness said, but stopped and pulled his gun and began to back up when the woman came at him waving the knife.

'I'm going to shoot you,' the police quoted him as saying. 'Go ahead and shoot,' they said she replied, still advancing.

The witness said the policeman retreated into the street and fired two shots, one of which hit a woman bystander, before he tripped over a traffic island and fell on his back against a car.

The police said he fired several shots when he stumbled, and one bullet hit the bystander in the chest.

Both versions agree that, after he fell, the woman kept coming, and was shot in the abdomen. Both women were taken to Washington Hospital Center.[20]

Corruption runs amuck in U.S. police departments and has for as long as records have been kept. Recently the Philadelphia police were wracked with scandal and, in Kentucky, an entire county government was found to be riddled with corruption. In the fall of 1970, one of the largest police-corruption cases in U.S. history was documented in the Knapp Commission Report:

We found corruption in the police department to be widespread. It took various forms depending upon the activity involved, appearing at its most sophisticated among plainsclothesmen assigned to enforce gambling laws. In the five plainclothes divisions where our investigations were concentrated, we found a strikingly standard-ized pattern of corruption. Plainclothesmen, participating in what is known in police parlance as a 'pad,' collected regular bi-weekly or monthly payments amounting to as much as $3,500 from each of the gambling establishments in the area under their jurisdiction, and divided the take in equal shares. The monthly share per man (called the 'nut') ranged from $300 to $400 in midtown Manhattan to $1,500 in Harlem. When supervisors were involved, they received a share and a half. A newly assigned plainclothesman was not en-titled to his share for about two months, while he was checked out for reliability, but the earnings lost by the delay were made up to him in the form of two months' severance pay when he left the di-vision.

Evidence before us led to the conclusion that the same pattern existed in the remaining divisions which we did not investigate in depth. This conclusion was confirmed by events occurring before and after the period of our investigation. Prior to the Commission's ex-istence, exposures by former plainclothesman Frank Serpico had led to indictments or departmental charges against nineteen plain-clothesmen in a Bronx division for involvement in a pad where the nut was $800. After our public hearings had been completed, an investigation conducted by the Kings County District Attorney and the Department's Internal Affairs Division—which investigation neither the Commission nor its staff had ever known about—re-sulted in indictments and charges against thirty-seven Brooklyn plainclothesmen who had participated in a pad with a nut of $1,200. The manner of operation of the pad involved in each of these situa-tions was in every detail identical to that described at the Commis-sion hearings, and in each, almost every plainclothesman in the di-vision, including supervisory lieutenants, was implicated.

Corruption in narcotics enforcement lacked the organization of the gambling pads, but individual payments—known as 'scores'—were commonly received and could be staggering in amount. Our inves-tigation, a concurrent probe by the State Investigation Commission, and prosecutions by federal and local authorities all revealed a pat-tern whereby corrupt officers customarily collected scores in sub-stantial amounts from narcotics violators.[21]

Political Criminality

Those drawn into active political participation may find them-selves outside the law and defined as terrorists or subversives for standing up for what they believe to be their rights.

A bomb exploded today in a tavern frequented by Roman Catholics (in Belfast, Northern Ireland) injuring 14 persons, police reported. Earlier, a 19-year-old Catholic working on a construction site was shot to death.

Police said the bomb, for which no warning was given, went off in the Starr Plough Bar, run by James O'Kane, a Republican who had been detained by Northern Irish authorities as a suspected terrorist. The bar was severely damaged. Residents in the Catholic New Lodge area searched through the rubble to help rescue the injured, some of whom were reported to be in 'serious' condition.

Police declined to speculate on the motive for the bombing attack. Observers theorized that the bomb was planted by extremist Protestants determined to wreck the cease-fire declared by the outlawed Irish Republican Army on February 10.

Earlier, Hugh Ferguson was shot by a gunman on a construction site in Belfast's Catholic Whiterock district. He was shot in the head, chest and legs and died in a hospital.

A stray bullet wounded a three-year-old boy.

The killing was the second in 24 hours. Some security officials thought Mr. Ferguson might have been the victim of an internal struggle in the Marxist official wing of the outlawed IRA.

James Breen, 45, a Catholic freelance photographer, was shot to death yesterday in Lurgan, County Armagh.[22]

Crimes of Status

Then there are those who opt-out: the derelicts, skid-row bums, bag ladies, winos, druggies, street people, and homeless men and women whose lives on the fringe of commerce and society often invoke legal repression. An alcoholic inhabiting Seattle's skid row tells us:

Well, I was pinched last Friday and they threw me in the drunk tank where I stayed until court time this morning. These Seattle police put you in the foam rubber drunk tank for maybe two-and-a-half to three hours. After that, on the weekends when there is no court, they put you in the cement tank. No beds or blankets. Sixty to seventy men in one of those tanks that was meant to hold maybe thirty-five. Some of those tramps were sick and going into DT's [delirium tremens] and the bulls [police officers] just ignored them— sometimes as long as thirty minutes. I don't know if they are lazy or just too mean to help a sick man. The general consensus amongst the jail population is that this is the hungriest jail in the country— even the southern jails give of quantity if not quality. All seems to revolve around the pleasure-pain process. But why penalize the homeless, tortured, the ill? I reiterate, and Jim, you're aware that in truth, none of us were slapped for being exuberant, jocuse, morose, bellicose, or comatose, but because of lack of a lousy $20 bail. My own stand is that booze has been with us as long as the 'oldest profession.' Since humanism is being back-seated (not without a struggle), money is what's respected!

I was surprised when they booked me, relieved me of my property, but no property slip or receipt was forthcoming. One of the few jails I've even been in where that happened. I had no bread so it didn't matter but others lost all they had. Jim, here's a random thought— I'm not a cop hater, strangely enough I get along swell with guys like Anderson and most, it's just that arrogance and Mickey Mouse vindictiveness irritates the hell out of me—especially when a dozen or more tell me they've been robbed by the same. In my career I've been robbed exactly six times—twice by guys I toasted and aided, the others by the police in Oakland, Los Angeles, San Francisco, and Minneapolis. A drunk is always a pigeon to all who trade on his weakness.[23]

For those who join the mainstream of commerce and society, there are other traps and hazards that may lead to criminal activities.

Kenny Butler was driving his truck by an alley where some girls were playing. He stopped his truck to make a delivery at a jewelry store near the alley. After delivering his parcel, Kenny stopped for a moment to watch the girls playing. His mind wandered for a moment and he found himself thinking of the unsatisfactory sex he had with his wife the night before. The next thing Kenny remembered was standing in front of the girls with his pants unzipped, displaying himself. Kenny had been 'in trouble with the police' before but this was the first time he has been arrested for 'flag waving' (as the prison inmates call it), or, in the language of the law, exhibitionism. For a previous offense of armed robbery, Kenny was put on parole. For this offense, Kenny served six years in state prisons and mental hospitals.[24]

Organized Murder

Kenny's act, like many other criminal acts, was spontaneous and idiosyncratic. Other forms of criminality are highly organized. An enforcer for a criminal syndicate, "Joey" tells the following in his autobiography:

Every member of organized crime is capable of doing many different things, but each is an expert in at least one area. Some guys are great gamblers. Others are super hijackers. Me? I kill people.

My official title is 'hit man,' but I guess you could think of me as a policeman. The Mob has its own social structure and we have to deal with our own internal problems. Let's face it, we don't have any place where we can sue somebody. I don't even call it murder. To me, it's just a job.

Actually, you might say crime is the family business. I grew up watching my father shuttle in and out of prison. That was when I learned that crime pays, no matter what anybody tells you. When my father was home, he made good money and we lived very well; when he was in jail, we barely survived. A lot of people today, they blame a person's background for everything he does wrong. That's bullshit. My cousin grew up in exactly the same environment I did and today, he's a cop. We both knew exactly what we were doing. He picked one way, I picked the other. But when I made the choice, I knew exactly what I was getting into, and I knew what I was getting out of.

My total is 38, 35 for money and three for revenge. I can remember each man that I hit. I can give you the order, the details, even the weather on that day. And I would not make a mistake. Number 18, for example, was a gambler who was discovered informing on the Mob. He had quietly been arrested and made a deal in order to keep himself out of a jackpot—which is our word for a jam. Certain things began to kick back and some people checked and found out my man was the source, so he had to go. I caught him in a small bar and I just walked in and blasted him with a .38. It was dark and I was wearing very nondescript clothing and that was it. I remember him. I remember them all. You never really forget.

But it doesn't bother me, not one bit. This is my job. It is my business. I shoot people and that's it. I never think of it in terms of mortality, although that may be hard for a lot of people to believe. I know the difference between right and wrong. And I know by most standards of morality that what I do would be considered wrong. But this doesn't bother me. I also know the difference between eating and starving, between having a pair of new shoes and a pair you have to stuff newspaper in just to keep from freezing. Believe me, I know.[25]

Mercy Killing

On November 11, 1973, a *New York Times* reporter wrote about a mercy-killing trial in New Jersey. The trial was of a 23-year-old man who had shot and killed his older brother: " 'I am here to end your pain George, is it all right with you?' He nodded yes—the next thing I knew I had shot him." In those words, Lester Syg-maniak told a Freehold, New Jersey, jury of the death of his 26-year-old brother, George, paralyzed following a motorcycle accident. The words "mercy killing" were not used in court, but the defense argued that Lester had acted only in response to anguished pleas from George. After a 6-day trial for murder, the Freehold jury deliberated just 2.5 hours before acquitting Lester. The grounds were temporary insanity. "I feel much better," Lester said after the verdict. "That's all I want to say now."

In 1984, a retired Army colonel stood trial for a similar offense. His son had tried to commit suicide by setting himself on fire. The father had saved him by turning the garden hose on him. But his son was left terribly scarred and disfigured and needed to be hospitalized. After numerous operations, and at his son's request, the father walked into the hospital one afternoon and told his son he had "found a solution to your problems." He showed the son a pistol and asked if he wanted him to use it. The son, who could not speak, nodded yes. The father shot him in the head, walked out into the corridor, and told the nurses his son was dead. He then sat down on a bench in the ward.

Conclusion _____

The preceding pages present a collage of different types of criminality. It is in the nature of a collage that one gets an impression—sometimes confusing and disjointed—but an impression, nonetheless. The most salient single point to be gained from the foregoing is that crime consists of an extremely varied and complex set of human social behaviors. To study it systematically, we need to know how much there is, how it is distributed, why some people are labeled criminal while others are not, and why some acts are defined in law as crime while others are not.

It is in the nature of science that we work with only small samples of the universe. It is, however, incumbent upon science to develop reliable knowledge about the entire universe and to make the best possible estimates. In this chapter, we have not been concerned with developing logically consistent categories of crime. The next several chapters take up this issue. We move from an impression of crime to a summary of the descriptive data on crime gathered by criminologists concerned with providing as objective and complete a description of crime as possible.

Data on Crime: Part I

Criminology is built on two great pillars: *facts* (or *data*) and *theories*. We must know what the facts are, and we must have theories that explain them. Unfortunately, neither facts nor theories come to us in prefabricated packages. We must discover both. In the process of discovering what the facts are, we also uncover some common misconceptions. As a rule of thumb, we must approach with caution facts gathered by people who have a vested interest in having the facts turn out a certain way. Novelists, journalists, and script writers for television and movies all have a vested interest in creating images of crime that are tantalizing, exciting, and even horrifying. Conjuring up a secret society that controls "organized crime" makes for good novels and films but is a serious distortion of reality.

Police departments, to some extent, share the same interest. To the degree that the police can convince the lawmakers and the general public that crime is a serious problem that threatens everyone's well-being, they are better able to prove the importance of their work, increase their budgets, and improve their work conditions. Thus, when the FBI approaches Congress in the spring to request an increase in its budget, we must approach with caution the claims made about crime and crime rates.

Politicians and judges may also share a vested interest in creating certain images of crime. If a politician is in office and has promised to "do something about crime," it may be in his or her interest to show a decrease in crime. A politician running for office may use the "crime problem" as a way of attacking his or her opponent in an effort to win the election. If a judge wishes to make legal decisions that increase the punitiveness of the law, then it is in his or her interest to spread alarm about crime.

The Chief Justice of the United States, Warren Burger, in an address to the American Bar Association, warned of the imminent danger of rising crime rates, especially crimes of violence: ". . . the statistics are not merely grim they are frightening. . . . Washington, D.C., the capital of our enlightened country, in 1980 had more criminal homicides than Sweden and Denmark combined with an aggregate population of over twelve million as against 650,000 for Washington, D.C., and Washington is not unique."[1]

Chief Justice Burger supported his conclusion with statistics on crime published by law-enforcement agencies in Sweden, Denmark, and the United States. Unfortunately, these data are neither gathered nor reported with an eye to accuracy. Rather, the information supplied by the FBI is strongly influenced by bureaucratic and political considerations. As a result, the data give "an entirely incorrect impression regarding criminality."[2]

In the United States, official crime data are published by the FBI as the *Uniform Crime Reports (UCR)*. These annual reports are the major source of data on crime used by politicians, media, and police departments. Unfortunately, these data are seriously flawed because the FBI and the police departments, whose reports comprise the basis for the UCR, have a vested interest in the outcome of the data.

Bias in Official Statistics _____

Studies of how the FBI crime statistics are obtained show consistently how the process in inevitably biased and leads to misleading information. There is scant attention paid to the problems of gathering accurate data. The data used for determining the extent and trend of criminality are "crimes known to the police." The FBI receives weekly reports of crimes known to have been committed from police departments throughout the country. The police rely primarily on reports from citizens that a crime has been committed. There is no requirement that a suspect be found or arrested, or that the crime even be investigated. The categories used in classifying acts as crime are arbitrary, inconsistent, and contradictory. As early as 1931, the Wickensham Commission warned that the publication of the *Uniform Crime Reports* was problematic:

> Nothing can be more misleading than statistics not scientifically gathered and compiled. The Uniform Crime Reports . . . make no suggestion as to any limitations or doubts with respect to the utility or authority of the figures presented. On the contrary they contain a graphic chart of 'monthly crime trends,' and along with them the bureau has released to the press statements quoting and interpreting them without qualification. It requires no great study of these reports to perceive a number of weaknesses which should impose a more cautious promulgation of them.[3]

That the statistics gathered by the police and reported to the FBI are not objectively gathered is evidenced by a number of studies on how these data are generated and collated. The crime categories used in the *UCR* are often ambiguous. For example, burglary requires the use of force for breaking and entering in many states, but the FBI tells local police departments to report the crime of burglary simply if there is unlawful entry.[4] Merging these two types of offenses makes statistics on "burglary" ambiguous. More important is the way the police departments are instructed to fill out the forms. In every instance, the instructions are designed to show the highest incidence of crime possible. The *Uniform Crime Reporting Handbook* states, "If a number of persons are involved in a dispute or disturbance and police investigation cannot establish the aggressors from the victims, count the number of persons assaulted as the number of offenses."[5]

In reporting homicides, the instructions to the police are equally misleading from the point of view of gathering scientifically valid information. The instructions tell police departments that they should report a death as a homicide regardless of whether other objective evidence indicates otherwise: ". . . the findings of coroner, court, jury or prosecutor do not unfound [change the report of] offenses or attempts which your [police] investigations establish to be legitimate."[6]

Equally problematic for using the *UCR* for scientific purposes is the degree to which crime rates are subject to political manipulation. Selke and Pepinsky report a longitudinal study of the police reporting of crime in Indianapolis that demonstrates how crime rates are made to fluctuate according to whether the people in political power want the rates to go up or down.[7]

Seidman and Couzens studied police reporting of the crime rate in Washington, D.C., during the time when Richard Nixon was using Washington as a demonstration city to show how his "war on crime" was effective. During this period, the police in Washington were under pressure to reduce the crime rate. The most common form of "serious" crime reported to the FBI by local police departments is felonious larceny (theft). For a larceny to be considered "serious" it must be of property worth more than $50.00. To create the impression that the "war on crime" was effective, the Washington, D.C., police began reporting most of the larcenies known to them as larceny involving property valued at $49.00, which kept them from being reported as felonies and, thus, kept the serious crime rate down. The Chief of Police said, "Either I have a man who will get the crime rate down in his district or I'll find a new man."[8]

No doubt the chief "found the man" who would get the crime rate, if not the incidence of crime, down. A number of other studies also show how crime rates are manipulated and poorly reported by police and the FBI, limiting their utility.[9]

Other problems with the *UCR* include the fact that only a small sample of criminal offenses is included in the report. The included offenses represent only a tiny fraction of the total array of criminal acts and they are disproportionately the crimes likely to be committed by the poor, male, and minority populations in the country. Completely absent from the *UCR* are data on white-collar crimes, consumer fraud, child molestation, wife abuse, and so forth.

The *UCR* also presents the data in misleading ways. By use of gimmicks like a "crime clock," the report misleads and distorts the reality of crime. This makes good newspaper copy and serves to give the law-enforcement agencies considerable political clout, which is translated into ever-increasing budgets, pay raises, and more technologically sophisticated "crime-fighting" equipment. It does not, however, provide policy makers or social scientists with reliable data. It also has the effect of creating fear and insecurity, which may inhibit people's ability to function fully in their lives. As Pepinsky and Selke conclude, "the police cannot and should not be expected to be objective about the compilation of reported crime statistics. The field is one of the few where those who are evaluated are responsible themselves for gathering their own evaluation data."[10]

Official statistics, then, must be used with extreme caution. This does not say that all official statistics are worthless. For example, in addition to "crimes known to the police," the *UCR* reports the number of arrests made each year. These data will tell us with reasonable accuracy what charges the police use when they make arrests. They cannot tell us how much crime there is or whether the rate of crime is increasing. Organizational considerations dictate the content of these data far more than do the reality of what is taking place. For example, when police make an arrest, they typically charge a suspect with a number of different offenses. This is done to increase the bargaining power of the prosecutor when he or she confronts the suspect with the charges. The charges brought by the police that appear in the arrest statistics, then, are a very poor reflection of the offenses actually committed. They tell us much more about police activity than they do about the amount, types, and trends of criminal activity. The arrest data are rarely used as an indication of how much crime there is; they are, however, often used as a measure of who commits crime. This usage is extremely misleading. Most policing takes place in a relatively small geographical area of the city. Not surprisingly, this is also where most arrests occur. Some of the more-common crimes for which arrests are made are public intoxication, gambling, and possession of weapons and illegal drugs. The residents of urban ghettos and slums are constantly surveyed by police. Thus, they are more likely to be caught in illegal activities. The police are not inspecting the middle-class homes and cars to see if their owners possess illegal weapons or drugs, are walking the streets intoxicated, or are having a Friday-night poker game.

Among criminologists, there is agreement that official statistics are suspect. There is disagreement, however, as to whether official statistics are more misleading than informative as an indicator of crime rates and trends. In the criminological literature, you will frequently find research reports based on official statistics that make assumptions about the validity of the data we have questioned here. We take the position that official statistics must be evaluated on a case by case basis. So, too, must one evaluate the conclusions of researchers on the basis of the validity of the statistical data employed. In general, criminologists or public officials who use official data to show an increase or decrease in crime rates or that one group of people commits more or less crime than another are making erroneous assumptions based on unreliable data.

Victim-Survey Data _____

There are data that provide a much better description of selected characteristics of criminality than do official statistics. Some of these data are gathered by government agencies; the most useful are the *annual victim surveys* conducted by social scientists under the auspices of the Department of Justice. While these surveys have their own shortcomings (which we will presently discuss), they are nonetheless quite useful for scientific purposes. Even with victim surveys, however, a word of caution is in order. While every effort is made to draw adequate samples and gather data as objectively as possible, the written reports are presented in a very unscientific manner. Typically the annual report of the Justice Department reporting the results of the victim surveys begins with language that is designed to alarm rather than enlighten: "In the first six months of 1984 there were one million three hundred thirty-five thousand victims of crimes of violence or personal property."[11]

Close scrutiny of the data reveals, however, that most of the "crimes of violence or personal property" are accounted for by (1) crimes against property that did not involve contact between the victim and the offender, (2) crimes that were not reported to the police, and (3) crimes that the victim considered too unimportant to warrant reporting to the police.

The first national victim survey was conducted in 1967. People were asked whether they or any member of their household were the victim of a crime. The questionnaires and the sampling procedures were designed by sociologists. This provided, in the words of a leading methodologist, "the most important innovation in criminological research in several decades."[12] The first surveys were a basis for improving the research instruments. Since 1973, victim surveys have been conducted every year. About 60,000 households and 135,000 individuals are interviewed each year. One of the most important findings from the victim surveys is that the crime rate from year to year is fairly constant (see Table 2.1). A compilation of the results of victim-survey data by Langan and Innes led to the conclusion that "the proportion of the population victimized by violent crime was fairly constant between 1978 and 1982."[13] Be-

TABLE 2.1   Victim-Reported Crimes (1973–1982)

Offense	Rate*									
	1973	1974	1975	1976	1977	1978	1979	1980	1981	1982
Rape or attempted rape	181	181	163	144	156	167	184	157	178	143
Robbery or attempted robbery	690	713	673	646	622	589	626	656	741	708
Assault or attempted assault	2,597	2,469	2,505	2,527	2,679	2,685	287	303	324	306
Larceny with contact	317	311	308	289	265	312	287	303	324	306
Larceny without contact	9,029	9,175	9,269	9,320	9,462	9,361	8,899	8,004	8,194	7,945

*Per 100,000 population.

tween 1982 and 1985, the criminal victimization rate *dropped* by nearly 700,000 to about 16 percent below the number of victims reported in 1981.[14]

It is particularly important to compare these findings with the official statistics of the *Uniform Crime Reports*. For 50 years, the *UCR* showed an increase in the amount of crime, although there were periods of fluctuation from one year to the next in which the rate for some types of crime declined. Criminologists questioned the official data and the claims of ever-increasing crime rates. They noted that the homicide rate, which they assumed was generally more accurate than for other reported crimes, did not vary greatly from decade to decade. Victim-survey data suggest that criminologists who questioned the reliability of official statistics generated by police departments were quite right to be skeptical.

Another important finding of the victim surveys is that, of the people who report being the victim of a crime, the vast bulk of the crimes committed against them are not very serious in terms of either personal or property damage (see Table 2.2).

If you look carefully at Table 2.2, you will see that in every instance the bulk of the reported victimizations are for crimes where there was (1) an attempted crime but no completed offense or (2) a crime without any personal contact (something stolen from a desk or a locker, perhaps). It is significant in evaluating the seriousness and prevalence of crime in America to also realize that, for every type of crime, there is less than a 50 percent chance the victim will report the crime to the police. When asked why they do not report the crime, victims say that the crime was "not important enough" or that "nothing could be done about it."

TABLE 2.2   Estimated Rate of Victimization by Seriousness of Offense (1982)

More-Serious Offense	Rate*	Less-Serious Offense	Rate*
Larceny with contact	306	Larceny without contact	7,945
Aggravated assault	931	Simple assault	1,708
Robbery with injury	220	Robbery without injury	310
Attempted robbery		Attempted robbery	
with injury	708	without injury	2,638

*Per100,000 population.

Source: Edmund F. McGarrell and Timothy J. Flanagan, *The Sourcebook of Criminal Justice Statistics* (Washington, D.C.: U.S. Department of Justice, 1984), 286.

These findings shows that it is very unlikely that anyone will be the victim of a crime in any given year. Over 90 percent of the respondents report that neither they nor any member of their household was the victim of a criminal offense. Indeed, over a lifetime it is unlikely that most people will be the victim of a serious offense. Judging from the results of the victim surveys, the most likely crime of violence that one will experience is a "simple assault," which is defined as "an attack without a weapon resulting either in minor injury (e.g., bruises, black eye, cuts, scratches, swelling) or an undetermined injury requiring less than two days of hospitalization." Simple assault also includes attempted assault without a weapon. Analysis of the results of victim surveys for a 5-year period (1978–1982) by Langan and Innes shows that the risk of being a victim of a violent crime in any given year is less than 3 percent. Furthermore, 2.5 percent of this is accounted for by being a victim of an assault. On the other hand, this estimate does not include the risk of being victimized by drunk drivers, child abusers, and probably a great deal of spouse abusers, which would not be reported on victim surveys. It also does not indicate the likelihood of being the victim of a crime in a lifetime. Still, the evidence is very persuasive that the risk of being victimized by crime generally and by violent crime particularly has been irresponsibly exaggerated by law enforcers, politicians, the media, and even some criminologists.[15]

Distribution of Crime Victims

The incidence of crime is not uniformly distributed. Official statistics indicate that crimes are committed against more men than women, more young men than older ones, more people who live in cities than people who live in small towns, and more people who live in lower-class areas of cities than people who live in middle- or upper-class areas. These findings, however, may be very misleading. Men are more likely to assault one another in public. Women are more likely to be assaulted in their homes. The former is therefore much more likely to get reported to the police and even to be mentioned as a crime on a victim survey. Assaults against children—child molestation and incest—are not as public as male-against-male assault. People with upper- or middle-class incomes are more likely to settle problems of aggressiveness by seeking private, professional help rather than having their assaults made public. To obtain better data on the relative incidence

A taste of drugs on the street. *(Angel Franco/Woodfin Camp & Assoc.)*

of assault as well as other types of crime, it is necessary to gather data from shelters for battered women or abused children, and even from hotlines where people call to report personal problems.

The victim of a crime varies to some extent by the type of offense. Women are more likely than men to be victims of rape. It is likely that this difference in reports reflects real differences, but the discrepancy is probably less than the data show, given the reticence of police to arrest for male rape and the reticence of male victims to report the offense. Women are also unlikely to report the offense. Rape statistics are therefore notoriously unreliable.

According to the results of victim surveys, violent criminal acts are committed approximately twice as often against males as they are against females. As pointed out, however, this may distort the number of offenses against women. Victims of spouse abuse may not even know that such acts are illegal or a particular incident may not be perceived by the victim or the assailant as a crime. Respondents may be fearful of reporting these incidents to an interviewer. There is some evidence that women whose husbands batter them go to great lengths to keep it a secret to avoid public embarrassment and further spouse attacks. We are unfortunately a long way from knowing how much hidden violence there is. Criminologists have become more sensitive, however, to the problems associated with accepting the picture of criminality as depicted by measures that are insensitive to the extremely complex web of human relations within which crimes occur.

Age, Race, and Crime

Victim surveys make it clear that there is a relationship between age, race, and the risk of being the victim of a crime. People between 16 and 24 years old are more likely to be victimized than those of any other age group. The risk of being a victim declines steadily after age 24. A higher proportion of blacks (4 percent) than whites (2 percent) are victimized by violent crimes. This finding follows from the more-general fact that the lower the social class, the greater the likelihood that one will *report* being the victim of a crime.

Arrest and Race

Arrest data indicate that young black males are disproportionately arrested compared to young white males (see Table 2.3).[16]

Chilton's recent study of arrests in Boston shows the relationship between age, race, and arrest.[18] He studied all arrests re-

TABLE 2.3 Ratio of Black to White Arrest Rates of Persons Under 18 Years of Age for Selected Offenses in the United States (1976)[17]

Offense	Rate*
Crime of violence	9.08
Property crime	3.14
Aggravated assault	5.69
Forcible rape	9.64
Other sex offense	3.22
Vandalism	1.23
Driving under the influence	.29
Drunkenness	.56
Runaway	.94

*Per 100,000 population.

ported to the FBI in 1968 and 1980. He found that, while the 15–19 year old age group constituted 7.4 percent of Boston's population, this group accounted for 32 percent of the arrests for robbery, assault, burglary, theft, and rape cases reported to the FBI in 1960. In 1980, this age group was 10 percent of the population and accounted for 37 percent of these arrests. The age group of 15–29 year olds accounts for 59 percent of all Part I arrests in 1960 and 76 percent in 1980.

Non-white males in Boston constituted less than 1 percent of the Boston population in 1960, but made up approximately 15 percent of those arrested for what the FBI defines as the most serious offenses. In 1980, non-white males were 4.5 percent of the population and accounted for 33.6 percent of the arrests.

The finding that young men are most often arrested for crimes such as theft, burglary, assault, and robbery is consistently reported by studies relying on arrest data supplied by police and other law-enforcement agencies. The finding that non-white males are more likely to be arrested for these crimes is also consistent from one study to another. These findings lead many to conclude that young males, and especially young non-white males, commit most of the crimes. This conclusion is very suspect. It is suspect first and foremost because the crimes of theft, burglary, assault, robbery, and rape are only a tiny fraction of the criminality that exists at any point in time. Completely absent from these statistics are white-collar and corporate crimes; crimes against women that occur in the family; and assault, rape, and battery perpetrated by family members against one another. The use of children for pornography or prostitution is not included. Of course, political and police corruption, organized crime, and crimes of the state—crimes to be discussed in the next chapter—are completely absent from these statistics.

The conclusion that young black (or non-white) males account for a disproportionate amount of crime is also suspect because these studies do not allow for police practices that are likely to bias the results.[19] Policing is a bureaucratic phenomenon.[20] Police departments make decisions on where to look for crime and whether or not to make an arrest. The police generally devote a greater amount of their surveillance energies to areas of the city where non-whites live. The finding that blacks are more likely to be arrested than whites is, at least in part, the result of a self-fulfilling prophecy. Black males are frequently arrested "on suspicion" and for possession of weapons. If the police concentrate in black areas where overpopulation and poor housing forces much of the social life onto the streets, then it is not surprising that the police discover more people who appear suspicious or are carrying weapons in black areas than in white. Approximately 80 percent of the arrests each year are for minor offenses like public drunkenness, gambling, disorderly conduct, and "suspicion."[21] The normal street life of American ghettos makes arrests for these kinds of offenses among blacks and lower-class whites a virtual certainty. That this same intensive surveillance accounts for the disproportionate arrest of blacks and non-whites for assault, burglary, robbery, and rape may not be completely explained by this institutional bias, but it no doubt contributes to a substantial amount of the difference. There is some empirical evidence that, when confronted with a suspected crime, the police are much more likely to arrest poor non-whites than they are middle-class whites for equally serious criminal offenses.[22]

Closer examination of Table 2.3 also reveals some interesting comparisons between white and black arrest rates. Hindelang, Hirschi, and Weiss conclude from these data that blacks are more likely to commit more-serious offenses than whites.[23] This conclusion, however is not supported by the data when they are examined in a broader perspective of what we know about crime.

First, we know from victim surveys that black women are more likely than white women to report rapes and assaults to the police.[24] Thus the higher arrest rate for blacks in these categories may be because of the fact that black women are more likely to report such an incident. Second, it is noteworthy that one of the most serious offenses in terms of harm to people and property is drunk driving. Here, the white arrest rate is four times as high as the black rate. Thus the conclusion that the arrest data, even with their bias, show a higher incidence of more-serious crimes committed by blacks than whites is not justified. Indeed, these qualifications suggest that, if all things were considered even for the kinds of offenses normally recorded by the police, the rate of white involvement in serious crimes may well exceed the rate of black involvement. One of the few studies in this area ever done compared, through observations rather than police reports, the delinquency of middle- and lower-class youths. It was discovered that, although these middle-class youths were never arrested and their crimes never recorded, they were in fact engaged in more-serious offenses as regularly and consistently as were the lower-class youths.[25]

Homicide

Generally speaking, criminologists believe that homicide statistics are among the more accurate data provided by law-enforcement agencies. The argument for this conclusion is that homicides are more likely to be reported and the consequence of the act (i.e., a dead person) is more difficult to hide. While this may be true, there are certain qualifications on the homicide rate as reported by the *UCR* that must be taken into account. As previously noted, the way the police are instructed to report a homicide—even if the coroner, prosecutor, jury, and judge do not confirm that it took place—makes the data suspect. Another indication that the police may overestimate the number of homicides is by comparing the results of victim surveys and police reports. The only year in which the victim survey asked respondents whether or not they or any member of their household had been the victim of a homicide was 1967. None of the respondents reported that they had been the victim, but the homicide rate estimated from respondents saying someone in their immediate family had been a victim was 3.1 per 100,000 population.[26] The *UCR* for 1967 reported a homicide rate of 5.1; almost twice the rate indicated by the victim survey. It is quite possible that the discrepancy is the result of consistent over-reporting by the police, much of which would be accounted for by the method of reporting.

By combining data from police reports, interviews with police officials filing the reports, and other sources, Riedel and Zahn were able to improve upon previous research.[27] They analyzed data for the period of 1968–1978. Their extensive report compares homicide by sex, age, race, region of the country, cities, and a host of other variables. Some of the most important findings are that (1) homicide rates show minor fluctuations from year to year and (2) from 1968–1978, the homicide rate rose somewhat (see Table 2.4).

Other data of interest from this report show that males are almost three times as likely as females and blacks are twice as likely as whites to be victims of homicide. The age group 20–49 has the highest homicide-victimization rate, while the elderly and the very young have the lowest.

The greatest proportion of all homicides takes place between acquaintances; the lowest proportion between strangers. Surprisingly, 56% of the victims of homicide in the family are men and

TABLE 2.4 Incidence of Homicide Victimization in the United States (1968–1978)

Year	Rate*
1968	6.0
1969	6.4
1970	6.4
1971	7.4
1972	7.6
1973	8.2
1974	8.8
1975	8.8
1976	7.7
1977	8.3
1978	8.6

*Per 100,000 population.

43% are women. In the cities this ratio increases to 70% male victims, 30% female (see Table 2.5).

Of the victims of acquaintance homicide, 84 percent are men and 20 percent are women. This pattern is the same for stranger homicides: 84 percent of the victims are men, 15 percent are women (Riedel and Zahn, 1985, p. 27.) Generally speaking, the same trends of victims are found in offenders: over 80 percent of the offenders are male; the age group that contains the majority of offenders is from 15–29; and blacks and whites commit about an equal number of homicides but because blacks constitute only 15 percent of the population, they are over-represented in the category of offenders.

TABLE 2.5 Sex of Victims in Three Types of Homicides in the United States (1978)

Sex	Type of Homicide (%)			
	Family	Acquaintance	Stranger	Unknown
Male	56.7	80.5	84.5	79.0
Female	43.2	19.4	15.3	20.1
Sex Unknown	0.1	0.1	0.2	0.2

Source: Adapted from Marc Reidel and Margaret Zahn, *The Nature and Pattern of Criminal Homicide* (Washington, D.C.: U.S. Department of Justice, 1985), 25.

As these researchers recognize, despite the care they took, there is still the possibility of bias in the overall rate. Nonetheless, it seems safe to conclude that the bias is consistent from one year to the next. Most criminologists conclude that although the data are far from exact, the trends in the homicide rate are a reasonably accurate estimate.

Our Criminal Cities

A 1974 report based on victim surveys in the nation's five largest cities (New York, Chicago, Philadelphia, Detroit, and Los Angeles) begins with this statement: "Nearly 3.2 million crimes of violence and common theft, including attempts, took place in the nation's five largest cities."[28]

The tone of the statement suggests, as it is clearly intended to, that "crimes of violence and common theft" are rampant. However, as was pointed out before, one must cautiously approach statements interpreting statistics that are designed for political purposes; these reports are issued by the Department of Justice. Going beyond the raw statements, we come to quite a different conclusion. For the five largest cities, as in the national surveys, 90 percent of the respondents report that neither they nor any members of their households were victims of any kind of crime in the preceding year. Less than 3 percent of the respondents report being the victim of a violent crime, even when the definition of "violent crime" includes acts that are not normally considered "violent."

A companion study of eight other large cities found essentially the same thing. The cities have a higher incidence of reported victimization than smaller cities, but the incidence is still far lower than would be expected from the stereotype of American cities as places where it is not safe to walk the streets at night. What these studies confirm is the conclusion drawn by Andrew Hacker:

> . . . there are at most three unreported robberies for every one divulged to the police, and in most cases the non-reporting victim will be poor and disillusioned about any increase in his safety. On this speculation . . . 300,000 robberies took place in New York throughout 1972. As the city has approximately 6 million residents, aged 16 and over, a New Yorker stands a chance of being robbed about once every 20 years. While the odds are clearly greater in [the lower-class areas of] the South Bronx, the Lower East Side, and Bedford-Stuyvesant, ironically the most noise about crime comes from [the

upper-class sections of] Parkchester, Bay Ridge and Staten Island, where the likelihood of being held up in an average lifetime is almost nil.[29]

Self-Report Surveys _____

Thus far, we have concentrated on data generated by official agencies and victim surveys. As was pointed out, these findings are important but of limited value because they cover only a fraction of the varieties of crime extant in our society. Victim surveys give us a good idea of who is victimized. For some offenses, they also ask the respondent to describe characteristics of the offender such as age, race, and sex. Official data tell us who the police arrest (with qualifications as noted) but do not tell us about people whose offenses escape police attention. One research technique developed by sociologists to reveal types of criminality ordinarily hidden from victim surveys or official statistics in the *self-report survey*. This research technique involves asking a sample of people to indicate whether or not they have committed certain criminal acts.

In 1946, Austin Porterfield administered a questionnaire to Texas college students. He discovered that over 90 percent of the respondents admitted to committing at least one felony.[30] Wallerstein and Wyle found similar results.[31] They administered questionnaires to 700 adults over the age of 15. The questionnaire consisted of 49 criminal acts punishable by at least 1 year in prison. Of the respondents 91 percent admitted committing at least one of the offenses. The men in the sample admitted committing an average of 18 offenses. The women admitted to an average of 11 offenses.

Since these pioneering studies, dozens of others have confirmed the original findings. High-school and college youth asked to indicate on a questionnaire whether or not they have engaged in a number of criminal acts from being truant to fighting, stealing, running away from home, and drinking while underage indicate a frequent involvement in such acts.[32] Most recently, Elliot and Huizinga conducted a national survey of youth that confirmed the earlier findings; over 90 percent of the respondents admitted to having committed serious criminal offenses.[33]

These data showed that virtually everyone sampled admits to having committed criminal acts. One finding from the studies that has produced a great deal of disagreement and controversy among criminologists is how to interpret the data.[34] On first brush, there appears to be little difference by social class in the propensity to violate the law. Because the vast majority of people sentenced to prison or juvenile institutions are from the lower classes, this fact was interpreted by some to mean that the difference between lower-class and other youth was not in the frequency or severity of their criminality, but in the biased law-enforcement practices of the police. Others pointed out, however, that the kinds of offenses lower-class youth committed were more serious and that they tended to commit criminal acts more frequently than middle- or upper-class youth.[35] Michalowski comments intelligently on the controversy:

> Recent studies using national youth samples and more sophisticated questionnaires have tended to confirm both interpretations. That is, there appears to be no significant difference between lower-class, working-class, and middle-class youth when it comes to self-reported involvement in property crimes (excluding robbery), drug offenses (either selling or using), status crimes such as truancy, runaway and underage drinking; or public disorder crimes such as carrying a concealed weapon, drunkenness, hitchhiking, and so forth. However, lower-class youth appear disproportionately among those reporting a high frequency of offenses. It should be noted, however, that high-frequency offenders accounted for less than 5 percent of the juveniles surveyed in each of the three social classes.[36]

The self-report studies tend not to ask about the more-serious forms of personal violence: murder, rape, assault with a deadly weapon, and so forth. Studies of college students reveal a substantial amount of what is called "date rape."[37] Meyer reports that over 20 percent of college women are the victims of rape or attempted rape.[38]

Self-report studies suffer some of the same shortcomings as victim surveys. Tapping the criminality of inner-city youth through self-reports is difficult. Most of the surveys are of local high schools, although recently we have data from national surveys that reduce the shortcomings of earlier studies. In the end, of course, one of the most serious limitations is the perception of the respondent in combination with the content of the questionnaires. Respondents may well not think that their act was criminal and therefore not report it. Child abuse, sexual assault on one's girlfriend or wife, rape on a date or at a "wild party" where "she was asking for it"—these may go unadmitted because they are not perceived as crim-

Shoplifting: the five-finger discount. *(Blair Seitz/Photo Researchers)*

inal by the respondent. If the questionnaire does not ask for offenses, they will not be recorded; for example, none of the questionnaires asks about driving while under the influence of alcohol. Evidence from participant-observation studies indicates that this may be one of the most common and most serious criminal acts committed by middle- and upper-class youth, yet it will not be recorded if it is not asked about. Even with the promise of anonymity, respondents may be reticent to admit that they have committed very serious offenses. The risk of persecution for something that has gone undetected would have to be weighed against the desire to answer a questionnaire honestly. It seems unlikely that many respondents would place the value of the questionnaire results above their own safety. Finally, the questionnaires do not tap that whole range of criminal offenses known as white-collar, corporate, and governmental crimes. In short, although self-report studies provide more valuable information about crime and delinquency, they provide only a piece of the puzzle that must be combined with many other pieces before the picture is complete.

Crimes Against Women

The most serious crime committed against women is violence. Violence against women includes assault, rape, and murder. Some of the facts relevant to these offenses are that[39]

1. Most of the crimes against women are committed by men. This is consistent with the fact that most crimes are committed by men.
2. There is, overall, about a 50 percent chance that the crime against a woman will be committed by a stranger. In 1982, out of 123,714 rapes or attempted rapes reported in the victim survey, 60 percent were perpetrated by strangers and 40 percent by nonstrangers. For assaults, 47 percent were perpetrated by strangers and 53 percent by nonstrangers.
3. The incidence of rape from 1973–1982 shows minor variations from year to year, but, like most other crime rates, it is quite constant (see Table 2.3). In 1973, the estimated rape-victimization rate per 100,000 females 12 years of age or older was 181; in 1982, it was 143.
4. Black and Hispanic women are more likely than white women to be rape and assault victims.
5. The lower the family income, the greater the likelihood that a woman will be the victim of an assault or a rape. The victimization rate per 100,000 white women from families with incomes under $3,000 a year in 1982 was 302; the rate for white women with an income of $25,000 a year or more was only 48. For black women, the rate for women from families with incomes under $3,000 in 1982 was 138; the rate for women from families with incomes over $25,000 was zero because there were no reported victimizations. For white women, the incidence of rape declines consistently with increased family income; for black and Hispanic women, the incidence is highest in the group whose family income is between $15,000 and $24,999.*

*The fact that black and Hispanic women from the middle-income group report a higher incidence of rape victimization than women from lower-income groups is a surprising finding of these surveys. There is possibly a biased result stemming from the relative ease of interviewing middle-income black and hispanic women compared to interviewing other lower-income groups. Whether this bias accounts for the difference cannot be determined at this time.

Other crimes for which women are most often the victim are incest and child sexual abuse. Data on these offenses are notoriously unreliable. Children who are the victims of incest, especially involving their father or a close relative, are reluctant to report these acts to the police. Families are often complicitous in a conspiracy of silence to protect both the offender and the victim. There is a reticence on the part of women or families to report sexual assaults of any kind because there remains a widespread belief that a woman who is the victim of a sexual assault is somehow stigmatized. Often the assumption is made that a woman who is a victim was somehow guilty of encouraging the assault. Empirical data clearly demonstrate the error of these assumptions, but their prevalence curtails the reporting and accuracy of the data. It is significant that, despite the institutionalized tendencies to under report, the incidence of reported sexual crimes is, nonetheless, very high.

Crimes Against Children

Infanticide is a crime that, until recently, has received scant attention from criminologists in the United States. It is one of the more-difficult crimes on which to gather reliable data. Like rape and spouse abuse, it often takes place in the family and may be concealed under the heading of "crib deaths." Also like rape and spouse abuse, it is more likely to be discovered when committed by lower-class and poor people than by middle- and upper-income people. Even with these qualifications, it is still clear that infanticide occurs with some frequency (see Table 2.6).

More common than infanticide are child abuse and child neglect. The U.S. House of Representatives Committee on Education and Labor estimates that 2,000 children die each year in the United States from physical abuse and neglect. This committee estimates that an additional 1.5 million children are the victims of abuse or

TABLE 2.6 Frequency of Infanticide in the United States (1979–1981)

1979		1980		1981	
Male	**Female**	**Male**	**Female**	**Male**	**Female**
104	66	114	96	108	112

Source: Statistical Abstracts of the United States, 1985.

neglect each year. Other commonly committed crimes against children are the use of children in the production of pornographic films and photographs and in child prostitution. At times, securing children for these purposes involves kidnapping as well. At other times, it consists of parents selling their children. Data on the incidence of these crimes is nonexistent. We do know, however, that child prostitution and the use of children in pornographic films is common in U.S. cities. Doubtless, thousands of children are victims of these types of crimes every year.

As with all types of crime, it is necessary to be cautious interpreting data gathered for political, rather than scientific, purposes. Recently in the United States, a hue and cry has sounded over the problem of missing children. Commentators on television and in newspapers are pushing this as a major social problem of the modern era. Estimates are bandied about to the effect that 2–3 million children are missing every year in the United States. These children, it is said, are sold into slavery for sexual purposes, raped and murdered, or turned into drug-crazed miniature Oliver's who steal or peddle drugs for slaveholder-like adults who exploit them. These claims are gross exaggerations at best. To begin with, states define a "child" very differently. In some cases, a person is a "child" until he or she reaches the age of 21; in others, the age is 12. We would hardly count as a "missing child" someone who is 18 years of age or older. Furthermore, of the 2–3 million children reported missing each year, 99 percent of them are "found" within 24–48 hours.[40] They are children who leave home temporarily. Of the remaining 1 percent, some of these are runaways who, although facing the world at a young age, nonetheless go off to make their own way. That some of these end up living "on the streets"—begging, selling drugs, and/or stealing—is no doubt the case. Other missing children are in fact kidnapped by a parent who does not have legal custody: It is a criminal act to be sure, but one that puts the behavior into a different perspective than one gleans from the propaganda perpetuated by special-interest groups. Very few of the truly missing children have been kidnapped; some are forced into prostitution or used in the making of child pornography. The latter category, however, is extremely small.

Child prostitution and pornography are not well researched, but what evidence exists indicates that it is most often the parents and not some stranger who force children to engage in prostitution or allow children to be used in the making of pornographic films or photographs. One of the few available studies describes a child of 3 years old being told by her parents to get on a bed and allow a man to have sex with her while the scene is filmed. The child asked the mother, "Do I have to Mommy?" The mother answered, "Yes, honey, we need the money."[41]

Victimless Crimes

An understanding of crime in the modern world requires that we understand acts that criminologists refer to as "victimless crimes." These include such things as smoking marijuana, being truant from school, obtaining an abortion after a legally defined term of pregnancy, practicing homosexual acts (which are still criminal in 25 states) or some types of heterosexual acts, gambling, and so forth.

The pioneer in studying victimless crimes, Edwin Schur, points out that in victimless crimes there are two distinct types of criminality: (1) crimes in which there is no complainant but there may be an objective harm to some people and (2) crimes in which those participating in the acts do not think they are harmed.[42] An example of a crime in which there may well be an objective harm but complainants are rare is bribery. A customs official bribed by smugglers to permit the importation of illegal substances (cocaine, for example) is as unlikely as the smugglers to complain. Nonetheless, one can argue there is considerable harm done. Illegal substances that are demonstrably harmful to people's health are allowed onto the market. People desiring the drugs may engage in other types of crime in order to obtain the money to buy them; people who are being exploited may fail to organize against the exploitation because the addiction to drugs supercedes political action. If there is not sufficient work for the population, drugs may serve to render a potentially revolutionary labor force complacent or they may give alienated youth an outlet that is less socially harmful than drinking alcohol or engaging in vandalism. The second type of victimless crime, that which is perceived by the participants as not harmful and a matter that they have the right to decide for themselves, is illustrated by homosexual relations between consenting adults and by abortion. There are those who say these kinds of acts are harmful to society. Others argue that they are beneficial. As with many acts defined as criminal by law, there is not a consensus. In Chapter 5, we will take up the issue of what are the implications of the fact that the law reflects a world in which people disagree over the legitimacy of defining particular

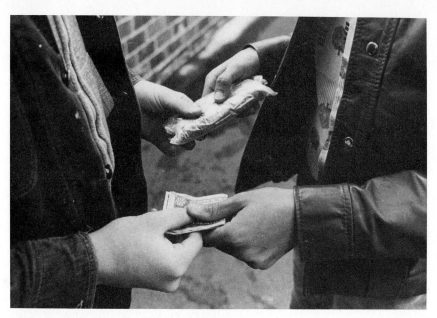

(*Jim Anderson/Woodfin Camp & Assoc.*)

acts as criminal. At the moment, we need only consider the types of acts defined as crime by law.

Victimless crimes are among the most difficult of all criminality to measure. Clearly, if two people agree to engage in a criminal act, discovering the criminality will be difficult. Other victimless crimes—prostitution, gambling, vagrancy, public intoxication—are equally difficult to count. Self-report surveys such as those previously reported may give us a clue as to the distribution and rate of some of these offenses, but at best these will only give a rough idea. Surveys of college students indicate that over 70 percent smoke, snort, or pop illegal substances with some regularity.[43] Smoking marijuana, snorting cocaine, and popping amphetamines is as widespread today as consuming alcohol was during prohibition. Illegal gambling, prostitution, bribery of public officials, and homosexual acts between consenting adults: The incidence of these and other victimless crimes is widespread.

It is estimated that 14 percent of American males and 4 percent of American females are practicing homosexuals.[44] In half the states, their practices are criminal. As recently as 1985, the United States Supreme Court upheld the right of states to make homosexual acts criminal.[45] The case is worth considering, for it bears directly on the issue of what constitutes crime and how criminologists must take into account the entire spectrum of criminal behavior when developing adequate descriptions and explanations of crime.

Michael Hardwick, as mentioned in Chapter 1, was arrested in his home for committing sodomy. The police officer who made the arrest entered the home because Mr. Hardwick had failed to pay a fine for drunkenness. He found Mr. Hardwick and another man engaged in oral sex. Mr. Hardwick appealed the case to the U.S. Supreme Court on the grounds that the sodomy law violated his right to privacy. The Supreme Court, in a controversial 5–4 decision, upheld the sodomy laws by denying that the right to privacy protected citizens against such prosecution. Sodomy is defined as oral or anal sex. In Idaho, Utah, Arizona, Oklahoma, Louisiana, Minnesota, Missouri, Michigan, Kentucky, Tennessee, Mississippi, Alabama, Georgia, South Carolina, Florida, North Carolina, Virginia, Kentucky, Rhode Island, and Washington, D.C., acts of oral or anal sex—whether committed by heterosexuals or homosexuals—are criminal offenses punishable by up to 20 years in prison. In five other states (Nevada, Montana, Texas, Kansas, and Arkansas) sodomy is a crime only if it is committed by homosexuals.

Oral sex, according to surveys of sexual practices among Americans, is practiced by over 70 percent of the population.[46] Thus, in 19 states, 60–70 percent of the population are habitual criminals who could be sentenced up to 20 years in prison. Or, in those states with habitual-criminal statutes, these people could be sentenced to prison for life without parole. That this seems outlandish and impossible should be considered in light of the fact that only a few years ago persons found with as little as a half-ounce of marihuana were sentenced to up to 25 years in prison for the crime of possession. Considering all the other offenses that people systematically commit (tax evasion, driving under the influence of alcohol, and so forth), the proportion of the population that are habitual criminals as defined in some state laws probably approaches 100 percent.

Frances Cullen says that "an adequate theory of the origins of deviant behavior must address two distinct questions: (1) What conditions motivate or predispose people to violate social and legal norms? and (2) What conditions account for the specific form that a deviant response takes?"[47] If he is correct, then it follows that "an adequate theory of deviant behavior" will have to be a theory of all human behavior. Correspondingly, it follows that any theory that purports to explain why some people commit crime and others do not must be judged according to its ability to explain *all* human behavior as well.

Until recently, abortion was another crime practiced by sizeable proportions of the population from all social classes. Abortion laws were revolutionized in recent years by U.S. Supreme Court decisions *(Roe v. Wade* and *Baker v. Carr)*. In *Roe v. Wade,* the U.S. Supreme Court ruled that the states could not make it a crime for a woman to terminate a pregnancy in the first trimester. The court also held that the states could legally restrict whether an abortion in the second trimester was in a hospital or a clinic, but that the decision to abort was still the woman's right. The court ruled that the decision to abort in the third trimester could be regulated by state law. Most states have passed legislation making it illegal to terminate a pregnancy after the end of the second trimester. The recency of these court decisions makes it impossible to know how many people are aborting illegally.

Prostitution is an extremely common type of victimless crime; it is also a controversial issue in criminology as to whether or not it should be categorized as "victimless." It is usually engaged between consenting adults, but it is arguable that the women who are selling sexual favors are nonetheless victims. The superb work on prostitution by Eleanor Miller brilliantly describes the life and times of under-class women who turn to prostitution as a means of escaping the oppression of mindless work, disrupted families, and economic hopelessness.[48] Miller also describes how prostitutes are caught in a web that includes selling and using drugs, shoplifting, and assisting in other forms of criminality.

Research on prostitution makes it very clear that prostitutes suffer from diseases, mental anguish, and degradation. To some extent, these consequences may be attributable to the fact that it is illegal. It is also argued that defining prostitution as illegal deprives people of their right to determine how they will use their own bodies. Prostitution is, then, a victimless crime in the sense that it takes place without a complainant, but it is also arguable that it is a crime that leads to a great deal of personal harm. Prostitution accounts for more arrests of women than any other crime. It is certainly one of the easiest crimes for the police to discover, which may account for its high arrest rate. On the other hand, millions of men and women engage in this crime annually, making it one of the most frequent violations of the law.

Cross-Cultural Studies _____

Cross-cultural studies are exceedingly difficult. We are often forced to rely on official statistics. As we have seen, official statistics are political footballs that get kicked about in an effort to score points rather than provide reliable scientific data. One of the most recent attempts to study violence cross-culturally began by writing to the embassies of foreign nations, enlisting help in gaining access to data on crime and violence rates. The authors report that, in some instances, they received letters telling how problems of crime and violence had ceased to be of any consequence: "This drastic reduction in the crime volume is due to various improvements in police service instituted by our government to improve peace and order, which is one of the notable achievements in the new order in our country that have helped evolve a new concept in police work since the imposition of martial law."[49]

The Archer and Gartner study also suffers severe limitations created by language translation. Categories that had one meaning to the people of a country were translated ethnocentrically into another meaning that would be attached to that behavior in the United States. Such ethnocentric bias creates real problems for comparative research and makes suspect any conclusions drawn from such research.

Even where there may not be deliberate manipulation of the statistics, comparing data from two countries is unreliable because of fundamental differences in how criminal acts are defined and, especially, how the statistics are recorded. In Norway, a crime is not recorded as a murder unless someone has been convicted. If a person who killed another is convicted of only negligent manslaughter or if it is found that the killing was the result of self defense or insanity, the killing is never recorded as a murder. In the United States, as previously stated, the act would be recorded as a murder if the police investigating the death felt it was murder, regardless of what the coroner, court, jury, or prosecutor decided. Thus, comparing the murder or homicide rate between Norway and the United States is entirely misleading. One suspects that similar recording differences would be found on careful scrutiny of the procedures used in various countries.

Cross-cultural data from victim surveys encounter some of the same problems of "definition." A survey of violent crimes in Norway a few years ago revealed an incidence of personal violence comparable to that in the United States.[50] The questions asked in both surveys were essentially the same. It is quite possible, however, that the interpretations given to the meaning of the questions varied. In Norway, a person might consider it an act of violence if someone shoved them while boarding a train; in the United States, a person might not consider this or any act short of being hit with a pick axe as an act of violence. This is, of course, an exaggeration, but the point is that comparing responses to possible criminal infractions cross-culturally can only be done with great care.

Perhaps the only finding from cross-cultural victim surveys that is worth reporting is that most countries seem to report about the same percentage of people victimized every year.[51] The studies are too new and too limited to allow any firm conclusions, but the data are suggestive.

We are in a somewhat better position to evaluate cross-cultural studies based on ethnographic data provided by anthropologists. A recent criminology text utilizes these sorts of data to great effect.[52] We will cover the results of these comparisons in later chapters, where these results will be applied to testing some of the current criminological theories.

Conclusion _____

Reliable scientific knowledge derives from making accurate observations and logically consistent theories that explain these observations. This chapter focused on some of the important facts discovered by criminologists seeking an accurate description of crime. Many of the facts fly in the face of commonly held ideas. Even people who should know better, such as the Chief Justice of the United States, often make erroneous statements about crime. It is imperative that we are able to differentiate between data that is scientifically reliable and data that is being generated and used for political or bureaucratic purposes. As Pepinsky and Jasilow put it, we must dispel the "myths that cause crime" if we are to ever gain an adequate understanding.[53]

By far the most difficult myths to overcome about crime in America are those generated by law-enforcement officials. It is in their interests to paint a picture of crime that corresponds with what they need and do. Police need not be consciously deceptive to dispense misinformation. Bureaucratic rules, a firm belief in the legitimacy of what they are doing, and a set of rules that systematically bias their work and the reporting of crime all add up to the generation of statistics that are misleading and perceptions of crime that are erroneous. The major source of crime statistics, the *Uniform Crime Reports,* published annually by the FBI, are misleading statistics that, unfortunately, form the basis for much of the misinformation used by the media, politicians, and reporters.

A more-accurate picture of who is the victim, who commits criminal acts, and the types of crime committed can be formed from the more-systematic and less-biased researches summarized in this chapter. These researches, however, cover only a small segment of the total amount of criminality. In the next chapter, we will discuss a wide variety of criminal acts not included in the official statistics, victim surveys, self-report surveys, or cross-cultural studies.

CHAPTER

3

Data on Crime: Part II

No doubt many people think that crime consists only of the kinds of behaviors discussed in the last chapter. This is understandable given the inordinate amount of attention such acts receive in the media. For criminology, however, the task of describing criminality only begins with delinquency, homicide, robbery, assault, rape, and theft. Criminology is the study of acts defined by law as criminal. One of the characteristics of modern legal systems is the expansion of criminal law to include a very wide spectrum of behavior.[1] In this chapter, we summarize the data on white-collar, corporate, public, state, and organized crime.

Corruption

Political and law-enforcement corruption are, in a sense, victimless crimes like those surveyed in the last chapter because they involve criminality between consenting adults. Because there is

57

no direct victim, these crimes are largely hidden from view. In another sense, however, we are all victims of corrupt practices just as all women are victims of rape whether or not they are themselves directly victimized. Our best indication of the variety and extent of crimes of corruption derives from (1) government hearings, (2) agency reports, and (3) participant-observation research. When social scientists research police or political corruption, they find that it is widespread at every level of government. Extensive researches in Seattle, Washington; Reading, Pennsylvania; Philadelphia, Pennsylvania; London, England; and a host of other cities reveals widespread corruption of police and politicians.[2] Journalistic accounts also support the findings of social scientists.[3]

The U.S. Attorney General's Office is responsible for investigating and prosecuting the violation of federal statutes under the Ethics in Government.[4] It issues an annual report on cases brought before the court under this act. These data, like other official statistics, cannot provide an accurate description of the extent of criminality of this type, but they are suggestive. The Ethics in Government Act covers election crimes, election fraud, criminal patronage offenses, and illegal campaign financing. This section of the Justice Department has only 24 full-time assigned attorneys. Three attorneys are responsible for investigating and prosecuting allegations of election fraud for the entire country. Needless to say, the ability of this minute staff to cover the field is extremely limited. Furthermore, this staff is limited to federal law violations that do not include state or local misfeasance or malfeasance in office.

From 1974–1983, the limited staff of this division obtained a total of 1,552 indictments against federal public officials (see Table 3.1). In a 3-year period from March, 1976, to January, 1979, the indictment and prosecution of corrupt public officials included

1. Six members of Congress.
2. Eighteen Executive Branch officials (including Richard Helms, Director of the Central Intelligence Agency).
3. One member of the Federal Judiciary.

Among the indictments brought were some that received widespread publicity: In 1983, the Public Integrity Section prosecuted Rita M. Lavelle, an Assistant Administrator for Solid Waste in the Environmental Protection Agency, for, among other things,

TABLE 3.1   Federal Indictments and Prosecutions of Corrupt Public Officials (1974–1983)

	Federal Officials									
	1974	**1975**	**1976**	**1977**	**1978**	**1979**	**1980**	**1981**	**1982**	**1983**
Indicted	59	53	111	129	133	128	123	198	158	460*
Convicted	51	43	101	94	91	115	131	159	147	424
Awaiting trial on December 31	1	5	1	32	42	21	16	23	38	58
State Officials										
Indicted	36	36	59	50	55	58	72	87	49	81
Convicted	23	18	35	38	56	32	51	66	43	65
Awaiting trial on December 31	0	5	30	33	20	30	28	36	18	26
Local Officials										
Indicted	130	139	194	157	171	212	247	244	257	270
Convicted	87	94	100	164	127	156	168	211	232	226
Awaiting trial on December 31	4	15	98	62	72	67	82	102	58	61
Others Involved										
Indicted	66	27	199	171	198	289	280	340	265	262
Convicted	56	24	144	144	135	252	202	294	249	257
Awaiting trial on December 31	0	2	70	83	71	69	87	70	72	77
Totals										
Indicted	291	255	563	507	557	687	721	878	729	1,073
Convicted	217	179	380	440	409	555	552	730	671	972
Awaiting trial on December 31	5	27	199	210	205	187	213	231	186	222

*The 1983 figures were reviewed to attempt to identify the reason for the substantial jump in prosecutions of federal officials. The explanation appears to be two-fold. First, there has clearly been a greater focus on federal corruption nationwide; second, there appears to have been more-consistent reporting of lower-level employees who abused their office, cases that may have been overlooked in the past. For reference, the U.S. Attorneys Offices were told: "For purposes of this questionnaire, a public corruption case includes any case involving abuse of office by a public employee. We are not excluding low-level employees or minor crimes, but rather focusing on the job-relatedness of the offense and whether the offense involves abuse of the public trust placed in the employee."

Source: Annual Report to Congress on the Activities and Operations of the Public Integrity Section, U.S. Department of Justice (April 1984), 40.

perjury before the U.S. House of Representatives and the U.S. Senate; U.S. District Judge Harry Claiborne was indicted in Nevada on charges of bribery, fraud, obstruction of justice, and making false statements on his income-tax returns; Anthony J. Buffalino was sentenced to a year and a day in prison for soliciting money from a defendant awaiting trial on the promise of having the defendant's sentence reduced; Sorkis Webbe and his son, Sorkis Webbe, Jr., and four others were indicted for vote fraud in Missouri—it was alleged that they had engaged in a successful scheme to affect fraudulently the outcome of a close legislative contest for the Missouri House of Representatives in 1980; and Allen Z. Wolfson and Louis Rocha, Jr., were charged with violations of campaign-financing statutes for contributions made through illicit conduits in excess of the $1,000 maximum allowed by law.

The exposure, if not the incidence, of public corruption reached its zenith during the administration of Richard M. Nixon. Leading members of Nixon's cabinet were indicted and sentenced to prison for a wide range of offenses from soliciting and receiving illegal political-campaign contributions to breaking and entering office buildings. Included among the high-level government officials who were found guilty of criminal acts while serving in public office were Attorney Generals John Mitchell and Richard Kleindeist; Presidential Advisors John Dean, John Erhlichman, Richard Halderman; and Vice President Spiro Agnew. Maurice Stans, one-time Secretary of Commerce who managed the campaign to reelect President Nixon in 1972, pleaded guilty to violating federal election fund-raising statutes and was sentenced to a year in prison. Richard Helms, director of the Central Intelligence Agency, pleaded *nollo contendre* to charges that he perjured himself before Congress.

Richard Nixon's presidency was one of the most scandal-ridden ever; but it was not unique. A review of scandals that involved criminal acts on the part of a president or his close advisors reveals that no president in U.S. history has escaped unscathed. George Washington enriched himself through land speculation and the use of the presidency for personal gain, including the illegal importation of Merino sheep smuggled from Spain. The Teapot Dome Scandal, through which Warren G. Harding and several cabinet officers made fortunes by selling federal land, is one of the more-famous acts of presidential corruption, but it is not the only one. Lyndon Johnson feared he would be put in prison if his connections to Bobby Baker were revealed. Bobby Baker was John-

INDICTED: Jay Turoff (left), former New York Commissioner of Taxi and Limousine Commission. *(Chester Higgins, Jr./The New York Times)*

son's assistant when Johnson was in the Senate, and Baker used his position in that capacity to shake down businessmen who wanted to put vending machines in public offices.[5] Even Dwight Eisenhower was embarrassed by his Secretary of State, Sherman Adams, who accepted a gift of a vicuñae coat from a government contractor. Eisenhower himself accepted gifts from businesspeople, which put him in the awkward position of a conflict of interests. During the first 5 years of Ronald Reagan's two terms as president (1980–1985), over 50 public officials appointed during his administration were forced to resign under suspicion of illegal behavior. Members of Congress are not often the object of surveillance, but, in the late 1970s, the FBI established a probe into the corruption of public officials. This operation was called ABSCAM. Based on information suggesting that some public officials were accepting bribes in return for legislative and political favors, the FBI used undercover agents to investigate the allegations. The FBI did not wait for a complaint or develop a case "after the fact." Rather, the agency targeted people it suspected of accepting bribes and, using undercover agents posing as people seeking political favors, attempted to bribe the officials. This policing method is very common in making arrests for prostitution, drug dealing, and receiving stolen property. It is less commonly used to catch upper-class criminals. The defendants in the ABSCAM case argued that the police entrapped them. Had this claim been upheld in court, the defendants would have been found not guilty. It was, however, denied, and a number of politicians were sentenced to prison.

In less than 2 years of investigation, the FBI uncovered evidence that culminated in the prosecution and conviction of ten persons, including U.S. Congressmen John Murphy (NY), Raymond Lederer (PA), Michael Myers (PA), Frank Thompson (NJ), Harrison Williams (NJ), John Jenrette (SC), and Richard Kelly (FL). In addition, a Philadelphia attorney, a Philadelphia city councilman, and a New Jersey State Senator were also prosecuted for accepting bribes.

There is no compilation of comparable state-level cases presently available. There are, however, an almost endless stream of revelations of bribery and corruption at the state and local level in police departments and among public officials. In Louisiana in 1985, the governor, his brother, and a number of cohorts were indicted for soliciting and accepting bribes. The Queens Borough President in New York City is alleged to have solicited and accepted bribes in connection with the awarding of contracts totaling more than a million dollars. In their ground-breaking research on toxic-waste dumping (outlined later), Block and Scarpitti discovered evidence of widespread political and law-enforcement corruption, which culminated in toxic contamination.[6]

White-Collar Crime

Criminologists speak of acts committed in the course of doing business by "a person of respectability and high social status" as *white-collar crime*.[7] Business and corporation activities are circumscribed by law in myriad ways. Not all legal obligations governing their activities are criminal. For example, if a company fails to live up to the terms of a contract, there are legal remedies for the person who has had his or her contract violated. Failure to fulfill the conditions of a contract, however, is not a crime unless there was fraud involved. Similarly, if a worker is injured on a job, the company may be liable for compensating the worker for his or her injury, but it has not necessarily committed a crime. If, however, the injury resulted from the company's gross negligence, then it may have committed a crime.

When we speak of white-collar crime, then, we are speaking of only those acts committed as a result of a person's occupation that are specifically defined in law as criminal. A professor who burgles people's homes on weekends is not a white-collar criminal since burgling homes is not a result of his or her occupation. A professor who misuses public funds (research grants, for example) would be a white-collar criminal. If landowners burn down one of their apartment houses in order to collect insurance, this is white-collar crime. If they burn it down in order to enjoy the flames and heat, it is not.

Occupational and Corporate Crime

White-collar crimes may be either occupational or corporate. *Occupational crime* consists of criminal acts done solely for the benefit or economic gain of the individual offender; corporate crimes are those committed for the benefit of the corporation. Examples of white-collar occupational crimes are embezzling, stealing employer's goods, insider trading on the stock market, blackmailing based on occupation-acquired information, misusing legally assigned funds (a lawyer who bilks an estate for which he or she is executor, for example), and bribe-taking by politicians and police.

Corporate crime consists of criminal acts committed in the course of doing business in which the principal benefactor is the corporation, not the individual. A tax accountant who fiddles the books to increase his or her own income is committing an occupational offense. When the books of a corporation are "adjusted" to hide income and avoid corporate taxes, this is corporate crime. When the heads of the largest electrical manufacturing companies in the United States agree to fix prices, this is corporate crime. It is also corporate crime for banks to transfer funds in excess of $10,000 without reporting the transfer to the appropriate government agency; for corporations to bribe government officials or make illegal campaign contributions; and for companies to steal trade secrets of competitors, to fix prices, to engage in fraudulent advertising, to fail to adhere to proper safety and health standards for employees, and to illegally dump toxic wastes. These are but a few of the practices engaged in by corporations that are violations of the criminal law.

The concept of white-collar crime was first suggested by Edwin Sutherland in an address to the American Sociological Association in 1939.[8] His more complete study was published in 1949.[9] Sutherland studied the criminal careers of the 70 largest manufacturing, mining, and mercantile corporations in the United States. The subjects were selected from lists composed in 1929 and 1938. At the time of the study, the average age of the corporations was 45 years. He found that each of the 70 corporations had one or more decisions against it for criminal activities: restraint of trade; misrepresentation in advertising; infringement of patent, trademarks, and copyrights; unfair labor practices; financial fraud and violation of trust; violations of war regulations; and assorted miscellaneous offenses. Two firms (Armour and Company and Swift and Company) each had 50 decisions against it. General Motors ranked third, with 40 decisions; Sears Roebuck and Montgomery Ward tied for fourth with 39 decisions each. The total number of decisions against the 70 corporations was 980, with an average of 14 decisions per corporation. As Sutherland points out, this makes most of the corporations he studied "habitual offenders."

Sutherland's findings of frequent violations of criminal law by the 50 largest corporations in the United States is repeated in subsequent research. Both occupational and corporate white-collar criminality is a way of life for most big businesses and many small ones as well.

In an exhaustive investigation published in 1981, Clinard and Yeager studied the criminal, civil, and administrative violations of the 477 largest manufacturing corporations in the United States as listed in the Fortune 500.[10] They reviewed the records of 25 federal agencies and compiled data on cases either initiated or completed against the 477 corporations during 1975 and 1976. In addition, 105 of the largest wholesale, retail, and service corporations were surveyed for a total of 582 corporations. The researchers found six main types of illegal corporate behavior: administrative, environmental, financial, labor, manufacturing, and unfair-trade practices.

Three-fifths of the 477 corporations had at least one legal action initiated against it from 1975–1976. Two hundred of the corporations, 42 percent, had multiple cases charged against them. Seventy-one corporations had multiple environmental cases, 61 had multiple manufacturing cases, and 37 had multiple labor cases. A few corporations accounted for the majority of the total violations: 13 percent of the companies cited accounted for 52 percent of the violations with an average of 23.5 violations per firm in the 2-year period.

One of the safest ways to assure profits in many large industries is to influence the passage of laws and government spending. The oil industry enjoys substantial tax advantages as a result of lobbying and political-campaign contributions. Lobbying and political contributions are perfectly legal. However, the law limits the amount a corporation can give to a political campaign. Many corporations violate this law in order to increase their influence with favored politicians. A congressional study of the Nixon presidential campaign of 1972 revealed widespread illegal campaign contributions, including over $100,000 illegally contributed by Gulf Oil. More than 300 major corporations were exposed as having given illegal campaign contributions.[11]

It is important to understand that both occupational and corporate crimes are being committed. It was a criminal act for Gulf Oil to give $100,000 in illegal money to the Nixon re-election campaign; this was a corporate crime. It was illegal for Nixon to accept this money; this was an occupational crime. Similarly, while Spiro Agnew was Governor of Maryland and later Vice President of the United States, he accepted payoffs from construction companies seeking government contracts. The companies committed corporate criminal acts; Spiro Agnew committed a personal criminal act.

The distinction between corporate and occupational crime is often a fuzzy one. Take a case involving former Attorney General Richard G. Kleindienst. When Kleindienst was Attorney General, the Los Angeles office of the FBI discovered that the teamsters union was about to sign an insurance agreement valued at more than 1 billion dollars. The FBI suspected that there had been payoffs and corruption of some union officials, including the then president of the union, Frank E. Fitzimmons. The FBI sought permission from the Attorney General to place an electronic-surveillance listening device in the room where insurance and teamsters officials were meeting. Mr. Kleindienst refused the request.[12] The teamsters union had played a central role through large campaign contributions and delivering votes in the presidential election of Mr. Kleindienst's boss, Richard Nixon.[13] After the meeting between the teamsters union and the insurers, the president of the teamsters, Mr. Fitzimmons, flew back to Washington on President Nixon's private plane. Several years later, Mr. Kleindienst, acting as a private attorney, received a $125,000 fee from the teamsters union for arranging another large insurance contract for the teamsters. Corporate, governmental, and occupational criminality are often so intertwined as to represent a fusion of several distinct sociological types of crime. In this case, there is evidence of white-collar occupational crime (the union officials), the political corruption of government officials, and the corporate crime of fraud on the part of the insurance companies. None of the participants, however, was ever prosecuted for these offenses.

In August 1985, Eli Lilly Company of Indianapolis pleaded guilty to mislabeling and not reporting the side effects of Oraflex, an antiarthritic drug the company introduced into the market in 1982. Dr. William Ian H. Shedden, former vice president and chief medical officer of Lilly Research Laboratories, was found guilty of failing to report information to the Food and Drug Administration concerning the safety of Oraflex. More than 1,400 people in Great Britain claim they were damaged or that relatives died from taking the drug. Lilly and Dr. Shedden were fined $1,000 on each of the 25 charges for a total fine of $25,000.

The most dramatic result of the trial of a corporation for the violation of worker health and safety regulations took place in Illinois, where five executives of Film Recovery Corporation were charged with murder and the corporation was charged with manslaughter in the death of an employee, Stefan Golab.[14] The court found that

> the conditions under which the workers in the plant performed their duties was totally unsafe. There was an insufficient amount of safety equipment on the premises. There was no safety instructions given to the workers. The workers were not adequately warned of the hazards and dangers of working with cyanide.

The trial established beyond a reasonable doubt that the executives knew of the dangers workers faced while working with cyanide. Three of the defendants were found guilty and sentenced to 25 years in prison and each of the corporations involved was fined $10,000. This case is unique in the annals of criminal trials of corporations and corporate executives with respect to both the charges brought against them and the severity of the sentences imposed. The Eli Lilly experience, in which relatively small fines were imposed for acts that created immeasurable harm, is much more typical of the legal system's response to corporate and white-collar criminality.

Arson

In 1979, there were 145,500 known incidents of arson in the United States. In the decade between 1965 and 1975, 10,000 homes were destroyed by arson in Detroit alone. One sociologist, James Brady, who has studied arson extensively, suggests we are in the throes of creating an "urban desert" of burned-out tenement houses, slum dwellings, and poor houses.[15] The National Insurance Service Office estimates that over $4 billion is paid out annually for arson fires. The Law Enforcement Assistance Administration estimates there was 325 percent increase in arson between 1965 and 1975. Each year, close to a thousand people die in arson fires: "Many of these are children or old people, unable to move quickly to escape the flames in the darkness. The buildings in which they died were typically unsafe, unhealthy, and in clear violation of fire and safety codes."[16] Brady quotes a *60 Minutes* special, "Fires for Profit," where it was said that "death by fire is a pauper's epitaph, as arsonists strike most often in inner-city districts of the poor."

These deaths and the destruction of the property caused by arsonists are almost entirely the result of corporate decisions. Banks "red line" areas of the city where they will not give loans on housing—thus making it impossible for owners to finance inner-city property. Arson is one way of recouping the potential losses by collecting insurance. Slum landlords who may own hundreds of apartments in the inner-city profit from the arsons by collecting insurance and being able either to construct new housing that can be rented for higher prices or to sell the bare land for more than the original building was worth.

The 1970s saw the creation of a new set of criminal laws directed toward American businesses. The Foreign Corrupt Practices Act (1978) made it a criminal offense for U.S. corporations to bribe agents of foreign governments. These laws were passed after the Securities and Exchange Commission disclosed massive payoffs by U.S. corporations to foreign officials:

- From 1969–1975, the Lockheed Corporation spent $202 million to bribe government officials in France, Germany, Turkey, Italy, the Netherlands, Japan, Saudi Arabia, Indonesia, and the Philippines.
- General Motors paid foreign governments $250,000 a year from 1970–1975. These payments were made to assure smooth business operations; for example, to expedite people and goods

through customs and circumvent bureaucratic hitches to business operations.

- The United Fruit Company (renamed United Brands) bribed Honduran government officials with payments exceeding $2.5 million and Italian officials with payments of $750,000. These bribes were to effect favorable business treatment, including low tax rates for the corporation. This scandal led to the suicide of a United Brands president and the resignation of the Honduran president.[17]
- From 1960–1978, 300 of the 500 largest corporations in the United States paid at least $1 billion in illegal political contributions and commercial bribery to foreign government officials, including the husband of the Queen of the Netherlands and the Prime Minister of Japan.[18]

As with most of our data on white-collar, corporate, and public crimes, we are left to estimate the extent of the criminality. More so than with other types of crime, law enforcement is inconsistent and dependent on the political ideology of those in power. There is reason to believe that there is as much bribery today as ever, but the only solid data we have come from the exposure of the Securities and Exchange Commission in the 1970s.

Money Laundering

In 1984 and 1985, the Justice Department began enforcing laws that require banks to report cash transactions over $10,000. These laws are supposed to make it difficult for people to avoid paying taxes on cash not reported to the Internal Revenue Service by transferring funds overseas to secret bank accounts. The laws also make it more difficult for drug traffickers to transfer large sums to pay for drug deals or to conceal profits. The Justice Department investigation revealed wholesale violation of these laws by most of the nation's largest banks and financial institutions. Chase Manhattan Bank was fined for failing to report billions of dollars in cash transactions. Crocker National Bank had to pay $2.25 million in fines for failing to report $3.9 billion in transactions. The Bank of America, the second largest bank in the United States, and E. F. Hutton, stock brokerage company were also found guilty of laundering billions of dollars to overseas bank accounts, and they were fined. Before the investigation wound down, dozens of banks and stock-brokerage companies were found guilty of criminally laundering more money in 1 year than robberies, thefts, and burglaries account for in 10 years.

Tax Evasion

Avoiding taxes motivates a substantial amount of white-collar crime. The Cartier Jewelers in New York, one of the most exclusive jewelers in America, conspired with its customers to avoid federal, state, and local taxes on the sale of expensive jewelry. Customers walked out of the store with hundreds of thousands of dollars worth of jewelry while the clerks wrote the sale up as going to a customer out of state. Empty boxes were then mailed to out-of-state addresses.

One of the most common forms of tax evasion is smuggling. Alcohol, cigarettes, furs—virtually all luxury items that are heavily taxed—are smuggled into the country and across state lines. New York State loses hundreds of thousands of dollars a year in revenue from items smuggled across its borders from states with lower taxes; especially profitable is the smuggling of cigarettes, alcohol, and even gasoline. It is estimated that bout 100,000 gallons of gasoline are smuggled each year into New York to avoid taxes. Another common technique to avoid taxes is for corporations to maintain "store-front" offices. In this scam, a company establishes an address that is merely a paper operation in order to avoid paying taxes. In 1985, the Illinois Insurance Department ordered 11 insurance companies to stop using "store-front" offices in Illinois to avoid taxes estimated at a loss of 5 million dollars a year to the state.[19]

Another form of tax evasion that is commonplace is the undervaluation of corporate property. A Senate subcommittee estimated that millions of dollars are lost each year from this form of evasion.[20] The subcommittee cited the case of the United States Steel plant in Gary, Indiana, which was underassessed by $119 million. This was part of a pattern of giving large corporations a tax break used by the tax assessor of Gary, Indiana, who systematically undervalued property.[21]

Factory Safety and Health

One of Canada's leading legal scholars recently described deaths and injuries incurred in the work place as "close to genocide."[22] Each year, the number of workers whose well-being is adversely affected by work-related conditions is two and a half times greater than the number of victims of violent crimes. Over 100,000 workers die from diseases and injuries received while at work. Donnelly estimates that 2.3 million workers suffer diseases and injury each year as a result of work conditions.[23] Not all of these are the result of corporate crimes, but many are. As Kramer notes:

> . . . over 100,000 deaths a year are attributed to occupationally related diseases, the majority of which are caused by the knowing and willful violation of occupational health and safety laws by corporations. . . . Additionally 14,200 workers are killed in industrial 'accidents' with two million more receiving disabling injuries . . . the majority of these deaths and injuries can be attributed to dangerous work conditions maintained by corporations in violation of federal law.[24]

The Office of Safety and Health Administration (OSHA) is responsible for enforcing safety and health laws, but it is hamstrung by a small staff of investigators responsible for overseeing hundreds of thousands of manufacturing, industrial, and construction sites. Even so, OSHA reports indicate that there are many violations of worker safety and health laws every year. In 1980, there were over 165,000 violations of health and safety standards in the mining industry alone.[25] It is not uncommon for a corporation to have a criminal record of thousands of violations spanning several years.[26] Reiman documents the case of an explosion that killed workers in a coal mine that had over 1,000 recorded safety violations. Inspections by the Nuclear Regulatory Commission of the Kerr-McGee uranium-processing plant in Gore, Oklahoma, disclosed 20 infractions of safety rules between 1977 and 1985. An inspector wrote on September 24, 1985, that "the plant's compliance with regulations and license conditions has been marginal . . . the total number of violations is excessive and the presence of repeated problems indicates a lack of management oversight."[27]

On January 4, 1986, "James Harrison died a horrible death . . . his lungs destroyed by an acid cloud that trapped him in Kerr-McGee's Gore, Oklahoma, uranium-processing plant."[28]

Donnelly estimates that the problem of worker safety and health is so widespread that almost every worker in the United States will be injured, contract a serious disease, or die over the course of a 35–40 year work career.[29]

In the coal-mining industry, over 15,000 miners are disabled each year by work-related conditions.[30] According to the annual report of the Secretary of Labor, 130 miners were killed by unsafe work conditions in 1980. These figures are expected to rise by 35–40 percent in the next few years as coal production increases to replace the high cost of oil. By the year 2000, one researcher estimates that over 42,000 miners will suffer injuries and 370 will die each year.[31] These figures do not even include the victims of "black lung" disease, which is the most common cause of permanent disability and early death among coal miners.

In the 1920s and 1930s, the Bureau of Labor Statistics developed a reporting system that was intended to collect information on every work-related injury, illness, or death. In the first years of reporting, 20,000 work fatalities were documented, along with 1,600 permanent disabilities, 100,000 partial disabilities, and 2,500,000 temporary disabilities. Based on the statistics from subsequent years, the National Safety Council reports that there is a rate of 43 accidents and illnesses per 1,000 workers each year. Their data indicate that the rate remained fairly stable from 1933–1963. The rate increased substantially in the 1960s, however, with the creation of a large number of jobs working with hazardous materials. In 1972, there were 100,000 deaths and 300,000 injuries annually resulting from working with hazardous substances. Of 500,000 asbestos workers in the United States, 100,000 are expected to die of lung cancer, 35,000 of pleural cancer, and 85,000 of asbestiosis. This amounts to 40 percent of all asbestos workers who will die as a result of their employment.

These findings on the hazards faced by workers are subject to many of the same problems as data on other crimes. Just as women who are the victims of rape or assault are reticent to report these findings, corporations whose workers are injured are reluctant to report the injuries. Furthermore, workers may not realize that the injury or illness is due to work conditions. For years, medical doctors working for coal-mine operators and cotton manufacturers lied to the workers about the origin of illnesses caused by coal dust and cloth fibers. Furthermore, the number of deaths, injuries, and illnesses attributable to the violation of criminal laws is at this point a matter of conjecture. As previously indicated, however, it is abundantly clear that a large proportion of the 2–3 million worker accidents, deaths, and illnesses each year in the United States are a result of corporate criminal acts.

Product Safety and Health

Both the products and the by-products of manufacturing are responsible for widespread death and disease. Much of this carnage is the direct result of criminal acts by corporations. Approximately 19 percent of all U.S. deaths annually (144,000) are attributable to air pollution, part of which is caused by corporate violation of pollution laws. The Consumer Product Safety Commission estimates that 20 million serious injuries—including 30,000 deaths each year—result from unsafe and defective consumer products such as spoiled food; unsafe drugs; and defective autos, tires, appliances, contraceptive devices, motorcycles, bicycles, and so forth. One of the more extreme examples in recent years involved the chemical company, Union Carbide. In 1984, an explosion at one of its factories in India killed more than 2,500 people, with thousands of others injured. Subsequent investigation revealed that (1) the company was aware that valves were leaking; (2) as early as 1978, a company report indicated misgivings about the safety of the plant; and (3) in 1981, a worker died as a result of improper safety precautions. Union Carbide admitted that a safer computer safety system was available and in operation at its other plants. The Indian government arrested, then later released, the president of Union Carbide. A number of Union Carbide officers were tried on criminal charges.

Many industries knowingly produce dangerous products that result in widespread death and illness. Sometimes these products are accompanied by fraudulent reports attesting to their safety. The pharmaceutical industry is probably the worst offender. A recent study by J. Braithwaite based on official records and interviews with corporate executives, law-enforcement agents, and others reveals a systematic pattern of law violation in the pharmaceutical industry that would be difficult for another industry to match.[32]

Braithwaite's analysis underscores the fact that corporate crime reflects corporate decision-making practices rather than the evil, malicious, or avaricious motives of individual corporate executives. Indeed, it is the bureaucratic nature of the decision that is the basis for the individual's ability to shirk responsibility. The top-ranking executives are often shielded from responsibility by an elaborate process that keeps them from knowing specifically about illegal practices. Corporate crime is, according to Braithwaite, firmly grounded in normal corporate activities.

Braithwaite's data span the globe from interviews and official records in Australia, Guatemala, Mexico, the United States, and Great Britain. Braithwaite found that the pharmaceutical industry world-wide was systematically and universally involved with fraud in the safety testing of drugs, with a pattern of criminal negligence in the manufacture of unhealthy and unsafe drugs, and with a history of bribery and corruption that was the worst in the world.

From 1972–1974, 74 percent of the U.S. clinical investigators in the pharmaceutical industry failed to comply with legal requirements. People who volunteered for experiments were not told of possible dangers and researchers failed to keep proper records of the amount of drugs used in experiments. Data on test results were fraudulently recorded and drug-company executives failed to report negative results and elevated positive results to mislead government agencies.

In foreign countries, American and British drug companies bribed and corrupted government officials to permit them to sell drugs banned in the United States and Britain—drugs known to be hazardous to health and drugs known to have no medicinal value.[33] For example, while paying compensation to victims of the Dalkon Shield in the United States and Britain, the manufacturers of this harmful contraceptive device continued to distribute it to women in the Third World. To accomplish a crime like this, drug companies bribe government officials, licensors, and doctors. They falsify claims in advertisements and promise cures they know cannot be expected.

The pharmaceutical industry may be, as Braithwaite maintains, the most habitual corporate offender in producing and distributing hazardous products, but it is not alone. The infamous recent cases of General Motors and Ford Motor companies knowingly producing dangerous automobiles is illustrative.[34]

In 1971, the Ford Motor Company produced the Ford Pinto. The company had test results that showed the Pinto was seriously flawed because the fuel tank was located too near the back bumper. Tests indicated that, even at low speeds, if the car were struck from behind, the fuel tank would burst into flames. The production scheduled was, nonetheless, met. The Ford Motor Company consciously calculated how many deaths and injuries would result from the unsafe nature of the Pinto. The executives estimated that 180 people would burn to death as a result of automobile fires caused by the faulty design. They estimated that there would be an additional 180 serious burn injuries and 2,100 burned vehicles.[35] The total cost to Ford of lawsuits from these production-design–caused deaths, injuries, and property damage was estimated by Ford executives at $49.5 million. Retooling for machinery and fixing the design fault so that the car was not dangerous was estimated to cost $11.00 per vehicle and a total of $137 million. The executives decided to produce and sell the dangerous car. As a result, from 1971–1976, hundreds of Ford Pintos exploded into fiery coffins in what otherwise would have been mere "fender-bender" accidents. The Ford Motor Company has paid out millions of dollars in damages, but it was found not guilty of murder in a trial brought in Indiana as the result of people killed in a Pinto crash.

In 1980, General Motors repeated the Ford experience. Their X-Body cars were found to have serious brake-locking problems. Production continued on schedule without correcting the dangerous error. Advertising of the cars failed to mention the problem. In 1983, the U.S. government reported 1,700 complaints and 15 deaths resulting from the tendency of the car's brakes to lock. The government sued General Motors for $4 million and accused the company of covering up the problem by providing false information to the National Highway Traffic Safety Administration. The government also charged that company officials gave statements under oath that they "knew or should have known" were false.[36]

Toxic Wastes

The illegal disposal of toxic wastes claims untold numbers of victims every year. Wastes must be buried or disposed of with great care to avoid polluting the land and endangering the health of millions of nearby residents. As a result of the high cost of disposing of wastes, there is a formidable business in illegal toxic-waste dumping.[37]

In 1983, the Environmental Protection Agency estimated that 150 million metric tons of hazardous toxic wastes were generated. Block and Scarpitti analyzed the EPA data. They found the estimate to be low due to the exclusion of the small manufacturers who are not under EPA control and the discrepancy between the 60,000 companies that reported they intended to generate hazardous waste and the EPA count of only 14,000 manufacturers. Illegal haulers and dumpers are not included in the survey. On-site disposal of toxic wastes is costly and cumbersome. A large number of illegal waste haulers, known as "midnight dumpers," dispose of the waste at lower prices by illegally dumping the waste into rivers, sewers, bayous, marshlands, farms, coal mines, ravines, mountain valleys, and unpoliced landfills.[38]

Child-Labor Market

Child-labor laws passed in 1938 and amended in 1961 and 1966 restrict the age and hours of child employment. Immigration laws restrict the employment of immigrants who do not have immigration cards permitting them to work. It is also illegal to employ people without paying the minimum wage, and the employer must contribute to Social Security, unemployment, and other federal and state programs.

The violation of these laws is rampant in America and most European countries. Illegal immigrants are employed at below minimum wage and are not provided with the legal benefits of employment. In 1970, the U.S. Department of Labor conducted a study of farm labor that found a total of 498 farms in violation of federal statutes restricting the use of child labor: 1,472 children under 16 years of age were illegally employed, most of them in jobs during school hours. The age of children employed illegally ranged from 3–15 years; the majority were under 13.[39]

A report in the *New York Times* on illegal immigrant labor described conditions for many illegal immigrant families as virtual slavery.[40] For the first time in recent history, two farmers in Georgia were charged with keeping an immigrant family under conditions of slavery.[41] Farmers in particular (but also some industries relying on unskilled labor) pay starvation wages to immigrants and keep them in perpetual bondage by holding over their heads the threat of reporting them to immigration authorities and having them deported if they refuse to work long hours at arduous, often unsafe, work for subsistence salaries.

The Federal law that is contained principally in the Fair Labor Standards Act of 1938 (as amended in 1961 and 1966) provides that "no producer, manufacturer or dealer shall ship or deliver for shipment in commerce any goods produced in an establishment situated in the United States in which . . . any oppressive child labor has been employed" (Sec. 12a).

Other relevant provisions

1. Require payment of time and a half for work over 8 hours a day for more than 40 hours a week (Sec. 4a).

2. Require permits for minors under 16 and make it a crime to employ minors while they should be in school.
3. Make it a crime to employ minors under adverse health or moral conditions.

The Friends Service Committee surveyed farm labor and the use of child labor throughout the United States in the 1970s.[42] It concentrated on the states of California, Washington, Oregon, and Maine. The committee found rampant violation of child-labor laws throughout these areas. They described the work done by children as

- Hard, tedious, mind-destroying, and illegal. Much of the labor is 'stoop labor,' picking strawberries, grapes, cucumbers, garlic, chili, cotton, and onions.

Temperatures in some places (Washington, Oregon, and California, particularly) range from 80–110 degrees. Work starts at 5 or 6 A.M. and continues usually for more than 8 hours. The children who work the fields miss school.

Observers documented that practically every farm they visited employed underage children who worked more than 8 hours a day under "adverse conditions" and during school hours.

In Aroostook County, Maine, 21,000 migratory workers are brought in each summer to do stoop labor and run the machinery necessary to harvest the potato crop. Six to seven thousand adults are augmented by 15,000 children of school age.

In California, the observers studied 229 children working in agriculture in six California counties. They summarized their findings:

1. The average hourly wage for children working in agriculture is $1.12; the average hourly wage for children working on piece rate is $1.04.
2. Of the children in the sample, 27.5 percent work without Social Security cards.
3. Of the farms surveyed, 19 percent failed to provide adequate toilet facilities.
4. Of the farms surveyed, 34 percent failed to provide adequate handwashing facilities.

As with most examples of white-collar crime, these findings only suggest the extent of the criminality. Violations of criminal law that involve child-labor and other illegal labor practices are found whenever researchers investigate. It is probably safe to assume, on the basis of these findings, that these crimes occur virtually everywhere in the labor market.

Seriousness of White-Collar Crime

The data speak for themselves. Faulty goods, monopolistic practices, and other violations are estimated by the Judiciary Subcommittee on Anti-Trust and Monopoly to cost consumers between $174 and $231 billion annually. One price-fixing case involving large manufacturers of electrical equipment (General Electric, Westinghouse, and 27 other electrical companies) "cost utilities, and, therefore, the public, more money than is reported stolen in a year."[43] Losses resulting from a conspiracy to fix prices among a group of plumbing manufacturers cost $100 million; major U.S. corporations admitted to the Securities and Exchange Commission that they made illegal payments of hundreds or millions of dollars in foreign payoffs:

> In 1979, nine major oil companies were sued for illegal overcharges in excess of one billion dollars. The companies were accused of either charging too much for products derived from natural gas liquids or 'banking' excessive costs on their ledgers, in order to boost consumer costs later. In contrast, the largest robbery in the history of the United States occurred in 1978 and involved the theft of $4 million from the Lufthansa airline warehouse in New York City.[44]

In contrast, the average loss through robbery from 1973–1984 was less than $100.[45]

> Many more people die as a result of corporate criminal activities than die from criminal homicides: The efflux from motor vehicles, plants and incinerators of sulfur oxides, hydrocarbons, carbon monoxide, oxides of nitrogen, particulates, and many more contaminants amounts to compulsory consumption of violence by most Americans. . . . This damage, perpetuated increasingly in direct violation of local, state and federal law, shatters people's health and safety. . . .[46]

If the cost of corruption, bribery, and fraud in government and business were calculable, the results would be staggering. There is also considerable intangible cost from the public's justifiable loss of confidence in the major institutions of their society and the sense of powerlessness engendered by the realization that "crime in high places" is out of control. All these costs and many others make white-collar, corporate, and governmental crime the most serious crime problem facing America. The failure to enforce existing laws adequately is a sign of the problem, not an indication that it is unimportant.

State-Organized Crime _____

State organized crime consists of acts defined by law as criminal that are committed by state or government officials in the pursuit of their job as representatives of the government.[47] This type of crime is discussed in detail in Chapter 13. A few examples will make the point that these types of crimes are as essential as mugging, robbery, and white-collar and corporate crime to the study of criminology.

Not surprisingly, statistics on state organized crime are hard to find. Statistics are kept by government agencies, and they are not inclined to gather data on their own criminal actions. Nonetheless, we know that many governments in the world maintain their power through the use of death squads, illegal incarceration, police brutality, and the like. In most instances, these are acts defined in the nation's own laws as criminal. Despite an avowed concern with the "crime problem," no government publishes data on how many crimes it commits. For these data, we must either make inferences from other reported facts or rely on observations.

One example of governmental crime is planned assassinations. In U.S. law, it is a crime to conspire to commit murder. At Senate Hearings held in 1976, it was admitted by U.S. government officials that they conspired to murder several heads of foreign governments, including Patrice Lumumba of Uganda, Kwame Nkuma of Ghana, Fidel Castro of Cuba, and Salvadore Allende of Chile. Evidence was also presented that the CIA enlisted the services of organized-crime figures John Roselli, Sam Giancanna, and Santo Trafficante, Jr., in the attempt to assassinate Fidel Castro.[48] Some of these heads of state were killed, although it is not clear who killed them or whether they were the victims of the CIA conspiracy. Nevertheless, the conspiracy itself was a crime.

The multinational corporation I.T.T. conspired with the U.S. government to overthrow the democratically elected government of Salvadore Allende in Chile. The coup that ensued ended in the murder of many people, including President Allende and the General of the Chilean Army, Renee Schneider.[49]

In 1954, officials of the U.S. government conspired with officers of the United Fruit Company to overthrow the legal government of Guatemala in violation of international and U.S. law. Jacobo Arbenz was elected President of Guatemala on a campaign of land reform for the peasants and jobs for the people of his country. The major target of the land reform was land owned and leased by the United Fruit Company, a U.S.–based multinational corporation. Reacting to the new government's land-reform program, the United Fruit Company mounted a strenuous propaganda campaign that falsely claimed an "Iron Curtain" had fallen over the country. A. A. Berle of the State Department claimed that Guatemala was "in the grip of a Russian-controlled dictatorship."[50] In fact, Arbenz rejected a communist ideology and was attempting to create a democratic, capitalist political/economic system, but one in which the poorest people in the cities and on the farms were provided a decent standard of living.[51] To do this, of course, it was necessary to reduce the profits of the U.S. multinational corporations that had grown fat with the help of a government complicitous in the exploitation of the people and their lands. Arbenz advocated a reformist ideology, not communism. Nevertheless, the Eisenhower administration approved a plan called Operation Success, which was organized, inspired, and financed by the CIA. In 1954, Castillo Armas—with money, arms, and assistance from the United States—overthrew Arbenz. Thomas McCann of United Fruit wrote that "United Fruit was involved at every level," in the CIA's successful Guatemalan coup.[52] John Foster Dulles, then Secretary of State, had been a senior partner of Sullivan and Cromwell—United Fruit's New York law firm—and its principal advisor on foreign operations. CIA director Allen Dulles was also a former member of that same law firm. Many others members and advisors to the Eisenhower administration had direct connections with United Fruit. Not the least of these was General Walter Bedell Smith, who was a close advisor to Eisenhower and a former CIA director. He oversaw the destabilization of the Arbenz government and later joined the board of directors of United Fruit.

During and after the 1954 coup, over 9,000 people were arrested. Many of them were brutally tortured. Over 1.5 million acres of land were returned to the large land owners, including, of course, United Fruit.

In 1984, the Central Intelligence Agency produced and distrib-

Former National Security Advisor, John M. Poindexter takes the oath before the House subcommittee. *(Wide World Photos)*

uted to people in Nicaragua a manual that advocated the murder of government officials; the murder of people opposed to the government to make it look like the government murdered them, thereby creating martyrs; the blackmailing of ordinary citizens to force them to work for guerillas opposing the government; the destruction of public property; the disruption of traffic by throwing nails on the road; and other criminal acts. The CIA was committing a crime by advocating acts that are against the law in its own country as well as against the laws of Nicaragua and the international court of justice. The acts advocated by the CIA caused untold harm and suffering to the people of Nicaragua. Throwing nails on the street, for example, destroys truck and automobile tires, which are in short supply in an impoverished country. Farm produce rots while waiting to get to markets where people are desperate for food. Products for export are delayed, reducing the country's economy and, in the end, lowering the standard of living, which is already one of the poorest in the world.

Internal governmental crimes include illegal acts by law-enforcement and intelligence agencies. Included in these are crimes such as a CIA program to intercept the mail of private citizens.

This operation lasted for over 20 years (1950–1973). The interception of a U.S. citizen's private correspondence without explicit and specific approval by a court is a criminal as well as a civil violation. The CIA, several postmaster generals, and one U.S. attorney general were conspirators in this illegal operation. In one year, over 13,000 private letters were illegally opened. As the FBI reports thefts, this would constitute over 13,000 offenses "known to the police." In the 1960s, officers in the U.S. Navy fraudulently reported the use of over $100,000 worth of jet fuel. In 1976, Senator William Proxmire exposed 95 defense and military personnel who were entertained by defense contractors at a cost of several hundred thousand dollars, which was added to the defense contracts approved by the people being entertained.

Today, however, other forms of state-organized crime pale in comparison to the crime of smuggling. During the occupation of Indo-China (Vietnam, Cambodia, and Laos), the French government and, later, the American government conspired with local and international narcotics dealers to smuggle drugs. Initially, the French depended upon opium smuggling to finance the colonial governments in Indo-China. In time, the opium and heroin production financed the French and the American wars against the Vietnamese.[53] The U.S. government today engages in the criminal smuggling of military weapons to clandestinely support right-wing governments. These crimes are discussed in detail in Chapter 13.

Political Crime _____

The concept of *political crime* refers to crimes committed by people in order to maintain or change existing political power relations. These crimes differ from bribery, corruption, and election fraud in ways analogous to the difference between occupational and corporate white-collar crime: Political crime is engaged in for the benefit of a social class, group, or organization rather than solely for the benefit of the individual who perpetrates the criminal acts.

In the history of all societies, groups in opposition to the existing power structure have struggled against government policies. Sometimes the opposition takes the form of legally protected rights: for example, the rights to speak out, to organize electorally, and to demonstrate peacefully. At other times, however, the opposition resorts to criminal acts. The history of America is, from one point of view, a history of riot, rebellion, and revolution.[54]

The United States was born from criminal action. The revolution of the colonists against British rule was a criminal act according to existing law. The revolutionaries won the struggle and thereby converted their crimes into acts of heroism. Other rebels in American history have been less successful. The attempt by the Southern states to secede from the Union failed, thus making the Southerners who participated in the Civil War criminal.

Native American (Indian) rebellions against the government have existed ever since the United States was established. The following are among the more-violent Native American revolts from the 18th–20th centuries:

1763   Pontiac's Rebellion
1763   Paxton Boys
1813–1814   Creek War
1814   Little Turtle's War
1831–1832   Sac and Foxe Rebellions
1833–1837   Blackhawk War
1835   Seminole War
1838   Revolt of the Cherokees
1849–1863   Navaho Rebellion
1866   Sioux Revolt
1876   Apache (Geronimo) Wars
1896   Wounded Knee
1905   Navaho

More recently, Native Americans on reservations openly fought federal agents in an effort to publicize the mistreatment of Native Americans and the violation of their traditional hunting, fishing, and other rights.

While Native Americans fought for their independence, culture, and property against transplanted Europeans whose control of the government and the national military force gave them the power to define the rebellions as criminal, farmers waged their own wars against the state:

1730   South Carolina residents tarred and feathered a   revenue officer.
1768–1771   Wars of the Regulators
1771   War of the New Hampshire Grants

1786–1788 Shay's Rebellion
1791–1794 Whiskey Rebellion, Pennsylvania
1799 Pries Rebellion

The most continuous source of riots, rebellions, and criminal political organizing in American history grows out of the conflict between workers and owners (see Table 3.2). Throughout U.S. history, workers have organized and violently struggled to gain safer and healthier work conditions, shorter hours of work, better wages, the right to bargain collectively, the right to form trade unions, and the right to have a voice in the management of corporations. Corporations, mine owners, and the government have, in return, often acted criminally in opposition to the workers' demands. During the workers' strikes, rebellions, and riots of the 19th century, owners and managers hired "strike breakers," who were well armed and paid to disrupt—by assault and murder—the workers' attempts to organize. State and local governments were complicitous with the owners and managers, and sometimes they sent police

TABLE 3.2 Worker-Owner Warfare (1870–1940)

1879	Molly Maguires (Ancient Order of Hibernians)
1874	Thompkins Square, New York
1877	Railroad Strikes
1866	Haymarket Square bombing
1892	Homestead strike; Coeur d'Alene, Idaho
1894	Pullman strike
1894	Alabama coal strike
1895	Streetcar strike, Brooklyn, New York
1901	San Francisco teamsters
1903–1904	Colorado labor war
1910	Bombing of *L.A. Times* by AFL
1912	I.W.W. Textile strike, Lowell, Massachusetts
1913	Michigan copperstrike; Colorado Coal War
1919	Centralia, Washington strikers; Nationwide strikes against railroads and steel; May Day Riot in Cleveland
1922	The Herrin Massacre; the Dearborn Massacre
1920–1930	Appalachian mining rights
1931	Chicago Eviction Riot
1932	Army Bonns Riots
1935	Southern Tenant Farmers Union
1935	Harlem riots
1936–1937	CIO sit-down strikes against auto companies
1937	Memorial Day Massacre at Republic Steel in Chicago
1937	Violent worker rebellions in Cleveland, Massillion, and Youngstown, Ohio

Policing the 1937 Flint, Michigan sit-down auto strike at the Chevrolet plant. *(UPI/Bettmann Newsphotos)*

and National Guard troops to join the strike breakers in attacks on workers; at other times, government officials "turned a blind eye" to the violence against the workers.

The first slave uprising in the U.S. was in 1712, although there is evidence of conspiracies prior to this in 1687 at Northern Neck, Virginia, and in 1710 in Surry County, Virginia. Black revolts against slavery, discrimination, exploitation, and repression have continued since that time.

1712 Uprising by the slaves of the Carmantee and Pappa tribes in New York

1728 Savannah insurrection

1730 Insurrection at Williamsburg, Virginia

1739 Three insurrections in South Carolina

1740 Gabriel's insurrection

1816 Camden, South Carolina, uprising

1819 Plot in Augusta, Georgia

1822 Denmark Vessey plot

1832   Nat Turner's insurrection
1841   The Creole case

Shortly after the end of World War II in 1945, America entered yet another period of law violation by political groups attempting to affect fundamental change in the structure of the government. In response, the government itself engaged in illegal acts in an effort to suppress the demands for change.

The Civil Rights Movement in the South, led by Martin Luther King, Jr., advocated and practiced "passive resistance." Those participating in the struggle violated the "Jim Crow" statutes in Southern states.[55] These laws prohibited blacks from eating at the same lunch counters, attending the same schools, riding in the same parts of the buses, or gathering in public places with whites. The response of the police and political leaders was to use practically any method, legal or illegal—including beating, killing, illegal arrest, and violation of rights to free speech and assembly—to suppress the movement and its leaders. As the decade of the 1950s continued, more and more people from all over the United States went to the South to work in the Civil Rights movement; their strategy was to force social change by violating the law. Some were murdered, but Southern police refused to investigate. In at least one incident, an informant/agent for the Federal Bureau of Investigation was complicitous in the murder of a white woman Civil Rights worker who was chauffering demonstrators from their homes to the demonstration.

In the 1960s, the struggle for civil and equal rights of the black people was joined by students, workers, and a diverse cross-section of U.S. citizens demanding an end to the war in Vietnam. Once again, political change was sought and criminal acts (demonstrating without a permit, desecrating the American flag, vandalism, and even murder) were committed in the process.

Law-enforcement agencies rushed to the defense of the established order by violating the law as well. Illegal arrests, the use of violence and coercion, and the murder of demonstrators and political organizers exacerbated the violence and criminality on both sides.

Blacks in ghettos and slums rioted. In 1964, Rochester, New York, Philadelphia, and New York City felt the heat of rioters in the slums and ghettos burning buildings, cars, and trash; looting stores; and vandalizing cars and apartments. In 1965, riots took place in the Watts section of Los Angeles; in 1966, in Chicago and Cleveland; and in 1967, in Newark, New Jersey, and Detroit. In 1968, the last year of major riots during this siege, the nation's capital, Washington, D.C., was joined by Baltimore, Pittsburgh, Chicago, and several other cities as the site of major racial and interracial violence, rioting, and rebellion.

The student revolts of the 1960s rarely reached the level of violence or the destruction of property characteristic of the urban riots, but they, nonetheless, involved hundreds of thousands of people in the commission of criminal acts. The Free Speech Movement at the University of California, Berkeley, touched off a series of demonstrations and police reactions that spread crime across campuses from east to west and from north to south. In 1967, the New York City anti-war demonstrations illegally occupied buildings; destroyed property; and violated municipal, state, and federal laws. That same year saw a riot at the Pentagon, near Washington, D.C., and demonstrations, riots, and rebellions at the Century Plaza Hotel in Los Angeles, in Oakland, and at San Jose State College. During the first half of the 1967–1968 school year, there were 71 demonstrations on 62 campuses. During the second half of the year, there were 221 demonstrations at 101 schools. Students and workers refused to be drafted; some went into hiding while others emigrated to Canada, Sweden, and other countries.

The police used riot squads, illegal arrests, criminal violence, and threats in response. Participants and movement leaders were killed under questionable circumstances in Greensboro, North Carolina. Mark Hampton, a leader of the black movement, was shot by police while asleep in his bed in Chicago. George Jackson, whose letters and writings from Soledad Prison in California were inspirational for the movement, was shot and killed by a prison guard.

While he was president in May 1971, Richard Nixon endorsed a suggestion that members of the teamsters union be brought in to physically assault antiwar demonstrators in Washington, D.C.

Organized Crime

The successful commission of some types of crime require organization, coordination, and specialization. The most frequently committed crimes of this type are smuggling, gambling, laundering money, and the illegal dumping of toxic wastes. These types of crime are referred to in criminology as *organized crime*. Each of these crimes may be attempted without creating or using criminal organizations. Furthermore, other crimes such as usury, receiving and selling stolen property, real-estate and stock frauds, and some forms of white-collar crime benefit from organization, coordination, and specialization. Thus, as with most criminal-behavior systems, there is overlap between the ideal type and the sociologically related phenomenon. The fact remains, however, that most crimes of smuggling, gambling, money laundering, and illegal dumping of toxic wastes are perpetuated by organized-crime networks.

Official statistics and self-report surveys are of limited value in generating reliable information on organized crime. Social scientists, using participant observation and interviewing research techniques do reveal that these forms of criminality are very prevalent.

In the everyday language of the police, the press, and popular opinion, "organized crime" refers to a tightly knit group of people, usually alien and often Italian, that runs a crime business structured along the lines of feudal relationships. This conception bears little relationship to the reality of organized crime today. Nonetheless, criminologists have discovered the existence of organizations whose activities focus on the smuggling of illegal commodities into and out of countries (cocaine out of Columbia and into the United States and guns and arms out of the United States and into the Middle East, for example); other organizations, sometimes employing some of the same people, are organized to provide services such as gambling, prostitution, illegal dumping of toxic wastes, arson, usury, and occasionally murder. These organizations typically cut across ethnic and cultural lines, are run like businesses, and consist of networks of people including police, politicians, and ordinary citizens investing in illegal enterprises for a high return on their money.[56]

How much organized crime is there? One measure of the presence of organized crime is the availability of illegal goods and services. The fact that illicit drugs such as cocaine, marijuana, opiates (heroin), and amphetamines are readily available throughout the United States and Europe is substantial evidence that organized crime is omnipresent. The problems associated with moving drugs from their source in remote regions of Columbia, Turkey, Ceylon, Thailand, or Mexico to Amsterdam, Stockholm, New York, and Seattle without having the goods confiscated requires a high degree of effective organization.

Arguing that the availability of commodities and services is directly related to an organization responsible for obtaining and distributing them is, however, tricky business. Certainly much prostitution is not controlled by an organization, but is supplied by individual entrepreneurs—usually a man and several women or, in the case of male prostitutes, simply individuals working on their own. The same thing appears to be true of the professional fence who buys stolen goods and sells them; it may be true of most people engaged in usury (lending money at interest rates above the legal limit) and in some illegal gambling.

Nonetheless, for many illegal commodities (e.g., drugs) and services (e.g., gambling), a large number of sociological studies show that these are criminal activities centered in organized crime.

In 1970, the Organized Crime Control Act was passed by Congress and signed into law by President Nixon. This law made it possible for the U.S. Department of Justice to employ new enforcement techniques to arrest, convict, and get information from people allegedly engaged in organized-crime activities. Between 1972 and 1984, the special task force in the Justice Department assigned to investigate organized crime arrested 376 people, of whom 265 were sent to prison or punished by fines and probation.[57] These data hardly touch the surface of people involved in organized crime.

Sociologists investigating organized crime in Europe and America discovered crime networks operating profitably and with impunity from prosecution virtually everywhere. An investigation in Seattle, Washington, exposed a crime network involving a former governor of the state, the county prosecutor, the chief of police, the sheriff, at least 50 other law-enforcement officers in the city and county: These were leading businesspeople, realtors, contractors, corporation executives, bankers, racketeers, gamblers, drug dealers, and drug pushers.[58] Investigations in Detroit, Texas, Pennsylvania, New Jersey, and New York revealed a similar pattern. Indeed, wherever sociologists or reporters investigate, they find crime networks organized to provide illegal goods and services. As Daniel Bell noted, this type of crime is "an American way of life."[59]

The volume of business generated by these illegal enterprises is comparable to the volume of business generated by the largest industries in the United States. The smuggling of drugs generates a gross volume of business of over $100 billion a year.[60] The largest corporation in the world has a gross volume of business less than that of illegal drug smuggling. Indeed, only ten nations in the world have a gross national product that exceeds the gross volume of business from cocaine, marijuana, and heroin. Traffic in illegal arms and military equipment may exceed the volume of drugs. Even the smuggling of cigarettes across state lines to avoid excise taxes constitutes a business of $400–500 million a year. Indeed, a single truckload of bootlegged cigarettes may yield $1,200–2,000.

Professional Theft _____

Professional theft is rare compared to other types of crime. It is impossible to estimate numbers with any hope of accuracy. It is significant, however, that professional thieves in federal and state penitentiaries at any point in time usually number only a handful of the inmates. This could be a testimony to their ability to stay out of prison. However, the estimate that the number of professional thieves is small is also evidenced by the fact that reports of professional theft in cities throughout the United States and Europe and the occasional discovery of professional thieves working for a number of years, suggest that the incidence is small. The fact that most arrests for crime are of people in the ages from 16–25 when, presumably, most of them will not have developed the skills and experience to qualify as professional thieves, further supports the position that professional theft does not account for large amounts of crime.[61]

Professional thieves are committed to crime as a way of earning a living; they accept prison sentences, fixing judges, and crooked attorneys as part of their way of life and, more often than not, specialize in particular forms of theft such as confidence tricks, safecracking, burglary, receiving stolen goods, robbery, shoplifting, check forgery ("laying paper"), or fraud. They identify with their own society, which has a hierarchy, a shared unique language, and an ethical code. The professional thief views his or her work with pride and sees theft as a legitimate enterprise.

Thieves rank their profession according to the complexity and training necessary to carry out the craft. Safecracking and confidence tricks rank at the top of the profession.[62] Shoplifting (boosting) and "small time" crimes like robbing from parking meters or forging checks rank near the bottom. Biographies of professional thieves reveal a similar pattern: The typical professional thief begins early in life learning how to steal; spends a good deal of time in juvenile and adult prisons; apprentices with an older, more-experienced thief; and learns the craft. He or she associates with other thieves for the most part, but may often have friends and even partners on the police force. The successful commission of crime depends upon wit and a highly developed intuitive sense

Living with a contra-
diction between con-
sumption and wages.
*(Robert Houser/Photo
Researchers)*

that can warn him or her of danger. For some of the professions,
like safe cracking and robbery, it is necessary to work in teams.
The safecracker needs a "point man" to be a lookout while the
safecracker (or boxman) opens the safe. Often safecrackers and
robbers will also engage a "finger man" who will keep an eye on a
particular store to see when there are the most customers, when
the "door shake" (or police) come by to check the store, when the
money is taken to the bank, and all the other things that would
make a prospective "mark" a good place to rob or break into.

Success with smuggling, illegal gambling, drug trafficking, and
other organized crimes depends on the ability to gain the cooperation of law enforcers. This is accomplished through attorneys who
specialize in criminal law and through "the fix"—being able to pay
off the police, the prosecutor, and the judge. Professional theft, like
many other types of crime, depends upon interconnections be-

tween the apparently noncriminal and the openly criminal segments of society.

Conclusion _____

This chapter surveyed a wide range of criminal acts and what we know about them. There is an immense research literature in criminology detailing the frequency and the quality of criminality that exists in the modern world. We know that white-collar occupational and corporate criminality is more costly, more serious, and probably more common than the criminality that occupies the attention of politicians, the police, and the media. This applies *only* to acts that are a violation of the criminal law. If one includes acts that are harmful but not criminal, then, of course, the picture would be even bleaker.

Interestingly, despite the fact that the public is bombarded with news about the crimes of the lower classes, public-opinion surveys indicate that the public is more concerned about white-collar crime. Marvin Wolgang's survey of people's attitudes towards different types of crime revealed the following:

> The seriousness score for the offense of a legislator who takes a bribe of $10,000 from a company to vote for a law favoring the company was 370. By comparison, a score of 339 was assigned to the burglary of $100,000 from a bank; a robbery at gunpoint in which the victim needed medical treatment was given a score of 361 . . . illegal retail price-fixing by several large companies is considered more serious than a personal robbery in which the offender intimidates the victim with a lead pipe and steals $1,000 (201 to 197). Factory pollution of a city's water supply resulting in only one person's illness carries a seriousness score . . . more than twice the score . . . assigned to a burglary in which the offender breaks into a private home and steals $100.00[63]

Research by criminologists reported in this chapter confirms the public's perception. The number of people who are harmed in some way by the criminal actions of corporations, governments, corrupt public officials, or entrepreneurs seeking to increase their profit margin is infinitely greater than the number of people harmed by burglary, theft, robbery, rape, and murder. Significantly, as was shown in the preceding chapter, the most serious personal crimes— such as murder and rape—are more likely to be committed by family members or acquaintances than by strangers, whereas the crimes surveyed in this chapter are almost always committed anonymously by agents who have little or no acquaintance with the people who are harmed.

While we have covered a vast array of criminal acts, it should be remembered that we can only briefly touch upon them. Each of the subjects covered in this chapter is the subject of volumes. Nonetheless, with this overview we are now able to move to some of the theoretical issues that occupy criminological inquiry. It was noted in the beginning chapter that criminology, like all the sciences, was built on two great pillars: facts and theories. We now have a grasp of some of the facts our theories must fit; let us, then, turn to the theories and see how they mesh with the facts.

CHAPTER

4

Criminal Law

Most people accept criminal law as a given. Like sky and earth, gravity and friction, it is just there. Criminology, however, cannot simply accept the law as given. It must investigate how the law came to be the way it is, why some acts are defined as criminal and others are not, what the difference is between civil and criminal law, and what is the legal definition of a criminal act. These are some of the questions that we take up in this chapter.

Definition of Behavior as Criminal

What constitutes crime changes over time and from society to society. "Even if you kill a man," the noted philosopher of law

H. L. A. Hart notes, "this is not punishable as murder in most civilized jurisdictions if you do it unintentionally, accidentally or by mistake, or while suffering from certain forms of mental abnormality."[1]

Anthropologists searching for universal norms find none.[2] The capacity of human beings to create different cultures in which different behaviors are defined as right and wrong is apparently endless. The history of every legal system is a history of social change. Acts defined as criminal at one historical juncture are acceptable behaviors at another, while acts that at one time are a matter of an individual's own choice are later defined as criminal. A few examples will help make the point: A little over 100 years ago in the United States, Africans were enslaved. It was a criminal act for black people to refuse to work for their owner or to leave their master without permission. It was also a criminal offense for anyone to hide or otherwise assist a slave to escape from a state where he or she was a slave. Less than 15 years ago, it was a criminal offense for a woman to obtain an abortion and for a physician to perform one, except under certain conditions—for example, if the pregnancy were the result of rape or if the mother's health were seriously threatened by the pregnancy. Since 1973, when the Supreme Court handed down the decision in *Roe vs. Wade,* a woman has the right to decide whether or not to have an abortion in the first trimester of her pregnancy and licensed medical doctors can legally perform an abortion.

Today it is illegal to grow, distribute, sell, or possess marijuana in most states. Utah, a state whose politics are dominated by the ultra-conservative Mormon church, and a few other states in recent years have lessened the penalties or decriminalized the possession of small amounts of marijuana altogether.[3] On the other hand, Nevada, where gambling and prostitution are legal, has some of the most severe penalties in America for the sale or possession of marijuana. In California, it is legal to grow marijuana for one's own consumption, and possession of less than 1 ounce is punishable by a fine of $5.00. Twenty years ago, California law was like the laws of most states today, where the growing or possession of even small amounts of marijuana is a felony for which people are still put in prison for long sentences.

In 1986, the United States Supreme Court upheld a Georgia law making it a crime for consenting adults to commit sodomy. This decision upheld the laws in 25 states, making it a crime punishable in some cases by up to 20 years in prison for homosexuals to engage in oral or anal sex—practices that are normal for homosex-

JOSEPH G. BROWN

Dear Friend:

Death row is a terrifying place. I ought to know. I spent 14 years there.

At one point, I came within 15 hours of being executed.

I am alive and free today because of a few courageous people who believed me when I swore I was innocent. These courageous people included lawyers, journalists, prison-reform activists, and friends who wouldn't let my conviction go unchallenged. And so they re-examined the evidence and confirmed what I had known all along—that I had been made a convenient scapegoat by the State of Florida.

The single-minded determination of this diverse group of supporters was the difference between me being free today or just another statistic on the long list of executions.

They made some key discoveries. They learned that the State's primary witness admitted that he had lied. They also found out that the prosecutor had suppressed important evidence—an FBI lab report that proved that the fatal bullet did not come from the gun I owned. And samples of the assailant's blood, found at the murder scene, did not match mine.

I moved a step closer to freedom when the Reverend Joe Ingle, Director of the Southern Coalition on Jails and Prisons, obtained a letter from one of the jurors. It stated that the Jury foreman told everyone to forget whether I was guilty or not. Convicting me would "get one more nigger off the streets."

The State of Florida finally released me because they could no longer sustain the lies, cover-up, and racism that put me on death row in the first place.

I know that what I am telling you runs contrary to everything you have always believed about America's system of justice. Our criminal justice system is widely believed to be the fairest in the world. And because of this widespread respect, many of us have come to think of it as being flawless.

"Justice is blind" the saying goes. The symbol of our legal system is a blindfolded lady holding a balanced scale.

I am living proof, however, that our system is far from perfect. It has serious flaws. And these flaws work primarily to the disadvantage of the poor and those whose victims are white.

ual and many heterosexual couples. In 17 of the 25 states, sodomy is a crime for both heterosexual and homosexual partners.

Americans legally wager almost $20 billion a year in Las Vegas, Reno, and Atlantic City, and at race tracks.[4] They also wager billions of dollars on state-run lotteries. On the other hand, for a bookmaker to accept a wager or someone to run a poker game is illegal and punishable by imprisonment.

The pharmaceutical industry legally produces billions of amphetamines that are sold in the illegal drug market.[5] Cigarettes, alcohol, and other drugs are also legally sold although their harmful affects are well known. Selling other drugs, such as marijuana, heroin, and cocaine, is criminal.

John DeLorean, an automobile executive with the Ford Motor Company, wreaked havoc on the Irish and English economies by borrowing millions of dollars from the British government, temporarily employing thousands of workers, and subsequently declaring bankruptcy when the automobile he was producing failed to sell.[6] These acts were not criminal, despite the misery and suffering they caused thousands of workers. However, when Mr. DeLorean was accused of conspiring to smuggle cocaine into the United States, he was charged with committing a major felony. Had he been convicted of these charges, he could have been sentenced to prison for the rest of his life. Why is it a crime to import a drug that many people want to consume while it is not a crime to close down unprofitable factories, devastating the economies of entire cities and jeopardizing the well-being of thousands of people?

Why are there no laws in the United States that would punish people for having more children than they can reasonably support? There are in China. Why are there laws prohibiting people under the age of 21 from drinking while there are other laws that make it a criminal offense for people over 18 to fail to register for being drafted into the Armed Services?

Our task as criminologists is not to understand these anomalies in a philosophical, moral, or ethical sense. Our task is to describe and explain what constitutes a criminal act and why some acts are defined as criminal while others are not.

Criminal and Civil Law

"The history of modern law," Jerome Hall writes, "is marked by the reception of ideas which originated in ancient Greece, were modified in medieval philosophy, and have been further developed since then in innumerable discussions and decisions."[7] Among the basic notions incorporated in Anglo-American law is the idea that criminal law is distinct from civil law in crucial ways. The state's role in civil law is to adjudicate between disputing parties. Under criminal law, the state is the injured party and it acts as an advocate against a person, group, or corporate entity. Contrary to civil law, for an act to be a crime there must be (1) a harm, (2) an act that is defined in law as criminal, (3) an act or omission to act that is causally related to the harm, (4) an intention to commit the act, and (5) a penal sanction (fine, imprisonment, or both) attached to the commission of the act.

Of all of these criteria, the "central feature that distinguishes criminal from non-criminal law is *mens rea* (intention)."[8] Civil law focuses on the injury done to someone but criminal law focuses on the intention of the defendant. Literally, *mens rea* means "guilty mind." The essential ingredient of the "guilty mind" for determining whether or not someone has committed a crime is that the person intended to commit the act. If the act was a mistake, if the person intended to do one thing but actually did another, or if the person was mentally incapable of intending to commit the act, then no crime was committed. Even with intent, if the act was impossible, then there has been no crime. In a famous English case, a man was tried for murder because he shot his gun several times into the body of an already dead man. The defendant did not know the object of his wrath was dead and he fully intended to kill him. But because it was impossible for him to kill an already dead man, he was found not guilty.

Probability Versus Reasonable Doubt

Criminal law also differs from civil law in the rules that govern its enforcement. In civil-law cases, it is sufficient to show that the harm caused was "in all probability" the result of the acts committed. In criminal law, the test of causal relation is much stronger: The harm must have been the result of the person's intentional actions "beyond any reasonable doubt." For example, if a manufacturer produces a birth-control device that is known to produce cervical cancer in women and a woman who uses the device contracts cervical cancer, it is probable that the use of the device caused the cancer. The court need not prove "beyond a reasonable doubt" that there was a causal connection in order to award damages to the woman. On the other hand, if the same company is being tried for murder or for causing "grievous bodily harm" as a result of manufacturing and selling the device, then the causal connection between the use of the device and the cervical cancer must be proven "beyond a reasonable doubt."

Compensation Versus Punishment

Civil law is concerned with making compensation to the victim. Criminal law is concerned with punishing the offender. In both cases, the perpetrator may be "punished." A corporation that has to pay $50,000 to a victim of corporate negligence is being punished, but legally the emphasis is on compensating the victim, not punishing the corporation.

Criminal law applies only to people directly involved in the commission of the illegal act. Civil law can be extended to people who may have had no knowledge of the act nor any direct responsibility for its commission. When the vice presidents of General Electric conspired to fix prices and violated federal statutes against unfair trade practices, the president of the corporation and the corporation itself were held civilly responsible for these acts, even though it was never proved in court that the top executives were aware of the illegal practices of the vice presidents. In criminal trials, however, it would have to be shown that the corporate executives above the vice presidents were aware of, and in complicity with, the acts.

Legality (Retroactivity)

Other differences between civil and criminal law that we should bear in mind include the fact that criminal penalties can include death, loss of citizenship, corporal punishment, imprisonment, probation, community service, participation in rehabilitative programs (Alcoholics Anonymous, for example), and cancellation of rights granted to every other citizen. Civil penalties cannot include any of these punishments. As a general rule, criminal law adheres strictly to the principal of legality that stipulates *nullum crimen sine lege* (no crime without law). The most important application of this principle is that no law can be passed retroactively. Today it is not a crime to sexually assault your wife in West Virginia. If the West Virginia legislature passes a law tomorrow that makes this act a crime, anyone who committed the act today or at any time before cannot be tried for the crime. In civil law, retroactive penalties are sometimes legislated.

Rules of Evidence

Finally, the rules of evidence in criminal and civil trials are significantly different. A centerpiece of criminal law is the protection of a defendant against self-incrimination. In civil law, a person may be required to produce incriminating documents, papers, and memos that are used as evidence against them.

A word of caution is in order, however, lest we give the impression that the distinction between criminal and civil law is always crystal clear. As Blum-West and Carter point out, the line between criminal and tort law cannot be drawn with a fine pencil.[9] Torts and crimes usually, but not always, require an intent. "Strict liability offenses" are those in which a person may be held responsible for committing the act, regardless of intent. For example, a newsstand operator who had pornographic literature for sale was held criminally liable even though there was evidence that the pornography had been placed on the shelves by a salesperson without the newsstand operator's knowledge. It is also clear that the penalties administered in tort cases not only are compensatory, but also are intended to serve as a sanction. Indeed, research by Nancy Frank on factory safety and health legislation established that the use of civil penalties for violations of factory safety and health laws was consciously chosen over criminal penalties because it was more efficient to administer penalties through civil, rather than criminal, law.[10] Nonetheless, the distinction between criminal and civil law is a starting point for criminology. It provides a broad spectrum within which to develop questions, theories, and research, even though it does not permit an absolutely iron-clad distinction between acts that are criminal and those that are not.

Process of Law Creation _____

The previously mentioned rules and principles give us the working definitions that characterize modern law. Most legal systems today incorporate most of these ideas in one way or another. In the following chapters, we will see that these rules may be ignored or explicitly negated, as was the case in Nazi Germany in the 1930s and 1940s and as is the case in South Africa today. We are concerned here, however, to outline the formal legal structure. We take up how the law works in practice in later chapters.

These principles and rules, then, give us the formal outline of criminal law and distinguish criminal law from civil law. They do not tell us, however, how it happens that some acts are defined as criminal while others are not. For an answer to that question, we need to look at theories of criminal law creation and examine the empirical data to see how well the theories explain the facts.

Theories of Criminal-Law Creation

One of the most influential theories of criminal law was set forth by Emile Durkheim in the 19th century. He postulated that

> the only common characteristics of crimes is that they consist . . . in acts universally disapproved of by members of each society . . . crime shocks sentiments which, for a given social system, are found in all healthy consciences. . . .
>
> The collective sentiments to which crime corresponds must, therefore, singularize themselves from others by some distinctive property; they must have a certain average intensity. Not only are they engraved in all consciences, but they are strongly engraved.
>
> The wayward son, however, and even the most hardened egotists are not treated as criminals. It is not sufficient, then, that the sentiments be strong; they must be precise.
>
> An act is criminal when it offends strong and defined states of the collective conscience.[11]

Durkheim's theory can be summarized as containing two grand hypotheses:

1. Criminal law represents the synthesis of the most deeply felt morality of a people. This morality is a reflection of the religious and customary values shared by "all healthy consciences."
2. Criminal behavior serves to establish the moral boundaries of a society and is most prevalent in societies where the moral order is undergoing change or is threatened for some reason.

Law as a Reflection of Shared Values

The argument that criminal law is a reflection of shared values and customs is perhaps the most common explanation for the origins of criminal law in legal and social theory. To evaluate the validity of this theory, we must first distinguish between the origins of criminal law and its status at a particular point in time. It may be that, at a particular time, the law reflects widely shared values and norms. Today, almost everyone in Western society agrees that there should be some state-supported system for protecting citizens from theft and assault. This does not mean, however, that the origin of the law can be traced to shared values. It is possible that the shared values are a result of the existence of the law rather than the reverse. We must investigate the emergence of Anglo-American law in England, for it was during this period that most of the characteristics of what has come to be modern-day American, Canadian, English, and most African legal systems were codified and systematized.*

Crime in Early England _____

Prior to the Norman Conquest of England (1066) for one person to kill another was "first of all an offense against the victim or his family and was therefore to be settled by suitable payment to the sufferers."[12]

What was true of murder was true of other crimes as well; if a man raped a woman, it was the responsibility of the woman's family (usually her father, brother, or husband because it was a patriarchal society) to demand compensation from the offender. In early England, then, what is today criminal was treated as a civil offense; it was customary to seek compensation instead of punishment.

When the Normans under William conquered England, the land they dominated militarily was not so much a single nation as it was a disunited collection of feuding kings who shared control of the people and the country with the Catholic Church. For the conquest to be of any value to William and the Normans, it was essential that the people be brought under the control of a centralized authority. William and his successors were to be engaged in several centuries of conflict with the existing fiefdoms in their efforts to unify England under a single monarchy. The criminal law as we know it today was created as a singularly effective tool in accomplishing this goal. Following the conquest in 1066, "crime came more and more to be regarded as an offense against the King's

_____

*Canadian law has, in English Canada, the English Common Law tradition and, in French Canada, the French Civil Law tradition.

Peace for which it was the right and duty of the state to exact punishment."[13]

There were good structural reasons why replacing customary practices with a criminal-law system such as we know it today was important for the monarchy. As long as interpersonal conflicts were handled by family, church, or feudal lords, the crown's power over the people was limited. Once the criminal law was created and acts such as murder, rape, and property offenses were brought under the control of the king, the allegiance of the people to local landlords was weakened. Furthermore, the crown established a system of courts with judges who came to minister "justice" and who thereby were a reminder of the power of the "one king."

> State law and crime came into existence during the time of Henry II as a result of this separation of State and Church, and as a result of the emergence of a central authority in England which replaced the authority of the feudal lords. Henry replaced feudal justice with state justice by means of justices in eyre, the king's peace, a system of royal courts, and a system of royal writs. Common law emerged as the law of the Crown available to all men. The myth that the common law of England is the law of the Anglo-Saxons is without historical foundation. The family was no longer involved in law and justice. The State was the offended social unit, and the state was the proper prosecutor in every case of crime.[14]

The transformation of English law from community to state and from civil to criminal was, then, the result of a struggle between the conquering Normans on the one hand and the coalition of feudal lords and the established Church on the other. Out of these and later struggles between landowners and mercantilists, capitalists and workers, criminal law originated, changed, and became what it is today.

Theft, Law, and Society

During feudalism, the conflicts between the crown, Church, and landlords were responsible for the emergence of criminal law. Most property offenses, such as theft or vandalism, were disputes left to the landlords. With the advent of commerce, however, there were major changes in the economic and social relations of the people. In Europe, trade became increasingly important for nations. Centralized states were replacing feudal fiefdoms and the state became increasingly dependent on merchants and the capital they generated. But the growing importance of trade between European nations created conflicts over who "owned" the goods that were being shipped. Before this time, "ownership" rested with the individual who had possession of the goods. But when a merchant entrusted the carrying of his or her goods to a clerk, did that merchant then give up ownership? It was the dilemma created by this sea change in economic and social relations that led to the creation of the laws of theft as we know them today.

A critical point in the history of the law of theft came in the Carrier Case decided in England in 1473:

> The facts are simple enough: the defendant was hired to carry certain bales to Southampton. Instead of fulfilling his obligation, he carried the goods to another place, broke open the bales and took the contents. He was apprehended and charged with felony.[15]

At the time of the defendant's arrest and trial for felony, no law in England made it a crime for a person to convert goods that he acquired legally to his or her own use. An earlier rule had applied to servants, but, prior to the Carrier case, it was not extended to include employees. Yet, despite this lack of prevailing common law or legislative enactment, a tribunal of the most learned judges in England decided against the defendant and found him guilty of larceny. By so doing, they established a new law, which favored the well-being of the emergent class of capitalist traders and industrialists.

The judges hotly debated the decision, as did legal scholars. Nobody could justify the new law as logically required by existing laws. It was possible, however, for the judges to create legal fictions that justified the decision. In this way, they protected the interests of the new mercantile class, not through their direct involvement in law creation but through the "perceived need" of the judges sitting on the highest courts of the time. The "perceived need," of course, represented the mobilization of a bias that favored the interests of the not-yet-dominant but soaring new economic class, against the interests of employees or people contracting to carry goods.

Following the Carrier case in 1473, the law of theft expanded and developed throughout the 16th, 17th, and 18th centuries. Over time, judicial interpretations expanded the legal definition of theft to include instances where an owner had never seen the goods, so long as the employee placed goods received in the owner's receptacle. The courts also broadened the interpretation of "servant" to include cashiers, clerks, and persons hired to transport goods from place to place.

> Growth [of theft laws] in the eighteenth century is so accelerated that it protrudes conspicuously from the pattern of the whole course of the criminal law. . . . It is in this century that one comes upon the law of receiving stolen property, larceny by trick, obtaining goods by false pretenses, and embezzlement.[16]

According to Hall, these laws emerged when they did because of Britain's colonial expansion:

> [British] colonies served a double purpose. They supplied raw materials. They also furnished a market for the sale of goods manufactured at home; and the home manufacturers were prompt to protect that market.
>
> The tremendous change in the organization of industry is the first development of major importance which closely touches the law of the eighteenth century. Trade became increasingly impersonal and free from supervision. . . . In the Middle Ages goods were produced by individuals, their families and neighbors, for local consumption. Next came regulation and close supervision by crafts and guilds in villages and small towns. . . . And, finally, with the Industrial Revolution came large-scale production.
>
> All this was accompanied by changes in the economic organization of society . . . the transition from an agricultural economy toward a dominantly manufacturing system.

First amendment repossession. *(Arthur Tress/Photo Researchers)*

There was another eighteenth-century development of the greatest importance, namely, the rise of credit and banking facilities and the use of modern instruments to facilitate trade. . . .

This growth in banking and the use of paper currency and instruments of credit affected the law of theft in several important respects. The effect upon the law of embezzlement was direct and sharply marked. . . . The Act of 1742, the first true embezzlement statute by a Whig parliament, anxious to protect the greatest Whig mercantile institution in the country . . . applied only to officers and servants of the Bank of England. . . . The second embezzlement statute, enacted in 1751, applied to officers and employees of the South Sea Company, and the third (1763) extended only to employees of the Post Office. . . . In 1799 . . . the first general embezzlement statute was enacted.[17]

What Hall describes in these passages, of course, is the emergence of a law to protect capitalists and capitalism. The interests that the laws of theft were designed to protect were the interests of the capitalists. The conditions that gave rise to embezzlement as a crime were (1) the expansion of mercantile and banking credit and the use of credit mechanisms, paper money, and securities; (2) the employment of clerks in important positions with reference to dealing with, and, in particular, receiving valuables from, third persons; (3) the interests of the commercial classes and their representation in parliament; (4) a change in attitude regarding the public importance of what could formerly be dismissed as merely a private breach of trust; and (5) a series of sensational cases of very serious defalcation that set the pattern into motion and produced immediate action.[18]

The transition from feudal economy to capitalist economy, the victory of capitalists over feudal landlords in a series of wars and contests for control of the state, the representation of capitalists' interests in parliament, and the changing social relations (the emergence of clerks, for example, who took money and other negotiable instruments in the name of their employer) coalesced to bring about a whole gaggle of new laws. Among them is today's laws of theft. None of these forces, however, reflected any consensus on the part of the people.

Trespass and Poaching

The work of Douglas Hay and E. P. Thompson lends further support to the theory that the emergence of English law was not a result of consensus but was rather the consequence of conflicts between various ruling classes and the people.

In 1723, England passed a law making it an offense punishable by death to engage in a wide range of activities—poaching, wearing a disguise while in an area where deer or horses were kept, damaging fish ponds, wounding or killing cattle, and so forth. Under feudalism, peasants living on manorial land had the right to hunt, fish, and gather wood on the lord's property. The emergence of capitalism, however, changed the serf to a wage earner and the lord's manor to a private estate.

> The historical movement which changes the producers into wage-workers, appears, on the one hand, as their emancipation from serfdom and from the fetters of the guilds. . . . But, on the other hand, these new freed men became sellers of themselves only after they had been robbed of all their own means of production, and of all the guarantees of existence afforded by the old feudal arrangements. And the history of this, their expropriation, is written in the annals of mankind in letters of blood and fire.[19]

To effect the transition to capitalism and alter the people's use of communal land, parliament enacted criminal laws imposing severe sanctions—including death—for "poachers and wood stealers." Despite these laws, people continued to exercise what they considered their "natural rights" to hunt, fish, and gather wood in the only available space—the lord's land.[20]

The Black Act greatly increased the number of offenses for which courts would impose the death penalty. This led many social and legal historians to conclude that some overwhelming problem must have elicited the Black Act as a response.[21] From the perspective that the law responds to social needs, the sudden sharp increase in harsh penalties for criminal acts suggests that the Black Act responded to some increase in the incidence and severity of poaching. E. P. Thompson tested this theory by examining the records available from courts and local sheriffs and the discussions within government. His research shows that the Whig party, which controlled the government at the time, responded to changing economic and political conditions brought about by the shift from feudal to capitalist social relations. Under feudalism, people had the right to kill some of the animals on local estates and to fish in the streams. The law dealt with violations of the rules of civil matters—i.e., wrongs by one person against another. With the development of capitalism, however, came a different ideology of private property and a changed set of class relations.

The act registered the long decline in the effectiveness of old methods of class control and discipline and their replacement by one standard recourse of authority: the example of terror. In place of whipping-posts and stocks, manorial and corporate controls, and physical harrying of vagabonds, economists advocated the discipline of low wages and starvation and lawyers advocated the sanction of death. Both indicated an increasing impersonality in the mediation of class relations, and a change, not so much in the "facts" of crime as in the category—"crime"—itself, as it was defined by the propertied. What was to be punished was not an offense between men (a breach of fealty or deference, a "waste" of agrarian use-values, an offense to one's own corporate community and its ethos, or a violation of trust and function) but an offense against property. Because property was a thing, it became possible to define offenses as crimes against things, rather than as injuries to men.

The functions of the severe penalties went beyond the mere threat of punishment. As Douglas Hay points out:

> The rulers of eighteenth-century England cherished the death sentence. The oratory we remember now is the parliamentary speech, the Roman periods of Fox or Burke, that stirred the gentry and the merchants. But outside Parliament were the laboring poor, and twice a year, in most countries in England, the scarlet-robed judge of assize put the black cap of death on top of his full-bottomed wig to expound the law of the properties and to execute their will.[22]

Hay notes further the sanctification of private property during this period:

> Once property has been officially deified, it became the measure of all things. Even human life was weighted in the scales of wealth and status: "the execution of a needy decrepit assassin," wrote Blackstone, "is a poor satisfaction for the murder of a nobleman in the bloom of his youth, and full enjoyment of his friends, his honours, and his fortune." Again and again, the voices of money and power declared the sacredness of property in terms hitherto reserved for human life. Banks were credited with souls, and the circulation of gold likened to that of blood. Forgers, for example, were almost invariably hanged, and gentlemen knew why: "Forgery is a stab to commerce, and only to be tolerated in a commercial nation

when the foul crime of murder is pardoned." In a mood of unrivaled
assurance and complacency, Parliament over the century created
one of the bloodiest criminal codes in Europe. Few of the new penalties were the product of hysteria, or ferocious reaction; they were
part of the conventional wisdom of England's governors. Locke himself defined political power as the right to create the penalty of death,
and hence, all lesser ones. And Sahftesbury, the enlightened ratio-
nalist who attacked both Hobbes and the Church for making fear
the cement of social order, at the same time accepted that the "mere
Vulgar of Mankind" might perhaps often stand in need of such a
rectifying Objects as the Gallows before their Eyes.[23]

Vagrancy Laws

The history of laws making vagrancy a crime further illustrates
the inadequacy of consensus theory. Vagrancy statutes in the 14th
century reflect the British monarchy's concern to protect the interests of the feudal landowners. The statutes provided that

> Every man and woman, of what condition he be, free or bond, able
> in body, and with the age of three-score years, not living in mer-
> chandise nor exercising any craft, nor having of his own whereon to
> live, nor proper land whereon to occupy himself, and not serving
> any other, if he in convenient service (his estate considered) be re-
> quired to serve, shall be bounded to serve him which shall him re-
> quire. . . . And if they refuse, he shall on conviction by two true
> men . . . be committed to goal till he find surety to serve.
>
> And if any workman or servant, of what estate or condition be,
> retained in any man's service, to department from the said service
> without reasonable cause or license, before the term agreed on, he
> shall have pain of imprisonment.[24]

In 1351, this statute was strengthened by the stipulation, "And
none shall go out of the town where he dwelled in winter, to serve
the summer, if he may serve in the same town."[25] These laws were
"an attempt of make the vagrancy statutes a substitute for serfdom."[26]

Gradually feudalism disappeared. In 1575, Queen Elizabeth I
granted freedom to the last serfs in England. After that, the state
acted first in the interests of the new landed gentry and then in
the interests of the manufacturing classes. Changes in vagrancy
laws reflected this transition. The breakup of feudalism coincided
with increased commerce and trade. The commercial emphasis in
England at the turn of the 16th century had particular importance

in the development of vagrancy laws. With commercialism came considerable traffic bearing valuable goods. In the mid-14th century, 169 important merchants plied their trade. In the early 16th century, 3,000 merchants engaged in foreign trade alone. England became highly dependent upon commerce for its economic surplus. Italians conducted a great deal of England's commerce during this early period. The populace despised them. Citizens attacked and robbed them of their goods. "The general insecurity of the times made any transportation hazardous. The special risks to which the alien merchant was subjected gave rise to the royal practice of issuing formally executed convenants of safe conduct through the realm."[27]

The new focal concern was even more general in its scope:

> Whoever man or woman, being not lame, impotent, or so aged or diseased that he or she cannot work, not having whereon to live, shall be lurking in any house, or loitering or idle wandering by the highway side, or in streets, cities, towns, or villages, not applying themselves to some honest labour, and so continuing for three days; or running away from their work; every such person shall be taken for a vagabond. And . . . upon conviction of two witnesses . . . the same [loiterer] shall be marked with a hot iron in the breast with the letter V, and adjudged him to the person bringing him, to be his slave for two years.[28]

In sum, the vagrancy laws constituted a legislative innovation designed to provide an abundance of cheap labor to England's ruling class during a period when serfdom was breaking down and the pool of available labor was depleting. They hit at the "idle" and "those refusing to labour." With the breakup of feudalism, the utility of these laws disappeared. The increased dependence of the economy upon commerce and trade made the former use of the vagrancy statutes irrelevant. In the early 17th century, the emphasis turned to "rogues," "vagabonds," and others suspected of criminal activities. During this period, the statutes embraced "roadmen" who preyed upon citizens transporting goods from one place to another. The increased importance of commerce to England during this period brought forth protective laws. The vagrance statutes originally aimed at providing serfs for feudal landlords became a weapon in this new enterprise.[29]

In the United States during the late 19th and early 20th centuries, vagrancy statutes were used, much as they had been in England, to create a labor force. The end of the Civil War left

Uncle Sam's kitchen.
(Burk Uzzle/Woodfin
Camp & Assoc.)

Southern plantation owners and Northern industrialists wishing to industrialize the South without an adequate work force. The Emancipation Proclamation and the passage of the 13th and 14th Amendments freed the slaves, but a system of wage labor did not exist. Also, there was unwillingness on the part of plantation owners or industrialists to pay wages where slavery had previously provided cheap labor. A solution to the dilemma posed by the abolition of slavery was to arrest "free Negroes" for vagrancy and then force them to labor by leasing them to landowners, mining companies, or industrialists.[30]

Enforcing the vagrancy statutes was but one of many ways criminal law was used to force ex-slaves to provide slave-like labor for the agricultural, mining, and industrial sectors of the Southern economy following the Civil War. Other criminal laws were developed and applied to former slaves. Enforcing these laws against ex-slaves also had the consequence of disenfranchising the black population and maintaining the economic and political control of the white population over the black.

The use of vagrancy statutes to create and control the labor force in the United States is not limited to the South or to the period immediately following the Civil War. Until very recently, during times of harvest people were arrested for vagrancy and given the option of either working as a farm laborer or being sent to jail.[31] These statutes were also used to control "undesirables." California used them to limit the immigration of unemployed persons during the depression.[32] Vagrancy statutes also came to serve the police as a catch-all to permit them to arrest, harass, or jail persons whom they found to be a nuisance or suspected of being potential criminals.

The very nature of vagrancy statutes as catch-all categories pinpointing a status rather than an act makes them swim in vagueness. The Jacksonville, Florida, ordinance, for example, reads:

> Rogues and vagabonds, or dissolute persons who go about begging, common gamblers, persons who use juggling or unlawful games or plays, common drunkards, common night walkers, thieves, pilferers or pickpockets, traders in stolen property, lewd, wanton and lascivious persons, keepers of gambling places, common railers and brawlers, persons wandering or strolling about from place to place without any lawful purpose or object, habitual loafers, disorderly persons, persons neglecting all lawful business and habitually spending their time by frequenting houses of ill fame, gaming houses, or places where alcoholic beverages are sold or served, persons able to work but habitually living upon the earnings of their wives or minor children shall be deemed vagrants and upon conviction in the Municipal Court shall be punished by 90 days imprisonment, $500 fine, or both.[33]

Because of the vagueness of the statutes and the unbridled discretion granted law enforcers, the enforcement of these statutes has culminated in a large body of appellate court decisions. In 1972, a group of people arrested under the Jacksonville, Florida, statute appealed to the U.S. Supreme Court arguing that their arrest was unconstitutional because the statute was too vague. Justice Douglas expressed the view of the Supreme Court supporting the defendants' appeal:

> Here the net is cast large, not to give the courts the power to pick and choose, but to increase the arsenal of the police. . . . Where the list of crimes is so all-inclusive and generalized as the one in this ordinancy, those convicted may be punished for no more than vin-

dicating affronts to police authority. . . . Another aspect of the ordinance's vagueness appears when we focus, not on the lack of notice given a potential offender, but on the efficacy of the unfettered
discretion it places in the hands of the Jacksonville police. Caleb
Foote . . . has called the vagrancy-type law as offering "punishment by analogy." . . . Such crimes . . . are not compatible with
our constitutional system. . . . Arresting a person on suspicion, like
arresting a person for investigation, is foreign to our system, even
when the arrest is for past criminality. Future criminality, however, is the common justification for the presence of vagrancy statutes. . . . The Jacksonville ordinancy cannot be squared with our
constitutional standards and is plainly unconstitutional.[34]

As a practical matter, the long, disreputable history of vagrancy
statutes in the United States ended with this decision.

Consensus Theory _____

The data from research on the origins of Anglo-American criminal law are inconsistent with the claim that criminal law is a
codification of customary beliefs and reflects a consensus in the
values held by "every healthy conscience." In short, Durkheim and
those who pursue this theory are simply wrong. As pointed out
earlier, however, this does not mean that, at any point in time, it
is an error to assert that there is consensus among a community
of people. The error comes when it is claimed that this consensus
explains why some acts are defined as criminal while others are
not.

It is also important to bear in mind that, even where there is an
apparent consensus, the lines separating agreement and disagreement are usually very ambiguous. Most people in the United States
would certainly agree that there should be laws against "violence," yet, as Skolnick points out, "Violence is an ambiguous term
whose meaning is established through political processes. The kinds
of acts that become classified as 'violent' and, equally important,
those which do not become so classified, vary according to who
provides the definition and who has superior resources for dissem-
inating and enforcing his decision."[35]

The importance of this observation is brought home by considering the politicization of aggression. In a speech on May 10, 1984,
President Reagan characterized the government of Nicaragua as
a government that supported and armed "terrorists and guerillas."

On the other hand, in that same speech he referred to the contras—a group of people fighting against the Nicaraguan government—as "freedom fighters." One person's "freedom fighters" are
another person's "terrorists and guerillas."

The strongly held and apparently universal belief in the dictum
"Thou shalt not kill" is a telling example of how slippery is the
notion of consensus.[36] Killing is not always against the law and is
in fact often praised as honorable. Soldiers kill in war time; exe-
cutioners pull the switch. Governments plot and carry out executions of government leaders in peace time and in war (see Chapter
13.)[37] Finally, it must be remembered that *not* to kill may itself
be a crime. A soldier who refuses to kill or a citizen who refuses
to serve in the military commits a crime.

Horowitz and Liebowitz point out the political nature of urban
ghetto riots and argue cogently that the distinction between criminality and political marginality is obsolete.[38] The point is that
what constitutes crime and deviance is the result of a political
process, not a simple reflection of agreed upon ideas of right and
wrong:

> . . . the decision to treat deviance as a social problem is itself a
> political decision . . . deviance theories [should be] about society
> and, therefore, politics, conflict, coercion and other such 'normal'
> concerns. . . . There is confusion about the line beyond which 'steal-
> ing' becomes 'looting,' 'hooliganism' becomes 'rioting,' 'vandalism'
> becomes 'sabotage'; when do 'reckless maniacs' become 'freedom
> fighters'? Are the everyday encounters between the policy and ur-
> ban slum youth throughout the world somehow stripped of their po-
> litical significance if what is happening is not defined as a 'riot' or
> 'disturbance'?[39]

Societal-Needs Theory _____

Another theory commonly proposed to account for the origins of
criminal law is that criminal law is a reflection of societal needs.
This theory, which is an application of functional theory, argues
that the existence of what Durkheim called a "social fact" should
be sought in the consequences it has for established social relations in society. Jerome Hall applied this theory to criminal law:
"the chronological order of the principal phases of legal change is
(1) a lag between the substantive law and social needs; (2) spon-

taneous efforts (practices) of judges, other officials, and laymen to make successful adaptations; and (3) legislation."[40]

The first question that should be asked about this theory is Whose needs? The term "society" is a confusing one. Every modern nation state consists of many different groups, social classes, and collectivities. To speak of "society" as though it were a real entity that existed outside the people who live together in a particular nation, state, county, or community is to assume what should be an empirical question: Does this collection of people constitute a "society" in the sense that they all share the same basic needs so that when a choice is made it is good for everyone? The answer for modern, complex societies divided by class, race, ethnicity, and gender is clearly no. Therefore, to speak of "societal needs" is to make the erroneous assumption that what is good for one group is good for another.

Hall's research on the emergence of the laws of theft provides important data relevant to this issue. He notes that "breaking the bales open and taking the goods assigned to him" was made a criminal act as mercantilism and commerce came to be important in Europe. Yet clearly the decision to make the person who broke open the bales a criminal was one that favored the merchant over the employee. Whether or not we agree that this was a "good thing," the point cannot be disputed that the law was making a decision in favor of the merchant and against the interests of the employee. Similarly, when the king decreed that people in villages could no longer hunt, fish, and gather wood according to the customary practice of treating "common grounds" as their own, the king was creating criminal laws in the interests of the nobility and against the desires, interests, and customary practices of the peasants and villagers. When the laws of vagrancy were passed in England and America—creating a labor force dependent on the landowners, industrialists, or mine owners—acts in the interests of the capitalists but antithetical to the interests of the workers were made criminal. "Societal needs" are nonexistent in such cases; it is the needs of one class of people in conflict with the needs of another. The state chooses sides and criminal law reflects this choice.

The fact that criminal law is inexorably a choice between one set of interests and another is not limited to the early history of the law, but it characterizes modern-day law creation as well. Even laws that, on the surface, appear to serve the needs of everyone often, upon closer inspection, turn out to be fraught with special interests that conflict with those of significant numbers of people.

In 1970, for example, legislation was passed that was ostensibly designed to curtail the growth and influence of organized crime.[41] On the surface, nothing would seem to come closer to fulfilling the requirement of a law meeting "societal needs" than a law designed to control organized crime. Analysis of the law-making process, however, reveals that even here those who influence and write the law were making important choices as to whose needs the law was to meet.

The Organized Crime Control Act of 1970 fundamentally changed many previously held sacred principles of criminal-law enforcement.[42] It vastly increased the powers of the federal government vis à vis state and local governments in law enforcement. Acts previously left to state and local governments were, with the stroke of a pen, transferred to federal jurisdiction. The federal prosecutor was given unprecedented powers through fundamental changes in the power of the grand jury. Among other things, after passage of this law, the federal prosecutor could send an uncooperative witness to prison for an indefinite period of time if the witness refused to testify after he or she was granted immunity. These changes, and others in this law, were revolutionary. They were also steadfastly opposed by many legal groups, including the New York Bar Association and the American Civil Liberties Union. Was this law, then, a reflection of "societal needs"? Controlling organized crime may be necessary for "society," but this law, like most laws, invariably contains qualities that conflict with the interests of some groups in the process of protecting the interests of others.

The idea that criminal law reflects societal needs appears, at first brush, indisputable commonsense. Closer scrutiny of the logic of the argument combined with empirical studies of the implications of the theory suggests, however, that this "commonsense" theory is not an adequate explanation of why acts are defined as criminal.

As scientists, we must abandon this theory just as we abandoned theories that said the sun moved around the earth, that all matter could be reduced to the four elements—fire, water, air and stone—or that gold could be created from rocks.

Ruling-Class Theory _____

Faced with the failure of traditional sociological theories, social scientists sought alternative explanations. One alternative—suggested by the work of classical political theorists such as Machiavelli, Pareto, Marx, and Weber—is that law is simply a reflection of the interests and ideology of the ruling class. Max Weber put it this way: "with government as an instrument or vehicle available to whomever can control or use it, opportunities for gain, whether pecuniary or political or other advantage, accrue to those who can use government."[43]

Marx made the point more succinctly and pointed the finger at the class of people most likely to control and use the government: "In every era the ruling ideas are the ideas of the ruling class."[44] For both Marx and Weber, the ruling class consisted of those who controlled the economic resources and political power. The opportunities for profit as well as the possibility of controlling the government and the law rested in the hands of those with political and economic power. Political power led to economic power and economic power led to political power. Thus the theory that the ruling class determined the content and functioning of criminal, as well as other, law made sense. As we have seen, the theory is also consistent with a large body of empirical data on the historical development of law.

This theory that is variously referred to in sociological and political science literature as the instrumentalist, ruling class, or elite theory finds some support from research into the "behind the scenes" machinations in the law-making process. Gabriel Kolko, John Braithwaite, and W. G. Carson provide fascinating research showing that laws, which on the surface are antithetical to the interests of the ruling class, were in fact laws sought by them. Legislation requiring meatpackers to comply with federal health standards in the production process was widely publicized as a moral campaign to protect the consumer. In fact, as Kolko's research proved, the legislation was sought after, lobbied for, and largely written by the nation's largest meatpacking companies. They sought the legislation because it gave large companies a competitive advantage over small ones. Large companies could distribute the added cost of regulation over a larger number of products, thus reducing the unit cost as compared to small companies. Also, the meatpackers wanted the laws as a symbolic measure that placed the government's seal of approval on U.S. meat, thus giving U.S. meatpackers an advantage over competitors for the European market.[45]

Similar results were found by Braithwaite in his study of the pharmaceutical industry: "the transnational corporations are prepared to support tougher regulatory controls where they can see that this will impose costs on local competitors which the transnationals already meet."[46]

W. G. Carson, in his study of early English factory legislation, found the same process: Large manufacturers supported legislation on factory reforms as a way of gaining a competitive advantage over small competitors.[47]

The studies cited thus far, and a large number of others, lend considerable empirical support to the ruling-class theory. The theory fails, however, when the entire spectrum of criminal law is surveyed because, although consistent with much data, it is contradicted by other findings. One of the areas of legislation that most clearly contradicts ruling-class theory is legislation making it a crime for employers and owners to interfere with the right of labor to organize, strike, and "collectively bargain." It will be remembered that in the 1800s and early 1900s it was in fact criminal for workers to engage in strikes and boycotts, or even attempt to organize into labor unions. Workers trying to wrest some control of the economy and their own lives from owners were put to prison, shot, beaten by police, and killed as criminals violating criminal laws.[48] The fact that these laws changed was a clear instance of law changing out of class conflict, but changing against the desires, ideals, and political organization of the ruling class. The major piece of federal legislation changing the status of labor unions in the United States was the National Labor Relations Act of 1934. Karl Klare described this act as "perhaps the most radical piece of legislation ever enacted by the United States Congress." He goes on:

> Enacted in the wake of great strikes of 1934, at an unusually tense and fluid historical moment, it represented, in the words of one historian, 'an almost unbelievable capitulation by the government' . . . a small number of the most sophisticated representatives of business favored passage of the Act on the theory that some such measure was essential to preserve the social order and to forestall developments toward even more radical change. Nonetheless, most employers, large and small, bitterly opposed passage of the Act.[49]

But, of course, the mere passage of the act by the legislature did not therefore change the legal order nor mean that the law would necessarily be effective: "the Wagner Act did not fully become 'the law' when Congress passed it in 1935, or even when the Supreme Court ruled it constitutional in 1937. . . . The Act 'became law' only when employers were forced to obey its command by the imaginative, courageous, and concerted efforts of countless unheralded workers."[50]

Ruling-class theorists, in turn, respond that laws such as the National Labor Relations (Wagner) Act are often supported by specific ruling-class interests. Although on the surface the laws are contrary to their economic interests, they in fact are in their interests. The aforementioned study by Gabriel Kolko of the support for meatpacking regulations by the large meatpackers is often cited as an example.[51] Furthermore, ruling-class theory argues, even when laws are against the short-term interests of the ruling class (capitalists in capitalist societies), they are essential for purposes of legitimacy. The state must appear to be representing "everyone" and thus occasionally placate unruly citizenry by passing laws against the ruling class as a demonstration of the neutrality of the state and the inherent goodness of the system. This perpetuates capitalism "in the long run" and serves the interests of the ruling class.[52]

The arguments of ruling-class theory have some cogency, but they are, nonetheless, limited. It is clear that some laws are designed by segments of the ruling class to subtly serve their interests.[53] On the other hand, it is fallacious to assume that the ruling class is one monolithic class with shared interests. To be sure, if threatened by the overthrow of the capitalist system or a rising tide of socialist revolutions in parts of its empire, the ruling class will tend to unite against the opposition, even at the cost of supporting causes and ideologies with which they do not agree; the history of Hitler's rise to power in Germany is in part a testimony to just this process. But the history of legislation is replete with examples of a divided ruling class struggling quite openly against itself for favorable legislation. Calavita's research on the history of immigration laws in the United States is a good illustration.[54]

In the 1800s, the burgeoning industrial revolution in the United States produced a demand for labor much greater than was available. One solution to a labor-shortage problem, from the owners' point of view, is to allow immigration from countries where there is a labor surplus. During the 1800s, U.S. immigration laws clearly reflected the state's adaptation of this solution. There is, however, a contradiction here: If the influx of labor grows beyond the numbers that can be easily integrated into the labor force, there is a potential for labor unrest as workers ban together to demand more jobs. In U.S. history, there was also the fact that workers from

Europe brought with them a conscious realization that the interests of workers and owners were inherently in opposition to one another, a history of involvement of socialist and communist politics. Thus, as the labor market was gradually filled and the initial phase of industrialization subsided, a large, unemployed, urban-labor force was left behind. Militant labor movements and open rebellion was one of the consequences. Some legislators and businessmen saw a solution to the unrest and rebellion in laws restricting immigration. Some industries, however, continued to depend on a large surplus-labor force for maximum profits. While the bankers and clothing manufacturers sought restrictions on immigration, the steel industry sought to keep immigration policies open. Eventually, the steel industry lost, and, in 1921, the nation's first general law restricting immigration was passed.

Can this be explained easily by ruling-class theory? It can, of course, if one argues that the "real interest" of the ruling class was restricted immigration. If the only evidence for this claim is the fact that the law passed, then the explanation is a tautology: The event is explained by the existence of the event.

On the other hand, to argue that the ruling-class theory is totally inapplicable to the legal process is to throw out the baby with the bathwater. Examples of ruling-class intervention in, and control of, the legal order abound: The asbestos industry attorneys recently drafted a piece of legislation that would make it illegal for employees to sue their employers or trade unions for damages resulting from illnesses caused by working with asbestos (this is an industry infamous for the health hazards to workers that is expected to claim at least 400,000 lives);[55] lawyers employed by the pharmaceutical industry played a major role in drafting anti-amphetamine legislation resulting from a hearing that disclosed systematic violation of drug laws in the industry;[56] representatives of the largest meatpacking firms in the nation controlled the legislation establishing meat-inspection standards for the industry;[57] the banking industry writes legislation ostensibly controlling banks; the aerospace industry participates in legislation setting safety standards for airplanes; and so forth. That there is ruling-class interest and influence in vast areas of law cannot be denied. That it is the only force responsible for law creation or law implementation, however, is erroneous. What is called for is not a theory that argues for either total control by the ruling class or no control at all, but one that recognizes both the strengths and the limitations of ruling-class influence on the legal order.

Pluralist Theory _____

In the light of these facts, it is tempting to go in the direction of the legal scholar, Lawrence Friedman, who articules a pluralist theory of law making: "what makes law . . . is not 'public opinion' in the abstract, but public opinion in the sense of exerted social force."[58]

This theory is correct as far as it goes; that is to say, it is consistent with the facts. The passage of criminal laws inevitably favors some groups' interests. As Thorsten Sellin put it, "Social values which receive the protection of the criminal law are ultimately those which are treasured by dominant interest groups."[59]

The problem is that this theory does not tell us how to determine which groups are dominant and will, therefore, be able to "exert social force" to create laws. If the only measure of whether a group or social class is dominant is that it succeeds in having its laws enacted, then the theory is simple tautology (see Chapter 4) and explains nothing. On the other hand, if the theory accepts a hypothesis from Hubert Blalock that "the possession of money almost automatically confers power in Western society,"[60] then the theory becomes a thinly veiled disguise for ruling-class theory, which, as we have seen, is wanting as a general theory of criminal-law creation.

Another shortcoming of pluralist theory is that much law making occurs through individual decisions. The "dominant interest" theory must assume either that all judges represent the same interests or that they are influenced by the same "exerted forces." Finally, legislation we previously examined (e.g., the Organized Crime Control Act of 1970) reflects the political infighting of government officials over different ideologies and can only be tautologically explained by the "interest group" theory.

Structural-Contradictions Theory _____

Thus far we have looked at three general theories of law creation: consensus theory, societal-needs theory, and ruling-class theory. Our method for evaluating these theories is consistent with the scientific methods outlined in the previous chapter. First, we evaluate the logical structure of the theory, then we examine the empirical evidence to see if it supports the claims implied by the theory. We have found that these three theories are not consistent with a substantial amount of the empirical data derived from systematic research on the law-creation process. This does not say, of course, that no evidence could be found that would support one of the theories. Indeed, we can find instances that partially support one or another of these theories. Hagan and Leon, for example, discovered that juvenile-welfare laws in Canada reflected widespread concern over juvenile welfare. And, as we saw above, ruling-class theory is also consistent with some but not all, cases of law creation.

In view of the failure of these theories, we propose a structural-contradictions theory of law making, which builds upon existing theory while explaining facts the others failed to do.

The starting point for the theory is that every society, nation, economic system, and historical period contains within it contradictions that are the moving force behind social changes—including the creation of criminal laws.

A contradiction results when the very process of responding to one set of a problems, demands, ideologies, or expectations embedded in existing social relations creates situations that are fundamentally antagonistic. Contradictions are inherent in social, political, and economic relations in every historical period and cannot be resolved within the existing social framework. The starting point for understanding criminal law is the articulation of the existing contradictions in a particular historical epoch.

This formulation assumes that it is people, not the "systems," "society," or "culture," who create law. It is people responding to contradictions but bounded by existing resources and constraints.[61]

The consensus, societal-needs, and pluralist theories assume that the state is a value-neutral "system" with an imminent intelligence directing social change. A more-accurate depiction sees the state as a set of interrelated institutions with specific roles and role occupants who make decisions. The decisions of the role occupants in the structure that create laws are a response to events external to the state. The passage of a law creates a response from groups external to the state, which stimulates further law-making action. The instrumentalist's observation that the "ruling class" puts pressure on the state to make laws that reflect that class' interests and ideology is correct. Because the economic elite of a society is better organized and can afford to purchase labor for the sole purpose of manipulating the state, this class is more likely than any other class to see its views reflected in law.

Repressive and exploitative law as well as law that contradicts the strongly held views of other groups or social classes, however, generates resistance. When the resistance leads to open conflict (for example, in the form of riots, demonstrations, and rebellions) the law will be used to respond to it. The response may be new legislation, new interpretations of old laws, or use of existing laws to repress or ameliorate the conflict. The ruling class will win some and lose some struggles in the face of such conflicts. An adequate theory of law creation must accommodate this fact.

At the base of the process are structural contradictions. These may be economic, political, social, or ideological. In capitalist economic systems, a basic economic contradiction is between the private ownership of production and the public nature of the productive process; that is, it is the "public" (workers) who must provide the labor that actually accounts for the production of the goods. Simply put, those who own the factory have the legal right to almost anything they want with their property and what it produces.[62] Without workers to produce goods, the factory is only an expensive shell. If both owners and workers insist on keeping everything produced by the combination of private property and public work, there is an irresolvable contradiction. The contradiction builds conflict between workers and owners into the system. The law is used in an effort to resolve that conflict.

The contradiction between the private ownership and the public nature of work is the root of conflict between owners and workers that has plagued America from its inception. We noted in Chapter 2 the prevalence of class, race, and labor strife over the years. In the beginning, the laws overwhelmingly favored the owners. Owners could set inhuman conditions of labor at whatever wages they chose to pay. Slavery and the exploitation of the labor of women and children were legal. It was a criminal act for workers to try to organize, strike to interrupt the work process, or interfere with property owners' right to do anything they chose with the property or the products produced with or on it.

The fact that these laws reflected neither consensus nor societal needs was clearly established when workers, slaves, women, and children rebelled. They blatantly violated the law and suffered imprisonment, beatings, and even death at the hands of law enforcers "upholding law and order." If ruling-class theory were correct, the situation would never have changed. There was a sufficient surplus of labor to enable owners to replace the "uppity" and recalcitrant with new immigrants or more slaves. For the most part, the owners opposed the workers' efforts unanimously because they saw any concession as a first step toward "socialism, anarchy and communism,"[63] and, more immediately, a threat to profits.

The conflict engendered a serious dilemma for those who occupied key roles in the state. There was widespread sympathy for at least some of the demands of the workers. A number of resolutions were proposed and tried. As is usually the case under these circumstances, a massive use of state force was one of the first efforts. Ideological haranguing about the criminality of anarchy and the necessity for living under "rule of law" accompanied the state use of force to suppress the conflict.

If the use of massive coercive force and the plea for "obeying the law in the interests of everyone" are effective, the law is unlikely to change. If law makers and those who own the economic resources must compromise, as they ultimately did in the case of workers' rebellions in the 1920s and 1930s, then the laws will change. If the ruling classes succeed, as they did against the Native Americans (through a policy of genocide and forced segregation), then the law changes to legitimize and codify the policies of increased repression.[64]

At the dawn of industrialization, manufacturers forced laborers to give up the practice of producing goods in their own cottages for the factory. The conditions of labor in the factories were inhumanly routine, boring, and oppressive. The workers rebelled and "machine smashing" was an almost universal practice as a way of fighting the changes. Laws changed to criminalize machine smashing and even being a member of the "Luddite" movement, which opposed the transition from cottage to factory industry. In the end, the workers lost and were forced to accept factory work in lieu of starvation.

In the 1930s, however, the years of riots, rebellions, and worker agitation against the oppressive and exploitative conditions of work were the impetus for legal changes that benefited the workers; collective bargaining, trade unions, and the right to strike were made legal by the National Labor Relations (Wagner) Act of 1933.[65] What was criminal from 1776–1932 was legal in 1933 as a result of the conflicts generated by contradictions in the political economy of the 19th and early 20th centuries. One attempted solution of law makers was the passage of a plethora of laws giving workers heretofore unheard of powers.[66]

Racism and Sexism in American Criminal Law

The history of racist laws in America is a history of contradictions and people's struggles with them. To legitimize slavery as an institution, white Americans defined people with black skin as nonhuman. They were not supposed to possess souls, human intelligence, or the capacity for civilized conduct. On the other hand, the institution of slavery demanded that black people as well as white people perform human tasks: building shelters, forming communities, raising children, and working. Without work, shelter, and procreation, the slave population was of no economic value. The work done, however, was not the work nonhumans could do or there would have been no necessity for slaves. It was "a system constructed on the contradiction between denying the humanity of Blacks but depending on their human qualities for the survival of the system."[67]

This contradiction, as Genovesse insightfully points out, led to the creation of laws that tried to make logical sense out of what was inherently illogical. Slaves could not testify against whites— even if the whites were accused of fermenting revolution among the slaves—because slaves were not human and only human beings had the right to appear as witnesses in court. Thus we have the bizarre example of an abolitionist white being set free in a trial because the only witnesses who could testify that he had incited the slaves on a plantation to rebel were the slaves themselves.

A similar set of contradictions characterize law and the legal order with respect to women. Women, like slaves, were denied the vote and the right to work. The U.S. Supreme Court in 1867 held that a woman who had successfully completed law school and passed the bar in Illinois had no right to practice law. The Court's opinion was that:

> The claim that [under the Fourteenth Amendment of the Constitution] the statute law of Illinois . . . can no longer be set up as a barrier against the right of females to pursue any lawful employment for a livelihood (the practice of law included), assumes that it is one of the privileges and immunities of women as citizens to en-

(Bettye Lane/Photo Researchers)

gage in any and every profession, occupation, or employment in civil life. It certainly cannot be affirmed, as an historical fact, that this has ever been established as one of the fundamental privileges and immunities of the sex. On the contrary, the civil law, as well as nature herself, has always recognized a wide difference in the respective spheres and destinies of man and woman. Man is, or should be, woman's protector and defender. The natural and proper timidity and delicacy which belongs to the female sex evidently unfits it for many of the occupations of civil life. . . . It is true that many women are unmarried and not affected by any of the duties, complications, and incapacities arising out of the married state, but these are exceptions to the general rule. The paramount destiny and mission of women are to fulfill the noble and benign office of wife and mother. This is the law of the Creator. And the rules of civil society must be adapted to the general constitution of things, and cannot be based upon exceptional cases.[68]

Garfinkle, Lefcourt, and Schulder point out:

Not only were women totally excluded from the practice of law as lawyers until the present century, but they were also excluded from the whole legal apparatus—as judges, jurors, and litigants—by the same rationale. The rule of common law was that juries consisted of 'twelve good men.' One exception was made: when a pregnant woman faced execution, a jury of twelve women was convened to decide whether she should be executed before or after giving birth to her child.[69]

In 1869, Sophia Jex-Blake and six other women sought admission to medical school at the University of Edinburgh in Scotland. In the midst of great controversy, threats of physical harm, and concerted opposition by male professors and students, the seven women were allowed to attend segregated classes, for a while. The university refused, however, to award the chemistry prize to the student with the highest marks, as was traditionally the case, because that year the student with the highest marks was a woman. The controversy grew so heated that the university ultimately reneged on its willingness to allow the women to attend. The women went to court for satisfaction. They received none. The court ruled that the university had the right to discriminate against women even though they could not discriminate against people because of their religion or race.[70]

Sexism at Edinburgh was not an isolated event. Women in the 1800s could not vote, attend law school, be admitted to practice law, or serve in parliament or city councils. By law, women were not considered "persons" and therefore were not eligible for, or covered by, laws applied to "persons"—only men were people in England in the 1800s, so far as the law was concerned.

That this changed is well recognized. What is not as well recognized is that it changed only when women violently and consistently opposed the oppression and exploitation institutionalized in the law. The view that the law gradually changed as customs and beliefs changed, or that the law became more fair and tolerant as the logic of a democratic society for all slowly worked its magic through legal reasoning, is simply mythical. It was the consequence of women willing to undergo humiliation, torment, imprisonment, and even death in the struggle for equality in law and society that wrought what changes have occurred. In the 1800s, as in the 1900s, the institutions perpetuated themselves with their built-in biases and blatant sexism as long as they were not challenged. Even when challenged, their changes were slow and piecemeal.

One hundred and fifty years of women's struggle for equality in law has brought changes but not equality. One authority estimates that there are over 800 pieces of blatantly sex-discrimina-

tory laws currently on the statute books in the United States today: in Wisconsin, a wife can be disinherited by her husband; in
most states, women cannot co-sign for a loan, but their husbands
can, even though the property is technically "communal"; in some
states, a man can still legally kill his wife if he catches her having
sexual relations with another man; in rape cases, courts allow evidence about the woman's "reputation" as admissible (a woman with
prior sexual experience is less likely to be believed if she claims
she was raped); and in most of the United States, it is not a crime
for a man to rape his wife or a woman with whom he is living. A
man who kills his wife for adultery stands a reasonably good chance
of being excused for his "understandable" reaction; a woman who
commits the same act under the same circumstances is less likely
to receive a sympathetic hearing. A black accused of raping a white
woman is much more likely to be convicted of rape than a white
man accused of raping a black woman, a black man accused of
raping a black woman, or a white man accused of raping a white
woman. Women continue to be seen in law and in practice as
"property" to be owned and controlled by men.[71] As recently as
1961, the U.S. Supreme Court denied a woman's appeal from conviction by an all-male jury:

> At the core of appellant's argument is the claim that the nature of
> the crime of which she was convicted peculiarly demanded the in-
> clusion of persons of her own sex on the jury. She was charged with
> killing her husband by assaulting him with a baseball bat. . . . The
> affair occurred in the context of marital upheaval involving, among
> other things, the suspected infidelity of appellant's husband, and
> culminating in the final reflection of his wife's efforts at reconcilia-
> tion. It is claimed, in substance, that women jurors would have been
> more understanding or compassionate than men in assessing the
> quality of appellant's act and her defense.[72]

Women's rights movements and struggles effectively changed the
law. Changing the law, however, does not guarantee changing
patterns of social relations. This requires more than appellate court
decisions and changing statutes. In 1954, the U.S. Supreme Court
decided in Brown vs. the Board of Education that segregated
schooling was unconstitutional. Since 1954, as David Freeman
shows, the most measurable impact of the decision has been as a
source of legitimacy for continued racial discrimination in schooling.[73] More recent court decisions also undermine the effect that
the Brown decision might have by unholding the right of different

school districts to spend vastly different amounts of money on education.[74]

Women's Movement

The women's movement in the 1970s and 1980s has influenced a host of laws and law-enforcement practices. In common law, the man had a right to sexual relations with his wife even if these were violent relations. This law still holds in most states. The contradiction between a man's freedom and a woman's right to her "life and pursuit of happiness" is apparent here. The mobilization of women into a vocal and visible political movement has brought some change in these laws; Oregon, New Jersey, Iowa, and Delaware have rewritten their laws. In those states, men who rape or otherwise are violent to their wives may be punished.

Traditionally, police departments have been reticent to enforce laws against rape. The women's movement has also changed this practice in a few places.

Perhaps the most important recent change to take place in the law with respect to women occurred when the Supreme Court decided in *Roe vs. Wade* that laws that restricted a woman's right to an abortion "during the first trimester of pregnancy" were unconstitutional.[75] Abortion laws had for years restricted a woman's right to determine her own destiny. They discriminated against the poor by making illegal abortions unaffordable and dangerous. The women's movement focused considerable attention on these laws, generating conflict between those who sought to maintain male dominance as to whether or not a woman should have a baby and those who sought to give the woman a right to choose. The conflict has not abated with the Supreme Court decision. Those opposed to the women's movement have become increasingly violent, bombing birth-control clinics and trying to physically and mentally intimidate women who seek advice and counsel. The women's movement, in turn, is striking back through legal channels and by mobilizing public and political sentiment. This issue, however, will not go away soon, and we can anticipate continued conflict because of the oppression of women and the struggle of those who benefit from that oppression to try to maintain their privileges and power.[76]

All of the following reflect the cogency of the structural-contradictions theory: debates over capital punishment and the U.S. Supreme Court's vacillation on this issue; the emergence of wife beating and child abuse as salient issues in criminal law; and the use of federal statutes to punish people for violating another's civil rights (where the states refuse to impose punishment even for murder or assault). The contradictions are spelled out in conflicts where political and judicial office holders attempt to resolve problems by changing the law. The contradictives are, however, structural. It is possible to relieve the conflicts and dilemmas temporarily, but the contradictions will continue to generate conflict.*

Conclusion _____

The very heart of science is the interplay between theory and data. In this chapter, we have looked at the process by which laws are created by legislatures and courts defining acts as criminal and delinquent. We have surveyed the major theories in social science and law and attempted to explain why some acts are defined as criminal. These theories include the consensus, societal-needs, pluralist, and ruling-class theories. We have argued that each of these theories fails to account for substantial and important facts revealed by systematic study of the law-creation process.

Alternatively, we proposed a structural-contradictions theory that attempts to synthesize major parts of existing theories in a fashion consistent with the logic of scientific inquiry and the facts revealed by empirical investigation.

Our theory is that people make laws. People construct conflicts, resolve disputes, and change the way we all relate to one another. But people do not create their reality on a clean canvas every 10 years. They, like the painter, must fit their creative efforts to the size and shape of their canvas, the paints they have, and the imagination they can marshal to envision alternatives.

As the creation of criminal law is concerned, the most important part of the canvas everyone inherits from the past is the set of

---

*A number of studies of civil laws demonstrate the utility of this theory. Whitt compared the relative efficacy of ruling-class, consensus, and structural-contradiction theories to account for changes in California law regarding the expenditure of tax money for public-transportation systems. Calavita analyzed immigration laws in the United States. Curran undertook a study of mine-safety legislation. Stearns investigated factory safety and health in Sweden. Donnelly analyzed the law affecting the workers safety and health laws in the United States. Sbarbaro looked in detail into the emergence of the Organized Crime Control Act in 1970. In each instance, the researcher concluded that the facts of the case supported the structural-contradiction theory but failed to support consensus, societal-needs, ruling-class, or pluralist theories of law making.

contradictions built into the political, economic, and social relations of a particular time. Contradictions are inherent in the structure of the political organization, economic system, and ideological structure. A contradiction is a set of relations that contains elements that cannot coexist without generating conflict and that, by their incompatible nature, undermine basic features of the society.

The existence of contradictions creates dilemmas and conflicts that the people in positions to influence and create law try to resolve. Because they generally limit their efforts to manipulating the symptoms of the contradictions (i.e., resolving conflicts and dilemmas), the resolutions generate further contradictions, conflicts, and dilemmas. In this way, the process of law creation becomes ongoing and dialectical.

5

Explanation and Description of Criminality

Science is a unique way of seeing and investigating the world around us. But it is not the only source of knowledge. Poets, novelists, playwrights, musicians, psychics, and theologians all provide ways of viewing the world that are more or less helpful aids to understanding. Science gains understanding by constructing data and theories that have a particular logical and empirical form.

It is commonplace in high-school textbooks to depict the scientific method as one that strives for prediction and control. This is a very misleading notion. Recent developments in the philosophy, history, and logic of science make it clear that the methods employed by scientists are not a search for ways of predicting and controlling the environment; rather, the methods are those of cre-

131

ating reliable methods for gathering data, constructing logically consistent theories, and testing those theories.[1] The founder of the modern-day philosophy of science, Karl Popper, points out that scientific theories are often unable to control the events they study.[2] Astronomers cannot control the movement of heavenly bodies. Physicists cannot control the laws of motion. Biologists can neither predict mutations nor determine precisely which species will survive and which will become extinct. Biology can tell us only that there will be mutations and explain why some species have survived and others have not.[3]

Another misconception is that science consists solely of the accumulation of facts. In the last four chapters, we presented a large number of facts that we know about crime and criminal law. But the scientific effort does not end with this process. As Poincare notes, "Science is built up of facts as a house is built up of stone, but an accumulation of facts is no more science than a heap of stones is a house."[4]

For an accumulation of facts to become part of the house of science, the facts must be intertwined with generalizations that answer questions. Why is A related to B? How did it happen that X followed Y and not Z? In scientific inquiry, there is an inevitable entanglement and mutual dependence of scientific observation with scientific theory.[5] As we shall see, theories lead us to ask different questions, and the formulation of the these questions is a critical part of the process of developing reliable scientific knowledge.

Some philosophers of science argue that the real measure of scientific progress is in the questions asked rather than in the discovery of theories or facts.

Constructing Scientific Theory _____

There is an old cartoon, showing two archaeologists reading hieroglyphics on the wall of a cave, that circulates among anthropologists. All the writings are pictures of animals and people doing various tasks. At the very end of the writing there appears a formula: $E = mc^2$. This, of course, is Einstein's famous formula, which summarizes his theory of relativity. There is considerable wisdom in this cartoon in that the discovery of scientific theory often involves great leaps of logic and imagination. Einstein himself described the way he discovered scientific theory as combining careful and detailed study of the facts with vast intuitive leaps that he hoped would "make sense" of the facts.

Everyone is constantly constructing theories. It is a rare conversation that does not involve someone asking, Why do you suppose . . . ? The answer to the "why" is the first step in constructing theory. The questions asked and the answers suggested start the process of science.[6]

Recall some of the facts in Chapters 2 and 3. What do you want to ask about those facts? Probably the most common questions asked are (1) Why do some people commit criminal acts? and (2) Why are some acts defined as criminal while others are not? But these are not the only questions that can be asked. Why do females have a lower official rate of criminality than males? Why do urban dwellers report being victims of crime more often than suburban dwellers? Why do the police arrest more young black males than they do older white males? Why do the police enforce laws that prohibit lower-class crimes more often than they enforce laws that prohibit middle- and upper-class crimes? There is an almost infinite number of questions that can be asked about the facts we have about crime. Some of these questions lead to fruitful research and others do not. Some of the theories proposed are useful while others are not. Ensuing chapters will look in detail at the major theories of crime and how well these theories account for the facts.

Theories can be judged more or less scientifically useful depending on (1) the value of the questions raised useful to the development of knowledge; (2) whether or not the theory is capable of being falsified; (3) how general the theory is; (4) whether or not the theory is consistent with the known facts; (5) how parsimonious the theory is—a theory that is complicated and difficult to translate into real life implications will be less desirable than a simpler one with clear-cut implications; and (6) whether the theory has implications for change. A theory of cancer that tells us there is nothing that can be done to change the incidence of this disease will be, other things being equal, less desirable than one that has implications for changing the effects of the disease.

In the ensuing chapters, we will use these criteria to assess the scientific utility of extant criminological theories. But can we apply the scientific method to the study of crime? Are the social sciences scientific?

It is sometimes alleged that a science of crime is impossible.

This argument asserts that social science is impossible for one or more of the following reasons:

1. Human affairs are too diverse and too complex to be explained by a set of propositions or laws.
2. Since human beings have a freedom of choice (or "free will"), then they cannot predict human behavior.
3. Since the scientist is part of what is being described and explained, objectivity is impossible, and therefore social science cannot be objective and scientific.
4. What is true of one social situation is not true of others since every situation is unique.
5. Since social events cannot be reversed, it is impossible ever to test any social theories.[7]

Mainly, these criticisms fail not because they are wrong, but because they misunderstand the nature of scientific inquiry. Human affairs are indeed complex; human beings are diverse; and the variety of human experiences, cultures, and ways of life are almost infinitely variable. But so, alas, is the physical and biological world. If complexity and diversity were incompatible with science, there would be no science of anything.

The second argument (because human beings can choose, their behavior is unpredictable) is partially correct. But it is precisely the task of social science to determine the available choices and the likelihood that an individual or a group will choose one path rather than another. When we say that people generally choose to work rather than to live in idleness, we are not denying that they make a choice, only that the parameters of their life—as imposed on them by the structure of society—limit their choice so that one alternative is far more likely to occur than any other.

That the observer is intimately involved in what he or she wants to explain is certainly true of all sciences. Except for astronomy and some branches of physics, the observer is intimately involved as a human being in the study of mammals, of anatomy, of biological evolution, and of disease epidemiology. Further, once he or she has a particular theory, the amount of distance a scientist has from the subject tends to become irrelevant. When two astronomers watch a sunset, but each has a different theory of the movement of the heavenly bodies, they see quite different things: One sees the sun moving away from the earth; the other, the earth moving away from the sun. At this point, they are every bit as personally involved in what they see as is the social scientist observing family patterns or criminality. The objectivity of science comes from a willingness to allow data to contradict our theories, not from being unconcerned about the outcome of research.

The fourth argument (social situations are unique and therefore inexplicable by general theoretical statements; misses the mark by assuming a nonexistent regularity in physical nature. No physicist would declare himself or herself able to tell you when the physical properties that comprise a particular building will reach a point where they no longer will support the building. The leaves of a tree never fall the same way two seasons in a row, and no theory of physics or botany can explain why they fall as they do. But this does not negate the possibility of physics or botany; it only means that at any point in time, there are limitations on what a science can tell us about the world in which we live. In social life there are "regularities that comprise what social scientists call 'social situations.' The individual may be unique but the coming together of the constraints and resources of his or her world make up a complex of what may be called the 'social complex' (or what ecologists call the individual's 'web of life') that limits the choices the individual can make. The individual's life history may be unique but the experience of living in urban poverty is not."[8]

Finally, the fact that social events are not reversible makes experimentation more difficult, but it does not rule out the possibility of a science, or there would be no science of astronomy or of evolution. We cannot reproduce the process that leads to celestial bodies or to the emergence of a new species, but we can, nevertheless, study these events scientifically. It is perhaps a unique asset to be able to reverse events in a laboratory, which accounts for some of the powerful results that have emanated from certain branches of physics and chemistry; but the inability to produce reversible experiments does not negate the credibility of astronomy, biology, or social science.

The previously stated similarities between social, physical, and biological sciences should not blind us to the fact that there are also some important differences. Social science, especially criminology, is by its very nature a political and moral discipline in that its conclusions (theories, facts, observations, and so forth) invariably have political and ethical implications. If research shows that the death penalty does not deter people from committing murder, the political and ethical implications contradict the policies of some lawmakers and the "intuitive faith" of many people.

If the police carrying weapons increase the incidence of homicide, the implications are that disarming the police might be a sound social policy. Physical and biological sciences sometimes run into the same problems of acceptance. (Galileo was tried for heresy for suggesting that the Earth went around the Sun, rather than the accepted theological belief of the time that saw the Earth as the center of the universe, which meant that the Sun must go around the Earth.) More often, however, the findings of the physical and biological sciences of today are accepted as reliable knowledge, whereas those of the social sciences are more controversial.

Events To Be Explained

Scientific inquiry begins with a fact or an event that needs to be explained. The more clearly articulated the event, the better we are able to judge the utility of the explanation offered. Typically, findings or events that are selected as "unusual" ones are those that do not readily "make sense" in our own or some other commonly held theory of how the world works. For Darwin, the unusual event that struck his attention was the fact that, in the history of life, some species survived while others disappeared.

In the preceding chapters, we discovered a number of facts that qualify as unusual findings, given the theory that most people have about crime: that almost everyone commits criminal acts; that people in business are as criminalistic as people in the ghettos; that spouse abuse is widespread; that the criminal acts of smuggling, gambling, and so forth, are not controlled by a Mafia, but are run instead by a network of otherwise legitimate members of society (businesspeople, lawyers, politicians, and law-enforcement officers); and that governmental crimes are ubiquitous.

Given a finding that appears unusual, the criminologist next raises questions. Let us take the finding that organized crime is managed and controlled by people who are generally thought to be legitimate members of society. Criminologists then may ask a methodological question: Is this finding generally true, or is it a unique characteristic of the research setting that led to that conclusion? Another question is theoretical: Why do legitimate members of society become involved in organized crime? This question should then lead to an explanation or a theory.

There is a very important lesson here that applies to every science and to most discussions people have about the world. It will usually clarify things considerably to ask (1) What is it that is being explained and (2) What is the explanation being suggested? Surprisingly, it is often difficult to get a clear and unambiguous answer to these questions, even in otherwise very insightful essays and commentaries.

To clarify what is meant by this point, let us take a ubiquitous problem—one that continues to be asked by philosophers, social scientists, and laypersons. Namely, it is the problem of explaining why some people in the world are wealthy while others are poor. This empirical observation is our event.

We can explain the fact that there are both poor and wealthy people in the world in many different ways. Adam Smith sought to answer this question with a theory about why some nations are wealthy and others are not. Some theologians theorize that it is simply "God's will." Many people believe that some people are poor and others are wealthy because some people are smarter, harder working, and luckier than others. The smarter, harder-working, and luckier people are wealthy, and the others are poor. Yet another explanation is that those who have the wealth are in a position to force those who do not to remain poor in order to serve the interests of those who are wealthy.

Each of these explanations, and hundreds more we might think of, is a "commonsense" explanation. None qualifies as a good scientific theory because each is stated in vague, general terms. To make one of these explanations scientific requires specifying more explicitly the relationship between the generalization and the event to be explained. For example, we can take the generalization that it is "God's will" and break it down into a series of interrelated propositions that comprise a theory. It might look like this:

1. There is a God.
2. God cares about human beings.
3. God has placed both good and evil on earth for people to choose between.
4. God judges whether a person is good or evil by the choices he or she makes between good and bad behavior.
5. Those who choose good behavior will be rewarded.
6. Those who choose bad behavior will be punished.
7. Poverty is punishment for bad behavior; wealth is reward for good behavior.

At this point, we can say we have a theory that explains the event. How good the theory is depends on the other criteria we outlined before: Is it generalizable? Can it be disproven? Is it useful in raising other questions we may want to answer?

1. *Generality* First, we assess a theory by looking at its generality. Other things being equal (as specified later), the more general the explanation, the better it contributes to the acquisition of reliable knowledge. Generality can be most readily judged by the range of events—other than the question that incited it—the theory is capable of explaining. The narrowest possible theory accounts for only a single event or finding. The most general possible explanation, by contrast, would be one that explains a wide range of other events.

2. *Parsimony* Second, we can look to the explanation's parsimony. Other things being equal, we should prefer more-parsimonious explanations to more-complicated ones. In part, this criterion of parsimony is simply the translation of the commonsense notion that one should not complicate things unnecessarily.

3. *Falsifiability* Third, we look to the explanation's testability. In the words of Karl Popper, "it must be possible for an empirical scientific system to be refuted by experience."[9] This is a crucial criterion, and one on which many theories fall short. Without the ability to falsify a theory, the possibility of establishing reliable knowledge is virtually eliminated.

   An explanation can of course be constructed in a variety of ways, all of which reduce the possibility of testing. The two more common moves made in the structure of explanations that reduce the explanation's testability is to make the explanation tautological or to add auxiliary hypotheses. We will return to this issue later in the chapter.

4. *Empirical Validity* Fourth is the criteria of empirical validity. Quite simply, does the explanation fit the facts? Usually we can be fairly confident that the explanation will fit the event that stimulated its creation (although this is not always the case, and the history of science provides some fascinating occasions when an explanation was not even consistent with the fact that stimulated its creation), but the real question is does the explanation fit facts that can be deduced from it but that were not part of the explanation's immediate concern?

5. *Implications for Change* Social science theory is by its very

nature political in the sense that it has political implications. Social science theories can be judged in part on their implications for social change. If we are faced with two theories of how to lower the crime rate—both of which are equally valid according to the other criteria previously specified, but where the implications for social change vary—we may be left to choose between them on this criteria alone. Suppose, for example, one scientific theory implied that the crime of rape could be greatly reduced by eliminating sexist propaganda in the media, but another equally valid scientific theory implied that the crime of rape could be greatly reduced by castrating all males between the ages of 16 and 23. Which theory would we choose?

The answer may seem obvious, but in fact it requires a moral decision that is not contained solely in the scientific knowledge. The best theories may well be those in which the moral implications for social change are clear cut and unequivocal. These are probably the rarest of social science theories as well.

Interrelatedness of Criteria

The five criteria for judging a theory's scientific utility are closely intertwined. The presence of one influences the absence of others. The possibility of assessing an explanation's empirical validity (how well it fits the facts it is supposed to explain) is determined by its logical consistency and its generality. If a theory is so limited in scope that it accounts for only the event that brought it forth, then its empirical validity may be assured but its generality is severely weakened and its utility as a scientific theory is thereby reduced. If the explanation is tautological, or if it has attached to it a series of auxiliary hypotheses that render it less testable, then its empirical validity cannot be assessed.

As an example, let us return to our simplified explanation of why some people are wealthy and others are poor. How does this explanation fare in terms of our criteria?

On the first two points, our theory fares quite well. It is, in fact, a very general explanation. We can, assuming the words have the general meaning they seem to convey, deduce all kinds of things from the explanation: Good people should be healthier than bad people; good people should be wealthier than bad people; bad people should be more likely to commit suicide and engage in acts of destruction than good people; good people should be happier and enjoy life more than bad people; and so forth.

Our theory is also quite parsimonious. We can scarcely hope to explain so much with fewer concepts or propositions.

Is our theory testable? No, it is not. We would need to have, at the very least, some specification of how to determine (at least in general terms) what "temptations," "evil," and "good" mean. Not all the terms in a theory need be defined in ways that permit the definitions to be fit into observations. Some terms (or concepts) can be treated as "primitive" and left undefined. For example, it would be reasonable to accept as undefined (beyond a kind of shared cultural meaning) the concept of "God" in the theory under discussion here. But we could not also do this for such key theoretical variables as "evil," "good," "reward," and "punish." We must submit these terms to more explicit definition than we did in the original formulation of the explanation. We might define them as follows:

- People who are good live by the Ten Commandments.
- People who are evil fail to live by the Ten Commandments.
- Rewards consist of enjoying such things as good health, economic prosperity, and the esteem of one's fellows.
- Punishment consists of being inflicted with such things as poverty, poor health, misery, and a lack of esteem.

If these definitions or some equivalent ones are reasonable translations from the original theoretical perspective and if they are consistent with the general context of the explanation offered, then they are acceptable. They do in fact create an explanation that may be testable. It is now possible to move from the explanation to the real world and see if the explanation holds water. Does it fit the facts? That is, is it empirically valid?

Unfortunately for the explanation offered, we run into the first major stumbling block at this point. The explanation, it turns out, is wrong. First, there is a historical document containing an abundance of evidence that the good guys do not always enjoy health, wealth, esteem, and happiness and that the bad guys often do. Christ and Job are but two of innumerable examples showing that those who live by the Ten Commandments do not inevitably enjoy the good things of life. They may in fact be severely punished. And there is abundant evidence to the effect that those who are bad—

that is, those who fail to live by the Ten Commandments—sometimes enjoy rather fully the rewards to be had by life.

So we come down to this: The explanation offered to account for social inequality meets very well some criteria of utility but fails ultimately in the text of its empirical validity. At this point, we are faced with a dilemma. We can, as we should, look for an alternative explanation, or we can change the present one so that it more clearly fits the facts it seeks to explain.

The first move (to seek an alternative) depends upon many things, not the least important of which is the availability of another possible explanation extant in the social thought of the times. The second alternative, for very human reasons, is the one most often taken. It is also the most dangerous. For it is precisely at the point when explanations fail to meet the test of empirical validity that there is a strong tendency to sacrifice one of the other criteria in order to create the illusion of empirical validity. In this example, those who believe the theory make one or more of the following moves in order to salvage it. They argue that

1. What appears as rewarding and punishing is not necessarily what is really rewarding and punishing. Material posses-

Alternatives to crime. (Alon Reininger/Contact/W. Camp & Assoc.)

sions, physical health, apparent happiness, and the superficial esteem of one's fellows are not the stuff of true rewards. The reward is in being good; the punishment is in being bad.

The problem is thereby solved. The explanation is no longer incompatible with the empirical evidence. It is, in fact, incapable of being incompatible with *any* empirical evidence. It is no longer testable. It is a neat tautology. Its contribution to reliable knowledge is now reduced by its logical structure, whereas before it was wanting for a lack of empirical validity.

We might have added an auxiliary hypothesis that would have the same effect. We might have argued that

2. Some people have the special wisdom and ability to choose punishment in order to help educate their fellows to the greater glory of life after death. Therefore those who appear to suffer may in actuality be doing this for the benefit of others.

The effect is the same. Contrary evidence is not possible and the explanation is not testable.

What we have described is of course not unique to this explanation. The creation of tautologies and the addition of auxiliary hypotheses to otherwise perfectly testable and logically defensible theories is a characteristic mode of protecting explanations in any discipline. But it is profoundly important to realize that they do not add to the explanation's scientific utility, but detract from it. It is better indeed to have an explanation that is wrong—that is, that fails to account for all the data—but that remains general, parsimonious, and testable, than it is to have an explanation that cannot be shown to be wrong but has an intuitive appeal. This is because, if an explanation is known to be wrong, we will continue to search for a better explanation. But if an explanation with intuitive appeal cannot be shown to be wrong, it may be accepted, and policies based upon it may be extremely harmful. The history of belief in capital punishment as a crime deterrent is a very good example of just this kind of logic.

Examples from the history of science are legion. Biologists in the 19th century were struck by the fact that some species survived while others did not. There were many theories proposed for this fact: Some were theological, some were scientific. None was capable of accounting for all the relevant data. Charles Darwin spent 5 years traveling around the world on a ship called the *Beagle,* gathering data on flora and fauna. When he returned to England, he wrote *The Origin of the Species.* Darwin proposed a radical theory that is summarized by the phrase, "the survival of the fittest." Darwin argued that the species that survive are the most fit. How are we to know which species are the most fit? There is an easy answer to that question: Those that survive are the most fit. The problem is, that answer is all too easy. Darwin did not make that mistake. "Fitness," Darwin argued, is determined by a species' ability to adapt to changing conditions in the environment. The species' ability to adapt, in turn, is determined by the kinds of physical and biological traits it manifests, as well as its habits. Fitness could then be determined by criteria that were independent of whether or not the species survived. In this way, the theory was capable of being disproven. If we could show that a species that was adaptable to a new environment had nonetheless become extinct, Darwin's theory would be wrong. Or, if we could show that a species that was ill-adapted to changes in an environment had nonetheless survived, the theory would also be wrong. Since we failed to disprove the theory, it has been widely accepted as a good scientific explanation.[10]

The tendency to think tautologically is so common that it is one of the most important things to look out for in explanations. A closely related tendency is to invoke teleological reasoning. This is the invocation of a casual agent to explain something without seeking a naturalistic cause. Suppose you read about the Black Toad of the Andies. This toad is a survivor. It lives in a climate in which it is almost impossible for anything to survive. The temperatures range from 110 degrees in the daytime to 40 degrees below zero at night. The toad survives in this environment because it is able to store an immense amount of heat during the day. Among other things, its color helps it do this. Then, at night, the toad is able to survive the extreme cold by living off the heat it stores up during the day. Suppose someone asks, Why is the toad black? It is tempting to say, it is black so it can survive in this very difficult climate. But this is not an explanation. It is merely a teleological subterfuge that avoids the problem of explaining the toad's blackness. To say that it is black so it can survive suggests either that something (God perhaps) designed it that way or that the toad had the ability to create a color that would enable it to live where it wanted to. Neither is satisfactory for scientific purposes. If we want to explain why it can survive, its color is an important part of that explanation. But we cannot explain why it has its color by the consequences its color has for its survival.

The three characteristics of bad theory—tautology, auxiliary hypotheses, and teleology—are central to an ability to distinguish objectively between various theories.

In the chapters that follow, we shall encounter a number of social science theories of criminal behavior. Some of them build scientifically useful theories; others do not. We will use these ideas about how to judge the quality of theories when we come to look at theories of crime.

Interrelationship Between Explanation and Description _____

> Were the eye not attuned to the sun
> the sun could never be seen by it
>
> —Goethe

A few years back, the idea prevailed that science was concerned primarily with the task of accurately describing the world without prejudice. The dictum was very wrong, both as a rule to be followed and as a description of how science gets done. Indeed, if it were necessary to describe the world without prejudice in order to be scientific, then science would be impossible. Believing it to be possible has led to some of the most unscientific and useless researches imaginable.

First, let us take up the question of whether it is possible to describe the world without prejudice.

The world is not composed of naturally occurring lumps and lines; the world is a complete and utter chaos until we impose some order upon it.[11] What the scientific effort does is make order out of chaos by creating abstract concepts and relationships explaining some of the events within the chaos. What we choose to look at depends upon the theory through which we do our looking. Take this for example: Would Johannes Kepler and Tycho Brahe see the same thing if they watched the Sun at dawn? Kepler believed the Sun was fixed and that the Earth moved. Brahe believed the Earth was fixed and that the Sun moved. Although the "objective reality" of the Sun at dawn might be the same for both men, what they see and for that matter whether they even attend the sunrise at all, is conditioned by the theory they have. The Pope would not have seen the same things had he been at Darwin's side when he spent 5 years on the *Beagle*. Darwin's observations were the basis for his evolutionary theories, which changed the direction of biological research and theory as well as the perception of the world held by most Western thinkers. The Pope, with his theory of creation, would doubtless not have seen the same things Darwin did during the voyage:

> It takes a special perspective to 'see' what is happening. Conversely, one does not simple 'see' what is going on unless one has a theoretical perspective from which the events taking place make sense. A chimpanzee cannot see what a physicist sees and, as we noted before, two physicists see different things if they operate with different theories. Thus theories are not only things that order our data, they determine what we see and what we count as data. The view that it is possible to have a science that is purely descriptive is nonsense. What one describes, what one sees as important, how one interprets what is seen and ultimately how one explains the events observed all depend on the theory (or more generally on the theoretical perspective) that one carries to and away from the observations. To deny that one has a theory is to admit that one does not wish to articulate precisely what the theory is; but observation is impossible without a theory operating at all stages of the descriptive process.[12]

Ironically, it has often been asserted that the most scientific procedure is to eschew any theoretical preconceptions in order to be free from bias. But, by so doing, we do not free ourselves from bias, we become slaves of bias; by so doing, we do not become more scientific. We make science impossible. By failing to articulate the theory, the possibility of exposing it to either logical or empirical scrutiny is avoided, but the theory remains a dominant, albeit unassessed, component of the research process.

The fetish with "pure description" often leads to a kind of theoretical wasteland in which we end by searching for "factors" that "cause" the event we wish to explain. The factors we select are presumably determined by the empirical data. Instead, the factors are determined by the unarticulated theory that we are unwilling to let see the light of day. Such a procedure of attempting to explain something by restoring to the dodge that there are a "multiplicity of factors" at work has been commented on critically by Cohen:

It simply asserts that this particular event is "caused" by this particular combination of concrete circumstances and that particular event by another combination of circumstances. This delinquency is caused by "bad neighborhood," "feeble-mindedness," and "drunken mother"; that delinquency is caused by "poverty," "broken home," "bad health," and "premature puberty." What makes these "causes" other than the fiat or "intuition" of the author? Nothing, if nothing more is offered. Probably, in many cases, the assertion that this complex of circumstances is causally related to that event rests upon implicit, inarticulate, "preconscious" theoretical assumptions in the mind of the author, but explanation lies precisely in making these theoretical assumptions explicit, showing their applicability to concretely or "phenotypically" different "special cases" of the general theory, and demonstrating that this particular complex or circumstances fits the conditions required by the theory.[13]

"Diagnoses" based on intuition in the absence of theory are likely to fall into the "evil causes evil fallacy." That is, by proceeding intuitively, we are likely to assume that things we consider bad must be caused by other things we consider bad—that corruption, for example, must be caused by greed or some other "bad" thing. Such diagnoses suffer most, not least, from the effects of the biases and preconceptions of the person making the diagnosis. Without explicit theory, implicit theory-like assumptions are nothing more than vague hunches.

It is sometimes assumed that explanations are found by discovering correlations between things. If we find that every time the moon is full the rate of violence goes up in Minneapolis, it may appear sensible to seek a casual relationship. Much fruitful scientific knowledge has emerged from just this sort of quest. The correlation, however, is a stimulus for searching for the underlying reasons why the two events are correlated. Discovering the correlation is not the same as finding an explanation for the event. There are many correlations that are spurious; there may be two or more events that occur together but that are not causally related to one another.

A related problem is encountered when we discover a series of correlations in a time sequence. Suppose, for example, that three weekends in a row your friend goes out to parties. The first weekend, she drinks scotch and water. She awakens on Monday morning with a terrible headache. The next weekend, she drinks vodka and water. Monday morning she awakens with another terrible headache. The third weekend, she drinks bourbon and water.

Monday morning she has another headache. What caused the headache? Obviously, it was the water. We know, of course, that it was not the water. If the place she went to drink and the amount of smoke in the room and the company she kept was the same for each of the parties, it could be one or a combination of those. We know enough about alcohol and headaches to think that the cause of the headaches probably had to do with the alcohol. But correlation between the water, which was the only apparent constant, and the headaches would have led to a premature conclusion about the causal relationship had we not searched further or had a better theory with which to start. As Hanson says:

> Causal laws . . . are not built up in the manner: (A then B), (A then B), (A then B), therefore all A's are followed by B's. This obscures the role of causal laws in our conceptions of a physical world. . . . The causal structure of the universe, if such a thing be, cannot be grasped simply by counting off even pairs, Noah fashion, and then summarizing it all with an umbrella formula.[14]

One way to summarize these points is to remember that description without explanation cannot create scientific knowledge. Description may lead to good predictions (the water and the headaches would be a bad prediction, but the violence and the full moon in Minneapolis would be a good one). But such predictions are the result of ignorance rather than knowledge. We can predict a good food crop when sun spots appear on the moon, but we have no idea why those two events should be correlated and our knowledge about other features of why crops grow and why the moon has sun spots suggests that there is no causal relation between them. Predicting is not sufficient.

Some of the most important theories in the history of science have not been particularly good predictors. Darwin's Evolutionary Theory predicts hypothetically: We can only predict the survival and extinction of a species if we can predict environmental changes. We can predict the extinction of Irish elks only if we can predict the Irish flood that will drown them all. But the biological theory of survival need not be held in limbo until we have a climatic-geographical-geological theory that accurately explains environmental changes. Such a theory would be necessary, though, if we insisted that all theories must predict. A good theory must have deducible, testable assertions about empirical events, but these may be events that have occurred in the past can be anticipated only hypothetically.

If we find that criminal acts are associated with high blood pressure, we may suspect that there is a causal relationship. No one would suggest that high blood pressure causes criminality; the suggestion that criminality causes high blood pressure might be more reasonable. Still we cannot assume that, just because there is a statistical relationship, one factor causes the other. To establish that, we need to develop a theory that can be empirically tested. If we have a headache and we know that taking aspirin will solve the problem, we may not care why aspirin takes away the headache. In science, however, we are not satisfied merely to find an association; we must seek to know why the association exists.

Science is not an inhuman enterprise that requires us to dismiss the human qualities of bias and selectivity. Science is a very human enterprise involving the selection of information and the explanation of why things are as they appear to be. The touchstone of science is to articulate explicitly how we arrive at our conclusions.

Conclusion _____

When choosing between alternative explanations—as we inevitably must—the most general, parsimonious, testable, and empirically valid explanation is always preferred. We will know how well a theory meets these criteria only when the explanation is articulated explicitly enough to permit deductions of matters of fact to be made.

Observations (or descriptions) must be linked to and derived from the theory if they are to contribute to the acquisition of reliable knowledge. This necessitates articulating the suppositions, hunches, pretheoretical conceptions, and so forth that underlie our research efforts. Engaging in this effort prior to gathering data will force us to abandon research efforts that contribute little or nothing to knowledge.

In this chapter, we have seen that every attempt to explain a phenomenon can be judged according to its scientific utility, which, in turn, requires that we ask about the explanation's generality, parsimony, testability, validity, and changeability. We have also seen that any empirical or descriptive study of crime must inevitably assume some theoretical or explanatory model. It is the specification of the various explanatory models that must constantly be integrated with the observations (the "facts") that is the hallmark of scientific inquiry.

The end product of the scientific endeavor is the development of a reliable body of descriptions and explanations. Crime and delinquency are social phenomena that have intrigued and haunted attempts at descriptions and explanations for as long as we have compiled records.

As guiding principles with which to approach the study of crime, the following conclusions may be drawn from the history of science:

1. Scientific inquiry is circumscribed by two overriding concerns: the development of (a) logically consistent explanations and (b) reliable and valid observations.
2. Descriptions and explanations are intimately interrelated. No science can develop without this intimacy between fact and theory.
3. Theories answer questions. It is necessary to articulate clearly what the question is and what the facts are.
4. Data must be evaluated to determine whether or not they are reliable and valid.
5. Theories must be checked for logical consistency and empirical validity.
6. Acceptance or rejection of research findings or theoretical explanations is determined by the best information and ideas currently available, not by the unobtainable search for an ultimate truth.

6

Criminological Theory: An Overview

Theories are nets cast to catch the world, to rationalize, to explain and to master it.[1]

"Science is a fascinating thing," Mark Twain once observed. "One gets such wholesale returns of conjecture out of a trifling investment in fact." The "wholesale returns of conjecture" to which Mark Twain refers are, in science, theories. Theories answer questions. They explain relationships between events and provide causal explanations. They tell us why or how it is that the facts we observe are as they are.

In Chapter 4, we asked the question, Why is it that some acts are defined as criminal while others are not? We analyzed the scientific utility of various theories and concluded that a theory of structural contradictions and the response of people to those contradictions was the best way to explain why the law defines some acts and not others as criminal. In the next four chapters, we examine theories of criminal behavior and criminality in the same way, that is, by looking at their adequacy as scientific theories.

In Chapter 5, however, we learned there are many questions that can and should be asked about crime. The questions we choose to ask and the approach we choose to take reflect our theoretical starting point—what philosophers of science call our "paradigm."[2] In the long train of criminological theory, two paradigms that make diametrically opposed assumptions vie for supremacy. These are the consensus paradigm and the conflict paradigm. Within each of these perspectives, there exists a number of particular theories. For example, from the consensus paradigm come the biological, psychoanalytic, and functional theories. From the conflict paradigm emerge the subcultural, cultural-transmission, anomic, and structural-contradictions theories. We have already encountered some of the different theoretical implications of the two paradigms when we examined theories of law making (Chapter 4). Consensus perspectives, as we saw, led to theories that emphasize how the law reflects the values and interests of "all healthy consciences." Conflict paradigms lead to theories that see differences in power, interests, values, and ideology as fundamental facts that must be taken into account if we are to develop adequate scientific explanations. Consensus theories see deviance as a defect in the people who deviate; conflict theories see deviance as a consequence of the way people and institutions react to the behavior of others. In the remaining chapters of this book, we will see how the different paradigms attack a variety of questions—such as why some people commit crime and others do not, why crime is distributed as it is within a particular society, and so forth. For now, however, let us look in more detail at the content, logic, and implications of the consensus and conflict paradigms as they apply to criminology.

Historical Sketch of Explanations of Crime _____

Before the birth of scientific criminology, explanations of crime were based on concepts like sin, demonology, innate depravity, and utilitarianism (the idea that people calculated the relative likelihood of pleasure and pain in deciding how to act). In England as recently as the 19th century, criminal indictments accused the defendant of "being prompted and instigated by the devil and not having the fear of God before his eyes."[3] There is a simple reason why these theories are viewed as prescientific: None of them seeks to check its theoretical claims against facts. The most influential of these perspectives in prescientific criminology (and one that still claims some advocates) was the utilitarian philosophy. As Chilton points out, it came close to being scientific because it based its assumptions on potentially observable facts, but it never subjected those claims to factual testing.[4] Significantly, advocates of prescientific criminology were more concerned with creating a system of law that would deter people from committing crime than they were with explaining how crime came about.

Until the period of the Enlightenment, religious explanations of crime dominated. The Enlightenment ushered in the frame of mind that characterizes scientific inquiry: The positivist belief that ideas could be judged by whether or not they were consistent with observations. While we accept this point of view almost unthinkingly today, it was a revolutionary idea at that time, for it challenged existing religious explanations of morality, human nature, the creation of human life, and the movement of the "heavenly bodies." At the forefront of the challenge to religious explanations of crime were Cesare Beccaria (1738–1794), William Godwin (1756–1836), and the Marquis de Sade (1740–1814).[5] These writers expressed vastly disparate views on crime but, like their counterparts in modern criminology, shared a naturalistic theoretical perspective that contradicted and challenged fundamentally prevailing religious explanations.

Cesare Beccaria

In 1764, Beccaria published his classic work, *Of Crimes and Punishments*. Beccaria challenged the prevailing wisdom on the cause and treatment of crime at almost every point.[6] Rather than seeing crime as a manifestation of sin or demons in possession of a person's soul, Beccaria sought a naturalistic explanation. In contrast to the prevailing practices of the time, he argued for incarceration rather than corporal or capital punishment. Beccaria's theories and penal policies were pursued and elaborated by many legal and social science writers who followed him, including the

English jurist, Jeremy Bentham, whose influence on criminal law and criminology was not great at the time by whose writings characterized the school of thought known today as the Classical School of Criminology. The basic theoretical idea of the Classical School is that people calculate the rewards and risks of their actions and decide how to act based upon what they calculate will bring them the maximum of pleasure and the minimum of pain. This theory derives from the paradigm of hedonistic philosophy that sees human behavior as determined by a computer-like calculation of pleasure and pain, which operates in everyone's psyche. The task of law, from this point of view, is to determine objectively how much pain must be threatened or inflicted in order to deter people from committing antisocial and criminal acts. To be maximally effective, the utilitarians argued, punishment should be administered severely, swiftly, and certainly.

William Godwin

Other writers basking in the aura of Enlightenment philosophy took a different tack. While the Classical School of Beccaria and Jeremy Bentham can be described as "administrative and legal criminology," the exact opposite point of view characterizes the work of one of the 18th century's most influential social theorists, William Godwin.[7] Godwin was the husband of a founder of the British feminist movement, Mary Wollstonecraft, and their daughter was the author of *Frankenstein*. Godwin's theory of criminology, although sharing some of the same Enlightenment perspectives of Beccaria's, argued that human behavior was determined by the material condition of one's existence and that crime was the result of the unequal distribution of property:

> Godwin was an unashamed materialist, who believed that human nature arose from social conditioning. He believed in determinism, the power of "Necessity," although he followed Hume in allowing some role for human choice within the framework of causality. His version of contract theory was both adventurous and novel. He accepted that there had been some such contract, although he denied that humanity was necessarily subject to any precedents, even of an "Original Contract." Also, he suggested that the people who made the contract might have been gravely disappointed by the atrocities which governments had committed since. For Godwin, humanity progressed towards perfectibility, towards the stage where people could manifest their natural disinterestedness and benevolence, un-

til the day when they could live according to the pure laws of Nature. Rousseau had been quite correct to describe the idyllic state of the "noble savage" in the time before civilization; but Godwin wished to suggest that this was an ideal which could also be reached after the extinction of government and property.[8]

For Godwin, it was the inequality and injustice of existing economic and political relations that caused some people to turn to crime. Contrary to Beccaria's theory, Godwin's theory claimed it was the abolition of government and property that would free human beings from crime by allowing everyone to live in their natural state of harmony and benevolence. Godwin argued that governments and laws inevitably favor the rich and oppress the masses. For Godwin, crime consisted of "offenses which the wealthier part of the community have no temptation to commit."[9]

Criminal acts were determined by a person's experiences. They were not the result of calculating pleasure, pain, and risk. The experiences, in turn, were conditioned by the inequality, poverty, and powerlessness of those who did not share the wealth and privilege of the ruling class. Although he concurred with the Classical School's opposition to capital and corporal punishment, Godwin brilliantly argued against incarceration and rehabilitation:

> Coercion could only alienate the mind of the prisoner, regardless of whether this was done with good intentions. It only conveyed a message—submit to force, and adjure reason. Be not directed by the convictions of your understanding, but by the busiest part of your nature, the fear of personal pain, and a compulsory awe of the injustice of others. To conceive that compulsion and punishment are the proper means of reformation is the sentiment of a barbarian.[10]

The Marquis de Sade

Writing at the same time as Godwin and Beccaria, the Marquis de Sade used the novel as the medium through which he expressed his criminological theories. De Sade saw human nature as both violent and criminalistic. The source of crime is that a few manage to usurp and exploit the property of the many and use the excuse of crime as a way of enforcing their rule. Thus, de Sade justified crime as an inevitable manifestation of the human condition and condemned the punishment of criminals as nothing more than a tool of the ruling class to maintain its power, privilege, and property. De Sade pointed out how even the most heinous of crimes—like infanticide and murder—are, at other times, in other places, taken as natural and even valuable forms of behavior. Crime was also seen, at times, as a justifiable act of class revolt.

The ideas of Beccaria, Godwin, and de Sade formed the foundation on which criminological theory and research would build for the next 200 years. The criminology of today reflects the agreements and disagreements culled by these early thinkers from the theoretical perspectives on crime and justice reflecting Enlightenment philosophy. Beccaria's theories were more congenial to the monarchists, dictators, and governments of the emerging economic and political systems of Europe and America. It was Beccaria, therefore, who was elevated to the pinnacle of a criminological pioneer; the ideas of Godwin and de Sade, however, survived as a counterpoint to the classical hedonistic calculus, challenging the domination of classical criminology.

The 19th century witnessed the development of numerous social theories that elaborated and developed these two basic paradigms. From the Classical School of Beccaria and Bentham, through the works of social theorists and researchers like Cesare Lombroso, Herbert Spencer, and Emile Durkheim was elaborated the theory that government developed to curtail the potential excesses of human behavior and to create order and harmony in human social relations. This school of thought formed the foundation of the consensus perspective, so called because it views society as based on a fundamental concensus about what is right and wrong and the ways people must conduct themselves in order to live in harmony, peace, and mutual well-being.[11] The assumptions of this perspective that underpin its theories are (1) that there is a consensus on fundamental values and norms and (2) that criminal behavior is suppressed by the state in order to create the well-being of everyone in the society. One variant on this paradigm, the functional theory, makes the further assumption that crime and deviance exist, in part, to establish or reaffirm the most important values in the society.[12]

In opposition to the consensus perspective, social theorists such as Max Weber, Karl Marx, Frederich Engels, Antonio Gramsci, and William Bonger followed the line of reasoning suggested by William Godwin. Rather than assuming a consensus or imagining that acts of crime contribute to the equilibrium of society, this perspective conceives of institutions such as government, state, and economy as reflections of conflict between different groups vying for power, material resources, and control of their own destiny.

This theoretical paradigm is referred to as the conflict perspective.[13]

The conflict perspective assumes that modern societies are composed of groups and social classes whose life conditions, values, interests, and opportunities inexorably generate conflict over what is right and proper (values and norms) as well as how resources should be distributed. In the conflict paradigm, three theoretical traditions are salient: (1) those that emphasize interest groups as the source of conflict, (2) those that see power and its manifestation in the interest of the powerful (or the "ruling class"), and (3) those who see the process of change through a struggle between different social classes and groups as the moving force behind law and criminal behavior.

More specifically, the differences between consensus and conflict theories can be summarized along the following lines:

1. The consensus paradigm invokes culture and the people's values and norms as more important in determining social relations than economic, political, and power structures. The conflict paradigm sees culture, values, and norms as more determined by, than determining, political, economic, and power relations. The difference between the paradigms on this issue is not that either denies the importance of the other; rather, it is a difference in emphasis and what one sees as primary in determining the character of social relations.

2. Because consensus theories begin with the assumption that there are commonly shared interests and values in a society, consensus theories tend to ignore the role of the scientist's own values, ideologies, and assumptions. Conflict theory sees the values and ideology of the scientist as forming an intimate relationship with his or her perspectives, theories, and policy implications. Both paradigms adhere to the value of objectivity in scientific research; for the conflict theorist, however, a necessary condition for achieving this objectivity is the explicit articulation of the values and assumptions of the theory.

3. The conflict perspective sees the changes and dynamics of society as best understood in terms of class struggle and dissension over how social, political, and economic relations should be organized. The consensus perspective attributes to "society" an independent (almost mystical) existence by which people collectively and unconsciously seek to maintain ongo-

ing social, political, and economic relations. This perspective creates mechanisms that automatically enhance harmony, order, and equilibrium.

4. Consensus theory assumes the present can be understood as a "system" of interdependent parts that must be analyzed in terms of their consequences for the maintenance of the system. Conflict theorists see the present as a brief moment in a historical process that can only be understood by understanding the resources, constraints, and social forces the present has inherited from the past.

5. Conflict theory sees crime and criminal law as the result of struggles engaged in by people responding to the resources and constraints imposed upon them by struggles that preceded their own reality. Consensus theory sees criminal law as a reflection of consensus on what is needed to make harmonious social relations possible.

Recent Developments in Criminology _____

The last 40 or more years of criminological theory (World War II to the present), as well as contemporary theoretical "confrontations and refutations," continue to reflect this basic split between conflict and consensus traditions. For a brief period in the 1950s, the consensus perspective–based functionalist paradigm dominated the field, but, in the 1960s, this paradigm was profoundly challenged by theories deriving from the conflict tradition.

Criminological Theory: 1950–1988

Immediately following World War II, criminological theory managed to put aside the age-old division between consensus and conflict theories. In the wake of the burgeoning economy, expanding educational opportunities for white males, and euphoria created by the end of the war, criminologists found research and theory congenial to the mood. "Juvenile delinquency" became the problem, and social psychological theories linked to the consensus paradigm provided the answer. The issue was to explain how—in a society where "every healthy conscience" agreed on the values of work, family, and conformity—some behaved aberrantly. The answers, set forth in the form of theories that will be discussed in detail in the chapters to come, were focused almost exclusively on juvenile delinquency and concerned almost exclusively with discovering the uniqueness of personal and social experiences shared by those who were "delinquent."

Criminology neither discovered nor created, though it may have contributed to, the fetish with juvenile delinquency that characterized the 1950s and early 1960s. Criminology expressed the same concern that Edward R. Murrow did when he asked on a radio program, "Who killed Michael Farmer?"; that John Bartlow Martin did when he investigated the senseless murder of a nurse in Ypsilanti, Michigan, by a gang of young boys and wondered *Why Did They Kill?;* that Warren Miller did when he depicted Duke Custis as the Warlord of the Royal Crocodiles in *The Cool World;* and that Harrison Salsbury did when he investigated gang life in New York for the *New York Times.*

In Britain, France, Germany, and the United States, delinquency was a national issue. Sociologists, criminologists, and psychologists dug into their theoretical traditions and research strategies and tried to shed what light they could upon this issue.

In the late 1960s and 1970s, all that changed, but not as a result of "solving" the delinquency problem either politically or intellectually. Delinquency, delinquent gangs, and adolescent deviance remain as ubiquitous and their causes as much a matter of controversy today as then. What changed and what was reflected in the emergence of a "conflict-oriented criminology" was the political climate in which criminologists worked. In criminology, the "crimes of the powerful"—ranging from the crimes of nation states; to the illegal and immoral acts of large corporations; and to the misuse of police and political office by local, state, and national power-holders—were increasingly examined.

The "crimes of the powerful" were neither invented nor created by sociologists and criminologists. They reflected the interests and concerns of journalists, politicians, and, to some extent, that omnipresent but difficult-to-pinpoint "public."

Sociologists and criminologists once again sought theoretical traditions, explanations, and research methodologies that could be applied to the issues. The most significant change to come out of this enterprise was a restatement of the degree to which all social sciences is, in the end, a statement of policy alternatives. Questions of, as Howard Becker put it, "whose side are we on," replaced the myth of an objective, value-free science of criminology. The search for a theoretical paradigm with value premises seeking to understand the plight of those who were usually labeled criminal (the poor and the lower classes) led, in turn, to study Marxist theory for clues that might help in understanding crime.

What was resurrected from past criminologies and sociologies was inevitably more divisive than had been the case in the 1950s; the historical reality of the 1960s, which was itself more divisive, was also reflected in developments in criminology. What emerged was a redirection of criminological inquiry; questions changed, and perspectives and paradigms emerged that challenged extant ones and re-evaluated research strategies. The major thrust of the works of conflict criminologists was captured by Taylor, Walton, and Young in their 1973 publication of the (unfortunately titled) _New Criminology_.[14] The critiques they generated against the reductionist, delinquency-dominated criminology of the 1950s hit a sensitive chord with young criminologists, who were trying to make sense out of the 1960s with traditional theories that no longer seemed plausible. The "new," or "critical," criminologists spoke to what was happening.

The conflict-oriented criminology of the 1960s and 1970s made an extremely important contribution by reacting against the narrowness of previous generations of criminologists. But much of what these criminologists argued were restatements of threads and themes that had been part and parcel of criminology since the time of Thomas More and William Godwin. Criminologist Frank Tannebaum said the following in 1938:

> American criminal activity must be related to the total social complex. The United States has as much crime as it generates. The criminals are themselves part of the community in a deeper sense and are as much its products as are poets, philosophers, inventors, businessmen and scientists—reformers and saints. If we would change the amount of crime in the community, we must change the community.[15]

Criminologists Hawkins and Waller said this in 1936:

> The prostitute, the pimp, the peddler of dope, the operator of gambling halls, the vendor of obscene pictures, the bootlegger, the abortionist—all are productive. All produce services or goods which people desire and for which they're willing to pay.[16]

Thorsten Sellin said this in 1938:

> Values which receive the protection of the criminal law are ultimately those which are treasured by dominant interest groups.[17]

Robert Merton, speaking of corruption, said this in 1938:

> The distinctive function of the political machine for their criminal, vice and racket clientele is to enable them to operate in satisfying the economic demands of a large market without undue interference from the government. Just as big business may contribute funds to the political party war-chest to ensure a minimum of governmental interference, so with big rackets and big crime. . . . In both instances, many features of the structural context are identical: (1) market demands for goods and services; (2) the operators' concern with maximizing gains from their enterprise; (3) the need for partial control of government which might otherwise interfere with these activities of businessmen; (4) the need for an efficient, powerful and centralized agency to provide an effective liaison of "business" with government.[18]

Robert Merton also argued, in the 1940s, that organized crime and political corruption were not economically distinguishable from legitimate business. Failing to recognize this, he said, led sociologists to some "badly scrambled" analyses.

Edwin Sutherland, as is well recognized, called for studies and theories of white-collar (corporate) criminality, professional theft, and the ubiquitous nature of crime across the class structure. Sutherland also presaged the critical criminology of the 1960s and 1970s by linking the crime problem to the political economy of capitalism. His studies of white-collar crime (see Chapter 3) led him to conclude that businesspeople had destroyed democracy and the free-enterprise system by their criminality. He suggested that an alternative system ("perhaps communism or corporatism") needed to be explored.[19]

Other criminologists of an earlier era investigated the presence of juvenile delinquency in all social classes. They thereby laid the groundwork for a critique of criminological theories that sought to explain crime and delinquency solely in terms of the deviance of lower-class youth.[20]

The point of all this is simply to emphasize that much of what was set forth as "new criminology" in the 1960s and 1970s reflected a criminological perspective advocated by earlier generations of criminologists and social theorists. This tradition may have been forgotten in the 1950s, but that does not negate its earlier existence.

But there was and is more to the "new criminology" than a resurrection of observations made in an earlier era. The critical criminology of the 1960s and 1970s went beyond the empirical observations and suggested themes of the 1930's critics to seek a link between criminological theory and broader social theory. In particular, the most important innovation and direction in the 1970s was to take seriously the possibility that criminological inquiry could be linked to conflict theory. In this effort, there were some side steps and false starts, but these were only the first efforts at developing a truly original perspective on crime.

The most important false start of conflict criminology was the building of a criminological theory around the idea that "in every era the ruling ideas are the ideas of the ruling class." Taking this beautiful piece of rhetoric literally led some to argue that crime was a result of the ruling class's attempt to maintain and perpetuate their own interests and ideology. The problem with this position, obviously enough, is that when it is unilaterally applied to law creation and law enforcement, it is patently false. Laws are created and enforced, and many are, at least on the surface, neither in the interests nor reflecting the ideology of the ruling class.

An equally untenable position is the social-psychological explanation of the cause of criminal behavior proposed by Taylor, Walton, and Young. This explanation claims that criminal acts are best understood as political statements of opposing oppression and exploitation. While such a view may have considerable merit as a rallying point for radical ideology, it has little merit as a criminological theory. To begin with, one must ask, is this explanation positing a conscious recognition on the part of those who commit criminal acts? If so, it is a little out of touch with the consciousness (false or otherwise) of most people who commit crime. It is precisely because it is so rare that Eldridge Cleaver's claim that he raped white women as a way of attacking white man's property is such a powerful statement.[21] Most criminals tell us rather how they share their captors' view that their acts are antisocial, immoral, and wrong. Others, professional thieves tell us that, although their acts are labeled criminal, they are simply doing business like other businesspeople.[22] While this may represent a reflection of the logic of capitalism, it can hardly be said that these offenders are striking back at capitalism—at least not consciously. If the theory is posited as an "unconscious motivation" for the criminal acts, then it is no more defensible than the Freudian interpretation of criminal acts as motivated by Oedipal complexes and neurotic needs.

Furthermore, the view that criminal acts can be understood as a reaction against oppression and exploitation fails to recognize one of the starting points for a radical analysis, namely, that the crimes of the powerful, of corporations and corporate executives, and of nation-states and political leaders, are ubiquitous. Just as it makes little sense to see the crimes of people like Nixon, Johnson, and Callaghan, or of companies like Lockheed, Gulf, and Rolls-Royce, as explicable in terms of "delinquent subcultures" or "labeling," it makes even less sense to see these acts as motivated by a desire to strike back at oppressors and exploiters.

Thus, the early efforts of the "new criminologists" to provide an alternative theory of crime fell rather short of the mark. Through it all, however, a theme began emerging, finally taking hold in the 1980s. This is the attempt to apply Marxist theory—but not the naïve, vulgar Marxism of the ruling-class theorists or the simplistic Marxist social psychology of the frustration-aggression hypothesis—to the study of crime. This is a criminology built on the dialectic as the starting point for analysis. It is a criminology that denies the deterministic nature of social theory but does not fall prey to the equally erroneous assumption of voluntarism.[23] In essence, the theory argues that people in all social classes respond

Political activists? *(Ed Lettau/Photo Researchers)*

to the contradictions of their historical condition. The responses may be criminal or noncriminal, depending upon the law. But whatever the moral or cognitive components these acts are best understood as people creating their own social world out of the contradictions in their existence.

In our society, laws are seen as resulting from the contradictions that inhere in the political economy of capitalism. The "ruling class" is central in the law-creation process, but it is not alone in the world: The ruling class and its political allies must take into account the extent to which the lower classes are demanding changes. Thus, Marx's analysis of the law governing the length of the working day stands as a prototype of legal innovation; it is the struggle of the ruling class against the working class over the length of the working day that lies behind the changing laws.[24]

The starting point, then, for that facet of the "new criminology" that holds considerable promise as a general theory of crime is not society but social relations reflecting and influencing economic and political organization. The new criminology follows the observation that our focus must be on whole political and economic systems rather than on nation-states or societies. The analysis focuses on class relations (as opposed to social class as a category) as these are created and sustained by particular political economies. And, finally, the methodology of the new criminology is not one of determinism as practiced by some social sciences, but is a methodology that employs an interactionist assumption of the dialectic. This latter point requires some elaboration.

Most social science assumes that, if we understand the causes, we will be able to predict behavior. Once someone possesses a certain biological predisposition or has had a certain configuration of experiences, his or her behavior is *determined*. The dialectical methodology makes just the opposite assumption. It assumes that people are constantly interacting with their environment and making choices in terms of what they see, understand, and experience at any point in time. The assumption is *not* that people are completely free, for people inherit resources and constraints as well as contradictions from the world in which they live. But, within the resources and constraints, people usually have many choices. Not all capitalist societies develop identically; some have extensive welfare systems and some have democratic governments, while others have extraordinary differences between the wealthy and the poor, with minimal welfare systems and totalitarian systems of government. Some poor children go to university, others to prison.

Social behavior must be understood in terms of people making decisions under conditions over which they have some, but not total, control. This perspective, the essence of the dialectic methodology, is one of the major legacies of the "new criminology" of the 1960s and 1970s.

Criminology is a reflection of the times. In capitalist nations, the 1950s were dominated by a view of the world that saw "society" as a real and living entity. "Deviance" was a manifestation of personal maladjustment. Delinquency was thus the focus of criminological attention, and theories of how people became delinquent made sense in the cosmology of the times. The 1960s forced a challenge to that view. To construct a criminology built upon ground different from the existing theory, we resurrected ideas and observations of several generations before. In the end, however, it is necessary to forge a criminology from quite a different set of materials if it is to be more than a restatement of the theses of Merton, Sellin, Tannenbaum, and Sutherland. It is necessary to link criminology to classical social theory in its most fundamental way. This involves the development of a dialectical analysis that seeks to understand how contradictions inherent in the political economy are linked to the incidence and distribution of criminality at a particular historical period.

Drugs and Society: An Illustration

To give substance to the difference between the conflict and consensus traditions in criminology, let us look at how each of these traditions treats the issue of illegal drugs.

Criminologists working within the functionalist and social-psychological paradigms assumed that there was societal consensus that illegal drugs—such as opium, heroin, marijuana, and cocaine—were dangerous and that the use of these drugs was a problem requiring state intervention. Beginning with this perspective, criminologists were led to ask

1. Why do some people take illegal drugs?
2. What is the consequence for society of illegal drug use?
3. Are people who take illegal drugs more likely to commit other types of crimes (theft, assault, and so forth)?
4. Can drug addicts be rehabilitated and, if so, what programs are effective?

Faced with the same facts, conflict criminologists asked

1. Why is the taking or selling of these particular drugs defined as illegal?
2. What is the effect of these laws on law enforcement?
3. Are the anti-drug laws enforced impartially, or are the drugs produced by established manufacturers exempt from the laws?
4. Is there a difference in the enforcement of these laws by race or social class of user?

The work of Alfred R. Lindesmith illustrates very nicely the difference between the conflict and functional theory. It also suggests some ways in which the two paradigms can be reconciled.

Lindesmith began his study of drugs by first limiting his inquiry to opiates and their derivatives, the most important being morphine and heroin. Lindesmith interviewed known opium addicts and searched an extensive literature for biographical and autobiographical accounts of opium addicts. He developed his theory of opiate addiction based upon these interviews and personal biographies. Lindesmith theorized that a person became addicted to opium only when he or she experienced the following process:

1. Taking the drug or having it administered.
2. Experiencing a euphoric feeling from the drug.
3. Recognizing that the euphoric feeling was the result of having taken the drug.
4. Ceasing to take the drug.
5. Experiencing "withdrawal distress" (usually severe headaches, retching, and nausea).
6. Recognizing that the withdrawal distress was caused by the cessation of drug use.
7. Taking more drugs to relieve the withdrawal distress.[25]

Thus Lindesmith attempted to answer the question of why some people become addicted to opiates and others do not. He did not, however, assume that drugs were criminalized as a result of "societal consensus." Lindesmith researched questions implied by the conflict perspective, namely, why was the taking of heroin (and other such drugs) criminal? His research led him to conclude that anti-opium laws emerged as a result of political power struggles, bureaucratic machinations, and legislative attempts to raise taxes and supervise imports.[26]

There is, however, another methodological facet of Lindesmith's theory that is incompatible with conflict theory. He assumed that we will be able to discover a process through which people have gone that makes them "inevitably" become addicts. The dialectical methodology of conflict theory makes the opposite assumption: once addicted, a person may be more likely than others to make the decision to go on using the drug, but the circumstances of his or her life will be persuasive forces in making that decision.

More recent research on the history of opium and anti-opium laws elaborates Lindesmith's findings and links these laws to the expansion of capitalism and colonialism in the 17th and 18th centuries.[27] It was the search for markets that led British and American travelers to develop the opium trade in Asia. Later, the importation of cheap labor from Asia to build railroads and develop mining in the West created a substantial market for opium in the United States. Initially, opium was treated as "just another product" that was readily available on the open market. People once literally "laced their tea" with opium, and patent medicines touted by salespeople as a cure for everything from headaches to heart attacks were heavily infused with opium because of the drug's incomparable pain-killing effects. In the 1800s, the Chinese government entered in to an agreement with the United States to outlaw opium importation. It was not until 1914, however, that the sale and distribution of opium and its derivatives were formally outlawed. This came about, as Lindesmith's research shows, as a result of a concerted effort on the part of law-enforcement agencies to impose stiff penalties on anyone, including medical doctors, who sold or administered opiates.[28]

Wayward Puritans

Another illustration of the difference between conflict and consensus theories of crime is provided by two different interpretations of witchcraft in Puritan New England. In his classic study, *Wayward Puritans,* Kai Erikson set out to test the Durkheimian (functional) theory that

> crime (and by extension other forms of deviation) may actually perform a needed service to society by drawing people together in a common posture of anger and indignation. The deviant individual violates rules of conduct which the rest of the community holds in high respect; and when these people come together to express their

outrage over the offense and to bear witness against the offender, they develop a tighter bond of solidarity than existed earlier.[29]

Erikson's analysis of three separate "crime waves" in the Puritan community led him to conclude that these (which included the infamous witch trials) (1) functioned to define moral boundaries of the community and (2) were created by the community in order to have that effect.

Erikson's explanation for the crime waves in Puritan New England links consensus and functional theories of crime. The consensus theory assumes general agreement on values, while the functional theory assumes that the consequences of an event or a relationship can be a clue to its cause. We noted earlier in this chapter that this logic can easily develop into a teleological explanation that imputes to "society" a rationality and causal force that it does not have. It is not "society" or some reified abstraction that brings about social change or creates crime waves, it is people acting. The issue must then be: Who created the crime waves, and why? Erikson assumes that the consequences of the crime waves were their causes. This teleological assumption is the classic error of functional thinking and is unacceptable as an explanation. Consequences must be described, but, unless we believe in a world where "societies" think and behave while people are mere automatons, the logic of functionalism cannot stand the test of good theory construction.

A re-analysis of the data presented by Erikson found considerable evidence that it was not "the community" that created the crime waves in order to establish "moral boundaries." Rather, each outbreak was the result of power struggles for control of the community's resources. "Deviance was indeed created for the consequences it had. But the consequences were not to establish 'moral boundaries' but rather to aid those in power to maintain their position."[30]

Furthermore, the fact that three separate, major "outbreaks of deviance" occurred in a relatively short period of time suggests that "society" was not very successful in this way of creating moral consensus.

These illustrations of consensus and conflict theory are sufficient to communicate the basic differences in their assumptions and implications. In the chapters that follow, the differences will be spelled out in greater detail and the implications developed in terms of specific theories of crime and criminality.

Conclusion _____

In this chapter, we traced the development of criminological theory. Criminology began in the period of history known as the Enlightenment. It was during this time that Europeans began looking at the world in a wholly revolutionary way. They developed the idea that how we view the world should be judged according to how well our views were supported by observations. Today this does not seem like a very radical idea. In the 16th and 17th centuries, however, this was very radical indeed, for it undermined the position of the most powerful forces in Europe, the church and the monarchy. It forced a reformulation of the conception of the Earth as the center of the universe and of man as the creation of God. It gave rise ultimately to the world-shaking beliefs of Galileo, Freud, Darwin, and Marx.

In criminology, Beccaria and Bentham took a step toward the scientific study of crime when they formulated policies dictated by what they theorized would work. They failed to develop a full-fledged scientific paradigm, though, because their system of thought was independent of testing. Their propositions were judged by logical and philosophical cogency rather than empirical validity.

William Godwin approached the question of crime from a different vantage point. The debate begun in these early stages of criminology has continued in various forms to the present day. Broadly speaking, the Beccaria school saw crime as a problem of a few people who deviated from otherwise agreed-upon norms; Godwin saw the problem of crime as linked to political and economic power.

Modern criminology takes its leads but not its content from these early explorations. Modern criminology is strongly influenced by the disagreements that emerge from the conflict and consensus theories of crime and criminal law. There is agreement that, whatever paradigm we work within, the paradigm must be able to generate theories that will best explain the real world. This is the ultimate test of a paradigm's utility. In Chapter 5, we looked at theories that try to answer why it is that some acts are defined as criminal while others are not. In the succeeding chapters, we take up the issue of how well the theories derived from the conflict and consensus paradigms can explain other questions relevant to criminology as a scientific discipline.

CHAPTER 7

Biological Paradigms

by Janet Katz and W.J.C.

The development of scientific criminology parallels the development of other sciences. It emerged during the Enlightenment with the naturalistic conception of the universe and the revolutionary idea that conceptions of how the world and people behave should be subjected to empirical observation. Theories that withstand the test of empirical observation should be accepted and built upon; those that do not should be abandoned. Initial forays into behavioral science looked to biology and medicine for guidelines. Not surprisingly, people interested in studying crime postulated that criminality was biologically determined. The search was on, then, for physical and biological characteristics that would differentiate criminals from noncriminals.

That search continues to the present day. In fact, in the last 10 years there has been a renewed interest in biological explanations among the public, press, politicians, and certain criminologists. Is this renewed interest the result of advances in the biological sciences, so that we can now identify criminogenic factors only imagined by earlier theorists? Or is this new popularity unrelated to any actual increase in our knowledge about crime and the human condition? Certainly the modern biological explanations for crime—such as the XYY chromosomal abnormality or the study of the autonomic nervous system—appear to be the sophisticated products of genetic and neurophysiology advances. But if they are premised on the same faulty assumptions or fall victim to the same methodological errors as the earlier theories of the "born criminal," the similarities between past and present theories may be far greater than the apparent differences. In the last part of this chapter, we will examine this resurgence and whether there is existing evidence to support its present popularity.

Early Studies of Biology and Crime

Looked at solely from the logic of scientific inquiry—which consists of the search for general theories that are tested by empirical facts—the scientific study of crime can be traced to the work of a European anatomist, Franz Joseph Gall (1758–1828).[1] Gall asked the question, Why do some people commit crime? He sought an answer in the presumed biological differences between criminals and noncriminals. Gall founded the school of anatomy known as phrenology, which postulated that biological differences in behavioral tendencies were indicated by the constellation of bumps on the head. His research did not survive careful empirical testing, and phrenology, like alchemy, died an early death. However, 70 years later, the idea that criminal behavior was rooted in biological characteristics was revived by an Italian physician, Cesare Lombroso.

Lombroso began his work in the shadow of biological discoveries spearheaded by Charles Darwin's influential work, *On the Origin of Species,* published in 1859. Lombroso reasoned that, if species survived because of their fitness, at any point in time some species would be disappearing as a consequence of their unfitness for the conditions of life. Applying this logic to humans, Lombroso hypothesized that some human beings were carrying with them biological characteristics that were suitable for precivilized man (aggressiveness, impulsiveness, insensitivity to pain) but antithetical to contemporary society.[2] These prehuman characteristics (for example, low cranial capacity, receding chin, long arms, insensitivity to pain, and so forth) indicated atavism, a reversion to an earlier stage of man's evolution. People possessing these characteristics were "born criminals."

Lombroso gathered his data in Italian prisons. Unfortunately, he did not conceive of the controlled experiment to see if the characteristics he found among prisoners would be found in a sample of noncriminals as well. When later researchers, especially Charles Goring, an English prison physician, replicated Lombroso's study in 1913, the findings did not confirm Lombroso's theory. Goring concluded that criminals could be characterized by generally defective physiques and intelligence, but that these differences did not support the theory that there were "criminal types" with specific stigmata that differentiated them from noncriminals.[3] The failure of Goring and other researchers to find any support ultimately brought Lombroso's theory of atavism to an inauspicious demise.

Two students of Lombroso continued his search for the "born criminal." Enrico Ferri (1856–1929) expanded Lombroso's typological approach by giving more attention to environmental and social causes of crime. Raffaele Garofalo (1852–1934) recognized that the definition of crime varied by country; therefore, a person might be a criminal in Italy but not a criminal in Spain.[4] Realizing this might have led Garofalo to question the premise upon which a biological approach to crime should be constructed. Rather, he resolved the issue by limiting the scientific study of crime to what he called "natural crimes," or those acts he believed all civilized societies would condemn. These acts violated two basic altruistic feelings that characterized human emotions—the sentiments of *pity* and *probity*. The sentiment of pity is the feeling of revulsion over the voluntary infliction of pain. The sentiment of probity, according to Garofalo, is the innate respect for that which belongs to others (that is, property). A "natural crime" was therefore an action that violated one of these two sentiments. Instead of emphasizing the physical anomalies that Lombroso did, Garofalo believed the criminal possessed a moral anomaly—an inherited lack of one or both of the sentiments of pity and probity. Misinterpreting Darwinian theory to fit his thesis, Garofalo concluded that the true criminal, by committing natural crimes, demonstrated his inability to adapt to social life.[5] The penalty for the lack of adaptation, according to natural selection, is extinction. For Garofalo, therefore, the logical solution was to aid natural selection by administering the death penalty, life imprisonment, or transportation (exile to far-off places such as America or Australia) as a way to eliminate the offender, and eventually all crime, from civilized society.

These early researches were highly speculative and based upon limited empirical data. When the data were gathered, they did not support the theory. This failure, however, has not deterred others from reformulating the theory to find a biological basis for criminality. In the 1930s, a Harvard anthropologist, Ernest Hooton, tried once again to establish a connection between physical-biological types and criminality. This time the research to test the theory was impressively massive.

Hooton compared 14,000 prisoners and 3,000 nonprisoners on numerous physical attributes. He concluded that criminals were both physically and mentally inferior to noncriminals and that these differences were inherited. Criminals, according to Hooton's interpretation of his findings, showed a greater probability of (1) tattooing (which Hooton characterized as "a practice of stupid and ignorant persons"); (2) light and brown eyes; (3) low foreheads; (4) narrow jaws, and (5) high, pinched nasal roots. Within the criminal population, the types of offenders were thought to differ significantly from one another; that is, murderers and bank robbers were assumed to have different physical characteristics.

Hooton's research contains many methodological shortcomings that undermine the validity of his data interpretation. By limiting the study to criminal prisoners, his data can tell us only about people in prison, which is obviously a small proportion of the total criminal population. The prison population is overwhelmingly a population of lower-class criminals. Any generalizations about the characteristics of prisoners, then, are limited to lower-class criminals at best. Hooton's data also show some important anomalies inconsistent with the conclusion that prisoners and nonprisoners differ significantly on certain physical traits. For example, there are greater differences between groupings of the nonprison population than there are differences between the prison and nonprison population. Hooton asserted that the differences between prisoners and nonprisoners reflected inherited inferiority among the prison population. Hooton's measures of "inferiority" were more a reflection of his bias than objective measures of cultural or intellectual inferiority. Tattooing, eye colors, low foreheads, narrow jaws, and pinched nasal roots are hardly evidence of inferior physical types.

Furthermore, Hooton made two fundamental methodological errors: (1) He assumed that because two observable phenomenon are correlated they are causally related and (2) he compared a large number of prisoners with a relatively small number of nonprisoners, which made statistical generalizations more complicated. The two samples should be comparable in terms of relevant variables such as class and age. At the time of Hooton's studies, the appropriate statistical adjustments were not known and it was not practical to compute them without computers, which of course did not exist.

The tendency to confuse correlation with causation in biological studies of crime is so pervasive that it greatly reduces the effect of the argument in every study conducted. When Hooton found, for example, that prisoners had lower body weights than nonprisoners, he argued that this reflected different inherited characteristics. One would think that a more plausible explanation would be the different eating habits of free and imprisoned populations. Regardless, the discovery of a correlation is only a staring point for theorizing about why the correlation exists; it is not evidence of a causal relation. Biological theorists prematurely assume a causal connection without first developing a set of theoretical propositions.

In his zeal to distinguish criminal from noncriminal types, Hooton ignored data that were inconsistent with his theory. Convinced that there were different physical characteristics of different types of criminals, he classified people according to the crime they had committed. In fact, over half the population had been in prison before for different offenses. Thus, a murderer in one week's research would have been a bank robber 2 years earlier. The confounding nature of this obviated any reliable conclusions from Hooton's classification system.

Despite the lack of evidence supporting a biological theory of criminal behavior, advocates of this paradigm emerge with predictable regularity. In 1949, a student of Hooton's, William Sheldon, published *Varieties of Delinquent Youth,* in which he described three basic body types—endomorph, ectomorph, and mesomorph—and the corresponding temperaments.[6] According to

Sheldon, endomorphs are short, round, and inclined to put on fat. In temperament, they are relaxed, and extroverted, and they tend to prefer a comfortable and easy life. Mesomorphs are athletic, muscular, and strong. In temperament, they are aggressive, assertive, and dynamic. Ectomorphs are lean, fragile, and slender. In temperament, they are introverted and shy, with a tendency toward physical and psychosomatic disorders.

Sheldon classified 200 boys sent to a rehabilitation home in Boston and compared them with 200 college students who were assumed to be nondelinquent. Sheldon found that the delinquent youths were decidedly more mesomorphic and less ectomorphic than the nondelinquent ones.

Another pair of Harvard criminologists, Sheldon and Eleanor Glueck, replicated Sheldon's findings. They compared 500 incarcerated delinquents, aged 9–17, with 500 youths in the same age group who were not incarcerated. The Gluecks added a fourth body type to Sheldon's three: a balanced type for boys whose physiques conformed to none of the original categories. Their research led them to conclude that, "Among the delinquents, mesomorphy is far and away the most dominant component, with ectomorphic, endomorphic and balanced types about equally represented."[7]

In the early 1970s, the Glueck study was replicated by Cortes and Gatti. They also found that delinquents are more mesomorphic than nondelinquents. They reported that 57 percent of their delinquent group rated high on mesomorphy while only 19 percent of the nondelinquents rated high on mesomorphy.[8]

These three studies (Sheldon, Glueck and Glueck, and Cortes and Gatti) spanned 23 years and consistently found differences between youths officially labeled delinquent and ones not labeled delinquent on selected physical characteristics. What does this correlation tell us? Unfortunately, not very much. The researches were so fundamentally flawed that the results are, at best, only suggestive and, at worst, very misleading.

Selecting a sample of persons labeled delinquent and comparing them to a sample of persons not so labeled in no way assures us that we are comparing delinquent and nondelinquent populations. The college students compared with the delinquents constitute a sample drawn from a population that is itself often involved in delinquent and criminal acts, from illegal drinking and drug taking to stealing, vandalism, and even rape. It is estimated, for example, that 20 percent of college women will be the victims of rape or attempted rape by male students.[9] How many college students escape the label of delinquency but are guilty of crime is unknown. What is known is that self-report and participant-observation studies consistently show that people who have escaped the label "delinquent" and are not incarcerated for crime nevertheless report a very high rate of delinquent and criminal acts (see Chapter 3). Thus it is possible that these researches are actually comparing delinquents in institutions with delinquents who are not in institutions. In this case, if there really is a difference in body type between the two groups, the interesting question is why institutionalized youths are more mesomorphic than noninstitutionalized youths. Again, the correlation between different body types tells us nothing about the causal relation. The answer to why there is a difference may well lie in the amount of food consumed by nonincarcerated people at such places as McDonald's and Burger King, which is not available to incarcerated people. Because it is also unknown in these researches of what the persons labeled delinquent were guilty, we cannot even compare frequency or seriousness of delinquency between the two groups. Sheldon reported that the boys in the rehabilitation home from which he selected his sample were "more or less delinquent" and were referred to the institution "as a direct or indirect result of some sort of delinquency."[10] The boys in Sheldon's "delinquent" sample all lived at the institution, but Sheldon does not tell us how he selected those boys from the entire population at the home. Cortes and Gatti used boys attending a private high school as the nondelinquent group. Are private high-school boys more likely than lower-class institutionalized boys to be endomorphs? These studies, in other words, truly do not include comparable groups of delinquents and nondelinquents, nor do they even touch upon a representative sample of the entire group of people who commit criminal acts. To clarify this, refer to the data presented in Chapters 2 and 3.

Finally, a number of other studies provided results that contradict the findings of the Sheldon, Glueck and Glueck, and the Cortes and Gatti studies. An investigation of a sample of Princeton University students found that these students scored higher on the athletic, aggressive scales (the mesomorph types) than the sample of boys defined as delinquent in the Sheldon study. Samples of bus drivers and truckers were also more mesomorphic than Sheldon's delinquent sample. And, finally, a study comparing the body types of delinquents with 400 army recruits showed that the recruits were more mesomorphic than the delinquents.[11]

Thus, the assertion that mesomorphy or any other physical or biological characteristic is correlated with crime or delinquency has never been established. In addition, a finding of a relationship between a particular body type and delinquency may still not provide evidence for a biological cause of crime, any more than the probable predominance of mesomorphs on football teams proves that playing football is a biologically determined behavior.

Heredity Studies

The theory that antisocial behavior could be inherited was very popular in the late 19th century.[12] Theorists were never very clear about exactly what is inherited. At the most extreme, hereditarians, or eugenicists, who followed the writings of Francis Galton, believed in the existence of "germ-plasm," an immutable inherited substance that predetermined all mental, moral, and physical characteristics. If a person committed crimes, that behavior would be passed on in the germ-plasm of his or her offspring, who would manifest similar antisocial behavior.

To demonstrate this position empirically, people turned to the

Heredity or politics? *(Jim Anderson/Woodfin Camp & Assoc.)*

study of family lineages, and from 1874–1926, 15 family studies were published. Each supposedly traced the descent of a particular family to demonstrate the genetic base of antisocial behavior.

The first of these studies—*The Jukes,* supposedly an account of six generations of this fictitiously named family—was written by Richard Dugdale.[13] Of the 709 members he found, Dugdale claimed that 76 were criminals, 128 were prostitutes, and 206 were on public welfare. Clearly, antisocial behavior was concentrated in this family, demonstrating to the reader that it was also inherited.

An equally famous family study was *The Kallikaks,* written by Henry H. Goddard.[14] This book supposedly traced the descendants of Martin Kallikak, who had an illicit encounter with a feeble-minded barmaid during the Revolutionary War before returning home to marry an upstanding Quaker woman. Following the offspring of both unions, Goddard found numerous paupers, criminals, alcoholics, and mentally deficient persons from the illegitimate union, but few, if any, from the legitimate one. Ignoring all the differences in social and economic circumstances experienced by the children of these two unions (and certainly not telling the reader that he had altered some of the photographs of the "deficient" Kallikaks to make them appear moronic and shifty), Goddard concluded that the genetic cause of antisocial behavior had been established.[15]

It should not be surprising that Goddard was one of the most avid supporters of a relatively new "science" in the early 20th century—eugenics—the science of the improvement of the human race through better breeding. According to this science, individual worth and potential were genetically determined; to improve the quality of life in the United States, one needed to improve the quality of the individuals in it. This inner quality could be easily determined by one's present station in life. Individuals, classes, races, and countries in power were obviously superior to these who, on the bottom of the status hierarchy, had only their defective genes to blame. Eugenicists were extremely busy putting their theories into practice in the first 30 years of the 20th century. To keep inferior people from immigrating, eugenicists helped in the passage of the 1922 and 1924 Federal Immigration restriction laws, which severely curtailed the entry of Southern and Eastern Europeans into the United States. For the "low-quality" persons already here (for example, the poor, the disabled, the deviant), efforts were made to reduce their numbers through institutionalization, marriage restrictions, and involuntary sterilization. Because heredity, not environment, was the cause of social ills, heredity needed altering.[16]

Today, one can see the weaknesses of both the family studies and the eugenics philosophy. The fact that family members have similar environments as well as similar genes makes it impossible to conclude that similar behavior is the product of genetics and not environment. But the history and impact of the eugenics movement (64,000 persons involuntarily sterilized, the increased number of miscegenation laws, the barring of thousands from this country even as the Nazi horrors threatened their lives) make it clear that theories need not be accurate to affect many innocent victims.

Even when these theories have been discredited, practices based upon them may continue to exist. In the early 1970s, evidence came to light that involuntary sterilizations might still be occurring in this country. In a 1972 federal case looking into the sterilization of two black children in Alabama, the court remarked:

> Over the past few years, an estimated 100,000 to 150,000 low-income persons have been sterilized annually under federally funded programs. . . . There is uncontroverted evidence in the record that minors and other incompetents have been sterilized with federal funds and that an indefinite number of poor people have been improperly coerced into accepting a sterilization operation under the threat that various federally supported welfare benefits would be withdrawn unless they submitted to irreversible sterilization.[17]

Emphasizing savings in welfare payments and vague standards like "fitness for parenthood," these practices targeted the same group at risk from the earlier eugenicists—low-income, black, and other minority women.

> Physicians themselves acknowledged the common practice in teaching hospitals of performing elective hysterectomies on poor black and Hispanic women as part of standard training in obstetrics and gynecology. [A rural doctor in South Carolina] refused all medical treatment to his female, financially dependent patients when they declined sterilization after their third child.[18]

Only if we believe that children of the poor are destined (or predestined) to poverty and public welfare does this response make any sense. Both past and present abusive practices locate the cause of poverty in its victims. The solution to poverty is then simply to reduce the procreative abilities of the present poor, rather than examine or change the complex social conditions that deny children of the poor the opportunity to succeed.

Twins Studies

While family studies have been abandoned, the effort to identify the genetic influences on crime has not.[19] One of the major problems with the study of genetic influence on behavior is the inability to control genetic variation. If one could create an experiment in which genetically identical persons were placed in different controlled environments, one might be able to distinguish genetically versus environmentally produced similarities and differences in behavior. Nature provides researchers with part of this experiment in the form of identical twins. Monozygotic (identical) twins are the product of a single egg and sperm and therefore are 100 percent genetically similar. Dizygotic (fraternal) twins, on the other hand, are the product of two eggs and two sperm and have the same genetic similarity as any two siblings (approximately 50 percent).

This biological fact led researchers to compare the similarity (or concordance) of behavior manifested by identical versus fraternal twins. Because both types of twins are raised together and exposed to similar environments, greater similarity in behavior among identical twins could be the result of greater similarity in genetic makeup. The first study, in 1929, to report greater concordance in criminal behavior among identical twins was *Crime as Destiny* by Johannes Lange.[20] Lange identified prisoners who were twins and then located and determined whether the remaining twin was also in trouble with the law. Of the 13 pairs of identical twins he found, 10 were concordant (77 percent); that is, both were criminals; of the 17 pairs of fraternal twins found, only 2 pairs were concordant (12 percent). He concluded that the significantly higher level of concordance for identical twins was due to heredity rather than environment. Until the 1960s, the majority of twin studies followed this methodology of identifying incarcerated twins and then locating their siblings. In a more recent study, Karl Christiansen used the Twin Register in Denmark to locate all the same-sex twins born between 1881 and 1910.[21] By then examining the Danish Penal Register for the names of any of the 6,000 pairs of twins he had identified, he was able to locate any twins with a criminal conviction. For the 67 cases where an identical male twin had a criminal record, 24 of them had twin brothers who were also listed in the

Penal Register (36 percent concordance). But of the 114 cases of fraternal male twins with criminal records, only 14 had twin brothers with records (12 percent concordance). For the female twins, the numbers were smaller, but the trend remained the same.

The vast majority of twin studies have reported greater similarity in criminal behavior for identical twins than for fraternal twins. Even so, it would be premature to conclude that heredity has been shown to be the cause of this similarity. Even Christiansen warned that his findings could not be used as proof that heredity explains the higher concordance among identical twins. The reason for this caution is the continued inability to control, and therefore remove as a possible factor, the environmental impacts upon two individuals who look to the outside world like the same person. While all siblings grow up in the same family and have generally comparable environmental and social backgrounds, identical twins have unique experiences. Often dressed alike, treated alike, and able to confuse friends and teachers, identical twins may experience an environment significantly more similar than same-sex fraternal twins. The similarity in behavior may be explained by this fact rather than by genes. Until that possibility is disproven, twin studies cannot be used with assurity to further the genetic argument. Furthermore, the Christensen study showed that 64 percent of the identical twins did *not* both appear in the penal register. This fact suggests that heredity alone cannot possibly explain criminality.

Adoption Studies

Another method used to examine the impact of heredity on criminal behavior is the comparison of adopted children with both their genetic and their rearing parents. If adopted children are more similar in behavior to their genetic (though absent) parents than to their adopted parents, it would provide support for the genetic argument. One of the largest adoption studies of its kind was conducted in Copenhagen, where all males born from 1927 to 1941 adopted by non–family members were identified and compared with both biological and adopted fathers.[22] Hutchings and Mednick concluded that the criminality of the adoptees' biological fathers was of greater importance than the adoptive fathers' criminality in predicting the criminality of their sons, although the effects were interactive (see Table 7.1).

While these studies are more successful in separating environ-

TABLE 7.1 Criminality Distribution of Adoptees According to the Criminality of Adoptive and Biological Fathers

Biological Father	Adoptive Father	Percent Adoptees Criminal	Number*
Not registered	Not registered	10.5	333
	Minor offender only	13.3	83
	Criminal offense	11.5	52
Minor offender only	Not registered	16.5	103
	Minor offender only	10.0	30
	Criminal offense	41.1	17
Criminal offense	Not registered	22.0	219
	Minor offender only	18.6	70
	Criminal offense	36.2	58

Note: The information for the "Minor offender only" category is relatively unreliable. It includes contacts with the police unrelated to asocial acts.

*Number = 965.

mental and genetic influences, they suffer from some potentially serious problems. Children are not placed in adopted homes in ways best suited for experimentation (for example, randomly) but in ways best suited for the child. The attempt by adoption agencies to match adoptive parents with genetic parents may result in less environmental differences between these two sets of parents than we might expect.

Autonomic Nervous Systems Studies

While the previous studies were predicated on the assumption that criminal behavior may be inherited, the inherited trait that would predispose a person to this behavior was left undefined. Can a person inherit greed? Does a person inherit an uncontrollable desire to rob strangers at gunpoint? Except for the early eugenicists, who believed every trait imaginable (from seafaringness to promiscuity to the ability to accumulate wealth) was inherited, researchers have left unspecified the actual genetic characteristic passed on to future generations. One exception to this is the research on the autonomic nervous system.

Sarnoff Mednick examines the way in which we teach children to behave in socially acceptable ways. If a child has been previously punished for aggressive behavior, contemplating further aggression should produce fear about the subsequent punishment.

Children learn that if they inhibit aggressive thought, the fear is reduced. They are, therefore, rewarded (by reduction of fear) for inhibiting aggression. Mednick believes that people differ in the speed and efficiency with which their bodies respond to the inhibition and consequent reduction of fear. Therefore, people differ in the extent to which they are reinforced or rewarded for inhibiting antisocial behavior. That fear response is controlled in part by the autonomic nervous system (ANS). Mednick hypothesizes that individuals with an ANS that recovers quickly from fear would receive immediate rewards for inhibiting antisocial behavior and would therefore learn acceptable behavior quickly. Those with a slow ANS would receive less reward for inhibiting antisocial behavior and would learn acceptable behavior more slowly. Mednick claims that his preliminary research supports this hypothesis since he found that those who get in trouble with the law possess an ANS with slower responses than law-abiding individuals'.[23]

Mednick follows in the tradition of another theorist who believes that the individual's ability to be socialized or conditioned is inherited and is one factor that differentiates the criminal from the noncriminal. In *Crime and Personality*, psychologist Hans Eysenck first described in detail his ideas about the role of heredity in criminal behavior.[24] Eysenck believes that particular aspects of personality have a biological base and there is a strong causative relationship between particular personality types and behavior. The two personality types of most interest are extroversion (characterized by people who are social, impulsive, outgoing, and assertive) and introversion (characterized by people who are shy, quiet, inward-looking, and controlled). Psychological tests allow subjects to be located on an introversion-extroversion scale determined, according to Eysenek, by genetic differences on the part of the central nervous system (CNS), which controls reactions to external stimulation. The CNS of extroverts works to lessen stimuli before they reach the cerebral cortex; the CNS of introverts works to magnify stimuli. Consequently, introverts will feel "overloaded" by outside stimuli and therefore attempt to avoid stimulus-producing situations. Punishment (a form of stimulus) will be seen as threatening by introverts, and they will strive to avoid it (via conforming behavior). Extroverts, with a poorly aroused cerebral cortex, will have a more difficult time establishing the connection between behavior and negative consequences (stimuli) and be more likely to perform illegal acts.

This, according to Eysenck, explains a phenomenon all parents have experienced—while a single reprimand is sufficient to curb one child's behavior, repeated punishments seem to have little effect on another. The two children are simply born with differing levels of conditionability; some learn quickly, others more slowly.

The empirical evidence to date does not conclusively demonstrate that extroversion occurs at a significantly higher rate among criminals nor that it has a genetic base. In addition, there is insufficient evidence to conclude that a person's susceptibility or predisposition to conditioning is a biologically determined, unchanging characteristic. Instead, it has been argued that a person's conditionability is a product of both biology and earlier environmental factors.[25] If an individual's ANS, for example, could be modified by the environment or by an individual's personality that is itself externally produced, then the causal order assumed by this approach could be in question.

On a more-general level, this theory reduces antisocial behavior to uncontrolled responses to insufficient conditioning. It deemphasizes the initial societal choices of which behaviors are to be extinguished by punishment and the fact that those who do violate this conditioning could be making rational choices.[26] In other words, the assumption of conditionability as an inherited cause of crime denies the concept of crime as rational behavior.

XYY and PMS Studies: Stereotypes and Crime

XYY is a chromosomal abnormality found in a minute number of men and hypothesized to be associated with criminal behavior. PMS (premenstrual syndrome) is a hormonal imbalance found in differing degrees in women and also supposedly related to criminal activity. While the groups under investigation (men versus women) and the biological abnormalities (chromosomal versus hormonal) differ, the underlying explanation for the alleged relationship between these biological oddities and crime are based upon stereotypic and unsupported views of men and women. The attempts to explain aggressive behavior in men because of an extra "male" chromosome and criminal behavior in women because of raging hormones are two examples of how an uncritical acceptance of stereotypic explanations for gender-specific behavior can influence both criminological research and public reaction. The XYY theory is predicated on the assumption that men are innately (chromosomally) more aggressive than women. Only if one assumes that the single Y of the normal male causes aggression (and the absence of a Y explains the lack of aggression in women) could one predict that an extra Y would make a man extra male-like, that is, extra aggressive. Premenstrual syndrome rests on the unproven assumption that women are naturally and inevitably the pawns of their hormones. Only if one assumes that female behavior is naturally irrational and emotional could hormonal imbalance be a satisfying explanation for female crime.

The average person possesses 23 pairs of chromosomes. One of these pairs determines an individual's sex. Two X chromosomes produce a female; an X and a Y produce a male. Occasionally, a person is born with an excess or a deficiency in the number of chromosomes, and this variation can occur in any of the 23 pairs. (Down's syndrome is a relatively common cause of mild retardation caused by an extra non–sex related chromosome, resulting in a total of 47). Variations also occur with the sex-linked chromosomes. Klinefelter's Syndrome is a condition of certain males who possess an extra X chromosome (XXY), and it appears to be related to some mild retardation and degeneration of certain sex characteristics. Another, seemingly rare variation is the possession of an extra Y chromosome—the XYY chromosomal abnormality.

In 1965, Patricia Jacobs and colleagues published an article, "Aggressive Behavior, Mental Subnormality and the XYY Male," which summarized their research at a Scottish maximum-security institution for mentally disturbed patients with violent or criminal histories.[27] Though the expected number of XYY men in the general population is .15 percent, their examination of 315 male patients revealed nine with the extra Y variation—3 percent of the total. The response to this finding was immediate. Hundreds of studies in prisons and mental hospitals followed, and researchers claimed that they too had found a larger than expected percentage of XYY men. The mass media focused on these reports and the publicity that resulted had tangible results. Richard Speck, the 1968 murderer of eight Chicago nursing students, was falsely reported as having the XYY variation. The California Center for the Study and Reduction of Violence—founded in 1972 and jointly funded by the state and federal government—set up a program to screen junior-high boys for the XYY chromosome. A few states passed laws to screen delinquent boys for use in sentencing decisions and, in 1968, a group of doctors started a massive screening of newborn male infants at the Boston Hospital for Women.

The potential impact is obvious. Boys with XYY configurations might be seen as greater threats and in greater need of confinement than XY boys convicted of identical offenses. The impact to newborns identified as XYY might have been even greater. The doctors planned to follow the development of the XYY infants. Serious ethical and moral questions were raised immediately (and were partially responsible for ending this study). Do you tell parents that their son has an extra Y chromosome and potentially affect how they raise their child? Or do you withhold information from parents who want to know why you find their son so interesting?

Some people believed that at last a simple, single cause of serious criminal behavior had been found. Something in the chromosomal makeup of these men caused violent, aggressive behavior. If we could locate these men, we would pinpoint the serious offenders. The remaining question is, 200 studies later: Does the research actually support the thesis that XYY men are more aggressive and violent than XY men? The answer is *No!*

Though inconclusive, these studies found a limited number of traits characteristic of XYY men.

1. XYY men tend to be taller than comparable XY men.
2. XYY men convicted of crimes are more likely to be guilty of property offenses and *less* likely than convicted XY men to have committed violent offenses.
3. The families of XYY inmates tend to have less history of crime or mental illness than the families of XY inmates.
4. The prevalence of XYY men appears to be higher in mental and penal institutions than in the general population.

But even these findings are inconclusive, given the methodological problems, which include inadequate control groups and lack of double-blind studies. This allowed the bias of researchers to effect the evaluation of subjects. But the problems are more fundamental than just nonrigorous methods. The research claims to find a slight relationship between an extra Y chromosome and institutionalization in mental and penal institutions. The explanation for this finding is what is most troubling. Because men are more aggressive (in our society) and men alone possess the Y chromosome, XYY men must be extra men, or extra aggressive. This analysis conforms to our stereotypic view of men as naturally more aggressive, so the researchers failed to consider other explanations. For example, XYY men have an increased probability for mild retardation, a characteristic of other chromosomal abnormalities as well (for example, the XXY configuration associated with Klinefelter's Syndrome). The increased institutionalization or increased likelihood of detection for antisocial behavior may have more to do with intelligence than with "criminal-like tendencies" or aggressiveness. Also, if XYY men tend to be taller as well as mildly retarded, they may make more visible targets for, and poorer respondents to, police questioning. But the extra X chromosome found in Klinefelter's does not fit our stereotypic explanation of male behavior. The similarities between XYY and other disorders are then ignored, and the press and the public are impressed with the "unique" qualities of the XYY male.

In addition, there is reason to question whether any actual syndrome is related to an extra Y chromosome. Certainly the significant number of XYY men leading perfectly normal and uneventful lives (an estimated ¼ million in the United States alone) does not support the existence of certain behavioral characteristics endemic to these men. Moreover, the importance of the XYY variation in explaining crime is seriously in question when we consider the rarity of the phenomenon. In 1976, Witkins and others examined all men born in Copenhagen between 1944 and 1947 who were over 6 feet tall; of the 4,139 men examined, they identified only 12 XYY men (and 16 XXY men). While they reported that XYY men were more likely to have criminal convictions than either XY or XXY men (XYY = 43 percent, XXY = 19 percent, XY = 9 percent), they concluded that the differences were due to lesser intelligence, not greater aggression.[28] In addition, do these very few men have any significant impact on the total crime rate? Obviously, even if these men were somehow controlled or confined, the problem of crime would have been virtually untouched. The popularity of the XYY myth, now on the decline, can be explained more by its support of stereotypic views of men than by its scientific evidence.[29]

Another biological theory of crime also rests on equally stereotypic views but is, in fact, gaining popularity with the public. This is the study of premenstrual syndrome as a cause of female criminality. While the XYY theory rests on the assumption that crime and aggression reside in the genetic code of men, PMS relies on a view of women as the helpless victims of raging hormonal imbalances.

While even Lombroso mentioned menstruation, the scientific

study of its relationship to crime is credited to Katharina Dalton and her 1961 research in an English women's prison.[30] There she interviewed 156 newly convicted women whose crimes had occurred within the previous 28 days. After obtaining information on their menstrual cycles, she calculated where in the cycle the women were at the time of the crime. Dividing the 28-day cycle into seven 4-day segments, she reported that 49 percent of the women either were in the premenstrual phase (4 days before the onset of menstruation) or were menstruating at the time of their crime (first 4 days of menstruation). If crime was unrelated to the menstrual cycle, only 29 percent of the crimes should have been committed during these 8 days. Dalton concluded that the hormonal changes either caused women to commit crimes (through feelings of aggression, irritability, or emotionality) or increased the likelihood of detection (through increased lethargy and carelessness), or both.

Julie Horney, in a re-analysis of Dalton's data, offered an alternative explanation for these findings.[31] Instead of concluding that this higher incidence of crime during the premenstrual and menstrual phases proved that hormonal changes cause an increase in crime, Horney argued that crime and subsequent arrest could produce these hormonal changes. The trauma of arrest and imprisonment could trigger early menstruation; later calculations would conclude that the woman was in the premenstrual phase at the time of the crime when, in fact, she was not.

Evidence exists that a variety of events—such as surgery, divorce, and even travel—can affect a woman's menstrual cycle; arrest is certainly traumatic enough to be included in that list. To support her thesis, Horney reviewed Dalton's claim that approximately 50 percent of female drivers involved in accidents were in the 8-day premenstrual/menstrual phase. This might support the notion that women are more lethargic and clumsy during this time. Horney found, however, that 50 percent of the female passengers involved in accidents were also in that same 8-day phase. Unless we wish to argue that the passenger's lethargy somehow caused the accident, it would appear that the trauma of the accident triggered menstruation, not vice versa.

The assertion that these hormonal changes cause crime through heightened aggression or tension defies Dalton's own findings that 155 of the 156 women examined were convicted of nonviolent crimes (in particular, theft and prostitution). In addition, claiming the hormonal changes that occur to some degree in all menstruating women explain violent crime is at odds with the enormous differences in the violent-crime rate for men and women.

As with the XYY theory, the popularity of the PMS theory far exceeds the empirical evidence. Articles on PMS have appeared in popular magazines, and PMS has been raised as a defense in a few criminal cases. In at least two cases in England, it was used by the defense successfully to reduce murder charges to manslaughter. But its success with the public and the courts is not evidence of its validity. Instead, its popularity may be attributed more to its support of the traditional view of women as innocent pawns of their biology than to the amassing of empirical data. While modern science is identifying certain physiological problems associated with menstruation, we need not conclude that these problems increase the probability of crime or mean a woman is less responsible for her behavior. The evidence does not support the conclusion that women are irresponsible during menstruation; the stereotypic view of women prevents the exploration of other explanations for Dalton's findings.

The assumption that women are controlled by their emotions while men are not has resulted in an absence of studies on emotional cycles in men. Preliminary evidence of these extremely rare studies is that men do appear to have regularly occurring emotional cycles.[32] Unless we wish to argue that both sexes are irresponsible at least part of the time and that mens rea is a figment of the legal imagination, it is illogical to conclude that hormonal menstrual changes make women more criminal or less capable of making rational decisions.

Biochemical-Factor Studies

PMS is not the only approach that looks to the body's production of hormones and the effects of glandular functioning on crime. The production of the male hormone testosterone has long been examined in relation to aggressiveness in males, particularly sexual assault. The research to date shows no consistent relationship between glandular dysfunction or varying levels of testosterone and sexual aberrations.[33] In addition, testosterone levels vary daily and seasonally, making comparative findings suspect at best. As a rule, men produce far more testosterone than needed for sexual activities. "[But this] excess doesn't necessarily mean more, better or specific kinds of sex."[34]

The research on testosterone levels and crime rests on a presumed causal order, that men with high levels of testosterone are more aggressive, domineering, or assaultive than men with lower levels. The data do not support such an assumption, however. Studies have found that males experience a drop in testosterone following a variety of stressful situations. Research on primates report that monkeys who become dominant in new social groups subsequently experience an increase in testosterone levels, while subordinate monkeys show a subsequent decrease in testosterone levels. Therefore, while there has been a reported correlation between testosterone levels and aggression in young men (though not in older men), it has not been established in any way that aggression causes a rise in testosterone, or that increased testosterone causes aggression, or both, or neither.[35] Regardless, modern science is today able to regulate normal balances (or inbalances) artificially, and sex offenders have been treated by reducing the level of testosterone or increasing the level of the female hormones estrogen and progesterone.

The popular saying "You are what you eat" has been taken seriously in recent years, and the roles of vitamin deficiencies, food allergies, and diet have been examined, particularly in relation to juvenile delinquents. Leonard Hippchen's study of delinquents points to the lack of sufficient quantities of certain vitamins, especially vitamin B, as a cause of a number of youth-related problems, including truancy, running away, and a general "restlessness."[36] Others argue that excessive levels of sugar and/or caffeine are common in institutionalized delinquents.[37] Hypoglycemia[38] (a low blood-sugar disorder), or allergies to particular foods[39] and additives are also suggested as causes of hyperactivity and violence among children.

While some researchers have found this relationship, others have found no differences between delinquent and nondelinquent populations on these nutritional components. It is certainly too soon to conclude that these factors are known to contribute to delinquent behavior. There may also be a link between nutritional deficiencies and social class. Poorer children may have greater vitamin deficiencies because of the expense of buying the varieties of food necessary for a well-balanced diet. In addition, the availability and relative low cost of fast foods could lead to excessive chemical additives and sugar in the diets of lower-class children. But the policy implications for research on diet and crime are significantly different from those of the previous discussions. The use of vitamin supplements and the reduction of refined sugar are not intrusive therapies in the same way that the use of artificial estrogen or XYY screening would be.

On the other hand, the type of antisocial behavior being examined in these studies—uncontrolled and seemingly irrational outbursts or drastic mood swings and restlessness—is extremely narrow. To impose this model on crime in general is to describe crime as some spontaneous and irrational action beyond the control of the individual. Yet our knowledge of crime tells us that this is an inaccurate picture. It defines crime as a nonrational maladaptive behavior, when, in reality, most criminal actions are quite rational and extremely adaptive for the individual. Is burglary, auto theft, corporate bribery, organized crime, armed robbery, or political corruption irrational behavior? Truly irrational antisocial behavior, behavior that is unpredictable and inexplicable to both society and the individual actor, is much rarer and often treated from its onset outside of the criminal-justice system.

Studies of Intelligence and Crime

While the development of intelligence testing and IQ scores is relatively recent, the assumption that intelligence and crime are interrelated has a long history. In 1913, Charles Goring discounted Lombroso's assertion that criminals were physically inferior to noncriminals and concluded that it was mental inferiority that differentiated the law breaker from the law abider. Goring's conclusions are representative of the theories searching for an inherited trait that characterizes criminals. Research indicates that physical traits fail to distinguish these two groups. But what about mental characteristics? The criminal may still be different, even inferior, to the noncriminal.

The assumption that criminals are mentally inferior leads to researching only a limited scope of criminal types: the street junkie, the unemployed mugger, the delinquent dropout. No one would seriously explain corporate crime, state crime, political corruption, or organized crime by mental inferiority. The variable of intelligence in many ways narrows the definition of crime and criminals. Upper-class crime is simply outside that definition and, once again, we have a theory that studies the behavior of one class while ignoring the similar behavior of other classes.

The relationship between intelligence and crime cannot be discussed in a vacuum. It must be examined in the context of the history of the intelligence concept in general. That history is plagued by problems in definition and measurement and the infusion of racism and class bias.

The earliest "intelligence hunters" concentrated on physical measurements of the skull or brain cavity. In the 18th and 19th centuries, craniologists measured brain and head size in order to rank the races. Because the researchers were white, it is no surprise that whites were consistently ranked as superior, blacks as inferior, and Indians and Asians as somewhere in between. While all these studies have since been rejected, at the time they provided scientific and purportedly impartial justification for discrimination, slavery, and colonialism.[40]

One of the fundamental problems with the early research was its two assumptions: that (1) human races can be ranked empirically from most to least intelligent and (2) the rank order is already known (white-Asian/Indian-black). All we need to do is select those characteristics that produce the correct ranking. If a measurement does not show that whites are most intelligent, then that measure is discarded for being unpredictive.

The measurement of physical characteristics declined in popularity when psychological testing was introduced. Here was a more-direct way to measure the "mental worth" of individuals and groups. In 1904, Alfred Binet (1857–1911) was commissioned by the French Minister of Public Education to develop a method of identifying children whose poor school performance suggested the need for special education. He did this by developing numerous tests that ranged in level of difficulty, to which he assigned an age level. The difference between the child's mental age (the age associated with the last tasks performed successfully) and the child's chronological age was the subject's intelligence quotient (IQ). Binet never claimed that this score represented "inborn intelligence." The number was simply an average of many scores. It represented neither a scalable entity nor a permanent feature. It was a pedagogical guide for helping the mildly retarded.

By the time IQ tests were introduced into the United States by people like Lewis Termin—who revised and popularized the test under its new name, Stanford-Binet—the meaning of IQ scores had changed. The score came to represent intelligence—a single quantifiable entity that was both fixed and inherited. Because smart and successful people seemed to produce equally successful children, intelligence must be inherited; because IQ scores were predictive of this same success, IQ scores must then represent intel-

Stealing the private property of a "public" utility. (Carl Weese/ Rapho/Photo Researchers)

ligence. IQ tests are still administered to thousands of American school children. The test scores correlate highly with school performance (which is not surprising, because Binet wrote and standardized these tests using scholastic achievement) and are often predictive of occupational success. What has not been demonstrated is that intelligence tests measure intelligence. Instead of being proof that intelligence exists, high IQ scores and success may both be the product of high socioeconomic status. Children in the upper classes are more likely to be successful in the adult world. They are also more likely to have the academic background that increases IQ scores. This is not sufficient proof that these children are more intelligent than their poorer counterparts. The same is true for differences in IQ scores between white and black children. The difference in scores proves neither that one group is innately more intelligent nor that the differences are inherited or unchangeable.

Stephen Gould identified two basic errors that have led to the claim that intelligence tests measure something inherited and permanent.[41] The first error is the equating of the inheritable with the inevitable. Intelligence is inherited in the same way that all human attributes are. But, to the geneticist, that does not mean a certain trait is predetermined, only that our genes provide for a variety of manifestations that emerge under different environmental conditions. It is only the untutored who believe that inherited must mean predestined.

The second error is a failure to differentiate *within* and *between* group variation. Some have asserted that, because heredity explains a certain percentage of variation among individuals within a group, it must also explain differences between groups. Arthur Jensen and William Shockley employed this logic when they argued that, because blacks as a group score lower than whites on IQ tests (approximately 15 points lower) and a certain percentage of the variation in test results among whites is a product of heredity, the variation between blacks and whites must be hereditary. This simply is not so. Gould used the example of growing corn to demonstrate the error in this logic. Suppose we plant two bags of corn with different mixtures of seeds of different strains and varieties in adjacent fields. One field we water daily, the other we ignore. At harvest, the field of corn we watered would have a variety of different types and sizes of corn. So would the other field, but the corn would be unhealthy and smaller in comparison. The difference in corn within each field is the product of different seeds (heredity). The difference between the two fields is the product of the environment. Simply because within-group (or within-field) variation has a genetic component, does not suggest that between-group variation also has any genetic component.[42] Therefore, differences in scores between blacks and whites is not evidence of hereditary differences in intelligence.

Francis Galton and Henry Goddard suggested that intelligence was transmitted by a single gene. We know that is not true. But many still believe that intelligence is largely an inherited trait that predetermines ability. Eighty years after Binet first introduced the psychological intelligence test, we still have no valid measure of intelligence or evidence that intelligence is a fixed inherited quality.

How does this apply to crime? One of the first groups to be given IQ tests were incarcerated populations—jailed prostitutes, delinquents, adult felons. Reports claimed that 30 to 70 percent of these people scored below the mental age of 13 (the score that purportedly indicated feeble-mindedness). The conclusion reached was that low intelligence was a cause of crime. These conclusions were a bit premature. First, prisoners are not representative of all criminals, but are only the select few who are caught, convicted, and imprisoned. Second, these scores and conclusions were reported before the scores of prisoners could be compared with the test scores of the general public. When this comparison was done, it raised serious doubt about the earlier results. Tests administered to 1.75 million army recruits during World War I showed that close to one-half of these recruits also scored below the mental age of 13. Clearly a mental age of 12 or below did not indicate feeble-mindedness, or one-half of those soldiers deserved the label. When we look at the actual questions, it is easy to understand why so many people score low and why they tend to be concentrated among the lower classes, or newly arrived immigrants. It is more difficult to understand how anyone could argue that these tests measure some abstract reasoning ability or innate quality. The following is a sample of some of the questions from the Stanford-Binet IQ test:

Alpha Test (8 excerpts)—Underline the correct answer.
1. Five-hundred is played with rackets/pins/cards/dice.
2. The Percheron is a kind of goat/horse/cow/sheep.
3. The most prominent industry of Gloucester is fishing/packing/brewing/automobiles.
4. Christie Matthewson is famous as a writer/artist/baseball player/comedian.
5. Chard is a fish/lizard/vegetable/snake.
6. Alfred Noyes is famous as a painter/poet/musician/sculptor.
7. Becky Sharp appears in *Vanity Fair/Romola/The Christmas Carol/Henry IV.*
8. Habeas corpus is a term used in medicine/law/theology/ pedagogy.

The argument that IQ is related to criminality remains a popular theory among some criminologists. Travis Hirschi and Michael J. Hindelang recently reviewed past research on IQ and delinquency, using both official and self-reported data. Even when controlling for social-class and race variables, they concluded that "IQ is an important determinant of delinquency."[43] Specifically, they asserted that IQ affects delinquency through its effect on school performance. Therefore, they believe that the existing research has demonstrated that delinquents have lower IQs than nondelinquents. Hindelang and Hirschi never established that IQ tests measure anything innate or whether it is simply another measure of school performance. Nor did they address the questions of where intelligence comes from, whether it is impervious to change, and what factors might produce that change. Answers to these questions would lead to different interpretations of the data. Because Hindelang and Hirschi believed that IQ tests measured some innate ability, a causal model of the three relevant variables can precede in only one way:

IQ→School Performance→Delinquency

Without the assumption that IQ is an *a priori,* an innate quality, independent but predictive of school performance, the theory falls apart. Delinquency may lead to poor school performance and subsequent low test scores. Or delinquency and school performance may affect each other so that delinquency leads to less time in school, which produces poor grades and makes delinquency more attractive, and so on.

Mental abilities cannot be reduced to a single factor, and it is questionable whether intelligence can be ranked. There is no evidence that it is a permanent trait with fixed parameters. Despite the unanswered issues, intelligence has re-emerged in the criminological literature as a factor related to juvenile delinquency and IQ tests are still the definitive measure of intelligence. Whether or not school performance is related to deliquency is an open question, but the implications of this relationship are fundamentally different than those that emerge from the questionable claim that delinquents are less intelligent than nondelinquents.

Current Status of Biological Theory _____

We might reasonably suppose that, like alchemy, biological theories of crime would disappear in the face of such a preponderance of contradicting evidence and logically flawed theories. Instead, as we noted in the beginning of this chapter, there has been a resurgence in the popularity of biological theory. This renewed interest coincided with the 1975 publication of a book entitled *Sociobiology,* written by E. O. Wilson. Wilson proposed that the biological, and in particular the genetic, base for behavior needs to be emphasized in order to understand human behavior. Trained as an entomologist, Wilson believed that the techniques and knowledge we have acquired from the study of animal behavior can be applied directly to humans.

> My overall conclusion from the existing information is that homo sapiens is a typical animal species with reference to the quality and magnitude of the genetic diversity affecting behavior. I also believe that it will soon be within our ability to locate and characterize specific genes that alter the more complex forms of social behavior.[44]

These social behaviors include (but are not limited to) religion, ethics, warfare, genocide, cooperation, competition, conformity, spite, patriarchy, homosexuality, and xenophobia. Wilson did not simply say that biology or our genes have something to do with our behavior. He postulated a direct genetic link to specific social behaviors and argued that human nature itself is a direct result of genetic adaptation to the physical environment. Wilson, using Darwinian theory, concluded that these social characteristics were the result of natural selection and reflected the optimal adaptation to our physical world. Wilson was not saying that patriarchy, xenophobia, or genocide were good, but that they were natural in some evolutionary manner. We may be able to change our behavior, but we will have to fight against our "nature" to do so.

This assumption that individuals enter the world with some pre-established disposition is the underlying premise of one of the few sociologists supporting a biological explanation for criminal behavior, C. R. Jeffery. According to Jeffery, behavior is the result of learning and learning is the product of an interaction between the physical environment and the brain.

> Learning is a psycho-biological process involving changes in the biochemistry and all structure of the brain. . . . The types of behavior (response) exhibited by an organism depends on the nature of the environment (stimulus) and the way in which the stimulus is coded, transmitted and decoded by the brain and the nervous system.[45]

He depicts this model of behavior in the following way:

Genetic × Environment = Brain × Environment = Behavior
Code   Code

Therefore, while the external environment certainly plays a role in behavior, it is limited by the unique and inherited capacities of the individual's brain and nervous system. We are not all the same and we will not respond to the world in similar ways. "We do not inherit behavior any more than we inherit height and intelligence. We do inherit a capacity for interaction with the environment."[46]

Once we recognize that behavior is controlled by the brain, our response to deviant behavior must also change. Specifically, Jeffery believes that we must abandon our current practices of responding to criminal behavior after it has occurred and turn instead to crime-prevention programs. If the predisposition to crime exists in the brain prior to criminal behavior, then the discovery of that predisposition could prevent crime.

> In order to implement a biosocial approach to crime prevention, we must have early diagnosis and treatment of neurological disorders. This means experimentation and research. It will mean brain scans and blood tests. It will mean tests for learning disabilities and hypoglycemia. All of this involves medical experimentation, intrusion into the privacy of the individual, and controversial and experimental surgeries and/or drug therapies.[47]

Recognizing the political dangers and public opposition if the government were to operate such a system, Jeffery suggests a private treatment system to parallel or even replace the current criminal-justice system. This he believes would remove the treatment of behavioral disorders, including crime, from the *political arena* (his emphasis).

More recently, two Harvard professors, one an economist–political scientist and the other a biologically trained psychologist, set forth yet another modern-day version of the biological theory of criminality. In *Crime and Human Nature,* James Q. Wilson and Richard Herrnstein suggest that biological predispositions in combination with certain unspecified environmental experiences explain why some people commit crimes and others do not.[48] When it was published in 1985, their book received an inordinate amount of attention from the press and politicians, despite the fact that it suffers from the same illogic and empirical shortcomings as previous research based in the biological tradition. The most basic flaws, as previously noted, are (1) the biased selection of data to prove theory rather than test it and (2) a failure to distinguish between correlation and causation.[49]

Speaking of Wilson and Herrnstein's selection of data to support their thesis, Kamin points out that, to make their point:

> Tiny snippets of data are plucked from a stew of conflicting and often nonsensical experimental results. Those snippets are then strung together in an effort to tell a convincing story, rather in the manner of a clever lawyer building a case. The data do not determine the conclusions reached by the lawyer. Instead the conclusions toward which the lawyer wants to steer the jury determine which bits of data he presents.[50]

Wilson and Herrnstein argue that constitutional and developmental factors predispose some individuals to criminality. These constitutional predispositions include age and gender (e.g., young males), mesomorphic body types, low intelligence, and aggressive personalities. Even including inadequate family life and poor school performance, they conclude that "individuals differ at birth in the degree to which they are at risk for criminality."[51]

A central thesis of the Wilson and Herrnstein theory is that biological traits such as impulsiveness, aggressiveness, and intelligence are inherited. They argue that research shows criminals share these traits disproportionately, compared to noncriminals, and that some societies have more people with a propensity toward crime (as a result of these inherited tendencies) than others. As evidence for their theory, they cite research they claim demonstrates that criminals are less likely to be willing to "defer gratification" than noncriminals.[52] To come to this conclusion, Wilson and Herrnstein disregard data that would contradict their theory and select evidence that is misleading. For example, they cite as evidence for their theory the alleged fact that crime is associated with people who are unable to defer gratification, a study they say shows that young people growing up in the 1960s were more willing to defer gratification than young people growing up in the 1980s. Because, they assert, the crime rate of juveniles was higher in the 1970s than in the 1960s, this alleged change in the willingness of the different groups to defer gratification supports their theory. As evidence, they cite a study comparing 50 juvenile delinquents institutionalized in Rhode Island in 1974 with 57 delinquents studied in the same state in 1959. This study revealed that 16 percent of the 1974 delinquents said they would save rather than spend a dollar if it were given to them, whereas in the 1959 sample of delinquents, 30 percent said they would save it. When the amount to be given to the delinquents was raised to $100.00, 48 percent of the 1974 subjects, compared to 58 percent of the 1959 subjects, asserted that they would save the money.

Wilson and Herrnstein interpret these findings as proof of the causal relation between deferred gratification and delinquency rates in the two periods. The empirical fact, however, is that the difference between the responses of the two groups of delinquents may be no more than one would expect to find as a result of sampling error or chance. Furthermore, even if the difference were significant, it would only indicate that the delinquents are better economists than Wilson and Herrnstein (despite the fact that Wilson has a Ph.D. in economics), for the value of a dollar in 1974 was 41 percent less than it was in 1959. It should not come as a surprise, and it certainly does not indicate any difference in a willingness to defer gratification, that intelligent juveniles (or adults) were less likely to save a dollar in 1974 than they were in 1959.[53]

Another study cited in support of their theory compared the responses of delinquents and high school students in Anglo, Chicano, and Mexican cultures. Wilson and Herrnstein report that, when these students were asked whether or not they would save or spend money, the delinquents were less likely than the nondelinquents to report that they would save the money. What Wilson and Herrnstein do not report is that this was only true when the sums were 25 cents and $2.00. When the sums were $20.00 and $200.00, the proportions of delinquents and nondelinquents reporting that they would save their money did not differ. In addition, many of the studies they report do not measure actual behavior, but only what respondents claim they would do in response to a question on a questionnaire. Neither we nor Wilson and Herrnstein can conclude that what people say and what people do are always the same.

Wilson and Herrnstein claim support for their theory from the fact that Japan has a much lower crime rate than the United States. They attribute this to biological differences that are infused in the culture. The Japanese are more introverted than the Americans; Wilson and Herrnstein see introversion as a biologically determined propensity. Cultural differences, they assert, grow out of biological differences. As evidence, they cite a single study, which was a paper-and-pencil test trying to measure personality traits of people in Japan and the United States. The study did, in fact, show that the Japanese were more introverted than the Americans. But this is the only fact from the study reported by Wilson and Herrnstein. It happens to be the only fact from the study that supports their theory. They fail to mention that this sort of personality testing has also shown that the people of Uganda and Ghana score as high on introversion scales as the Japanese, and these cultures have crime rates much higher than those of the United States.[54]

Wilson and Herrnstein also fail to advise readers of the fact that the same personality test provides a score for an individual's tendency towards "psychoticism." The paper cited by Wilson and Herrnstein points out that the Japanese have the highest score of any culture on this trait. The countries scoring the lowest on this trait are Canada, the United Kingdom, and the United States. All are countries with higher official crime rates than Japan. Psychoticism, according to the study, is associated with brutality, insensitivity to the feelings of others, and self-centeredness. Presumably, these traits would lead to a much higher crime rate in Japan than in the United States if biological traits are inherited and manifested in responses to questionnaires. Because these data contradict the Wilson and Herrnstein theory, the authors conveniently ignore the data.

Their overall goal is to provide a comprehensive explanation of why certain individuals commit crimes and others do not. But, as they admit, they examine only the traditional street crimes of murder, rape, and theft, while reluctantly ignoring embezzlement, political corruption, and fraud (due to a paucity of research). Murder, rape, and theft are certainly serious crimes that need investigation, but they are not representative of all serious crimes. Wilson and Herrnstein's individualistic approach to criminology is therefore limited to a select few individuals. This is not to imply that people of all classes are not capable of commiting traditional street crimes. It is to assume that class position does effect the type of crime chosen, through its effects on opportunity, profit, ease, and so forth.[55] An executive vice-president "can" commit burglary, but the opportunity, profit, and ease of embezzlement will make the latter type of theft more desirable. On the flip side, the out-of-work laborer cannot choose embezzlement. The end result is that traditional street crime is predominantly a lower-class behavior.

Are persons of one class or one ethnic background born with constitutional and genetic criminogenic factors significantly different from those of other classes and backgrounds? Wilson and Herrnstein accept this possibility when they hypothesize that Japan's low crime rate may be the product of constitutional traits inherent in the Japanese psychology. In particular, they suggest that the high intelligence and introverted personality traits of the Japanese produced both the low crime rate and the specific cultural characteristics usually credited with that low rate.

To accept this explanation for low crime rates, it seems logical to accept biological explanations for high crime rates. And, if one limits, as Wilson and Herrnstein do, the definition of crime to traditional lower-class street crime, (so that only members of the lower class could cause high crime rates), one is left with a theory of crime that could be accused of racism and classism.

Class and Race Bias

Biological theory offers a seemingly simple and straightforward solution. Some people are biologically predisposed to crime. Find these individuals, cure or isolate them (depending upon their condition), and crime will be reduced. It is not an issue of politics, fairness, opportunity, or class. It is a scientific problem, best handled by the scientific community, not politicians or lawyers. Enrico Ferri argued this 60 years ago. C. R. Jeffery echoes him today, "We must approach the crime problem as a behavioral problem and not as a political problem."[56]

But crime is a product of a particular political and social milieu. To ignore that leads to a fatal misunderstanding of the nature of crime. Behaviors may be good or bad; that has little to do with their designation as crime. To aim a gun at a stranger and demand money is bad, and it is also a crime. To expose knowingly one-half million school children to asbestos because of the profit is also bad, but it is not a crime. As we have seen in Chapter 4, the definition of acts as criminal is a political process. To deny that crime is a social construct does not make the study of crime apolitical. It simply provides "scientific" support for the existing definitions of crime without recognizing that alternative definitions exist.

A half century ago, Garofalo recognized the political nature of crime. His attempt to deal with this fact was an artificial and arbitrary distinction between "natural crimes" and all other crimes, claiming that only the former were universal and biologically explained. Today we can see that his solution is without empirical justification. He demonstrates neither that natural crimes are of a biological origin nor that they are more objectively real and universal than the excluded crimes.

Jeffery repeats Garofalo's illogic by arguing that not all crime can be subsumed under biosocial criminology. Specifically, he believes his approach is best reserved for street crimes, the traditional personal and property crimes committed disproportionately by the lower classes (which look suspiciously like Garofalo's natural crimes). "Perhaps organized and white-collar crime should be regarded not as problems in criminology but as problems of politics and economics."[57] Jeffery argues that there are different causes and solutions for crimes committed by members of different social classes. (Forty-five years ago, Edwin Sutherland criticized criminology for its failure to include white-collar crime under its umbrella. Jeffery advocates its removal once again.) Wilson and Herrnstein fall victim to the same class bias by limiting their analysis to traditional lower-class crime. While they allude to the possibility that upper- and middle-class criminals may also share genetic traits with lower-class criminals, the weakness of their approach becomes clear when those excluded upper-class crimes are re-entered into the analysis. Is Richard Nixon a mesomorph? Do the corporate executives of the Manville corporation have low intelligence? Are embezzlers suffering from psychopathic personalities?

Some biological theorists limit the applicability of their explanation to "irrational" crime. But the very definition of rational and irrational turns out to be a value judgment. The machine smashing of the 19th century was seen as typically senseless vandalism by property owners. To the rioters themselves, their actions were very rational.[58] For agricultural laborers and workers in cottage industries, these were the acts of persons whose very livelihood was threatened by industrialization. For the factory workers, these were the acts of a new industrialized work force protesting and rioting for (and sometimes achieving) improved working conditions. In 1967, three physicians and leading advocates of psychosurgery suggested that some of the violence and looting accompanying the urban riots of the mid-1960s might be the product of organic brain dysfunction.[59] During the Revolutionary War, only a minority actually fought against the British, although everyone suffered under the same laws. Could the difference be organic brain dysfunction? What is rational and irrational depends upon our perspective and often our class.

Racist assumptions are also characteristic of most biological theories of crime. Lombroso's theory of criminals as representative of an atavistic throwback to more primitive man reflected the racial biases of the time. He argued that the reversion to more primitive beings or inferior animals was consistent with the known principles of selection, which were interpreted to mean that human beings came from apes through a process of gradual evolution. People living in less technologically developed parts of the world—people less capable of living in a higher form of civilization than white, European "man"—were assumed to represent linkages closer to the ape. The thesis proposed by Lombroso was that the reversion to primitive beings could be recognized among criminals by the existence of specific physical anomalies or stigmata that corresponded to those stereotypically attributed to people of

African heritage. Lombroso reflected the colonialist and imperialist policies of 19th-century Europe and infused these prejudices into his theory.

Racist views dominated the cultures of 19th century Europe and America. Even before Darwin and the misinterpretation of his theory by social scientists, "degeneration theory" argued that humans originated from a single source, but the different races were a result of degeneration from that beginning. Of course, to 19th-century Europeans, the white race had declined the least, the black race the most. Following Darwin's theory of evolution, "recapitulation theory" replaced degeneration theory and demonstrated once again how a scientific proposition can be used to justify racism. According to this theory, a developing individual passes through his or her own evolutionary past—a series of stages representing adult ancestral forms in their evolutionary order. If adults of "inferior" races were similar to the children of superior races, this was proof that the inferior groups were at a stage of evolution already surpassed by these superior (that is, white) children.[60] Lombroso's theory then was only an explanation for differences in people that was based on a fundamentally racist foundation. Lombroso was obviously unable to prove his assertion, but the stereotypes have survived for centuries without evidence to support them.

Recent attempts to resurrect biological theories of crime are less blatant in their racist, sexist, and classist assumptions, but they are nonetheless inflicted with these biases. Wilson and Herrnstein implicitly suggest that the higher incidence of crime among poor, young blacks in America may be evidence of biologically inherited propensities. They argue that if we can show a correlation between physical or biological characteristics and crime, then we must assume a causal link: "If it turned out that more criminals were, say, redheaded and freckle-faced, we would be on the train of genetic correlates of crime, just because redheadedness and freckles have a genetic basis."[61] This logic is truly astounding. It suggests, because persons with black skin make up a disproportionate number of people living in poverty, that the black skin, which is known to be genetically determined, must be the cause of the poverty. This cause is supposedly independent of racism, colonialism, slavery, or any other social-historical facts. If blonde women were the object of pervasive discrimination, had been enslaved for 300 years, had come from an area of the world that was colonized and enslaved, and had committed more crimes than nonblonde women, would we be justified in assuming that it was the genetic characteristics of blonde women that caused them to commit crime? Obviously not.

Conclusion _____

Biological theory reduces criminal behavior to uncontrolled but predetermined response by a human organism. Not only is this an inaccurate depiction of crime in general, but also it distorts the relationship of biology to human behavior. We are biological creatures, but that does not mean we are ruled by our biology or that biology and environment compete for control of our actions.

An assumption of many of the biological theorists is that biological (and, in particular, genetic) means innate and permanent. It is this premise that allows us to discuss criminal potential or assume we can detect it prior to the onset of crime. This is true for the sociobiologists who argue that certain human traits (for example, aggression) are universal and the natural product of evolution, as well as for those who argue that the genetic code of specific individuals predisposes them to maladaptive behavior.[62] Both approaches assume that certain behaviors are more natural and therefore more expected than other behaviors, either for specific individuals or for the species as a whole.

In his book *Violence*,[63] Graeme Newmen concluded, because the brain mediates aggressive behavior (being the mediator of all behavior), that aggression may be caused by an internal mechanism: specific neural systems that are inherited and organized to evoke violent behavior. Thus there is such a person as a "born killer," to use Newmen's own phrase. But it is illogical to conclude that some brains are innately organized to be aggressive, simply waiting for the appropriate trigger from the environment. A leading anthropologist, Ashley Montague, points out that there is no such thing as an innate basic aggressive circuitry.[64] Although neural systems can be organized by experience to function as aggression, an individual learns to be aggressive in the same manner that he or she learns to inhibit aggression. One is not a natural state, the other culturally imposed. Both are within our biological potential.

In a similar fashion, there is no persuasive evidence to support Wilson's contention that we are genetically programmed for aggression simply because we are often aggressive. Genetic potentials do not lead to inevitable outcomes. Violence, sexism, and racism are biological only in the sense that they are within the range of possible human attitudes and behaviors. But nonviolence, equality, and justice, are also biologically possible. What predominates in a particular society, historical period, or individual is not determined by biological predispositions, nor is the presence or absence of these qualities explained by theories deriving from the biological paradigm.[65]

At the very dawn of scientific inquiry, criminal behavior emerged as a focus of attention. The unprecedented growth of knowledge from viewing the heavenly bodies and even human evolution through the lens of science led to the optimistic belief that applying the same techniques to the study of human problems would quickly render them historical curiosities. The zeal with which criminality was studied utilizing the biological model was exceeded only by the development of legal systems to implement the presumed accumulation of knowledge. Unfortunately, the optimism was premature and the emphasis was misplaced. Two hundred years of research and theorizing about the possible relationship between biological, physical, genetic, and hormonal factors related to criminality has yielded no lasting evidence that there is a causal relationship between biology and criminality.

For the biological theorist, the starting point for the study of crime is the individual. He or she becomes the basic unit of analysis, and his or her physical or genetic codes become the ultimate components. The characteristics of society are seen simply as the sum total of the characteristics of its individual members and the individuals, in turn, the product of their genetic codes. Societies are aggressive because the individuals in these societies are aggressive. Crime and even war, the most organized form of aggression, are thus seen as the products of clusters of hostile, aggressive individuals. Economics, politics, culture, and social relations are all reduced to the sum total of individuals and their biological makeup.

This form of analysis is called reductionism—the attempt to study the whole (human history) by reducing every event to the behavior of its parts (people), as if these parts exist separate from, and unaffected by, the whole.[66] The history of this effort to study an individual as an encapsulated entity, driven by genes, neural circuits, or hormones, and only tangentially affected by larger social forces, is a history of scientific failure.

Behavior is criminal because there is a law. Law is not God-given and immutable for all times and places, as we have seen. There is nothing inherent in any behavior that determines it is criminal. It is, therefore, illogical to suppose that there is something in the biology of those who commit criminal acts that differentiates them from those who do not. When we recognize the political and economic processes determining what acts are defined as criminal (see Chapter 4) then the biological paradigm is obviously misdirected. To look for crime's cause and meaning in the biology, physique, IQ, or genetic code of an individual and not in the broader mosaic of social, political, and economic relations in which the individual is enmeshed, gives crime an ahistorical reality that can only lead to unscientific and false theories.

Does this mean, then, that we must abandon the search for explanations of criminal behavior, or does it mean that we need to look elsewhere? It was in large part in reaction to the failings of the biological paradigm that social scientists in the 20th century turned to psychiatric theories to answer the age-old question of why people commit crime. It is this body of research and theory to which we turn in the next chapter.

8

Psychiatric Paradigms

Is crime an uncontrolled or symbolic expression of basic human urges? Do criminals sometimes harbor an unconscious sense of guilt so overwhelming that they actually seek the punishment that their misbehavior brings? Do delinquency and crime stem from disturbances in the relationships between parent and child that are necessary for the development of adequate inhibitory controls? Does the frustration of instinctive impulses create mental conflicts that erupt into aggressively criminal responses?

From a psychiatric perspective, each of these questions would be answered affirmatively. The explanation of any particular case of criminality consists of locating the specific sources of frustration, the impediments to the development of controls, the mental conflicts, and the wellsprings of guilt that these led to the antisocial behavior in question. There is also the assumption that the most important period of development is early childhood (before age 5). Thus most psychiatric research focuses on delinquency. The typical rehabilitative effort undertaken within this framework is establishing a therapeutic relationship with the offender through which controls can be developed, guilt relieved, and mental conflicts resolved. The implied preventive strategy is to structure experience, especially interpersonal relationships within the family during early childhood. The ego and superego should then develop "normally," so that frustration and guilt do not become major emotional problems.

Freud and Crime

The contemporary psychoanalytic perspective stems largely from Sigmund Freud's efforts to weld psychiatric concepts into a process by which certain experiences led naturally and inevitably to their consequences in an individual's behavior. Freud went considerably beyond the work of his predecessors and contemporaries and developed a statement of process that made human behavior of any kind a logical deduction from a more-general theory. Freudian theory is not, specifically, a theory of criminal behavior, but Freud's clinical experience with neurotics led to the application of psychoanalytic theory to crime and delinquency. Freud's most direct personal involvement in the theoretical problems of crime and delinquency is represented by a paper that presents crime as a neurotic type of disorder.[1] In suggesting that the offender may commit offenses because of an unconscious desire for guilt-relieving punishment, Freud was suggesting that criminal and deliquent offenses, like neuroses, were outgrowths of repression and self-directed aggression.

Most contemporary psychoanalysts who specialize in crime and delinquency depart from Freud's original formulation, making a clear distinction between the symptoms of neurosis and those of criminal behavior while recognizing the possibility of both occurring together and intertwining.[2] Most theorists suggest that neuroses represent inwardly directed aggression, whereas "in the delinquencies, aggression is always directed toward the outside."[3] Karl Eissler, a major figure in psychiatric theories on crime, refers to inwardly directed and outwardly directed aggression as "autoplastic" and "alloplastic," respectively, but the difference in the etiology of the two types is by no means clear.[4] Eissler, in fact, suggests that the "alloplastic disorders" grow out of the "same constellation" as the neuroses, "namely, frustration of the growing child."[5] In a similar vein, Kate Friedlander states that "the unconscious conflicts which we find in neurotic or delinquent children and adults are identical and so far no specific conflict constellation has been described to explain why one particular person becomes delinquent and not neurotic and vice versa."[6] Nonetheless, the distinction between crime and neurosis is apparently more than a distinction between "surface" symptoms. August Aichhorn, Karl Eissler, and others contend that criminal behavior must be transformed into a neurosis before it will yield to successful treatment.[7] And some attempts have been made to describe the dynam-

Labeling and self-image. *(Thomas S. England/Photo Researchers)*

ics of character formation that lead to a delinquent, instead of a neurotic, reaction to the stress of internal mental conflicts.[8]

Two major theoretical perspectives relevant to crime, in addition to Freud's emphasis on becoming "criminal from a sense of guilt," have emerged from the psychiatric paradigm. There are also many isolated "interpretations" of particular crimes within the general psychiatric framework that fall into neither of these two major perspectives. Psychoanalytic theory is exceedingly provocative of novel interpretations, and its very ambiguity is a rich source of varied insights. Limitations of space preclude the discussion of more than these two major perspectives. The first emphasizes the failure of the delinquent to develop adequate ego and superego controls; this failure is attributed to the absence of normal emotional ties in early childhood. The second represents a development, less psychoanalytical, that elevates the "frustration-aggression" principle to the position of a central postulate in the explanation of delinquency.

Faulty Ego and Superego Development

Psychiatric theory postulates that each individual is endowed with a cluster of "pleasure-seeking" (that is, libidinal, or sexual) impulses, which Freud called the id (and sometimes the "criminal id," thereby emphasizing the antisocial nature of these postulated impulses or instincts). The control of these impulses is achieved, according to Freud, by the development of an ego out of restrictive experiences with the external world and by the development of a superego, an internalization of social standards accomplished by "identification" with the parent. There is the clear recognition in Freud's writings that these developments may be disrupted in various ways, especially by a disturbance in the normal emotional relationship between parent and child in the first few years of life.

August Aichhorn, a Viennese teacher who founded an institution for delinquent boys in Oberhollabruun, Austria, following World War I, detected in the basic ideas of Freud a clue to the problem of delinquency and its treatment, as well as a key to the problem of the neurotic disorders that were the primary focus of Freud's attention. Aichhorn adapted psychoanalytic theory and practice to the peculiar problems of delinquents. If there could be a "founder" of the psychiatric tradition in criminology, Aichhorn is the most appropriate candidate. His perspective is well summarized by Anna Freud with a minimum of extraneous detail and technical psychoanalytic terminology:

August Aichhorn, in the introduction to his book, *Wayward Youth*, emphasizes the pathogenic significance for social maladjustment of faulty ego and superego development. Internal and external factors which prevent the normal growth of the various ego functions act as a hindrance to the 'primary adaptations to reality' which Aichhorn regards as the indispensable basis and background of a development on social lines. Internal and external factors, on the other hand, which interfere with the emotional development of the child and prevent him from attaching his feelings to permanent love-objects (the parents or their substitutes) prevent, as Aichhorn explains, the second step in social development, i.e., adaptation to the cultural standards of the community of which the child is expected to become a member. Where normal emotional ties are missing, there is little incentive, nor is it possible for the child to model himself on the pattern of the adult world which surrounds him. He fails to build up the identifications which should become the core of a strong and efficient superego, act as a barrier against the instinctual forces and guide his behavior in accordance with social standards.[9]

Aichhorn proposed, following Freud, that a child lives according to the "pleasure principle," that is, "lives according to its instinctual demands, which are directed exclusively toward the attainment of pleasure and which ignore reality."[10] Because of repeated contact with "difficulties that stand in the way of instinctual gratification or because of the pain that may result from the gratification of instincts in a manner prohibited by society,"[11] the pleasure principle is gradually subdued. The "psychic apparatus is thereby forced to adapt itself to reality."[12] The educator or parent, according to Aichhorn, can assist in this developmental process by "providing incentives for the conquest of the pleasure principle in favor of the reality principle."[13] They may provide such incentives either by allowing the child to "experience increased pain following forbidden instinctual satisfaction" or by providing a "substitute gratification";[14] for example, love and affection may be given by the parent in response to the child's curbing his or her impulses.

However, "if the parents bestow affection without asking any return by way of renunciation, the child does not need to exert himself. Assured of love, he lacks the incentive to give up pleasure of favor of reality."[15] The result is "an unsatisfied need for love" and kind of "hate reaction" described by Aichhorn as "concealed," which manifests itself in the youngsters becoming "liars and intriguers; they tyrannize over their comrades in secret."[16] The background of this reaction, Aichhorn proposes, lies in the fact that "the parents, disappointed in each other, expend too much libido on the child. The child feels that this love is not given to him for his own sake and reacts to it by becoming dissocial."[17]

On the other hand, "if the child suffers too much from punishment or severity and is not compensated for this by the parents' love, he is forced into opposition and has no further incentive to submit to their demands and thus to subject himself to the reality principle. His main object is to resist authority. Rebellion against his parents, teachers, and society—the assertion of his ego against them—becomes just as great a source of pleasure to him as the gratification of his instincts."[18] This pattern constitutes another of Aichhorn's types of "hate reaction," the more common one, according to Aichhorn. This "type hates the environment quite openly, without any attempt at concealment."[19] Aichhorn further comments that "the great majority of children in need of retraining come into conflict with society because of an unsatisfied need for tenderness and love in their childhood,"[20] while suggesting that "the type 'delinquent due to excess of love' is not often seen in the training school. However, he is found disproportionately often in middle-class home."[21]

Aichhorn interprets both types of "hate reaction" as failures in the development of the ego or reality principle and the unrestrained operation of the pleasure principle. In summary, the formulation suggests that a gradual training of the child by the parents, characterized neither by an unloving harshness nor by an excess of indulgence, is necessary for the development of ego controls that curb the pleasure principle. In the absence of such ego controls, a "hate reaction" occurs, and the child becomes dissocial or delinquent. In a word, Aichhorn sees the delinquent as unsocialized.

> Any factor which interferes with the establishment of a firm mother-child relationship and with consistent handling of primitive instinctive drives will hinder this process of ego development. Separations of any length of time before the age of three, lack of interest or lack of time on the mother's side, personality defects in the mother which make her inconsistent during the periods of feeding, weaning, and the training for cleanliness, all may lead to a disturbance in ego development, which will be the more severe, the graver the environmental defect and the stronger the child's instinctive drives.[22]

The developmental process by which such early family experiences lead to aggressively acting out behavior are not, unfortu-

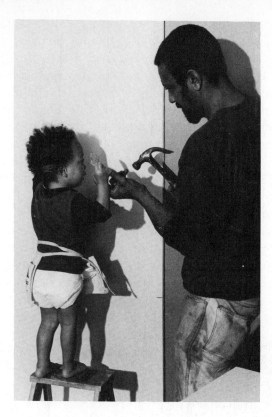

Learning to work.
*(Frostie/Woodfin
Camp & Assoc.)*

nately, subject to direct empirical verification, but are usually clinically inferred. Analysts make certain that the cases they handle fit the explanation that they expected to account for the behavior. In Aichhorn's formulation, the central concepts—such as pleasure principle, instinctual impulses, ego, reality principle, and hate reaction—are inferred from the behavior which these concepts are supposed to explain. The data presented by Aichhorn do *not* therefore constitute a test of his formulation, but should be seen as merely illustrative of his conceptual scheme. The only nontautological empirical test of the adequacy of the Aichhorn formulation lies in the association between delinquency and family circumstances. The frequent occurrence of such family circumstances was noted or inferred by Aichhorn in his experiences with training-school delinquents, which led to the formulation of his theory. Hence, the association of family conditions and delinquency is not tested independently but is based only on finding the relationship that was assumed and taken into account in constructing the theory.

Aichhorn's strategy for retraining delinquents is subtle and complex, but the essential outlines may be presented here briefly. It is first necessary for the "educator" (the term Aichhorn used, along with "worker," to refer to what has since come to be called a "therapist" or a "counselor,") to draw the delinquent into a positive transference to him.[23] Briefly, this means that the youngster must be persuaded to trust, respect, and "like" the educator; positive transference is "the tender feeling for the teacher that gives the pupil the incentive to do what is prescribed and not to do what is forbidden."[24] In the language of other traditions, we might say that the educator must become a significant other or a positive-reference person for the delinquent. It is then possible, shifting back into Aichhorn's terminology, for the educator to provide those incentives to the renunciation of the pleasure principle that were not adequately provided by the parents. Thereby the educator aids the youngster in the development of ego controls and, hence, the avoidance of further delinquency. Also, once positive transference has been established, "the teacher . . . offers traits for identification that bring about a lasting change in the structure of the ego-ideal."[25] This strategy of rehabilitation for delinquents points to the essentially social nature of the Aichhorn formulation; his rehabilitation technique is presumably a technique of interpersonal influence, contingent upon the establishment of a positive bond between the educator and the youngster. How is it, then, that Aichhorn places so little emphasis upon interpersonal influences other than those of the parents in early childhood and of the educator in rehabilitation?

Why, for example, does he not give emphasis to the interpersonal peer influences impinging on the child in later childhood as affecting the process of becoming involved in delinquency or in avoiding such involvement? Aichhorn apparently recognized such influences, but he does not give them any prominent place in his scheme. Because of his overwhelming emphasis upon the crucial significance of events in early childhood, an emphasis stemming from Freud, Aichhorn assigned to peers an insignificant role in the etiology of delinquency. The early family experiences that forestalled the development of ego controls created a condition referred to as "latent delinquency"—a predisposition to delinquency.[26] However, Aichhorn explains that "this does not mean that every child so predisposed will become delinquent. Bad company, street influences, and the like, factors which are not the underlying causes of delinquency, but the direct or indirect provocation, also play a part."[27] At another point, he comments "we know that 'bad company' can influence a child toward delinquency, but it can be no more than a precipitating cause in a situation where the delinquency is latent."[28] Aichhorn was apparently led to introduce the concept of latent delinquency and considerations of "bad companions, street influences, and the like" from his observation that "thousands of other children grow up under the same unfavorable circumstances (overly strict or overly permissive family relations) and still are not delinquent."[29]

The concept of latent delinquency is an auxiliary hypothesis that provides a curious contrast to other features of Aichhorn's formulation. Discussing the failure to develop ego controls, Aichhorn indicates that the youngster fails to develop the *capacity* to control his or her pleasure impulses and hence must remain unsocialized and childish. But this is apparently not what Aichhorn intends us to understand. Rather, in view of his latent-delinquency concept, Aichhorn is suggesting that the failure to develop ego controls will still allow the child to exercise such controls, that is, to become "latent" rather than a "manifest" delinquent. Hence, the scientificability of Aichhorn's argument is considerably weakened by the latent-delinquency concept—strictly speaking, Aichhorn is *not* saying it is the absence of ego controls stemming from disrupted parent-child relations that leads to delinquent behavior; rather, these circumstances give rise to a predisposition to delinquency that may not be manifest at all—the ego may be functioning after all. Whether or not the delinquency becomes manifest, according to the implications of the latent-delinquency concept, depends upon the nature of other circumstances that are not fully specified but may include "bad companions, street influences, and the like."

Aichhorn weakens his theoretical formulation still further. The latent-delinquency concept suggests that the lack of parental love in early childhood and the proposed consequent lack of ego controls, should at least be a necessary condition for crime, even if not a sufficient condition. But Aichhorn's own analysis of cases suggests this is not the case. In his exploration of clinical cases, Aichhorn does not always interpret manifest delinquency as stemming from the absence of ego controls. By a *post facto* interpretation, delinquency is also attributed to "a neurotic basis."[30] "The psychic processes which determine behavior are not functioning harmoniously,"[31] that is, mental conflicts and "psychic traumas."[32] Aichhorn is not then presenting the absence of ego controls as a necessary condition for delinquency, as the concept of latent delinquency suggests. In his analysis of cases, he actually follows a procedure not unlike the multiple-factor approach commented on critically in Chapter 4; Aichhorn in fact suggests that "we must approach the situation without prejudice and preconceived ideas"[33]—the kind of nontheoretical, nonscientific approach presuming that cause can be intuitively perceived.

In spite of the logical difficulties in Aichhorn's formulation, and perhaps because of his lack of insistence on the universality of his theory, he has had many students and followers throughout Europe and the United States who have attempted to apply, extend, and elaborate the original formulation. The thread of continuity between Aichhorn and his followers in the psychiatric tradition lies primarily in the continued emphasis upon the "pathogenic significance . . . of faulty ego and superego development" and the implications of disturbed parent-child relationships. Building on the foundation provided by Aichhorn, new therapeutic approaches have been explored. The role of the father, especially in the etiology of male delinquency, has received greater attention than is found explicit in Aichhorn's work.[34] New sources of delinquency have been suggested, for example, the unconscious encouragement of misbehavior by parents.[35] As representative of those followers of Aichhorn who have elaborated and modified the perspective that he introduced, we shall consider briefly the work of Fritz Redl and David Wineman.

Redl and Wineman

Redl and Wineman acknowledge Aichhorn as the inspiration for their work. The emphasis continues to be on the failure to develop adequate ego and superego controls. Furthermore, the roots of these defects are located, as in Aichhorn, in defective parent-child relationships, especially relationships lacking in affection or characterized by negligence, rejection, or cruelty. Redl and Wineman have described in greater detail than others the meaning of "the ego that cannot perform," that is, specifically what the failure of ego controls implies. The following list is adapted from their longer and more fully elaborated list of behavioral manifestations of a "weak ego":

1. Low frustration tolerance; the child "breaks into disorganized confusion" when faced with even mild frustration.
2. Extreme reactions to fear and anxiety; the child takes flight or tears off "on a binge of general wild behavior and destruction" when faced with even mild fear situations.
3. Low "temptation resistance"; "even mild action potentials

along the line of mischief or delinquency are easily mobilized" in the child.

4. "Excitement contagion"; "exposure to almost any type of excitement is 'catching.'"
5. Lack of care of possessions; the youngsters "lose, destroy, mislay, break possessions."
6. Lack of realism in regard to rules and routines; rules "would be interpreted in a persecutional way."
7. Inability to "learn from experience"; failure to modify behavior that had previously led to "inconvenient consequences."
8. Excessive fear of failure; the child is so afraid of failing that he will "withdraw from some fields entirely, or develop terrific resistance against even 'trying' under the most favorable circumstances."
9. Unrestrained conceit after a "success"; eager to seek somebody less successful to mirror their own achievement, with "no restraints of tack left."
10. Giving up or attacking in the event of a mistake; the child reacts to criticism or a mistake by saying "What's the use?" or by acting in such a way that "the person who administers criticism immediately is pushed into the role of a hostile, mutilating, depreciating adult."[36]

Interestingly, although children with weak ego development apparently show numerous signs of lacking realism in their contacts with the world around them, this was not wholly true of their assessment of social reality, that is, their conceptions of how others feel about them and skill in "sizing up what 'goes' and what 'doesn't go' in a group of contemporaries." Redl and Wineman report that their weak-ego children "show an amazingly wide range of contrasting behavior along this line. Most of them show . . . amazing acuity of social perception in battle relevant areas," but simultaneously show "most severe disturbances of this same function in certain other areas, toward certain people, and under specific conditions."[37]

Such detailed descriptions as those supplied by Redl and Wineman are valuable in specifying the applicability limits of a theoretical formulation. All delinquents are not characterized by behaviors such as these, and there is no implication the theory should fit cases that cannot be so described—that delinquents with quite different behavioral characteristics should have experienced neglect, rejection, cruelty, or lack of affection when very young. These detailed theoretical formulations are attempts to explain the same behavioral phenomenon. We shall call attention later to certain similarities and differences between the description of delinquents by Redl and Wineman, Cohen, and Cloward and Ohlin, whose formulations point in different etiological directions.

A single theory may not explain all types of delinquency and crime but may pertain to a special type, identified by its characteristic behaviors. Detailed descriptions are valuable because they pinpoint ambiguity in theoretical concepts. Whereas the psychoanalytic literature typically characterizes the function of the ego as reality orientation, it is clear that the ego-weak children described by Redl and Wineman were quite selectively rather than generally lacking in reality orientation. It is clear, in other words, that these youngsters were sometimes quite discriminating in perceiving and acting upon social reality. This suggests the possibility that the syndrome of behavior symptoms alluded to is not well described, for it does not suggest a *general* lack of reality orientation, but only a highly selective lack. Such qualification calls into question a theory that explains a generally weak ego.

Redl and Wineman have, in most respects, retained the terminology and substantially the same theoretical assumptions as those elaborated by Aichhorn. But the term "delinquency" has acquired a more specific and restricted meaning in the work of Redl and Wineman. By their more detailed description of the behavior characteristics of the problem boys with whom they deal and about whom they write, Redl and Wineman have narrowed their scope to the type of delinquent that has been called an "unsocialized aggressive," in contrast to Aichhorn's attempt to encompass all delinquency within a psychoanalytic framework. It is characteristic of the psychiatric tradition generally to assume that criminal or dissocial acts represent a type of spontaneous and natural response to underlying emotional problems, that is, as responses that do not need to be learned. This assumption appears to be much more tenable with respect to the behavior of the unsocialized aggressive than with respect to crime in general.

Frustration-Instigated Behavior

To Aichhorn and his followers, the aggressiveness of criminal behavior is attributed to unrelieved frustrations in early childhood. Thus there is the postulation of a connection between frustration and aggression, but the point of Aichhorn's formulation is that these frustrations are inevitable in the process of becoming socialized. It is the failure of the parents to strike a suitable bargain with the child—to give affectionate attention and love in return for the child's renunciation of other impulses that are proposed as being responsible for delinquency. In some other formulations, still within the psychiatric tradition, a direct link is postulated between frustration and aggression. A wide variety of hostile and aggressive acts—including those involved in crime, delinquency, intergroup conflict, and war—have been interpreted as either a direct or a symbolic reaction to frustrations.[38]

Freudian theory suggests that considerations of propriety (operating through the individual's superego) may lead to the inhibition of an aggressive reaction toward the real or imagined source of frustration. In a roughly similar way, hostile and aggressive impulses not only may be inhibited but also may be "repressed" (removed from conscious awareness). However, although the aggressive reaction may be inhibited and hostile emotions repressed, the theory proposes that the aggressive "energy" generated by frustration is not thereby dissipated; rather, it remains temporarily latent and will eventually find expression in less-direct ways. It may be expressed, the theory suggests, in symbolic and nonthreatening ways against the real or imagined source of frustration; or it may be unconsciously displaced onto another person or object symbolic in some sense of the source of frustration. Thus, to reiterate an oft-repeated story, a man is severely frustrated by his employer but, not being able to "talk back," gripes at his wife when he comes home. The wife represses a hostile response to her husband and scolds her son instead. The boy inhibits his aggressive feelings toward his mother, but "takes it out" on the dog. The dog does not snap back at his master but vents his pent-up feelings on the cat who, having no inhibitions against reciprocating the aggression of the dog, hisses and scratches right back. Although this illustration indicates the general notion of displacement, it does not make clear the assumption that aggression is displaced onto other persons or objects that are in some sense *symbolic* of the source of frustration. Thus, it might be suggested that a mother—frustrated by a deserting husband—is more likely to "take it out" on a son, who resembles the father, than on a daughter, who does not. And, presumably, the child frustrated by his mother is more likely to be hostile toward his female teacher or other

female adults than toward his peers. However, the symbolism involved in displacement may be idiosyncratic, that is, a symbolic
resemblance unique to the individual himself or herself. Therefore, the nature of aggressive displacement generated by any particular type of frustrating source is neither explicit nor implicit in
psychiatric theory. And, because of the fundamental notion of the
theory is that the aggressive feelings and the whole process of displacement may be unconscious (and even characterized by "resistance" to self-recognition), direct empirical verification of such
processes is impossible.

Norman Maier—a psychologist who makes a distinction between motivated behavior and frustration-instigated behavior and
thereby departs from the underlying theoretical presuppositions of
Freud, Dollard, and others—maintains that the responses to frustration are varied. These responses commonly include nonaggres-
sive, although otherwise undesirable, symptoms:

> Thus, an insecure child may show regression through bed-wet-
> ting, speech defects, whining, excessive timidity, and non-construc-
> tive play. He may show aggression by stealing, excessive fighting
> with other children, destructiveness of property, destructive play,
> and associating with rough gangs. He may have personality traits
> that are characterized by such terms as negativism, selfishness, an-
> tagonism, and uncooperativeness. The presence of behavior fixa-
> tions would be indicated if he showed repetitive action such as
> thumbsucking, nail biting, compulsive stealing, phobias, and ste-
> reotyped reactions in any of the behaviors listed as regressive or
> aggressive. Finally, resignation would be indicated by a marked
> tendency to withdraw from the group, being uncommunicative, and
> lacking interest in the surroundings.
>
> All these classes of behavior have a common cause and a common
> remedy. A given frustrated child might show any combination of
> these traits, but so long as the traits fall within the scope of the
> frustration process, the pattern expressed is of secondary impor-
> tance. If this is the case, it means that in therapy attention should
> be directed from the symptoms and what they mean to search for
> the sources of frustration.[39]

This latter view—the nonspecificity of the response to frustration
(except that the response is some kind of "behavior problem")—is
apparently more common than the frustration-aggression hypothesis among psychiatrically oriented correctional workers and researchers in the field of crime. For example, in their study com-

paring delinquent with nondelinquent siblings, Healy and Bronner stressed their finding that almost all of the delinquent siblings felt thwarted and rejected. The behavioral manifestations traced to such frustrations, however, were diverse and included withdrawal and other behavior problems as well as "aggression."[40]

At least one proponent of the proposition that frustration contributes to involvement in delinquency and crime presents his formulations with extreme caution and specifically suggests that frustration constitutes only part of the process of becoming delinquent. Leonard Berkowitz suggests:

> The thwarted person may have learned other, non-aggressive modes of response which inhibit illegal hostile actions. Before we can predict the likelihood of anti-social aggression, we have to know (1) whether the individual blames people other than himself for the frustration, (2) the extent to which his hostile behavior has been reinforced in the past by parents and/or peers, (3) the particular forms of aggression that had been reinforced most frequently, and (4) the extent to which he has interiorized moral standards opposing anti-social conduct. Frustrations are important in the development of delinquency and criminality but are not the sufficient cause of such behavior.[41]

The same writer specifically recognizes the necessity of social support for continued involvement in crime and delinquency: "Unless a person is extremely susceptible to intense emotional arousal and possesses unusually weak inner controls, he will not engage in recurrent criminality without the approval of some friends and associates."[42]

Interestingly, Berkowitz provides an interpretation for the behavior of the "unsocialized aggressive" delinquent that differs theoretically, though not empirically, from the formulation stemming from Aichhorn and currently represented by Redl and Wineman and Samenow. Berkowitz suggests that, unlike older boys who experience frustrations and subsequently direct their aggressions (directly, indirectly, or symbolically) toward the perceived source of frustration, "The boy who has been exposed to severe parental rejection in early childhood, on the other hand, may generalize his feelings beyond his parents to many other people including his peers. In a sense, he does not differentiate too well among the people around him; all are frustraters (real or potential) and all are not to be trusted."[43]

Thus, the more-generalized aggressive response of this special type of delinquent is attributed not to the absence of all ego controls, but to the inability of this child to differentiate between people at the time when severe frustrations were experienced. Berkowitz carries his description further:

> The rejected child has not obtained the love and protection he desired from his mother and father. . . . He wanted to be cared for by them but, instead, received only harsh rebuffs. Growing up not trusting and even fearing his parents, he regards everyone around him as a potential frustrater. The boy then goes out into the streets and to school with a 'chip on his shoulder.' He expects unfriendliness from others and this is what he frequently gets. If he becomes a delinquent or criminal, he will be an unsocialized or individual offender rather than a socialized gang member.[44]

Berkowitz asserts, however, that "the frequently thwarted individual does not possess a life-long-accumulated pool of aggressive energy. . . . Rather . . . his past history of frustrations increases his sensitivity to further deprivations. He is quick to perceive thwartings, perhaps even when other people would not see them."[45] By incorporating cognitive variability into his frustration-aggression formulation, with respect both to the failure of the very young child to differentiate between persons and to the increased cognitive sensitivity to frustration as a consequence of repeated frustration, Berkowitz presents a theoretical explanation for the behavior of the unsocialized aggressive delinquent that differs notably from that of Aichhorn in suggesting that such children also fail to develop strong "ego controls."[46] But this appears to be an incidental part of his formulation. It should be noted that Berkowitz' discussion of crime and delinquency is not limited to the unsocialized aggressive. His general frustration-aggression formulation encompasses frustrations other than those imposed within the family in early childhood. In fact, he specifically mentions "culturally induced frustrations"[47] and takes note of the frustration aspects of the formulations of Merton and Cohen[48] (see Chapter 9).

Berkowitz recognizes that some aggression is learned and instrumental. Maier conceptualizes essentially the same distinction in terms of motivated behavior and frustration-instigated behavior, a distinction that can best be described here by considering two contrasting cases from his discussion:

> A five-year-old child is found to be taking keys whenever he can find them. At first he does this openly. When his actions meet with

disapproval, however, keys continue to disappear, but now they are more difficult to recover—some were not recovered until after the behavior was corrected. After 9 months this behavior is sufficiently troublesome to warrant special consideration.

Since the stealing is primarily confined to appropriating specific objects and there are not characteristic signs of frustration, the behavior appears to be a problem in motivation. The child just needs keys very badly. In the light of this interpretation, it was recommended that the child be given a large set of keys for his very own . . . a ring of keys was obtained and the child was delighted. He now preferred his own keys to those of other people and he never again molested the keys of others. . . . He used his keys to turn an imaginary lock on his tricycle, just the way his daddy did with his car.

In contrast, let us take the twelve-year-old boy who is frequently reported for stealing in school. He has been lectured and punished by the parents (including severe whippings) but the behavior continues. The parents have done their best and are at their wits' end. Signs of frustration also are present. The child is uncooperative and uncommunicative. He lies to escape punishment, does poor work in school, and has undesirable companions. His younger sister, however, is a joy to the parents. She offers no behavior problems, does good work in school, is frequently praised, and is held up to the boy as an example. One might say she has earned the privilege of being both father's and mother's pet. In this case, the parents' behavior rather than the boy's seemed to require correction because their behavior was creating a frustrating situation. To win the parents' cooperation, the boy's side of the question was presented. The father recognized that he had a preference for the daughter. He set out to correct things. Much was made of the male side of the family. The father took the boy for walks, fishing trips, etc. Gradually the boy began to respond to his father as a companion and together they discussed questions of mutual interest. At no time, however, were morals or stealing discussed or mentioned. Nevertheless, stealing almost immediately disappeared, grades in school improved, and the boy spent much more time at home working on constructive projects.[49]

In general, Maier suggests two types of delinquency—motivated (instrumental or goal directed) and frustration instigated (an end in itself)—"any satisfaction that occurs may be in the form of relief, not in the form of consummation."[50] Unfortunately, Maier has not provided unambiguous behavioral clues to differentiate the two types. His suggestions for this include (1) the presence or absence of other symptoms of frustration (regression, hostility, fixation, resignation, and so forth) and (2) the success or failure of reward and punishment in modifying the behavior.[51] In addition to recognizing non–frustration-instigated delinquency (instrumental delinquency), Maier also explicitly notes that "all frustration-instigated behavior is not delinquent."[52]

The general view that frustration-instigated behavior includes criminal or delinquent acts provides an added perspective to Aichhorn's formulation. The general frustration hypothesis does not locate the source of crime necessarily in the early years of childhood. The general view also provides a perspective that has been incorporated in somewhat different ways into sociological formulations—most notably those of Cohen and of Cloward and Ohlin (see Chapter 9). However, the very generality of the basic concepts of frustration and aggression decreases the value of such a broad formulation as a theoretical explanation for crime. Furthermore, once it is recognized that the response to frustration may take several forms, it is not sufficient to point out that criminals are frustrated (who is not?); it is also necessary to specify why some people respond in a criminal way to their frustrations.

The frustration-aggression theory manifests a tendency characteristic of psychiatric explanations of crime and delinquency to resort, in the last analysis, to a multiple-factor approach. The work of David Abrahamsen exemplifies this tradition. Abrahamsen maintains that crime is the result of multiple factors that can be summarized in two "laws":[53]

1. A person's inherited characteristics set the limits on what a person can do and the environment determines what and how he or she will do it.
2. Criminal behavior is the sum of a person's criminal tendencies (T) plus the person's total situation (S) divided by his or her resistance (R) to criminality.

$$\text{Criminal Behavior} = \frac{T+S}{R}$$

If you were to substitute *any* behavior for "criminal" in these two "laws," we would have as adequate an explanation for any other behavior as we have for crime. For example,

> Political behavior is the sum of a person's political tendencies (PT) plus the person's total situations (S) divided by his or her resistance to political behavior.

$$\text{Political Behavior} = \frac{PT + S}{R}$$

Any behavior can thus be "explained." The problem with such a formulation is that, because it explains "everything," it explains nothing. Obviously, the theorist or researcher can plug into the equation anything he or she wants as "criminal," "political tendencies," "total situations," and "resistance." Theories such as this are logically more akin to the theories of why some people are rich and some poor (see Chapter 4). Then they are adequate scientific explanations.

Criminal Mind

A variation on psychiatric theory that persists, despite an overwhelming amount of evidence contradicting it, is the theory that criminals and noncriminals possess different personalities. The most recent and currently most influential statements of this position are found in works by Yochelson and Samenow.[54] Based upon 15 years of research in a mental hospital, Yochelson and Samenow, "abandoned the search for causes, discarded mental illness as a factor in criminality, threw out psychologic and sociologic excuses"[55] and dealt instead with what they call the "criminal mind." The criminal mind, according to the authors, is one that (1) thinks concretely rather than conceptually; (2) compartmentalizes life "almost beyond [the therapist's] comprehension"; (3) simultaneously expresses extreme sentimentality and extreme brutality; (4) creates its own reality, which is abnormal though not psychotic; and (5) does not sustain feelings of guilt sufficient to act as a brake on impulsive behavior.[56]

It is of course impossible to survey all incidences of criminality. In this way, all research findings are tentative because they are based upon a sample rather than the entire universe. Some samples, however, are so biased that the results are immediately suspect. Yochelson and Samenow generalize on the basis of intensive experience with inmates in a mental hospital who have committed crimes. The discovery of a criminal personality among such a unique subset of the total population of people who commit crime hardly justifies generalization. Not only are the people studied unique, but also other research shows that the fact they have been institutionalized in a mental hospital affects their view of the world and their personality.[57]

There has been a great deal of research comparing criminal and noncriminal responses to personality measures. Without exception, these researches show no significant differences in the personalities of criminals and noncriminals when the bias of the investigator is controlled.[58]

We need only recall the varieties of criminality outlined in the first three chapters to realize the futility inherent in efforts to discover a criminal personality. It would be miraculous if General Electric, Ford Motor Company, or factory owners found guilty of manslaughter for violating safety and health regulations, or the millions of college and high-school students who consume illegal drugs were all found to possess a criminal personality.

This is not to say that involvement in different types of crime may not result in differences in world views and perceptions. Indeed, a consistent finding in sociological research is the way that the work we do influences our world view and thus our personality. A recent work by Malin Akerstrom provides considerable insight by examining the similarity in attitudes and values of businesspeople and professional thieves.[59] This approach, however, is not confined to the assumption of across-the-board personality differences between criminals and noncriminals. Rather, it is a search for similarities and differences to be found by comparing people involved in different occupations and lifestyles.

The failure to discover any discernible differences between criminal and noncriminal personalities does not apparently affect those who say that such a difference should or must exist. As Jerome Miller observes, "The inadequate attempts to update the search of 'criminal man' . . . suggest that perhaps we are asking the wrong questions. The research gets hazier, less reliable, more unscientific, and more ideological, even as our sophistication in scientific method grows."[60]

Conclusion

The psychiatric tradition is distinguished by its conception of criminal behavior as unlearned, spontaneous, and stemming from early childhood experiences. It is also characterized by an emphasis on the family. More than other theoretical paradigms, the psychiatric tradition focuses on psychic forces and mental processes operating within the individual, rather than on interpersonal influence, culturally prescribed behavior patterns, and socially imposed control. Finally, the psychiatric tradition stresses, to a greater extent than other theories, the potential therapeutic value of individual counseling and psychotherapy, that is, of treating individuals and their families.[61] Two of the formulations discussed here—the Aichhorn formulation and the hypothesis of frustration-instigated delinquency—illustrate these characteristics of the psychiatric tradition only in their relative emphasis on these points; none of the writers represented in the preceding discussion completely overlooks the possibility that, for example, criminal behavior may be learned from associates or crime may be affected by socially imposed controls.

We have not, of course, been able to present in this brief discussion an exhaustive account of all psychiatric formulations in the literature of crime. Those presented have been selected first because of their widespread acceptance among psychiatrically oriented researchers and correctional workers in the field, and second because of their broad influence among those, like social caseworkers, who are not specialists but who must work with people accused of criminal and delinquent acts. Psychiatric theory provides a framework for the clinical practitioner that may be empirically false but organizationally useful. The optimism inherent in this approach is supported by case histories selected by those who practice the art, but faith in such a flexible, encompassing framework can not be shaken by these evaluations. While the flexibility, ambiguity, and ready availability of auxiliary interpretations that characterize the psychiatric perspective have made this approach attractive to many, these same characteristics render it, at best, incomplete as a scientific explanation and hazy with regard to implications for social change.

The clinician, the therapist, the counselor, and other clinical practitioners do not ordinarily see criminals or delinquents on the streets, but in a prison, clinic, or training-school setting. He or she does not ordinarily hear the everyday conversations of thieves, white-collar criminals, or drug addicts, but hears instead their most introspective views of themselves and of their world when they are urged by probing questions to reveal their innermost thoughts and feelings. Clinical practitioners see, in other words, a very restricted segment of the criminal world, but they see that segment very intensively. Unfortunately, because of the nature of their professional responsibilities, all too often they do not study noncriminal populations and compare them with anything except a stereotyped view of the "normal personality." One of the perplexing questions posed by clinical observations in theory building is the degree to which noncriminals, if examined in a similar way with equal intensity, would reveal in their innermost thoughts and feelings the same frustrations, struggles with guilt and jealousy, emotional tangles and personality configurations that are found among criminals. The question, then, is not simply what problems criminals face—because noncriminals face problems, too. The question is, do some people resolve their problems in criminal ways while others resolve them noncriminally?

For the purposes of developing general theories of crime, the psychiatric paradigm leaves much to be desired. In practically every attempt to construct a general explanation of why people commit criminal or delinquent acts, the psychiatric approach introduces tautologies and auxiliary hypotheses that limit the utility of the theory.

9

Social-Psychological Theories

For centuries, criminologists have searched for biological or psychological characteristics that differentiate people who commit crime from those who do not. The assumption of this line of reasoning is that, if differences can be discovered, we will also discover the cause of crime. Literally thousands of researches spanning over 200 years have consistently failed to discover significant differences between criminals and noncriminals in any personality, biological, anatomical, or psychological constellation of traits.

With hindsight to improve our vision, the reason for the failure of this search is as obvious as is the fact that one cannot produce gold from lead. Criminal behavior is not a characteristic of individuals; it is a legal category created by others and attached to particular types of behavior. The alchemists had a theory that all material substances were reducible to gold. That theory was wrong. Those who search for biological, psychological, or anatomical characteristics of criminals have a theory that there is a difference between criminals and noncriminals other than the criminal behavior itself. That assumption is as wrong as the alchemists'. There are two reasons for this. First, as previously mentioned, crime is a legal category imposed by the state onto the behavior of individuals. It is illogical to suppose that, simply because one group says the behavior of another group is criminal, that the group labeled criminal will possess a unique personality, biology, or anatomy. The government today also defines what is a legally binding contract, but we do not set about searching for differences in the personality or biology of people who engage in contracts. It would be a miraculous coincidence if the state inadvertently defined as criminal acts that were committed only by people with some unique biology, personality, or anatomy. Indeed, if that did happen, the most interesting scientific puzzle would be to explain how the state managed such a feat. If the other sciences accepted a definition generated by legislators and, therefore, determined by the political process in which different interests, power relations, and economic considerations dictated the outcome of that definition, no one would then propose to discover the properties of that defined thing. Yet, in criminology, those who seek biological and psychological explanations of criminal behavior are doing just this.

The second fallacy of these theories is that they assume what is demonstrably false: that some people commit crime and others do not. As the facts presented in the preceding chapters make abundantly clear, everyone commits some sort of crime. As Schwendinger and Schwendinger point out, when self-report studies "uncovered an unexpected amount of middle-class delinquency," criminology was thrown into "crisis."[1] It was not just the discovery of middle-class delinquency that caused the crisis for behavioral theories; it was also the middle- and upper-class criminality of businessmen and politicians, the income-tax crimes of untold millions of middle- and upper-class taxpayers, the spouse abuse of men and women, the date rapes perpetrated by college men, the crimes of the state, the widespread violation of laws prohibiting the possession and consumption of drugs such as marijuana, cocaine and amphetamines; the legal restrictions on consuming untaxed liquor that generates a multi-million dollar business in bootleg and blackmarket alcohol; it is the common practice of driving while under the influence of alcohol. These and hundreds of other acts render behavioral theories incapable of generating valid scientific knowledge because they start from false premises.

Another major shortcoming of biological and psychological paradigms is that they are conspicuously silent and, at times, blatantly sexist in regard to the question of women and crime.[2] In the modern world, women of all ages are less likely than men to be arrested for criminal acts. These theories often end by trying to explain this by reference to women's "more-passive" biological nature, their inherent tendencies to be "less aggressive," and their socialization into roles that emphasize socio-emotional behavior. This logic has led some sociologists to suggest that the increasing influence of the women's movement accounts for an increase in the criminality among women.[3] There is reason to doubt the reliability of arrest rates. Research on juvenile gangs reveals widespread delinquency among young women attached to delinquent gangs.[4] Shoplifting is fairly commonplace, and women account for a disproportionate number of the offenders; Horwitz found in a survey of 335 women in Delaware (see Table 9.1) that 30 percent admitted to having shoplifted one or more times.[5] The criminality of women is not limited to crimes against property. In the 18th century, two of the most famous and successful pirates of the Carribean—whose criminality involved murder, assault, and plunder on a scale rarely documented in the annals of criminality—were

TABLE 9.1 Self-Reported Frequency of Shoplifting Among Adult Women Who Admit Shoplifting at Least Once

Frequency of Shoplifting	Percent	Number
Once	42.3	41
2–3 times	29.9	29
4–6 times	15.5	15
7–10 times	5.2	5
11–15 times	3.1	3
More than 15 times	4.1	4
	100.0	97

Source: Caryn B. Horowitz. (1986). "Factors influencing shoplifting activity among adult women." Unpublished Ph.D. dissertation, University of Delaware.

women.[6] Women, then, are criminal often enough to disprove any biological or psychological theory that claims male characteristics account for criminality. Nonetheless, their lower rate of criminality must still be explained.

Theoretical Developments

Deficiencies in the biological and psychological paradigms lead most criminologists to favor theories that stress a social dimension as the cause of criminal behavior. The most respected theorists of the early 20th century, Willem Bonger, Edwin Sutherland, Robert Merton, Frank Tannenbaum, and Thorsten Sellin, developed their paradigms in response to the inadequacies of the prevailing ones. They assumed that the explanation of why some people commit crime and others do not lay in the social experiences of the individual, not in his or her biological or psychological makeup.

The most influential social-psychological theory of crime for the last 50 years—the differential association theory—was proposed in 1928 by Edwin H. Sutherland. The essence of the theory is found in the name; it means that the degree to which a person associates with criminal or noncriminal behavior patterns is at the root of criminal behavior.

Differential Association Theory

Sutherland's starting point was a conflict orientation to society. He conceived of society as made up of different groups and social classes who believed in and adhered to very different beliefs about what was right and wrong. As a result, Sutherland argued, people were exposed to a variety of behavior patterns. Some of these patterns were criminal, some noncriminal. As a general principle, Sutherland theorized that, if a person associated more with attitudes and behaviors favorable to the violation of law than with attitudes and patterns unfavorable to the violation of law, he or she would be more likely to commit criminal acts than a person whose associations were the reverse: "Criminal behavior is learned in association with those who define such behavior favorably and in isolation from those who definite it unfavorably . . . a person in an appropriate situation engages in such criminal behavior if, and only if, the weight of the favorable definitions exceeds the weight of the unfavorable definitions."[7]

Schematically, the theory may be summarized as a ratio between associations with attitudes favorable and unfavorable to the violation of criminal law:

$$\frac{\text{Procriminal Attitudes}}{\text{Anticriminal Attitudes}}$$

Sutherland elaborated the theory by noting that not all associations with either criminal or anticriminal attitudes are equally influential. He suggested that associations varied according to priority, duration, frequency, and intensity. Priority is defined in terms of how early in life the associations occur; duration refers to how long a period is involved; frequency is how often the associations occur; and intensity, in Sutherland's words, "has to do with the prestige of the source of a criminal or anti-criminal pattern and with the emotional reactions related to the association."[8]

Viewed from the standpoint of the criteria specified in Chapter 4, differential-association theory meets several of the criteria for good scientific theory. It is parsimonious; that is, the theory succinctly states and proposes to explain a wide range of behaviors in a single, straightforward generalization. It is very general and seeks to account for "all criminal behavior." It is amenable to empirical investigation and, we shall see, has generated more empirical research than any other single theory in criminology. Because it proposes a set of propositions that can, at least in principle, be operationalized so that we can look at real events and experiences to see whether or not the theory is correct, it is capable of empirical verification. The ultimate question that the theory must face, then, is that of its empirical validity: Do the facts we know about crime and criminal behavior fit the theory?

Testing Differential Association Theory

Most of the research that tests the theory employs questionnaires and surveys. The typical research method is to distribute questionnaires to two groups of juveniles, one incarcerated, the other enrolled in school. The questionnaires consist of questions asking each respondent to indicate whether or not they have engaged in acts defined as criminal and associated with other people who engaged in acts defined as criminal.

One of the earliest studies employing the method of self-reported delinquency was conducted by James F. Short, Jr.[9] Short administered questionnaires to a group of high-school students and a group of youths in a detention center for juvenile deliquents. He asked the respondents if they had (1) committed any of a list of acts defined as delinquent and (2) if they "ran around" with friends who committed delinquent acts. Short found a correlation between having delinquent friends and committing delinquent acts. The correlation was highest for girls 16 to 17 years old who were in the detention center (.606); it was next highest for boys 16–17 years old who were in the detention center (.581). For boys under 15 years old, the correlation was only .355. Short did not report the correlation for younger girls.

By social-science standards, these correlations are relatively high. They are statistically significant; we would not by chance expect to find correlations of this magnitude if there was not a similar relationship in the entire population from which the samples were drawn. These correlations do not mean that there is any causal relationship. This kind of theory test applies the logic of the negative: If we fail to find a correlation, then the causal claims of the theory are disproved. If we find a correlation, there may be other explanations for it. In other words, finding a correlation is a necessary implication of the theory, but it is not sufficient to rule out the possibility that something else underlies the finding.

Then, too, with a single research there is always the question of whether subsequent findings will confirm the original ones.

In the 1960s, Gary Jensen utilized the findings of the Richmond Youth Study conducted in California to further test the differential-association theory. In the fall of 1964, 17,500 students entering junior- and senior-high schools were administered questionnaires. This sample represented a much larger survey and relied on more-sophisticated questionnaires than Short's study. Jensen studied the responses of 1,588 nonblack males who were given the questionnaires. Respondents were asked whether they had ever committed selected acts of delinquency and, if so, how often. They were also asked if they associated with people who had committed delinquent acts or had attitudes favorable to criminality. Jensen found that 20 percent of the respondents with no delinquent friends had nonetheless committed one or more delinquent acts. In addition, other measures of association with attitudes unfavorable to crime yielded the same finding; significant numbers of people with little or no association committed delinquent acts.[10]

Using the same data base, Travis Hirschi measured the intensity of associations by developing an index of the person's attachment to people with attitudes favorable or unfavorable to criminality.[11] Hirschi's interpretation of his findings is exactly the reverse of what the differential association theory would lead us to expect: He found that the more intense the relationship a boy had with friends who were delinquent, the less likely he was to engage in delinquency.

A recent re-analysis of the Richmond Youth Survey by Matsueda comes to a different conclusion.[12] Matsueda argues that the Jensen and Hirschi tests were inadequate because they failed to control for association with criminal attitudes but inferred attitudes from association with people who engaged in criminal behavior. As Matsueda points out, simply counting friends is a rather crude way of testing for associations with criminal behavior patterns. Also, Matsueda added a more sensitive measure of delinquency by relating the degree of involvement with the association with attitudes.

Matsueda utilized techniques enabling him to control measurement errors that were not controlled in the Jensen and Hirschi studies. These techniques provided evidence that the ratio of attitudes favorable to delinquency compared to attitudes unfavorable to delinquency was the variable most highly correlated with delinquent involvement. Matsueda concludes, "tests of the specific hypotheses formulated here confirm the theory of differential association."[13]

Questionnaire Studies

There are numerous serious problems with researches that purport to test social-psychological theories of criminal behavior by employing questionnaires. These questionnaires account, in part, for the contradictory findings of various studies. As with most social science research, researches take "a short cut in data collection and base their methods on individuals reports of their own behavior" rather than on observations or objective measures of the person's behavior.[14] How much confidence can we have that a person will respond truthfully to a questionnaire asking if he or she has committed criminal acts? Certainly we can presume that, even under the promise of anonymity, high-school students might well be reticent to admit serious criminal acts.

Perhaps more limiting is the fact that these studies presume to test a hypothesized causal process by examining the correlation between current associations and past behavior. This is just the reverse of the direction the theory proposes. It is quite possible that persons who have engaged in delinquency and been caught will then seek friends and associations with attitudes favorable to the commission of delinquent acts.[15]

Furthermore, the distinction between delinquent and nondelinquent is an arbitrary one in these studies. Because almost all of the respondents admit to involvement in some delinquency, the studies do not, in fact, have a sample of nondelinquents with which to compare the delinquent sample. The self-report studies thus end by comparing people who are "more delinquent" (as measured by those who admitted delinquencies on questionnaires or those who were incarcerated in detention centers) with people who admit fewer delinquencies or are not incarcerated. Thus, these studies do not represent a test of a difference between delinquents and nondelinquents at all. What differences, in association with delinquent attitudes, that are discovered between the groups compared in these studies is more likely a consequence of the arbitrary definition used to distinguish between delinquents and nondelinquents. For example, it may be that those youths most likely to be apprehended and sentenced to a detention center are the ones perceived by the police and social-welfare workers as associating with "bad company." And it is a reasonable assumption that those youths who admit to greater involvement in delinquency are those who see themselves and their friends as "delinquent."

A participant-observation study of a middle- and lower-class delinquent gangs found that—although the real incidence of delinquency and the seriousness of the delinquencies were the same for the two gangs—the lower-class gang members were much more likely to be arrested and thought of themselves and one another as "delinquent," while the middle-class gang members were perceived by themselves and by others as being "good boys" who were in no way "delinquent."[16] Had questionnaires been given to the boys in these two gangs, the lower-class gang members would very likely have responded that most of their friends were delinquent and that they frequently and intensely associated with attitudes favorable to the commission of criminal acts. The middle-class gang members, however, because they did not define their own acts as delinquent (even though they were not only delinquent but also extremely harmful to others), would have responded that their friends were not delinquent and that they did not associate with attitudes favorable to the commission of criminal acts. The extensive study of delinquent gangs in Los Angeles by Schwendinger and Schwendinger also provides evidence that these differences are determined by the way the gang members and their friends are perceived rather than by the real involvement in delinquent activities.[17]

Differential Association and Adult Criminality

In a classic study of drug addiction, Alfred R. Lindesmith found that people became addicted to opiates (especially heroin) if they went through a specific process (see Chapter 5).[18]

Lindesmith employed the research technique known in sociology as "analytic induction." The essence of this method is that the researcher gathers data and develops generalizations to fit the data in hand, modifying the theory to incorporate any new data that contradict the working hypothesis. Eventually the researcher is satisfied that enough cases not requiring modification have been explored and the findings are then ready for publication and further research. Lindesmith documented the fact that the drug users in his sample were "hooked" once they underwent the process he describes. He also reported that a review of the literature (including autobiographies of drug users) failed to turn up anyone who reported kicking the habit once the cycle of addiction was completed.[19]

The process described did not involve association with attitudes favorable to the violation of criminal law or, for that matter, an attitudinal change. Lindesmith reported cases of people addicted to opiates who were administered the drugs in a hospital following an accident or illness. The addiction was not the result of any association with attitudes favoring criminality. Many of the addicts were advocates of anticriminal attitudes before and after addiction. The addiction that led to the criminality was, in some cases, quite accidental. These findings are inconsistent with what we would expect from differential association theory. In addition, the fact that the occupational groups with the highest rates of opiate addiction are medical doctors and pharmacists—occupational groups that certainly have their share of criminality but whose members, one assumes, do not associate with more criminal than anticriminal behavioral attitudes—would seem also to contradict the theory.

Donald Cressey's study of the process by which some people come to embezzle utilized the same research techniques as Lindesmith's study.[20] His findings also contradict differential association theory. Based upon the analysis of the case histories of 133 embezzlers, Cressey concluded that people who embezzled have a nonshareable financial problem that they realize can be solved by embezzling. The person then develops a rationalization that justifies the embezzlement while in a position of trust, which includes knowing how to embezzle.

The possession of a "nonshareable financial problem" suggests a lack of communication and intimacy with others who might communicate "attitudes favorable to criminality." It is possible, however, as Cressey argues, that the association with attitudes favorable to committing crime exceeds the association with attitudes unfavorable to committing crime through secondary sources such as books, television, films, and newspapers. This argument weakens the theory's scientific utility considerably. It is difficult to imagine a case in which it cannot be argued that someone was exposed to procriminal behavior patterns through secondary sources. As a result, any data that contradicts the theory can be explained by attributing an unknown quantity of exposure to media or to unknown, even imaginary, people providing attitudes favorable to committing crime. In an extreme form of this argument, if someone sees a Charles Bronson or Clint Eastwood film that glorifies criminality, it can always be argued ex post facto that the experience was so intense that this association overwhelmed all previous anticriminal associations. A theory with such a catchall logic is no theory at all. Clearly everyone, even monks in monasteries, associates with some procriminal attitudes. Without a clearer specification of what the associations must involve, the theory explains nothing.[21]

In a study of shoplifting, Mary Beth Cameron observed and interviewed women shoplifters in Chicago and Indianapolis. She found two types of shoplifters: boosters and snitches.[22] Boosters were professionals whose livelihood depended upon shoplifting. Snitches were mainly women who supplemented the family budget by engaging in the "five-finger discount" from time to time. Cameron found no evidence that the snitches ever communicated with anyone about their shoplifting or that they ever associated with others who were shoplifters or who expressed attitudes favorable to shoplifting or any other criminal acts. In fact, Cameron found that when snitches were caught and realized their shoplifting might be found out by others, they stopped shoplifting.

Research on corruption does not confirm the differential association theory. Case histories of politicians and policeofficers who accept bribes document a process of involvement that is often a matter of the person coming to realize that corruption is the only way to be successful. Etzioni's insightful study of the corruption rampant in political-campaign contributions documents how success and failure as a politician depends upon the willingness to accept illegal contributions.[23] A study of political and law-enforcement corruption in Seattle reports a case of a politician who had, until the waning days of a campaign for U.S. Congress, steadfastly refused to accept illegal campaign contributions. When he realized, however, that a $50,000 illegal contribution was likely to make the difference between winning and losing the election, he succumbed.[24] Similar case histories appear in studies of municipal and law-enforcement corruption; all of these make the differential association theory untenable.[25]

There are scores of well-documented cases of criminal acts committed by persons whose biographies contradict the differential association theory. A case in point is Lowell Lee Andrews, an 18-year-old, 300-pound honors student at Kansas University, who one day came home from school and shot his mother, father, and sister. After he killed them, he set fire to the house to make it look like that was the cause of the deaths. He drove back to school and tried to fix an alibi by being seen at his rooming house and a movie theater. Under interrogation, he confessed to the murder and was executed after a trial at which teachers and life-long acquaintances testified that Lowell was a religious, studious, responsible boy who was never in any kind of trouble. Testimony suggested that the principal identifying quality of Lowell was that he was a loner who read incessantly and was highly intellectual. The writer Truman Capote, who interviewed Lowell Lee while he awaited execution, described another facet of Lowell's character that acquaintances, relatives, and teachers did not see: "the secret Lowell Lee, the one concealed inside the churchgoing, biology student, fancied himself an ice hearted master criminal: he wanted to wear garish silk shirts and drive scarlet sports cars; he wanted to be recognized as no mere bespectacled, bookish, overweight, virginal schoolboy; and while he did not dislike any member of his family, at least not consciously, murdering them seemed the swiftest, most sensible way of implementing the fantasies that possessed him."[26]

Another case concerns a man named Charles Griffith and his daughter, who was injured in a freak accident when she was 1 year old. For 2 years, she lay comatose, unresponsive to touch or sound. She suffered irreversible brain damage. Until the accident, Griffith said "She never had her heart broken. All she knew was laughter and good times. And now she just lies there. She just lies there." Griffith visited his daughter in the hospital every day. Then, on June 19, 1985, at 9:00 P.M., he sat beside her bed for 2 hours before pulling a pistol from his pocket and shooting her twice in the heart. He immediately surrendered to the police.[27]

Charles Griffith committed first-degree murder. Others, faced with suffering relatives, children, or spouses, do the same thing. Some receive lengthy prison sentences; others are slapped on the wrist. They all commit criminal acts. To explain these acts by differential association is to create a land of the Mad Hatter in which words mean whatever we want them to mean and bear no resemblance to commonsense.

Stuart Palmer's research on murderers, which involved extensive interviews with persons convicted and sentenced to prison, revealed that these law violators were no more likely than the general public to have associated with attitudes favorable to the violation of criminal law.[28]

Literally thousands of cases that contradict the theory could be cited. One more will provide an example from a different sort of crime. An FBI agent named Richard Miller was arrested and accused of spying. In interviews after his arrest, he confessed to a number of petty crimes from stealing candy bars to selling products taken from a relative.[29] Nowhere in Miller's background was there the slightest hint of associations with attitudes favorable to crime. He graduated from Brigham Young University and was recruited by the FBI because he had a "clean background" and was committed to religion and conservative political ideologies. He was a reliable and respected FBI agent for 20 years prior to his arrest. Again, to see this case as supporting the differential association theory stretches the meaning of an explanation beyond sensibility.

Finally, the differential association theory cannot account for the fact that most people who are involved in crime as a major part of their lives at one point in time become less involved as they grow older. This applies to juvenile delinquents, who have peak years of law violation between 15 and 24, but most of them reduce their involvement in criminality after these years. Some cease it entirely. Harry King spent 45 years as a professional thief (known among thieves as a "boxman") specializing in safecracking. At age 60, however, when he was released from an Oregon prison after serving a 5-year sentence, he decided to quit his life of crime. He went straight until his death 5 years later. But he never renounced the values and attitudes that made him a thief; he always defended the integrity of the thief's culture and way of life and condemned the hypocrisy of a society that proclaimed honesty while judges and police held out their hands for bribes. Only his criminality changed, not his attitude. To the degree that his associations changed, they did so after he decided to stop committing crimes, not before.[30]

Differential Identification and Reinforcement Theory

Recognizing the logical and empirical problems of the differential association theory prompted the development of variations. Daniel Glaser suggested substituting "differential identification" for differential association.[31] Glaser's argument is that it is the degree to which people identify with criminal or noncriminal behavior patterns that determines whether or not they will commit criminal acts, even though they may not associate more with one than the other. The argument has the merit of linking criminal theory to an impressive body of social-psychological theory stemming from the symbolic-interactionist paradigm; it fails, however, to account for criminal behavior any better than differential association. The previously cited cases—for example, the mercy killing and the decision of a criminally involved person to change his life to a noncriminal one—are as incompatible with the idea of differential identification as they are with differential association.

C. Ray Jeffrey—borrowing from the psychology paradigm variously known as reinforcement, operant conditioning, and behavior modification—postulated that a person became criminal when he or she was reinforced more often for criminal than for noncriminal behavior.[32] Gordon Trasler, Hans Eysenck, Robert Burgess, and Ronald Akers each developed the application of this paradigm to criminology. Akers' theory was typical of the entire school, but it was unique in that it linked reinforcement theory to differential association; he called his theory differential reinforcement. People commit crime, Akers postulated, when criminal acts are reinforced and they cease to commit crime when they are punished. This simplistic notion is of course reminiscent of the classical school of criminology developed by Beccarria and Benthan (see Chapter 6). Akers, however, adds considerable sophistication to the classical school by adding notions such as "schedules of reinforcement" and disparities in reinforcing stimuli. The heart of the theory, however, remains the principle that "a person will participate in deviant activity . . . to the extent that it [the activity] has been differentially reinforced over conforming behavior and defined as more desirable than, or at least as justified as, conforming alternatives."[33]

The basic problem with this theory is that there is no independent measure of whether or not a particular experience of behavior is reinforcing. If a behavior is repeated, then it was reinforcing; if it is not repeated, then it was not reinforcing. The logic is infallible, but it is inadmissable as a scientific explanation. The theory cannot be false no matter what the empirical research reveals. It has exactly the same logical structure as the previously discussed theory that argued that some people are rich because they are moral, and they are obviously moral because they are rich. Explanations such as these, tautologies, are of little scientific utility.

Tests of reinforcement theory are often conducted in university laboratories. The typical procedure is to observe the behavior of animals (pigeons, rats, and chimpanzees are favorite subjects) or children. The subject is given a task to perform, and, if he or she performs the task correctly, a reward is given. If the subject continues to perform the task, it is assumed that the reward was reinforcing; if the subject does not repeat the task, it is assumed that the reward was not reinforcing. The author accompanied his son Jeff to an experiment conducted at the University of Washington in the 1960s, when reinforcement theory was prominent in psychology. The task assigned was for a child to place a marker in the correct hole at the sound of a note. If the marker was placed in the correct hole, the child was given an M & M candy. Jeff learned quickly and placed the markers in the correct hole. He was rewarded each time, until he completed the task and had a handful of M & M's. He was then dismissed. On leaving the laboratory, he dropped the M & M's in a trash can. When asked why he did that, he said, "I hate M & M's." This may not be a typical case, but it illustrates the problems inherent in observed-behavior theories that leave out the subjective experiences of the individual and the choices he or she makes.

Until it is possible to specify what is reinforcing and what is not, what is punishment and what is not, and what experiences are independent of the events (crime) to be explained, the theory is of little use as a scientific proposition. What is rewarding for one person at a particular point in time may not be rewarding for him or her at another point in time; and what is rewarding for one person may not be rewarding for another. The reinforcement theory of crime is not even useful as a "principle" or "starting point" because it specifies so little that is amenable to investigation and therefore confounds the issue by posing as "scientific" when it is in fact the reverse.

Control Theories

A somewhat different twist in criminological theory derives from asking Why *don't* people commit crime? rather than Why *do* people commit crime? Because, as we have seen, virtually everyone commits crime, it might seem that the question is a bit silly. Perhaps it is. If we assume that there is always something to be gained by committing criminal acts but that some people, nonetheless, refrain from doing so, then the question makes sense. Travis Hirschi takes this as his starting point and theorizes that people who refrain from committing criminal acts are "bonded," or tied closely, to people who see criminality as unacceptable behavior.[34] Hirschi is not simply restating Sutherland's theory in the reverse. He is arguing that it is not the number or quality of associations that keep people from committing criminal acts, but rather it is the close interpersonal attachments to people who disapprove of criminality. Hirschi places the locus for the most important bonding in the family.

Early studies by Hirschi and Jensen and by Wiatkowski supported control theory.[35] Comparing self-report surveys of juveniles who reported involvement in delinquency with measures of attachment (bonds) to school and family revealed significant differences between those students labeled as delinquent and those labeled as nondelinquent by the researcher. In our earlier discussion of self-report studies, we noted the problems with this type of research and the tenuous nature of any conclusions drawn from it. Among the many difficulties is that those people labeled delinquent are almost certain to express less "bonding" with parents or school than those not so labeled. Is this a consequence or a cause of being labeled delinquent? None of the researches reported to date controls for this; without this control, the data are suggestive at best. Furthermore, the results are inconsistent even using these questionable techniques. Matsueda, in a re-analysis of the same data used by Hirschi, found less support for control theory than for differential association theory.[36]

Family Relations and Delinquency

To the degree that there is any merit in control theory, it is more adequately conceptualized and researched by those advocating the theory that family relations explain why some youths commit crime and others do not.

Sheldon and Eleanor Glueck devoted years of research to the exploration of the causal nexus presumed to operate between family relations and juvenile delinquency.[37] Their principle study was a comparison of 500 delinquent boys with 500 nondelinquent boys. They compared these 1,000 young people on responses to questionnaires, psychological tests (such as the MMPI), family background, physical characteristics, and a host of other variables. They concluded that the most important difference between the delinquent and nondelinquent boys was the type of family relations they experienced while growing up. The class bias of the researchers was apparent throughout. They conceived of "good families" as those that expressed and communicated middle-class values of thrift, deferred gratification, obedience to authority, cleanliness, and politeness. They conceived of "bad families" as those that were too restrictive or too permissive (following Aichhorn), or set examples of sloppiness and bad work habits. They found statistically significant correlations between delinquency and bad families and nondelinquency and good families as they defined them.

The Gluecks' research task was formidable. Unfortunately, some fundamental flaws in their research design rendered their findings and interpretations suspect. As with so many studies comparing delinquents and nondelinquents, there is no adequate distinction made between the two groups. Delinquents are assumed to be incarcerated and nondelinquents are assumed to be in school. However, this assumption is simply false. Also confounding the study is that the "normal" and "abnormal" family characteristics used reflect the Gluecks' own bias as to what families should be rather than an objective criteria. Perhaps the most limiting aspect is that they misused statistical procedures for assessing the differences. It is axiomatic that, if we wish to compare two groups on characteristics that differ by taking a sample from each group, the sample size must correspond to the proportions found in the general

Ossining, N.Y., the town that Sing Sing built: more than a generation gap. (Arthur Tress/Woodfin Camp & Assoc.)

population.[38] This creates a particular problem for the Gluecks' study. Accepting that less then 20 percent of the juvenile population is ever officially declared delinquent, then the correct statistical comparison would be to have five times as many people in the nondelinquent sample as in the delinquent sample. On the other hand, because we know from self-report studies that over 90 percent of the juveniles who are not incarcerated admit to committing serious criminal acts, then the samples would have to have ten times as many people in the delinquent category as in the nondelinquent category. Either way, the Gluecks' studies are seriously flawed.

The sociologist F. Ivan Nye improved upon the Gluecks' theory and research in several ways.[39] Nye did not argue that family relations were the cause of delinquency. He recognized that unrecorded delinquency had to be considered in any test of the proposition that family relations were causally related to delinquency. Furthermore, Nye suggested specific ways in which the family might inhibit, or contribute to, the etiology of delinquent behavior: (1) defining what is right and wrong behavior, which leads to internalizing social controls; (2) making the child an extension of the family and thereby indirectly controlling the individual by making him or her want to avoid embarrassing or "letting down" the family (this variable is similar to Hirschi's notion of bonding); (3) utilizing direct controls in the form of rewards and punishments; and (4) contributing to the child's "need satisfaction" by aiding or inhibiting success in school, sports, peer relations, and career choices.

Nye's grand hypothesis is that the degree to which the family succeeds in creating delinquency-inhibiting or delinquency-producing relationships will determine the likelihood of delinquency. His research, unfortunately, did not test these rather subtle relationships. Rather, as an index of the existence of all these positive (or negative) features of family life, he was forced to include whether or not the marriage was the first or second, was intact, and was "happy." The assumption was that happy marriages were more likely to produce a nondelinquent environment. Nye did, indeed, find a significant difference between happy marriages, whether or not they were the first or second, and nondelinquency.

A central problem is that there is no control for the effect of law-enforcement agencies and family dynamics, which increase the likelihood that wayward youth will be placed in custody not as a result of their behavior but as a consequence of their families' behavior. It is axiomatic that families that are more focused on their children and able to present a good front to the community are more likely to intervene before official agencies (police or welfare agencies) are needed.[40] To what degree the correlation between officially labeled delinquency and family relations reflects this difference is not controlled for in these studies. Other research indicates, however, that this may be the crucial variable. We may, in fact, be seeing a correlation that is simply a reflection of class bias rather than a causal link in the etiology of delinquency.

It is significant that these studies were conducted during a time when the family in Western societies was more stable than it is today. Single-parent families, divorce, and separation are now more common. More and more children are being raised in what used to be called "broken homes," a characteristic that formerly carried considerable stigma. It is arguable that today the impact of family relations on delinquency and crime is considerably less than it was 30 years ago. Unfortunately, the answer to that question must await further research.

Situational Variables

Some theorists argue that the difference between those who commit criminal or delinquent acts and those who do not is determined by situational circumstances rather than previous experiences, personality, or relationships. In this view, everyone will commit a crime if the circumstances are right and no one will if the circumstances are wrong. Short and Strotdbeck outline what they call the "group process" in delinquency and crime.[41] Matza speaks of "drift," where people engaged in noncriminal activities develop delinquent or criminal alternatives to conventional behaviors.[42] Sykes and Matza argue that it is the prevalence of shared "techniques of neutralization" that differentiates those who commit crime from those who do not.[43] And Albert Cohen, in an imaginative study of working-class gangs, suggests that delinquency emerges as a solution to problems when the youths engage in a gradual process of "mutual conversion"; each member suggests some mildly deviant act that, if picked up on by other members, may lead to deviance as a part of the gang's everyday activities.[44]

These theories are among the greatest paradoxes facing the social-scientific study of crime. On the one hand, these theories are intuitively provocative because they are consistent with the experiences of many people who commit crimes but for whom crime never becomes a "way of life." On the other hand, they are probably, of all criminological theories, the most difficult to test. One can scarcely imagine being in a position to observe groups of youths or adults sitting around drifting into, or mutually converting one another to, delinquency or crime. If the researcher were so intimately involved in the criminality, he or she would also be implicated. After-the-fact interviews suggest that a process such as the one described is often involved, but the data are subject to the problems of memory and always sensitive to diverse interpretations. These theories, however, are the only ones in the social-psychological tradition that are consistent with the fact that people move in and out of delinquency and crime as youths and adults, that almost everyone commits some criminality at different times in his or her life, and that often this is a transitory event. Despite the potential value to be found in this paradigm, we are forced to conclude that—at this point in research on crime and delinquency—situational theory must be viewed as an imaginative speculation awaiting systematic research and development. Until the theory is formulated in a way that permits systematic observations that can test validity, it remains an intriguing speculation without verification.

Conclusion _____

There are literally dozens of social-psychological theories that attempt to explain why some people commit criminal acts while others do not. These theories emerged in an attempt to find an alternative to psychological and biological theories of crime, which ignored the social component in the etiology of deviance. Unfortunately, as we have seen, the logical structure of these theories and the built-in biases of the researches have failed to provide a body of knowledge that is any more satisfactory than the theories they sought to replace. In large measure, this results from the shared fundamental flaw of earlier theory construction; these theories ask why some people commit crime without recognizing that (1) crime is a politically defined behavior that is not sociologically or social psychologically unique and (2) most people commit criminal acts and the question therefore makes little sense.

The harshest lesson for any science to learn is that the nature of reality is such that not all questions are equally amenable to exploration. We must develop our science in different directions if we are to overcome the shortcomings of conventional approaches to crime. In the next chapter, we turn to yet another approach to the study of crime and criminality—sociological paradigms that try to avoid reducing criminality to the behavior of individuals by focusing on the structure of social relations.

CHAPTER

10

Sociological Tradition: Normative Paradigms

The last three chapters looked at biological, psychiatric, psychological, and social-psychological theories of criminal behavior. These are behavioral theories. They have in common the fact that they ask the question: Why do some people commit crime and others do not?

When behavioral theories are examined through the lens of the philosophy and history of science, some important logical and empirical flaws are exposed. As a group, these theories are either empirically false (they cannot account for the known facts about crime) or are tautologies (they are true by definition). In either case, they fail as scientifically valid theories. Behavioral theories are analogous to prescientific speculations in other fields. Seeing the world as flat led to what today we know to be erroneous explanations of why ships that went to sea never returned. It was not wind, tide, or ship construction, but the fact that the ship sailed off the end of the earth, that was postulated. The theory that the sun circled the earth held back the development of astronomy for centuries, as did the theory that there was a substance called "ether" that occupied the space between the heavenly bodies. Alchemists who asked how we could convert lead to gold negatively contributed to the advance of knowledge by demonstrating the futility of the quest. In each of these and hundreds of other instances, the development of reliable knowledge was held back because the wrong questions were asked. Criminology is held back in the same way.

Let us look again at some features of Darwinian evolutionary theory that illuminate the points being made. Darwin began his inquiry with the known fact that some species survive and others do not. Had all species survived, his inquiry would have been aborted long before he sailed on the *Beagle*. Had Darwin followed the logic of behavioral criminology, he would have sought the answer to why the dinosaur became extinct by looking only at characteristics of the dinosaur (association with attitudes favorable to extinction, more DYY chromosomes than the Duckbill Platypus, and so forth). Darwin was, however, too well-steeped in the logic of science to fall prey to this illogic. He sought to discover how the dinosaur's environment changed so that the species had to either change or become extinct. The species was unable to adapt, and it ceased to exist. Thus Darwin discovered an important principle and a valuable scientific theory.

The implications for criminological inquiry are profoundly important. E. P. Thompson's seminal work on crime in 17th-century England showed how peasants living in small villages depended on hunting, fishing, and wood gathering from common land owned by the king. When the king passed laws giving this land to his nobles (in order to assure their allegiance), he also decreed that persons gathering wood, hunting, or fishing on these lands were henceforth criminals and could be punished by death, even for blacking their faces so they could not be seen at night. Those who continued what were formerly customary practices among the peasants suddenly were criminals, guilty of "poaching," "trespassing," and "stealing wood." We would never come to an understanding of the crimes of trespass, poaching, and stealing wood if we looked only in the 18th century at characteristics of the "criminal" peasants.

Among behavioral criminologists, there is an implicit agenda that is rarely articulated but has dire consequences for the corpus of generated knowledge. This is the assumption that "real crime" consists of acts that are universally disapproved and about which there is consensus.[1] This assumption is false, as we have seen in the preceding chapters. What constitutes the image of the "crime problem" at any particular time depends on how crime is treated by the media, politicians, and law-enforcement agencies. In the 1950s, the governments of the Scandinavian countries (Norway, Sweden, Denmark, and Finland) campaigned against the high rate of death and injury resulting from drunken driving. They passed stringent laws against drunk drivers. In a few short years, the crime of drunken driving was moved from relative obscurity in the public consciousness to a position where it was viewed as second in seriousness only to murder.[2]

In the United States, it was a coalition of conservative politicians and law-enforcement officials who—in the 1960s and 1970s— elevated the crime problem from a matter of only minor concern to one of considerable public notice. But it never did reach the level of national focus that the politicians, media, and law-enforcement agencies sought.[3]

Furthermore, social movements or moral crusades may arise that focus on particular types of crime, and this too will have an effect on how the problem is perceived. Organizations like MADD (Mothers Against Drunk Drivers) in the United States are having a decided effect on how the crime of drunk driving is perceived relative to other offenses. The women's movement, as pointed out earlier, has been responsible for a public redefinition of rape and spouse abuse as social problems as well as for changes in law. In recent years, the issue of "crime in the streets" was created almost entirely by politicians seeking to increase law-enforcement powers and detract from other social problems—such as poverty, race discrimination, and war—that were, before the political campaign, viewed by the public as more-important issues than crime.[4] From 1976–1980, white-collar and corporate crime were raised to the level of major social problems as a result of political scandals spanning several years. These scandals forced the resignation of Vice-President Spiro Agnew, President Richard Nixon, Attorney Generals John Mitchell and William Renquist, and numerous other high-level government officials. When Jimmy Carter was elected president, he encouraged the FBI and other federal law-enforcement agencies to pursue white-collar criminals diligently. White-collar crime became a national issue and opinion surveys during this period showed that the American public saw this type of criminality as more serious than other types, such as burglary, theft, and assault.[5] When Ronald Reagan was elected president, however, the emphasis of the federal law-enforcement agencies changed dramatically. There was a concerted effort to reduce the emphasis on white-collar crime and emasculate the agencies responsible for enforcing laws against business. The enforcement of work-condition laws by the Office of Safety and Health Administration, for example, was drastically curtailed through bureaucratic changes.[6] Crime, then, had a very different tenor from 1980–1988 than it did from 1976–1980. It is, then, political changes that determine what is viewed as "real crime." For criminologists to assert that there is some "universal crime problem," or some type of behavior that is the "real" or "true" crime, is to ignore the political nature of criminality and the relative nature of human values and norms. Research into the causes of crime is often useful in that it yields data that helps us answer other questions, even though they contribute little to an understanding of why people commit crime.

This is not to say that it is unscientific to ask why people behave in different ways. Not everyone smokes marijuana; drives under the influence of alcohol; or commits rape, murder, stock fraud, or crimes against workers. It is defensible to ask why some people commit specific types of crime and others do not. But when the question is phrased this way, it brings into sharp relief the fact that our research is not focused on "crime" per se, but rather on behaviors that we have reason to believe are psychologically or sociologically homogeneous. These behaviors will usually include some acts that are defined as crime and some that are not. Thus, if we want to learn about corporate criminality so that we can develop behavioral theories, we would have to study decision making in corporations. This would include decisions that are in violation of the criminal law as well as decisions that are not.

In most states of the United States, and in some countries, it is not a crime for a man to sexually assault his wife or someone with whom he is living in a conjugal relationship. It is, however, a crime for him to assault other women sexually. To understand why some men sexually assault women while others do not requires studying sexual assault, whether or not it is defined as crime. To do otherwise invokes the questionable assumption that sexual assault against a wife in Texas has a different cause than it does in

Arizona because the laws in these places differ. If we want to know why some people smoke marijuana, we would want to study the process by which people come to smoke marijuana in Nevada, where it is legal, as well as in Pennsylvania, where it is a felony. It is illogical to assume, because something is a crime in Arizona and Pennsylvania but not in Texas or Nevada, that the cause of the behavior is different.[7]

Thus, the most fundamental error of behavioral theories is that they look for an explanation of those behaviors labeled criminal as a result of political decisions. Because behavior has been labeled criminal by agencies does not provide adequate scientific categories. If behavioral theories are to succeed scientifically, they must begin not with legal definitions but with sociologically or psychologically definable categories of human behavior. These are difficult to discover, and the awful truth is that social-scientific efforts to discover such typologies are notoriously unsuccessful.

Sociological Paradigms _____

Sociological theory tries to avoid the pitfalls of behavioral theory by searching for characteristics of the social structure that can explain variations in the distribution and content of criminality. We must be careful, however, not to confuse sociological paradigms with psychological or social-psychological theories created by sociologists. As Cohen notes:

> Much of what travels under the name of sociology of deviant behavior or of social disorganization is psychology. . . . For example, Sutherland's theory of differential association, which is widely regarded as preeminently sociological, is not the less psychological because it addresses itself to the question: how do people become the kind of individuals who commit criminal acts? A sociological question would be: What is it about the structure of social systems that determines the kinds of criminal acts that occur in these systems and the way in which such acts are distributed within these systems.[8]

Robert Meron was overly optimistic when he suggested in 1938 that the search had ended for behavioral theories that explain deviant behavior by biological or psychological characteristics. But he captured the essence of the sociological endeavor when he sought an explanation for why deviant behavior varied in different social structures and in different parts of the same society.[9]

For sociological theories to be successful, as Albert Cohen points out in his classic study of delinquent boys, we must begin with "facts our theories must fit."[10] And we must ask questions that are logically consistent with those facts.

Facts Our Theories Must Fit

We know that almost everyone commits crime, but that males have a much higher incidence of reported crimes than females. We know that what is defined as crime is determined by political processes. We know that there are profound differences within historical periods, cultures, and nations as to the kinds of acts defined as criminal and the frequency with which these acts are committed. Poor, unemployed ghetto residents do not engage in insider trading on the stock market, violation of factory safety and health laws against their employees, or the laundering of money through unnumbered Swiss bank accounts. Rarely do Wall Street bankers or chief executive officers of corporations snatch purses, burgle houses, or steal luggage from subways. Middle-class women are more likely to shoplift than middle-class men. Lower-class women are more likely to engage in prostitution than lower- or middle-class men. Police and politicians are more likely to take bribes than college professors. College professors are more likely to misappropriate funds from government research grants than assembly-line workers at Ford or General Motors.

Good theory must begin with these regularities in mind. Sociological theory asks why different nations, states, or historical periods produce different levels of crime. Until recently, the dominant sociological paradigm sought an answer to this question through an analysis of the normative system and its effects upon people in different historical and cultural periods.

Normative Theories

Norms are the ideas about right and wrong institutionalized by a people's culture and history. Norms cover a wide spectrum of behaviors from the relatively trivial to the profound. Some norms are codified into law while others remain customary practices or, as William Graham Sumner called them, "folkways."[11] Norms dictate whether cars should be driven on the right-hand or left-hand side of the road; whether food should be eaten cooked or raw, with hands or utensils, or in sexually segregated or collective dining areas; whether one person has the right to assault another if he or she is insulted; whether a man has the right to punish his wife or children physically should they fail to do what he tells them; and whether the state can execute criminals. These and an infinite variety of other ideas vary from one time and one culture to another. One of the classic traditions in sociology takes the analysis of norms and their explanatory power as its starting point.

The most influential normative theory in sociology was articulated by the French sociologist, Emile Durkheim. In 1897, Durkheim proposed a theory of suicide that explained variations in rates by the degree to which people internalized and found their web of life consistent with the dominant norms of their society.[12] He suggested that the normative integration of a society would lead to four sources of suicide: altruistic, fatalistic, egoistic, and anomic. Altruistic suicide, according to Durkheim, stemmed from the acceptance of self-sacrifice norms for the improvement of the whole society or for specific other individuals. Fatalistic suicide was the result of accepting the inevitability of events overwhelming individual choice. Egoistic suicide resulted from a normative system that emphasized the importance of the individual in shaping and making history. Finally, and most interesting sociologically, Durkheim depicted anomic suicide as that which results when some segments of the population are not sufficiently integrated into the normative system and experience "normlessness." Durkheim did not try to explain individual suicides; rather, he sought to measure different societies in terms of their normative integration and to see if their suicide rates varied as would be expected in terms of his theory. The data generally supported his conclusions, although the research techniques used in the 1800s were not sufficiently developed to permit very conclusive results. Later research using more-sophisticated methods has *not* confirmed Durkheim's findings. His theoretical perspective, however, especially the idea of anomie in his theory of suicide, has formed a central part of some sociological pradigms and lasted beyond the particular research he presented in support of his theory.[13]

Durkheim did not apply his theory to crime. That task remained for Robert Merton, who published the very influential paper "Social Structure and Anomie" in 1938. Merton began his classic application of Durkheim's theory to deviant behavior with these words,

"There persists a notable tendency in sociological theory to attribute the malfuntioning of social structure primarily to those of man's impervious biological drives which are not adequately restrained by social control."[14]

Merton proposed that an alternative paradigm was a derivative of Durkheim's anomie theory. He suggested that every society inculcated in its citizenry sets of goals that were deemed worth striving for. In Western societies, the most important goal, according to Merton, was success, which was defined in terms of striving for wealth, power, and privilege. But society would be an uninhabitable anarchy if the only norm governing people's behavior was a goal people were taught to seek. Goals must be accompanied by norms governing the means by which the goals are to be legitimately achieved. In America, for example, years of "deferred gratification" while obtaining an education is a legitimate means to achieving the success goal. Inheriting money or winning the lottery are also examples of this. Stealing, murder, arson, receiving stolen property, or bribing politicians, however, is an illegitimate means to achieve the goal of success. People situated at different places in the social structure have different access to the means for achieving the goal. For some, the goal is immediately accessible. They only need to implement the means available to them (attend university at their parent's expense and take a position in their family corporation upon graduation) in order to attain the culturally prescribed goals. For others, however, the goal of success may be difficult, if not impossible, to attain. A teenage youth who must choose between getting an education and helping his or her destitute family by taking a job is not in the same position relative to the means to achieve the goals as the son of a successful corporation's chief executive officer.

Deviant behavior (including criminal behavior) is one solution to the discrepancy between goals and means. Not all adaptations are deviant—some people conform to goals and means even though their chances of achieving the goals by legitimate means are negligible. Other adaptations (retreatism or ritualism) are deviant but not criminal. Merton catagorized the range of possible adaptations as (1) conformity, (2) innovation, (3) retreatism, (4) ritualism, and (5) rebellion. These possibilities he set forth in a table showing the relationship between the adaptations and the degree to which the person accepted or rejected the culturally prescribed goals and means:

	Goals	Means
Conformity	+	+
Innovation	+	−
Retreatism	−	−
Ritualism	−	+
Rebellion	±	±

Merton's anomie theory tells us that we should find a higher incidence of deviance in societies where there is a malintegration of goals and means. Further, he argues, we should find the highest incidence of deviation within a particular society in social classes and categories in which there is a poor fit between the goals learned and the access to the means for achieving the goals. Conversely, societies or social classes in which the shared goals are readily available by the prescribed means to achieve them will have a lower rate of deviance.

As an example of criminal deviance, Merton uses the innovations of white-collar criminals. If the goal of business success is not available by legitimate means, illegitimate means (stock frauds, insider trading, poor protection for workers) will be invented to achieve the goals. Corrupt machine politics is another example in which the goals of success are, for some, inaccessible by legitimate means. The creation of innovative, deviant means by establishing political machines that dispense favors (even cash) in return for votes and party loyalty is an innovation that is criminal but successful.

Unfortunately, Merton's theory does not go far enough. He fails to specify any means by which we could tell where to expect what kinds of deviation. The violation of criminal law by corporate executives conspiring to fix prices or defraud the government on contracts is difficult to explain. Indeed, one might logically expect that deviation in those instances would never occur, because the goal of success by any reasonable objective standard has been achieved and employing illegitimate means (violating the law) jeopardizes the goal as it increases the likelihood of success. Nor does Merton's theory tell us which of the adaptations is likely to occur under what circumstances. Because the option of "conformity" is always open to those who cannot succeed by legitimate means, we have no way of knowing why some societies or groups generate more deviance than other societies or groups.

Merton's anomie theory is, in reality, merely a taxonomy of adaptations rather than an explanation of the frequency and distribution of the adaptations.[15]

Opportunity Theories

Richard Cloward and Lloyd Ohlin extended Merton's anomie theory and applied it to juvenile delinquency.[16] They tried to explain different likelihoods of deviation by pointing out that not only was access to legitimate means differentially distributed in a society and between societies, but also there was differential access to illegitimate means. Not everyone associates, or is familiar, with possible ways of committing criminal acts to achieve cultural goals. A youth raised in a ghetto is more likely to become familiar with hustlers, drug pushers, and prostitutes than a middle-class youth from Des Moines. The specific techniques and knowledge needed to achieve success (especially money) through these illegal means is more likely to be available to ghetto, rather than middle-class, youth. Knowledge about smuggling guns or drugs may be acquired by police officers, but it is not likely to be an innovation that housewives will discover as a means to increase or enhance their success. Cloward and Ohlin suggest that delinquency is concentrated in the lower classes because opportunities to achieve success by legitimate means are greatest. This does not mean that all lower-class youths will be blocked from success by legitimate means nor that all lower-class youths will find illegitimate means readily available to them. Those that do, however, are candidates for delinquent behavior.

Cloward and Ohlin's stress on opportunity as an ingredient in the etiology of crime is often overlooked. It is certainly a necessary condition. By definition, if a person does not have an opportunity to commit crime, that person will not. Opportunity theory goes further, however, and argues that the learning of criminal means to legitimate goals is as critical as blocked goals in the process of becoming a delinquent. But this hypothesis is inconsistent with the fact that much delinquency and crime is apparently a spontaneous individual adaptation. Whatever access to illegitimate means Lowell Lee had before he killed his family (see page 241) was knowledge about life, death, and the power of guns that everyone has. Furthermore, youths who have ready access to the cultural goal of success through legitimate means are often delinquent. Middle-class delinquency is as prevalent as lower-class delinquency. It takes different forms (vandalism instead of theft; drunk driving instead of shoplifting), but it is nonetheless delinquent, with serious and harmful consequences for the health, safety, and property of others.[17]

Subcultural Theories

In complex societies, sociological research reveals that there is not a uniform value system. Rather, there are innumerable value and normative systems that compete with one another and are shared by people in different social classes and groups. Some of the earliest research on crime and delinquency in the United States focused on the criminality of immigrant groups. The argument was presented that immigrant populations often had a higher incidence of criminal behavior than non-immigrant groups because their shared norms were criminalistic.[18] Others argued that the immigrant groups did not bring criminal values; their values clashed with the host country's and created a strain that resulted in criminal behavior.[19]

This theme is often taken up by lay writers who seek a simplis-

Subcultural themes: Ode to a brother. *(Barbara Rios/Photo Researchers)*

tic explanation that has the ring of commonsense. Writers on organized crime who believe there is a Mafia or Cosa Nostra in America attribute the characteristics of these organizations to cultural patterns brought over by Sicilian immigrants. Susan Griffin proposes that rape is a product of a male culture that sees a woman as property and a man as having the right to take and use a woman's body as he sees fit.[20] Griffin's observation is echoed by Scully and Marollo. After observing that "empirical research has repeatedly failed to find a consistent pattern of personality type or character disorder that reliably discriminates rapists from other groups of men,"[21] they go on to argue that rape results because "traditional socialization encourages males to associate power, dominance, strength, virility and superiority with masculinity."[22]

There is a temptation to agree with explanations that have an intuitive ring of truth. It is certainly true that male culture depicts women as objects, usually inferior objects who need to be protected and are the rightful property of men. There is also a good deal of evidence that men not only think they have the right to have sex with any women, but also believe a woman "really" wants to be forced to have sex.[23] These myths persist despite an overwhelming amount of evidence to the contrary. We must be cautious, however, in accepting facile explanations. If this theory about rape were accurate, it would follow that most men would at least approve of rape and, if given an opportunity that was free from punishment, a majority of them would engage in it. The facts do not uphold this view. The percentage of women who are raped is alarmingly high, but in America it is nowhere near universal. Allan Griswold Johnson estimates that 20–30 percent of women 12 years and over will be the victim of a violent sexual attack at some time in their life. Most will be attacked by people who are not strangers.[24] Supporting these estimates are Meyer's findings that 20 percent of college women are the victims of rape or attempted rape.[25] These data, when combined with the aforementioned data on the frequency of spouse rape, are indicative of the fact that rape is extremely common; any general theory of criminal behavior must take this fact into account. Furthermore, the fact that middle- and upper-class men, including college and university students, frequently commit violent sexual attacks must also be accounted for. If subculture theory were sufficient to explain rape, the frequency of rape would be higher than these data indicate. Furthermore, evidence exists that, even when there is little risk of being punished, most men will not commit rape. In the South, where the rape of black women by white men was culturally permitted, and punishment was nonexistent among the dominant white culture, most white men did not rape black women.[26] Another fact inconsistent with this theory is that we do not find a uniformly higher incidence of rape in cultures that encourage masculinity and the oppression of women.[27]

Wolfgang and Fercutti extended this idea when they proposed that violence was attributable to a subculture in which violent reactions to conflict were normal. Wolfgang's research on homicide in Philadelphia revealed a striking difference in the incidence of homicide rates.[28] Nonwhite males aged 20–24 had a rate of 54.6 homicides per 100,000 population, compared with only 3.8 for white males of the same ages. Nonwhite females had a much higher homicide rate than white females (10.2 compared to 6.6), and nonwhite females even had a higher rate than white males (10.2 compared to 3.8). Wolfgang did not control for police bias in this study. It is quite likely, given what other studies demonstrate about police bias, that the differences in rates are in part accounted for because the police and prosecuting attorney are more likely to charge nonwhites with homicide but to reduce the charge for whites to manslaughter or even lesser offenses. These qualifications notwithstanding, the differences in homicide rates are significant and supported by research by Chilton and Riedel and Zahn.[29] Wolfgang and Ferracuti pursued the study of violence cross-culturally and discovered that "pockets of violence" existed in many different countries. Hagan points out:

> in Colombia *La Violencia* has claimed thousands of lives in a wave of violence that spanned several decades. In Sardinia the *Vendetta Barbaricina* provides another bloody example of a long tradition characterized by deadly quarrels. And in El Salvador violence has become so commonplace as to stimulate the expression *la vida vale nada,* 'life is worth nothing.'[30]

Wolfgang and Ferracuti explain that this tendency is more characteristic of some parts of society than others as a result of a subculture of violence; a set of norms supportive of violence exist outside the mainstream of societal norms. This theory seems plausible on first look. To test it, we would have to develop measures of the existence of a subculture supporting violence, other than the fact that violence (or homicide) was prevalent. Unfortunately, Wolfgang and Ferracuti do not present such data. Rather, their research ends in a tautology: The subculture of violence is assumed to exist and to explain the higher incidence of homicide because there is a higher incidence of homicide. The degree to which this sort of logic can end in a theoretical bias based upon racial stereotyping rather than upon data is illustrated in a study by Hindelang.[31] He argues that violent crimes (rape and assault) are common among blacks because violence is "more accepted and expected by blacks in social interactions and hence are less often construed as crimes and/or reported to either the police or to survey interviewers as crimes."[32] Yet his own data show that race differences in crime are greatest for the least-violent crime—robbery—and least for the more-violent crimes. Thus his own data contradict his theory, but he fails to see this in his zeal to support the theory. The subculture of violence theory, as Andersen points out, "rests upon ideological assumptions which denigrate the black community, its mores and values. The problem with this explanation is that it turns attention away from the relationship of black communities to the larger society and it recreates dominant stereotypes about blacks as violent, aggressive, and fearful. Although it may be true that rates of violence are higher in black communities, this observation does not explain the fact."[33]

Researches that investigate the presence of norms supporting violence and crime consistently contradict the claims of those theories that try to explain criminality in terms of social class and ethnic or racial groups. In a study of attitudes towards crime, Peter Rossi and others found considerable consensus across racial, ethnic, and social-class lines with regard to the seriousness and importance of criminal acts.[34] Erlanger, relying on data gathered for the President's Commission on Violence, found no significant differences by race or social class in attitudes towards personal violence.[35] Ball and Rokeach compared three categories of men: (1) those who had experienced a high degree of participation in violence at some time in their lives, (2) those with moderate involvement in violence, and (3) those with no history of violence. They asked people in each of these groups to answer questions designed to establish approval or disapproval of violent behavior. They found no significant difference between the three groups.[36] These studies indicate that, at least according to survey questions, there is widespread consensus on norms with regard to violence that cuts across racial, ethnic, and social-class lines. These norms are apparently even shared by those who have engaged in considerable violence. These researches indicate that the subcultures of violence and crime theories are suspect. These findings must be interpreted cautiously, however. Substantial research indicates that people responding to questions tend to respond in ways they think are wanted by the researcher.[37]

Subculture theories also fail to recognize the degree to which middle- and upper-class violence is hidden. Some current estimates are that one out of every four married women is a victim of wife-beating. Assaults on children are estimated to take place in one out of every eight families in the United States. Victim surveys indicate that one in very thousand women is the victim of a rape in every year. Assaults on the street or in public bars are common.

Governments and political groups engage in violent acts continuously. At this writing, there are over 300 military conflicts going on in different parts of the world. School buses filled with children, government buildings, airplanes, police cars, restaurants, and private residences are blown up almost daily. Governments are overthrown through violence, and union officials gain power by threatening violence against the membership or against opposition leaders. Government intelligence agencies plan and execute assassinations of foreign leaders and conspire to effect violent coups.[38] The U.S. CIA planned the assassination of Fidel Castro, even entering into a contract with leaders of organized crime to accomplish this. The CIA also plotted the assassination of Trujillo, Lumumba, Diem, and scores of other foreign leaders. In 1985, the French government assigned undercover intelligence agents to destroy an environmental group's ship (the *Greenpeace*) in order to curtail opposition to nuclear tests the French were conducting in waters near Australia and New Zealand. The agents carried out their assignment and, in the process, murdered one of the crew members. The South African government's police systematically torture suspects and indiscriminately fire weapons and tear gas at school children and people attending funerals.[39]

Are the bureaucrats who make the decisions for these government organizations, street gang members who engage in mugging or street fighting, and upper-class husbands who physically assault their wives all part of a subculture of violence? Theoretically, it is unlikely that this is a very good starting point for explaining violent behavior.

Delinquent Gangs as Subcultures

Walter Miller suggests in his paper "Lower Class Culture as a Generating Milieu of Gang Delinquency" that it is the values of the lower class that creates delinquency. This theory is typical of

normative theories that "explain" crime or delinquency by refer-
ring to the fact that it exists and then postulating that differences
in values account for the differences in behavior. The crucial question is whether the assumed differences in values between lower-
and middle- or upper-class culture can be demonstrated independently of the observed differences in behavior patterns. Without this
independent measure, the theory is simply a tautology built on
stereotypes.

Albert Cohen improves considerably on the logic of subcultural
theories when he describes a set of circumstances and conditions
shared by working-class youth in America. He sees this set as
characterizing the process by which working-class youth create a
delinquent solution. Cohen's starting point is that all behavior is
problem solving. To understand working-class delinquency, he argues, we must understand what problems these youth face and
how gang delinquency functions as a solution to the problems.
Working-class youth, Cohen says, share a set of values that limits
their ability to succeed in institutions dominated by middle-class
norms. He argues that lower-class culture emphasizes spontane-
ity, short-run hedonism, emotional expressiveness, physical aggressiveness, and a disdain for property. Middle-class values, by
contrast, emphasize the importance of personal control, deferring
of gratification, respect for property, containing one's emotions, and
verbal confrontations rather than fighting in dispute settlement.
Working-class youth, like all youth in Western societies, are forced
to attend schools dominated by middle-class teachers espousing
middle-class values. Working-class youth are then judged by middle-
class values from the moment they enter school. Thus, working
class youth share a problem of adjusting to this conflict of values.

Cohen tries to develop his theory so that it will explain how
delinquency is sometimes a solution to this problem. He argues
that working-class youth, interacting with one another and sharing the problem of adjusting to unfair standards, will seek support
for deviant actions that legitimize their own values and display
their disdain for the values of the middle-class. If a group of
working-class youth are in "effective interaction," they will ten-
tatively suggest deviant acts that are partial solutions; if these
suggestions are supported by others, the solution of a full-fledged
delinquent culture may result. In this way, Cohen explains not
only the emergence of delinquent subcultures but also their content. He points out that much working-class delinquency is not
goal directed but simply expressive behavior. This delinquency is

often oriented to the destruction of private property, the sacred cow of middle-class America. Working-class youth also display their disdain by flamboyant displays of cars, clothing, and public rudeness.

As a theory of working-class delinquency, Cohen's is clearly superior to most others we have discussed. He provides a clear definition of what he wishes to explain and does not claim more for his theory that any theory can deliver. He gives us an explanation for the differences between middle- and working-class delinquency and why the content varies. Cohen does not assume, as so many other theorists do, that middle-class delinquency is nonexistent. Nor does he argue that working-class delinquency is ubiquitous. He assumes what the facts show—that middle-class delinquency is as prevalent as lower- and working-class delinquency, that the type of behavior engaged in varies, and that not all youths engage in all types of delinquency. He then tries to explain the content and the distribution of the differences.

As a theory of a particular type of delinquency, Cohen's is no doubt the most viable we presently have. There are, however, many problems. The description of working- and middle-class cultures is a reflection of middle-class stereotypes rather than a sociologically accurate depiction. Middle- and upper-class youth who prolong their entry into the work force (by attending college and enjoying the immediate gratification of leisure time, freedom from the drudgery of unskilled or semiskilled labor, the economic support of their parents, and the status of being a college student) can hardly be said to be "deferring gratification." The working-class youth taking menial jobs or hustling to earn money may be showing a great deal more responsibility than his or her middle-class peer. Working-class culture is extraordinarily heterogeneous. As Gans' research on New York's "urban villages" shows, even a vast, heterogeneous city produces small enclaves of ethnic and racial communities that share middle-class values as universally as middle-class communities.[40]

If working-class delinquency is a solution to problems of adjustment to middle-class standards in school, then what are the "problems of adjustment" faced by middle-class youth that lead them to involvement in delinquency?

Cohen's theory is extremely difficult to test. To know whether or not working-class youth engage in delinquency through the process of "effective interaction" would require participation in the interaction processes of juvenile gangs as they go about deciding on their everyday activities. This sort of direct observation is unfortunately never available. Even studies of delinquent gangs that manage systematic observations over long periods of time are unable to get close enough to the participants in the early stages of delinquent behavior patterns to document the process.[41] The study of the Roughnecks and the Saints described earlier, however, provided some evidence that in the decisions made by these gangs to engage in particular delinquent acts, there was a process of "effective interaction" similar to that described by Cohen.

Cohen's theory completely ignores working-class women. Again, he limits his theory to boys and is therefore immune from criticisms that ask more of the theory. One suspects that the logic of seeing working-class youth faced with peculiar problems of adjustment should apply to females as well as males. The female solution to the problems of adjustment less often takes the form of delinquency. Why?

Differential Social Organization

Edwin Sutherland's differential association theory, discussed in the last chapter, explains criminal behavior as a result of learning attitudes favorable to the commission of crime. This is a social-psychological theory because it focuses on the social learning experiences of individuals. The theory also contains a sociological dimension, however, through the implication that wherever people are situated in the social class structure determines the likelihood that they will be exposed to attitudes favorable to committing or not committing different types of crime. Lower-class youth in urban ghettos, so the argument goes, are more likely to associate with attitudes favorable to committing street crimes, white-collar workers to attitudes favorable to committing white-collar crime, and government officials to attitudes favorable to committing state crimes.

Differential social organization is little more than a simple tautology. We know that different types of crime are located in different social classes. To explain this difference by simply saying that there are different norms in different classes explains nothing. Research in different social classes does not support the contention implicit in this theory, that people in different classes see their particular type of criminality as excusable but they see other types as wrong. As previously pointed out, criminal acts of all kinds (violence, fraud, drug violations) are widely distributed throughout the social classes. Differential social organization is thus wrong as a matter of fact—different types of crime are not the exclusive domain of any social class, except when it is impossible for people in one class to have access to the social position necessary to commit the crime—and there is no evidence that criminal attitudes vary significantly by social class. Short of such evidence, the theory is merely a tautology.

Women and Normative Theories

Normative theories in the sociological tradition share with behavioral theories a tendency to ignore the data on the relationship between women and crime.[42] As Leonard says, "Theoretical criminology is sexist because it unwittingly focuses on the activities, interests and values of men, while ignoring a comparable analysis of women."[43]

How to account for the distribution of female delinquency and crime must be a central concern of any criminological theory. Women in lower-class communities are as blocked as men from the achievement of culturally prescribed goals (success). Official statistics and self-report studies suggest, however, a much lower incidence of crime among women.[44] When this fact is confronted at all, which is rare, it is usually "explained" by some vague, often sexist, reference to the alleged fact that women learn different goals and are socialized to be docile and unaggressive. This explanation flies in the face of the fact that although crime and delinquency are less prevalent among women, they are not nonexistent. Shoplifting, violence, prostitution, drug use, embezzlement, and other white-collar crimes are too frequently engaged in by women for differences in socilization to be an adequate explanation. The challenge for criminological theory is to account for the fact that there is some criminality among women, but not as much apparently as their is among men. Why this is so is an important fact not addressed by the normative theories.

Functional Theories

In his classic work on suicide and criminal law, Durkheim proposed not only the anomie theory mentioned earlier, but also a functional explanation for crime. Crime occurred, he argued, because it strengthened and clarified the moral boundaries of the community. It is important to grasp the logic of this argument.

Durkheim argued that what he observed as a consequence of criminality, an increase in solidarity among those who observed the deviant acts, was the cause of its occurrence. In a similar vein, Susan Brownmiller argues that rape occurs because it "keeps women in their place."[45] The fact that women are raped may have, as a consequence, an increased dependence of women on men to accompany them and be with them in order to deter would-be rapists. It is illogical and inconsistent with what we know about rape to argue that it exists to "keep women in their place." This is like arguing that handicapped persons exist to establish physical normality. One consequence of the fact that there are people with physical handicaps may be that those without handicaps can define what is normal by reference to those who are handicapped, but to argue that the handicap occurred because of this "function" is a logical absurdity.

The classic form of the functionalist theory is to argue that an observed consequence is the reason for the existence of the social fact.[46] Kingsley Davis applies this logic to prostitution.[47] He argues that prostitution exists because it reduces the strain of finding a sexual partner. Prostitution functions to maintain equilib-

Suicide: A way out. *(Richard Falco/Photo Researchers)*

rium in social relations by providing an alternative to normatively approved sexual expression. Whether a lack of prostitution would produce strain in social relations and whether the existence of prostitution reduces that strain are empirical questions that functionalist theory never addresses. It fails to address them because it assumes the validity of the theory without testing it. It also assumes that the strains produced by prostitution are less important than those reduced by its existence. Functional theory is, in the last analysis, guilty of reifying society and attributing to it a self-regulatory mechanism that does not exist. It assumes that there is some "automatic, self-regulating mechanism in . . . society that blindly yet purposefully" creates social relations.[48] But "society" is simply an abstract depiction; it does not have a reality beyond that of the people who comprise it. "Society" cannot act, make decisions, have purpose, or create social relations. It is a more or less convenient way to refer to collectivities of people; it cannot explain why those people behave the way they do.[49]

Discovering the consequences of social facts such as crime and criminality is an important part of sociological study. Analyzing these consequences and attributing causal force to them is logically unacceptable in scientific analysis.

Conclusion _____

The titles of some of the leading sociological works on crime in the last 40 years demonstrate the normative paradigm and its hold on criminology:

1. "Delinquent Boys: The Culture of the Gang" (Albert Cohen)
2. "Social Structure and Anomie" (Robert Merton)
3. "Lower Class Culture as a Generating Milieu of Gang Delinquency" (Walter Miller)
4. "Subterranean Traditions of Youth" (Gresham Sykes and David Matza)
5. "Middle Class Culture and Delinquency" (Edmund Vaz and Joseph Scott)
6. "Techniques of Neutralization" (Gresham Sykes and David Matza)
7. "The Subculture of Violence" (Marvin Wolfgang and Franco Ferracuti)

8. "Delinquency as a Failure of Personal and Social Controls" (Albert J. Reiss, Jr.)
9. "Illegitimate Means, Anomie and Deviant Behavior" (Richard Cloward and Lloyd Ohlin)
10. "The Conflict of Values in Delinquent Areas" (Solomon Kobrin)

The assumption underlying these sociological theories is that the existence of norms and values explains behavior. The paradigm begins with people acquiring beliefs about right and wrong and then adjusting their behavior to fit these beliefs. If behavior varies from a set of standards generally agreed upon by society, then it must be because some people for one reason or another (learning, frustration, or failed socialization) do not share the norms and values of "all healthy consciences." When Durkheim and Merton argue that "normlessness is a structural characteristic of societies or classes of people that accounts for criminal behavior," they assume that an explanation for the criminality must be found in the norms and values.

The theory often flounders on the rock of tautology. If behavior is caused by norms and values, then different types of behavior must be caused by the distribution of norms and values in the society. When this is added to the functionalist belief that patterns of behavior occur because they are functional for the maintenance of existing social relations, then we have a theory that is incapable of disproof and therefore violates the first canon of good scientific theory. As we have seen, the assumption that norms and values underlay behavior has never been demonstrated with regard to the difference between criminal and noncriminal acts, nor has the assertion that deviance is functional been demonstrated beyond the tautological assertion that because it exists it must be functional.

Other sociological paradigms hold more promise. They do not assume that norms and ideology are irrelevant to human behavior, but they do not see them as independent of other features of social relations. We turn to these theories in the next chapter.

Crime and Social Structure

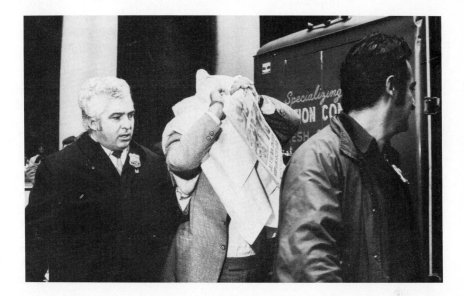

The theme running through this book is that good theory must be consistent with established fact. As we have seen, facts give rise to an infinite number of possible questions and explanations. One of the great contributions of the normative theories surveyed in the last chapter is the conception of crime as normal behavior; a point of view much more consistent with the facts of crime than with those theories that treat criminal behavior as some sort of abnormality. Indeed, the normative sociological tradition emerged as a reaction against biological and psychological explanations, which began with the assumption that criminality is abnormal behavior.

Viewing crime as normal behavior, however, is only the starting point. It does not follow that, if crime is normal, people who commit crime do so because it is normative in their culture, class, or ethnic group. Lower-class black males in the United States, French-

Canadians in Quebec, Palestinians in Israel, black males in South Africa, and Catholics in Northern Ireland all have the highest official crime rates in their respective countries. Does this mean that these groups all share a procriminal culture? Hardly. Most lower-class black males are no more likely than white upper-class males to commit criminal acts, unless we tautologically define as crime only those acts most likely to be committed by people in the lower classes. If norms could explain the difference in the official crime rates of these groups, then norms would also have to explain why upper-class males (medical doctors) are more likely to violate anti-abortion laws.

A theory of behavior that purports to explain all criminality must account for the incidence of the entire range of criminal acts. White-collar, corporate, state-organized, and political criminality is widespread. Mass political movements are also a mainspring of vast amounts of criminal behavior. The American revolutionaries who terrorized the British were criminals by the law of the land. So were workers who in the 1920s fought for their right to collectively bargain and strike, students who violate trespass and other laws while demonstrating against war or apartheid, farmers who mobilize civil disobedience, civil-rights activists who protest segregation and commit criminal acts in the course of opposing oppressive and discriminatory laws. These criminal actions cannot be casually dismissed while focusing on mugging, burglary, and assault. Indeed, the possible connections between these varieties of criminality can only be explored by seeking the interconnections.

The history of rebellions, revolutions, and struggles spanning the globe and involving almost every nation of the world is illustrated by the data summarized in Chapter 2. The modern-day incidence of burglary, robbery, and assault pales in comparison with the seriousness of involvement in criminal acts documented by these events.

The data and observations made in the last few chapters bring into sharp relief the necessity for a paradigm that integrates the political nature of criminal law with the social character of criminal behavior. It is a reasonable starting point to realize that the criminality of the lower classes and the powerless ethnic groups is normal behavior, but this does not explain the criminality. We still must explain why the official crime rate for certain types of crime is higher for some classes and groups of people than it is for others. Why do lower-class black males have a higher official crime rate for burglary, assault, and robbery while upper-class white males have a higher official crime rate for corporate, political, and white-collar crimes? Why are white male college students rarely arrested for rape despite the fact that "date rape" is experienced by 20 percent of female college students?

These, then, are some of the basic facts and questions theories must address. We have explored the strengths and weaknesses of different explanations—biological, psychological, psychiatric, social-psychological, and normative. None of the explanations proposed stands up to the test for good scientific theory, either logically or empirically. It was the recognition that these paradigms were contradicted by empirical data and lacking in logically consistent theories that led social scientists in the 1960s to seek explanations in characteristics of the social structure. The result was the creation of a conflict-theoretical tradition that asked different questions and posited different explanations for the known facts about crime and criminal law.

Structural Theories _____

Social structure consists of the institutionalized constraints and resources existing at a particular historical period. It does *not* include an individual's ability or his or her personality. Social structure includes such things as how work and labor are organized and divided (for example between owners and workers, men and women, minorities and majorities). It also includes the social class structure and where people are in the political and economic hierarchies of social class. Each of these, and myriad of other structural features characterizing different historical periods, determines the *constraints* and *resources* of the various groups and individuals that make up a particular society.

The structural tradition in criminological theory has its historical roots in the works of Thomas More, William Godwin, and Willem Bonger (see Chapter 6). In recent years, this paradigm developed under various names: "radical," "critical," "Marxian," "conflict," and "new criminology." This renaissance of the structural tradition was in response to the changes taking place in world politics and economics following World War II. Faced with the facts of the civil-rights movement, where people struggling for place in society could only exert their rights by violating the criminal law and being sent to prison, sociologists were made aware that not all crime was contained in the violence and property offenses of urban ghetto youths. Confronted with the widespread use of illegal substances by their students and their own children, for which some people were being sent to prison for 20 or more years, criminologists had to recognize that the legal system was not always an expression of community values and norms. With the breakup of colonialism as part of the world order and the emergence of new nations built on the criminality of "terrorists" who fought the exploitation of colonial nations, sociologists were confronted with facts with which consensus theories of law and behavioral theories of crime could not rest comfortably.

During periods of paradigm revolution in scientific inquiry, theories sent to rest on dusty back shelves are resurrected. In the 1960s, Howard Becker dusted off and built on the works of Frank Tannenbaum, Edwin Lemert, and Alfred R. Lindesmith.[1] Becker applied their ideas and research methodologies to the study of deviant behavior among jazz musicians. His work led to the publication of an extraordinarily influential book, *The Outsiders*.[2] In his book, Becker called for a reorientation of criminology recognizing that deviance or crime was a label attached to people by those with the power to do so.

This perspective came to be known as "labeling" or "societal-reaction" theory. It led to a spate of work on the process by which laws are made and people are labeled deviant. Most important, it reflected Edwin Sutherland's far-sighted observation that criminology was not just the study of criminal behavior but was also the study of why acts get defined as criminal and what kinds of acts are punished. By restating this point, Becker presaged the sociology of criminal law, for it was in this context that it once again made sense for sociologists to research and theorize about how laws are created and enforced. It also marked a change that ushered in an era of sociologists recognizing that their work ineluctably took sides and forced criminologists to ask, Whose side are we on?

Labeling School

Clarence Schrag insightfully summarized the basic propositions of the labeling perspective as follows:

1. No act is intrinsically criminal. It is the law that makes an act a crime.
2. Criminal definitions are enforced in the interest of powerful groups by their official representatives, including the police,

courts, correctional institutions and other administrative bodies.

3. A person does not become a criminal by violating the law. Instead, he is designated a criminal by the reactions of authorities who confer upon him the status of an outcast had divest him of some of his social and political privileges.

4. The practice of categorizing people into criminal and noncriminal categories is contrary to common sense and empirical evidence.

5. Only a few persons are caught in violations of the law although many may be equally guilty.

6. While the sanctions used in law enforcement are directed against the total person and not only the criminal act, the penalties vary according to the characteristics of the offender.

7. Criminal sanctions also vary according to other characteristics of the offender, and for any given offense they tend to be most frequent and most severe among males, the young . . . the unemployed or underemployed, the poor educated members of the lower classes, members of minority groups, transients, and residents of deteriorated urban areas.

8. Criminal justice is founded on a stereotyped conception of the criminal as a pariah—a willful wrongdoer who is morally bad and deserving the community's condemnation.

9. Confronted by public condemnation and the label of an evil man, it may be difficult for an offender to maintain a favorable image of himself. [If labeled by the authorities as criminal] the offender comes to see himself as an enemy of society engaged in a war in which right is more on his side than on society's.[3]

These observations constituted a fundamental challenge to the prevailing paradigms of the time. If we accept the outlook of the labeling school, we cannot continue to seek the causes of criminal behavior in the individual offender. The focus of attention shifts profoundly from the offender to the system of justice that defines acts as criminal and labels some people criminal.

As Becker was writing his seminal work on labeling, others were embarking on the systematic study of the criminal law and arguing for a reorientation of criminological inquiry that gave priority to studying the legal process.[4] A study of vagrancy laws demonstrated the political and economic forces shaping the emergence and changes in these laws. Austin Turk analyzed the relationship between criminality and the legal order, and Richard Quinney constructed a theory of criminality focused on the how the "social reality of crime" is constructed. These schools emerged between 1960 and 1970, profoundly affecting the way criminology was being done.

At the same time, sociological theory also was undergoing a radical transformation. Ralf Dahrendorf published a seminal paper, "Out of Utopia," which argued that sociological theory was distorting reality when it depicted society as characterized by consensus, social harmony, and "tendencies towards equilibrium."[5] Dahrendorf argued that society in fact contained inherent conflicts of interests and ideologies; was constantly responding to internally generated tensions; and was held together, not by a tendency toward equilibrium, but by force and the exertion of power. C. Wright Mills challenged conventional sociological paradigms by studying "the power elite," consisting of a coalition of military and industrial power holders whose decisions determined the shape of society and the distribution of resources.[6]

The paradigm revolutions in sociology spilled over into criminology and led to the development of what Michalowski describes as two different forms of conflict theory: a functional-conflict theory characteristic of the works of George Vold and Austin Turk and a "power-conflict theory" that built on the classic works of Weber and Marx. The latter theory was applied to criminology in the United States, England, France, Canada, West Germany, Africa, and Latin America.[7]

Functional-Conflict Theories

Michalowski makes a useful distinction between functional-conflict and power-conflict theories. He summarizes the central notions of the functional-conflict theory as containing the idea that:

1. As a function of both natural human diversity and the group nature of human life, society consists at all times of a number of groups with divergent goals and interests.
2. This diversity of goals and interests places various groups in conflict with one another.
3. This conflict is characterized by a constant process of moves and countermoves as groups seek to achieve their own goals

and thwart the efforts of those who would jeopardize this achievement.

4. This process of checks and balances tends toward an equilibrium that is recognized as social order while, at the same time, it provides the underlying forces for social change.[8]

George Vold and Austin Turk took up the challenge of applying functional-conflict theory to criminology. Vold described society as "a congeries of groups held together in a shifting but dynamic equilibrium of opposing group interests and efforts."[9] Austin Turk echoed this in 1969 when he described social order as "an always tenuous approximation of an order, more a temporary resolution of conflicting notions about right and wrong and of incompatible desires."[10]

Turk went on to argue that "criminality is not something which anyone does but rather something that happens in the course of interaction among various parties."[11]

As Michalowski points out, the functional-conflict perspective mistakenly treats all conflict as equal;

> Forms of conflicts such as those arising from ethnic and subcultural diversity are viewed as similar to those arising from fundamental differentials in power such as those based on class or gender. . . . In the formulations of both Vold and Turk power is abstract and universal, disconnected from the concrete distributions of economic, political and social resources. . . . The division of modern societies into classes with differing access to the means of production fades into the background, as does the use of political and economic power to generate ideologies in justification of inequality . . . the vision of endemic conflict that informs the theories of Vold and Turk leaves little room for development of a radical vision aimed at building societies characterized more by liberation and justice than by power and domination.[12]

Power-Conflict Theories

The power-conflict paradigm is an elaboration of Max Weber's sociology of law as applied to criminology. The starting point for this perspective is the recognition that not all groups in conflict are equally powerful and the task for sociological understanding is to explain which groups are able to force their will on other groups. Writing in 1938, Thorsten Sellin responded to the rise of fascism in Europe and the cultural diversity in America brought about by immigration in the late 1800s.[13] He observed quite accurately that the cultures brought from Europe were repressed by the dominant culture of the United States, just as the cultures defined by the fascists as "alien" were decimated. In Sellin's theory, in contrast to Vold and Turk, it is not sufficient merely to point out that conflict and power struggles are ubiquitous in human social relations. We must go on to describe and explain who wins and who loses in the struggle.

The power-conflict approach was supported by a number of other researchers on law and crime—in particular the study of theft by Jerome Hall and the study of vagrancy by the author.[14] These studies contributed to the ongoing search for criminological theories that resonated with the reality of the times. This search led to the development of a Marxist criminology, which has undergone several phases in the ensuing 20 years.

Marxism as Instrumentalist Theory

The search for a Marxist alternative to conventional criminological inquiry led to some rather oversimplified interpretations. The most important oversimplification was an attempt to build a criminological theory around Marx's rhetorical observation that "in every era the ruling ideas are the ideas of the ruling class." Taking this rhetoric literally led some to argue that the criminal law was merely a way of keeping the lower classes in their place, forcing a surplus labor force and maintaining the power and privilege of the rich. In this theory, the "explanation" is simply that the powerful define as crime what they want and need to protect themselves and those who commit crime are the victims of this system.

Taylor, Walton, and Young, in their timely book *The New Criminology,* took the logic a step further and tried to explain the criminality of working- and lower-class people as political statements that were an attack on the exploitation and repression of the system.[15]

These two propositions—that criminal law is merely the reflection of ruling-class interests and ideology and that working-class criminal behavior is a political statement against the oppression and exploitation of an unjust system—served to stimulate considerable research and critical appraisal; they did not, however, withstand the test of empirical and logical scrutiny. Critics were quick to point out that many laws opposed by members of the ruling class are passed, and that working-class criminality does not appear to the participants to be a political statement. Most people who commit property crimes explain their criminality in very materialistic terms. Akerstrom's detailed study of the verbal interpretations given by criminals finds that they typically talk about the advantages that accrue from a life of crime compared to the disadvantages of the life they would lead as a "square john."[16] A professional thief, Harry King, who specialized as a safecracker, was politically a right-wing conservative whose criminality was justified because of its consistency with capitalist ideology, not as an attack on the system.[17] The same theme comes through time and again in accounts given by professional thieves.[18] On the other hand, people convicted of sexual crimes explain their behavior as "impulsive acts" over which they have no control.[19]

Thus the early efforts to construct a criminological paradigm on the shoulders of Marx and Engels fell short of the goal. Through it all, however, a theme began to emerge that, only in the late 1970s, showed promise of creating a theoretical paradigm that would take into account the shortcomings of traditional criminological theory without falling prey to equally bad theorizing. This perspective rested on the development of Marxist theory from Gramsci, Poulantzas, Althusser, Foucault, Habermas, and a host of European scholars in the Marxist tradition.

Marxist Theory

Marxist theory can legitimately claim to have developed the most sophisticated analysis of social structure and its impact on groups and individuals. It is no doubt the most widely misunderstood social theory in the Western world. Critics often depict Marxist theory as one that invokes a simplistic economic determinism, that is, as a theory that reduces everything to economic conditions and economic motivations. Reading Marx and those who have developed the tradition, it is obvious that this depiction is a gross distortion. The bedrock of Marxist methodology is the dialectic. The dialectic sees people responding to, effecting, and changing the constraints and resources that exist. As such, the theory is totally in opposition to any determinist theory. It gives people a central place in shaping and directing their own lives and creating their social structure. It is not a paradox; it is the starting point of the theory that people inherit a particular social structure but react to and change it.[20]

Marxist theory is also often accused of being an instrumentalist paradigm, that is, seeing a ruling class as the sole determining force in history making. The truth is that Marxism begins with the antithesis of instrumentalist theory: "social life in capitalism is a product of forces that occur behind the backs—without the conscious understanding—of social actors, including those in the dominant social classes. The Rockefellers and their colleagues certainly benefit from capitalism as a social system but they do not control it."[21]

In Anglo-American social thought of recent years, the works of Fred Block, Isac Balbus, James O'Connor, and Alan Wolfe were fused with earlier writings of Marxist criminologists to provide a backdrop for the development of Marxist criminological theory in the works of Platt, Takagi, Michalowski, Chambliss, Seidman, Greenberg, Galliher, Schwendinger, Cohen, Taylor, Walton, Young, Hall, Pearson, Levy, and a plethora of other writers.

Marxist theory begins with the observation that every human group faces the same fundamental problem: how to organize its labor. Without the conversion of the natural environment to usable products—food, shelter, and clothing—human beings cannot survive. There are an infinite number of ways that people may organize their labor. In Marxist theory, how they do this is called the mode of production. The mode of production created may allow each member to seek, horde, and consume everything that he or she acquires. Or a group might organize the production and distribution of products equally among all the members of the group, regardless of how much each person contributes. They can create groups of people who take most of the production for themselves and redistribute only enough to keep those who produce goods alive for further production. Or, if there is an unlimited supply of people who are producing, they can organize the distribution so that some people consume all that is produced and others die from lack of food, shelter, and clothing.

Every historical era contains examples of groups that organize the acquisition and distribution of the products of people's labor differently. In the long train of human history, however, most of the forms of social organization created by communities fall into five modes of production: egalitarian, slave, feudal, capitalist, and socialist. Most, but not all, societies have created modes of production resulting in social classes that have different shares of the goods.

One of the problems facing every society in which there is an unequal distribution of wealth and power is that those social classes who receive more of the products will strive to retain their privileged position while those social classes who receive less will strive to increase their share. This simple and obvious fact results in every class society being graced with a fundamental contradiction: How do we maintain class relations that ineluctably produce antagonisms and conflicts between different classes of people? The people with the control of the resources generally also have access to more effective tools of physical coercion. One solution, then, is for the upper class to enforce the continuation of the unequal distribution of goods by coercion. Raw force, however, as Max Weber demonstrated, leads to an uneasy truce between the social classes: "the demands and interests of the dominant class must take into account the limits of direct manipulation imposed by a historical social formation."[22]

A more clever way of organizing people to accept an unequal distribution of goods is to convince them somehow that this is the right and proper order for the world. In the history of the world, there are many intriguing ways that a tacit acceptance of inequality has been accomplished, at least for short periods of time. At times, people have been convinced that those who have more of the resources are linked to gods and therefore they not only have special powers but also an inherent right to a privileged position. Other groups stress rewarding those in power because they are especially gifted or hard working and contribute more to the collective good than those who are not in power. The range of mechanisms by which inequality is made legitimate is an impressive commentary on human ingenuity.

In the part of the modern world that is industrialized and urbanized, it is law rather than religion or charismatic leadership that serves as a principal source of both legitimation and coercion. It is law that maintains inequality in the distribution of the products of labor. The law defines the rights, duties, and responsibilities that people have to one another and to existing institutions. One facet of the law that is central to maintaining existing social relations, including inequality, is the definition of some acts as criminal and the punishment of people who engage in these acts.

In some modern industrialized societies, the people who make the laws (those who occupy positions in the state and government) are almost identical with those who control the productive processes (what Marx calls the "means of production"). In the Soviet Union, for example, the Communist party holds most of the positions in the state bureaucracy and is also in control of the means of production. In countries with a capitalist mode of production the state and government are formally separated from those who own and control the means of production—the capitalists and the managers of capital. This difference makes for some extremely important differences in the way criminal law works and in the effect it has on these different societies (see Chapter 4).

States within which there is a separation of the owners of the means of production and the state officials who pass and enforce the laws, enjoy some autonomy from the dominant economic class. History shows that, when adjudicating disputes between classes, the state will usually be persuaded by the interests and actions of the dominant economic class. Thus, if we had to predict the most likely outcome of a dispute between owners and laborers, the own-

(Burk Uzzle/Woodfin Camp & Assoc.)

ers would win the dispute when the state adjudicates. This, however, would not always be true for, on occasion, the state will—in the interests of establishing legitimacy or maintaining peace—act in ways that are contrary to the interests and wishes of the dominant class. In the United States, for example, the owners of the means of production vociferously opposed giving women the vote in 1920 or workers the right to organize collectively in 1932, but the state acted independently, believing that it was necessary to avert the possibility of more-severe upheavals. Even in South Africa—where rule by a minority white population is enforced mainly by the sheer coercive force of government troops, police violence, and massive repression—the ruling class is occasionally forced to concede rights and privileges to the underclass black majority in the face of widespread revolt and rebellion.[23] Thus, in the Marxist paradigm, law in capitalist societies is seen as a reflection of class struggle that attempts to maintain simultaneously institutions that facilitate the accumulation of capital and a relative level of social peace.

Recent years bear witness to a proliferation of theories that build upon the Marxist paradigm. What we have described so far is a core of ideas that represent the starting point and agreed-upon assumptions of most criminological theory in this tradition. The remainder of this chapter and the next will outline the major theories in the Marxist tradition. As we shall see, these theories differ on a number of points, including the degree to which the state is autonomous from those who control the economic and productive forces. As Piers Beirne notes, the factors that determine the degree of state autonomy "have as yet been inadequately theorized."[24]

Crime and Economic Conditions

In 1905, the Dutch criminologist Willem Bonger published a seminal work titled *Crime and Economic Conditions*.[25] Bonger's work began from the Marxist position outlined earlier. He applied this perspective and theorized that crime varied depending on the degree to which a society was structured around capitalist or communist modes of production. The capitalist mode of production is structured around individual accumulation, competition, and a struggle for survival at the expense of one social class over the others.

Bonger saw four classes emerging in capitalist societies: the bourgeoisie, the petty bourgeoisie, the proletariat, and the lower (or lumpen) proletariat. He described the bourgeoisie as a class of people for whom the idea that predominates is "to gain money, always more money. This thirst for gold is not quenched when the man has arrived at a point where he can live a luxurious life and gratify all his caprices. Thanks to capitalism, it is possible to amass wealth without limit, so that the capitalist is never satisfied, however enormous may be the sums which he has gained."[26]

The petty bourgeoisie consisted of small shopkeepers and farmers. This class of people aspired to become the bourgeoisie and was in competition with it. Lacking capital and power, however, their position vis à vis the bourgeoisie dooms them to failure and generates hostility toward the capitalists: "As in the case of the bourgeoisie, the relations which the different members of the petty bourgeoisie have among themselves are determined by the economic system: fierce competition, life in a little circle where ideas cannot be broadened, all this breeds envy, hatred, and meanness."[27]

The proletariat class does not own or control the means of production. All they own is their labor, which they must sell in order to survive. The labor of the proletariat thus becomes a commodity just as the products made in factories are commodities. The proletariat sells one commodity (their labor) in order to purchase other commodities (food, housing, clothing, and so forth). The proletariat of Bonger's description (at the turn of the century) was poor, badly housed, often hungry, and burdened with large families. They had little power to form labor unions and virtually no opportunity to move into the petty bourgeoisie or the bourgeoisie. Their life was dismal and without hope.

Even worse off was the lower proletariat. This was the class of people who not only did not possess the means of production, but also were simultaneously unable to sell their labor. For these people,

continual poverty and the permanent fear of dying of hunger destroy all that is noble in man and reduce him to the condition of a beast, without any aspiration for higher things; for those who have come to this state from the more favored classes become more and more degraded and have soon lost the little knowledge they acquired in earlier periods. Servility and lack of self-respect are necessary to the poor if they are to get the alms they need to keep them alive, since they occupy no place in the economic life. Between then and the workers there is an enormous difference; they have no feeling of solidarity in the social life.[28]

According to Bonger, the prevailing personality type produced by capitalism was what he called "egoism"—a personality that strives for self-attainment and places only secondary importance on providing support or aid to neighbors. Bonger argued that, regardless of socialization designed to change this, in a capitalist economic system those who would ultimately gain control of the means of production would be those who behaved in the most egoistic fashion. In communist societies, he continued, the emphasis is on aiding the community rather than the individual. People who are most esteemed and highly regarded (and esteem and regard are the only external rewards available because everyone shares equally in the resources) are those who give the most to others, thus producing the character type of "altruism" as the dominant personality. Bonger theorized that in societies based upon equality and sharing—in which altruistic personalities dominated—we would find very low crime rates and a generally harmonious society. By contrast, in societies based upon inequality

Riding the subway in the affluent society. *(David M. Grossman/Photo Researchers)*

and competition—in which egoistic personalities dominate—we would find high rates of crime, deviance, and disharmony.

In support of his theory, Bonger presented a summary of the existing anthropological data comparing societies with different modes of production; that is, societies in which the organization of economy and politics differ from the capitalist societies of Europe. In his review of the anthropological data, Bonger found substantial support for his theory. Without exception, the anthropological reports of capitalistic, pre-industrial societies revealed societies that were extremely conflicted with ongoing problems of deviance, crime, and violence. By contrast, communistic societies revealed a consistent tendency to be harmonious and relatively free of conflict, crime, violence, and disruptive forces. Bonger cited the study of the Eskimo by Nassen as illustrative:

> The only thing that makes him [the Eskimo] really unhappy is to see others in want, and therefore he shares with them whenever he has anything to share . . . *his first social law is to help his neighbor.* . . . Good humor, peaceableness, and evenness of temper are the most prominent features in his character. He is eager to live on as good a footing as possible with his fellow-men and therefore refrains from offending them and much more from using coarse terms of abuse. . . . His peaceableness even goes so far that when anything is stolen from him, which seldom happens, he does not as a rule reclaim it even if he knows who has taken it. The result is that there is seldom or never any quarreling among them.[29]

Among some North American Indians, Bonger found further support in the anthropological research of G. Catlin, who reported:

> I have roamed about from time to time during seven or eight years, visiting and associating with some three or four hundred thousand of these people, under an almost infinite variety of circumstances; and from the very many and decided voluntary acts of their hospitality and kindness I feel bound to pronounce them, by nature, a kind and hospitable people . . . and under all of these circumstances of exposure, no Indian ever betrayed me, struck me a blow, or stole from me a shilling's worth of my property that I am aware of. [Yet] there is no law in their land to punish a man for theft—locks and keys are not known in their country—the commandments have never been divulged amongst them; nor can any human retribution fall upon the head of a thief, save the disgrace which attaches as a stigma to his character, in the eyes of his people about him . . . in these little communities. . . . I have often beheld peace and hap-

piness, and quiet, reigning supreme, for which even kings and emperors might envy them.[30]

Living among the Iroquois for much of his life, Lewis H. Morgan wrote:

> All the members of an Iroquois gens were personally free, and they were bound to defend each other's freedom; they were equal in privileges and in personal rights, the sachem and chiefs claiming no superiority; and they were a brotherhood bound together by the ties of kin. Liberty, equality, and fraternity, though never formulated, were cardinal principles of the gens. These facts are material, because the gens was the unit of a social and governmental system, the foundation upon which Indian society was organized. . . . If a man entered an Indian house in any of the villages, whether a villager or a stranger, it was the duty of the women therein to set food before him. An omission to do this would have been a discourtesy amounting to an affront. . . . Hunger and destitution could not exist at one end of an Indian village or in one section of an encampment while plenty prevailed elsewhere in the same village or encampment.[31]

Bonger cited a number of other anthropological studies that make the same point: Societies based upon the principles of equality and sharing invariably exhibit personality types and values that emphasize the importance of being kind, generous, and considerate of others, whereas societies based upon competition and the acquisition of goods and wealth create personalities and values that stress egoism and a lack of concern for the well-being of fellow human beings.

At the time of Bonger's writing, there were no modern societies that had implemented communistic or socialistic modes of production. The Russian Revolution did not take place until 1917. The world then consisted primarily of societies based upon tribalism, feudalism, and capitalism, with many societies in the throes of undergoing a transformation from the one to the other. Thus Bonger could not compare these with modern-day societies. He was, however, able to compare types of capitalist societies and particularly capitalist societies that were changing in different ways. He hypothesized—given the emphasis in capitalist societies on individual achievement and self-worth—that during times of economic upheaval, crime would increase. This should be true whether or not the economic system was contracting or expanding. In times of economic improvement, people would suffer anxiety and estrangement because of the pressure created by having to succeed in a competitive world. In times of contraction, people would be equally anxious because of an inability to provide for themselves and their families. Bonger surveyed crime rates in European capitalist countries during periods of rapid expansion and contraction and found that there was indeed a correlation between these periods and a rise in the crime rate.

Bonger wrote before the science of anthropology developed reliable methods for observing and recording the cultures of nonliterate people. As a result, the anthropological studies he cites must be read with caution. It is significant, however, that a survey of hundreds of anthropological studies conducted since Bonger postulated his theory lends considerable support to his proposition.[32] The suggestion that there is a difference in personality type that intervenes between the structure of equality and the behavior of the individual is less easily demonstrated. Indeed, cross-cultural studies reveal a surprising variety of personalities and inconsistent results with respect to attitudes toward self-aggrandizement versus cooperativeness.[33] Bonger's data comparing different types of crime by occupation, society, and degree of poverty are naturally limited to the quality of the data available to him. More relevant to the question of whether the organization of economic and political structures is associated with levels of criminality are the recent studies testing this proposition.

Crime and Inequality

Several recent studies explore the relationship between the incidence of violent crimes and the degree of inequality in society. Judith and Peter Blau find that income inequality and violence are highly correlated.[34] These findings are replicated by Wallace and Humphries' analysis of urban crime and capital accumulation.[35] John Braithwaite compares homicide rates cross-culturally and finds that homicide is highest in countries with the greatest degree of inequality.[36]

Similar results emanate from studies of rape conducted by Julia and Herman Schwendinger. The Schwendingers suggest that rape is a consequence of female powerlessness under capitalist development. Under capitalism, women constitute a reserve labor force that elevates men to a position of political and economic domination and renders women powerless and men able to take advantage of this powerlessness to act violently. The social-control agencies tend to be indifferent to this sort of crime unless forced to act by public-interest groups. Thus we find a higher incidence of rape under capitalism than under other social forms.[37] Julia and Herman Schwendinger, like Bonger, support their argument in part by anthropological data that shows rape is (1) not universal but (2) linked to the economic system. They analyze anthropological data from four nonindustrialized societies: the Mbuti, the Lovedu, the Mpoto, and the Baganda. Based upon this survey, they conclude that the coalescence of exploitative modes of production culminating in class societies "either produced or intensified" sexual inequality, violence, and rape.[38]

James Messerschmidt adds the observation that it is not only the capitalist mode of production, but also patriarchy that accounts for rape and violence against women. He faults the work of the Schwendingers for placing an unwarranted emphasis upon the mode of production and ignoring the equally important role of the hierarchical relationship between the sexes. Western societies, being both capitalist and patriarchal, Messerschmidt argues, have the highest incidence of violence against women (including rape).[39]

Research on the criminality of lower-class women by Eleanor Miller adds impressive support to the theories that link criminality to economic conditions and the mode of production. Miller interviewed and observed the life of women in Milwaukee who worked in the illegal economy, combining prostitution, theft, selling drugs, and a variety of other illegal "hustles" as a means of survival. In attempting to explain how women are recruited into "the Life" (as they call it), Miller begins with the observation that the recent official crime rate of women in the United States has shown a significant increase. This increase is interpreted by some sociologists as a consequence of the women's movement and women's increased involvement in the work force.[40] But, as Eleanor Miller points out, the increase is not in crimes committed by women who are in the work force, but rather in for property crimes committed by women who are *not* in the work force. She offers another explanation:

> socio-economic factors . . . have left underclass women and the households they often head in greater need over the last two decades than in the immediately preceding period. Furthermore, in the light of research that suggest a correlation between the property crime rate of women and certain major jolts to the economy that we

know had important consequences for women's labor force participation, it suggest an examination of the historical relationship between aggregate changes in women's labor force participation and
their criminality . . . it is important to note that the women who
entered the labor force in large number in the 1960's were, for the
most part, women who had not traditionally worked, older white
women with children. Does their entry into the labor force disadvantage in any way less educated, minority women already in the
labor force or desirous of entering the labor force? My hunch is that
it does. Moreover, this occurred at a time when those jobs that were
often the lot of this group, jobs such as farm laborer and domestic,
were becoming more and more scarce.[41]

Miller's research lends considerable support to Marxist theories
because it elaborates the forces that lead women caught in the
bind between scarce employment opportunities and unacceptable
family relations to survive on the fringes of society through a combination of illegal activities. These activities include prostitution,
drug selling, shoplifting, and other forms of criminality that provide an uncertain economic life and an omnipresent possibility of
arrest and sentence to prison.

In a recent work, Michalowski elaborates and builds upon the
Marxist theory. He begins with the proposition that the distribution and types of criminality are related to the mode of production.[42] He argues that, in state societies, a primary function of the
law is the maintenance of the mode of production. From the perspective of crime study, Malinowski suggests, three options for human action exist in any society: conformity, rebellion, and deviance. The law is concerned with rebellion and deviance because
these acts threaten the prevailing mode of production. In egalitarian societies (examples of which exist in preindustrial societies),
law-like institutions are primarily concerned with seeing that all
goods and privileges are distributed equally; in feudal societies,
the law focuses on protecting status and property relations; in capitalist societies, the law concentrates on controlling acts of rebellion or personal maladaptation that threaten the existing social
order or the private ownership of property and personal safety.

Adolescent-Subculture Theory

A much-improved explanation and description of juvenile delinquency has recently emerged from the Marxist tradition in the
work of the Schwendingers. In their seminal work on adolescent

subcultures and delinquency, they take into account a number of the "facts theories must fit" that other researchers have ignored. They recognize, for example, that delinquency is prevalent among most adolescents in one form or another. They also take into account that the quantity and type of delinquency varies depending upon social class, sex, and region.

Extensive research on adolescent subcultures in Los Angeles, as well as the compilation of findings from other studies, reveals consistent patterns of adolescent subcultures. In communities throughout the United States, we find young people in adolescent subcultures of street-corner, intellectual, and socialite types. These three prototypes go under different names: street-corner gangs are variously referred to as Greasers, Ese Vatos, Dudes, Honchos, Hodads, and Homeboys; intellectual subculture members are called Edges, Brains, Pencil-Necks, Egg-Heads, Book-Worms, Intellectuals, and Encyclopedias; and socialite subculture members are tagged with such names as Soshes, Elites, Shiddities, Colleges, Ivy Leaguers, Swingers, and Preppies. In each instance, the group is somewhat segregated sexually, but there are complementary female and male subcultures.

The Schwendingers explain the emergence and content of adolescent subcultures in terms of structural conditions that produce these groups. They summarize their theory thus: "In our theory we propose that certain *stratified networks* of adolescent groups mediate the relationships between macroscopic social processes (including socioeconomic conditions) and the modal patterns of delinquency occurring among peer groups. These delinquent patterns involve life-cycle changes and learned outlooks in adolescent groups on all class levels."[43]

The starting point for the explanation of delinquency proposed by the Schwendingers is that adolescence is a period in which a large proportion of the population is not integrated into the work force. These people are the target of advertizing campaigns urging them to consume and compete in the economic system, yet they are kept in school and dependent upon their parents for most of their income and consumption capacity. They are judged by their peers according to their ability to be independent from their parents but nonetheless to acquire sufficient consumer goods—from drugs to automobiles to clothes. Thus, adolescents are caught in an impossible contradiction. They are kept out of the labor market and are dependent upon parents for money, but they are judged by peers in accordance with their independence from parental values and control:

> Adolescents, in general, have no independent economic status in advanced industrial societies. This lack of independent status in the United States is rooted historically in advanced capitalist developments. Taken together, the replacement of living labor by machines and the technical and scientific revolution limit the expansion both of the unskilled labor force and of the labor force as a whole. Because they are generally employed in unskilled jobs, children and adolescents have been particularly affected by these developments. Therefore, since the 1930's, youth have been gradually but not completely eliminated from the economy—first in basic industries, and last in agriculture. They have been excluded because job markets are influenced by economic developments as a result of the changing composition of capital and its decreasing need for unskilled labor.[44]

The changing nature of, and the relationship of adolescents to, job markets place this age-segmented group of people in a unique position in the social relations created by the political and economic structures. As a consequence, these people develop their own linguistic worlds, each with its own internal logic. The languages, the meanings, and the ways adolescents create to cope with their particular relation leads to a variety of delinquent subcultures influenced by the social-class background and peer interactions. Some of these are highly delinquent, others less so. Only a few (the full-fledged "edges") escape involvement in delinquency.

A number of other studies support the general conclusion that delinquency is a consequence of the peculiar role in the economic and political structure assigned to adolescents. David Greenberg points out that under industrial capitalism, adolescent labor is delegitimized and displaced—which leads in turn to the creation of status anxieties and conflicts, and delinquency represents a solution for those most affected by these changes.[45]

The works of the Schwendingers and Greenberg are ground breaking in that they recognize the necessity to begin with the widespread nature of delinquency among youths and explain patterns and types of delinquent subcultures. They do not propose to answer the unscientific question of why some people commit delinquency; they focus instead on the question of what the varieties of adolescent subcultures are and why they have the shape and distribution they do.

In this regard, it is important to be sensitive to the fact that simply because a theoretical formulation purports to be a Marxist approach, does not guarantee it escapes the inherent flaw of asking an untenable social-psychological question. Colvin and Pauly carry the analysis of adolescent roles in capitalist societies one step further in what they claim is an effort to develop a Marxist theory.[46] They begin with the observation that the relationship a person has to work is critical in determining how that person relates to questions of authority, alienation, and a variety of other interpersonal relations. They cite evidence that the structure of family relations (the degree to which they are authoritarian, for example) are "profoundly shaped by parents' encounters with workplace compliance structures."[47] That is, the way people are treated and expected to relate to employers and fellow workers greatly influences the patterns of social relationships in other spheres, especially the family.[48] It follows from this that the content of parent-child relations will vary considerably by social class. In addition, Colvin and Pauly argue, the school structures its power and social control relations in terms of the social-class background of the students. They argue that different social-control patterns in schools are "designed for the various labor needs of capitalist industry."[49] They theorize:

> The more coercive the control relations encountered in these various socialization contexts tend to be, the more negative or alienated will be the individual's ideological bond and the more likely is the individual to engage in serious, patterned delinquency . . . coercive controls create an alternative orientation toward authority. They create negative ideological bonds and open the individual to entry into peer associations that reinforce patterned delinquent behavior.[50]

Colvin and Pauly acknowledge that there have been no studies that trace the process from work-place control to the etiology of delinquency in families. They note, however, that:

> In addition to Kohn's findings [that social control relations vary by social class] . . . a national survey of self-reported family violence found significant inverse associations between class-related variables (income and occupational prestige) and parental violence toward children and a significant positive association between unemployment and parental violence toward children. These findings suggest class differences in coerciveness of family control structures.[51]

Colvin and Pauly make the classic error that we have seen over and over in the literature on delinquency and crime: They assume that delinquency is primarily a lower-class phenomenon when all the evidence indicates it is not. They qualify their observations with the caveat that they are addressing "serious, patterned delinquency," but this hardly suffices. In the research on two delinquent gangs (the Roughnecks and the Saints) reported earlier, it was clear that the drunk driving and vandalism engaged in by the Saints (the middle-class gang) was at least as serious and as patterned during the high-school years as was the delinquency of the working-class Roughnecks. Furthermore, if the Colvin and Pauly theory were correct, we would expect all lower-class youth to be engaged in "serious, patterned" delinquency. While it does seem that almost all youths engage in delinquency, the frequency and distribution of "serious, patterned" delinquency among all lower-class youth is a myth perpetuated by middle-class social scientists. Thus, even within the Marxist paradigm, we find unacceptable theorizing based upon fallacious attempts to explain individual delinquency or criminality. Rather we should remain faithful to the idea that it is structured patterns of behavior, not individual adaptations, that must be explained if we are to develop adequate theories of crime, criminal law, and criminality.

Conclusion

The analyses of the relationship between social structure, crime, and criminal law are a significant advance in scientific inquiry about crime. With few exceptions they are consistent with the overall pattern of crime in modern industrialized societies. They provide theoretical frameworks that take into account the fact that criminality is widely distributed in the social structure and different types of criminality characterize different social classes or groups. They avoid the errors found in other paradigms of crime by not seeking to explain individual adaptations but being satisfied with linking characteristics of the social structure with differences in crime rates and the distribution of crime. By noting the differences in the power and economic potentialities of women and men, for example, they are able to explain why women have lower rates for most conventional crime. From these theoretical paradigms, it is also clear why upper-class men commit most of the corporate and white-collar crimes and lower-class men are more likely to be involved in crimes of burglary, robbery, and theft. What these theories lack, however, is an articulation of the specific characteristics of different types of social structures that can explain the dynamics of the process by which laws and criminal behaviors are produced. For this, we need to turn to an analysis of the characteristics of social structure independent of particular economic or political relations that can be applied to different types of society. This can be accomplished through an understanding of the *contradictions* and *conflicts* inherent in different forms of political, economic, and social relations. Developing and applying this paradigm is taken up in the chapters that follow.

12

Crime and Structural Contradictions

In this chapter, the effort is made to set forth a theory that is consistent with the scientific principles outlines in the preceding chapters. To accomplish this, we must build upon the paradigms that have gone before; we must work "on the shoulders of giants." Science is not cumulative in the sense that each fact is added to a pile until at some magic moment the pile automatically reveals its inner truth; science *is* cumulative in that the shortcomings of previous research and theory make possible the creation of new paradigms, the raising of new questions, and the development of improved techniques for gathering and analyzing data.

One conclusion to be drawn from the analysis of our knowledge about crime is that the structural tradition holds the greatest promise of leading to reliable scientific knowledge. It asks questions amenable to systematic investigation and capable of leading to reliable knowledge, for it assumes that criminal behavior is a response of groups and social classes to the resources and constraints of the social structure rather than the adaptation of individuals to personal biology, psychology, or social experiences. Our theory therefore draws from the structural tradition for its starting point. We seek to answer questions about why criminal behavior exists, why it is distributed as it is, and why it varies from place to place and from one historical period to another. We do not seek to answer why Johnny steals and Bobby makes airplanes, why one politician accepts bribes and another does not, or why one manager violates health and safety regulations and another does not. We understand that paradigms trying to explain individual criminal behavior are bound to end in either tautologies or empirically false theories. Either way, they are unsatisfactory as explanations. We wish to avoid this by focusing on questions that seek to understand the relationship between crime and social structure. Such an approach holds the most promise for the development of a reliable body of scientific knowledge.

Contradictions and Conflicts _____

A contradiction exists in a given set of social relationships (political, social, economic, and ideological) when, in the normal course of events, existing social relations simultaneously maintain the status quo and produce the conditions necessary to transform it. That is, when conforming to one set of demands, goals or institutionalized processes creates situations that are fundamentally antagonistic to the existing social relations.

Under these circumstances, "contradictions tend to intensify with time and cannot be resolved within the existing social framework."[1] Every historical era, every society, and every human group in the process of constructing ways to survive invariably creates contradictory forces and tendencies that serve as an unseen force moving the group toward new social, political, and economic relations. Change is thus an inexorable part of every human group.[2] To understand this, it is essential that we adopt an attitude toward social life that flies in the face of conventional wisdom. We must accept the fact that social life is contradictory, that opposites exist simultaneously, and that people both create their own history and are created by it. "The world is not to be comprehended as a complex of ready made *things,* but as a complex of *processes.*"[3]

The contradictions lead inexorably to conflicts between groups, classes, and strata. The conflicts reflecting contradictions are manifested as antagonistic relations that reflect the struggle of people to deal with contradictory social, political, and economic relations. The following are examples: workers go on strike, women demonstrate against unequal pay, farmers march on Washington, small landowners take up arms against agribusiness, and Indians barricade themselves on their reservation against federal agents.

Every historical era has its own unique contradictions and conflicts. The most important conflicts existing in a particular time and place are those that derive from the way the social, economic, and political relations are organized. The following are the most basic characteristics of any human group: how people make a living, the work they do, the way they organize their labor to produce the things that are useful and necessary for survival, and how they distribute the results of their labor and organize power relations. People may create a political organization that strives for equality or one that creates vast differences in wealth between the rich and the poor. People may create a political structure that allows every member of the community a voice in every decision or they may organize their politics so that only a few people have the right to decide. There exists an apparently infinite number of possible combinations and permutations.

For an understanding of crime, it is the way people organize their economy, politics, and social relations that must be the starting point for constructing an adequate theory.

Criminal behavior is generated because of the contradictions that inevitably arise in the course of life. The type of crime, the amount of crime, and the distribution of crime in a particular historical period and society depend upon the nature of the existing contradictions, the conflicts that develop as people respond to the contradictions, and the mechanisms institutionalized for handling the conflicts and dilemmas produced by the contradictions.

As we saw in Chapter 4, the emergence of criminal law can be understood in just these terms. That is, criminal laws emerge, change, and develop as people attempt to respond to conflicts generated by contradictions in the political and economic organization of their world. It will be recalled, for example, that in capitalist economies there is a basic contradiction between the public nature of production and the private ownership of the means of production. Goods cannot be produced unless people can be forced, coerced, encouraged, cajoled, or persuaded to do the necessary work. This is the public nature of production. Under capitalism, however, the ownership of the goods produced does not reside with those who produce them but with those who own the means of production— the tools, the factories, and the necessary knowledge. This leads inexorably to conflict, which invariably changes the existing relationships. As workers struggle to increase their share of what they produce and owners struggle to maintain or increase their share, workers and owners are locked in conflict, each seeking to increase their share of the surplus.

The public production–private ownership contradiction—combined with a political organization of democratic, electoral politics—led in the formative years of industrialization in the United States and Europe to ubiquitous conflict between workers and owners. These conflicts were responded to politically by the passage of innumerable laws making it a crime for workers to organize collectively against owners, to strike, to refuse to work, and so forth. The attempted solution, it must be stressed, was *not* attending to the contradictions that generated the conflicts, it was focusing solely on the conflicts created by the contradictions. This attempted "solution" to the conflict did *not* suffice to silence worker demands. Indeed, the more oppressive the laws became, the more virulent the workers' rebellion. In the 1930s, another political tack was tried—laws giving workers the right to bargain collectively and to strike under certain circumstances were passed. Other laws restricted these rights and gave the government the right to arbitrate and, under certain circumstances, to intervene. We also saw how the behavior of women seeking the vote, the right to determine their own economic role in society, and even their right to decide whether or not to bear children were defined as criminal.

One way to resolve the conflicts generated by a class society is to define some groups or classes of people as less than human. This resolution, however, generates its own contradictions on an ideological level. To convince people that they live in a just and fair society, ideologies of equality, and freedom, and the inherent integrity of the individual may be promulgated. Yet the treatment of some people as less than human is a useful way of maintaining a compliant labor force. If some people—because of their race, gender, or age—are treated as though they are less human than others, then conflicts are inevitable. Dealing with these conflicts then becomes part of the state apparatus. Laws are passed that institutionalize differential access to the resources. Some people are legally prohibited from full participation in what are ideologically touted as the fundamental rights and privileges of all. Thus, when slaves or women are defined as less than human and denied their rights, the structure of political and economic relations is ripe for the emergence of conflicts. The criminal law will respond in an attempt to resolve these conflicts; some responses will be increasingly repressive, others will be ameliorative. In time, slaves were freed, women got the vote, and workers earned the right to strike. But, in the interim, there was conflict defined by law as criminal.

As Sutherland once pointed out, an understanding of the processes by which the criminal law is created is also an answer to the question of why there is crime. There is crime, in this sense, because there is law that defines certain acts as criminal.

We want to go beyond this, however. We want also to be able to answer why the types of crime differ between sexes, social classes, ethnic groups, and age groups in a particular society, and we want to be able to know why crime varies by type, frequency, and intensity from one society or historical period to another.

Political Economy and Structural Contradictions

The major forms of economic organization in the modern world are capitalism and socialism. The major political forms are democratic and authoritarian governments. Sociologically, these political forms do not coincide in fact with the political depiction that characterizes public discourse. For example, it is commonplace in capitalist countries to equate democratic political forms with capitalist economic forms and authoritarian political forms with socialist economic systems. This simplistic characterization is totally erroneous. Some of the most authoritarian governments in the world are capitalist (Chile, South Korea, Costa Rica, Guatemala, and Brazil) and some of the most democratic in terms of public participation in decision making are socialist (China, Cuba, Yugoslavia). Whether or not a particular country exhibits authoritarian or democratic tendencies is a matter to be determined by objective asessment, not by political rhetoric.

Most societies today exhibit a mixture of these economic and political organizational forms. It is more accurate, in fact, to conceive of modern-day societies as those that vary along continua on the dimensions of economic organization (capitalist to socialist) and political forms (authoritarian to democratic). All societies represent a set of social relations characterized by attempts to resolve conflicts generated by contradictions inherent in the social structure. It is unlikely that those who have the power to make decisions in different nations will all make the same choices when faced with alternative ways of resolving conflicts. As they make different choices, different mixes of economic and political structures emerge.

In everyday political rhetoric, the Unites States and the Soviet Union are usually contrasted as representing "capitalist democracy" and "socialist authoritarianism," respectively. Although neither society meets the criteria for being purely capitalist, democratic, socialist, or authoritarian, the characterization nonetheless alerts us to the different types of contradictions and conflicts we can expect to find in these different forms.

The law responds to the contradictions and conflicts inherent in the established institutions and social relations. The attempt by workers, groups suffering discrimination (such as women, Native Americans, African Americans, Chicanos, gays, and lesbians), minorities, and the underclass to organize and demand an end to discrimination is met by resistance from the owners, who see in each of these efforts a threat to their control over what is "rightfully" theirs—the control of their property, their privileges, and the products produced by the machines, factories, and talents that they own. The dilemma for capital, the state and government is how to resolve the conflicts (see diagram on p. 305). Note that it is the *conflicts* that precipitate the dilemmas for the different actors in this drama and it is conflicts that people attempt to resolve. The contradictions are too fundamental: To resolve the contradictions necessarily requires changing fundamentally the organizational form of the political, economic, and social relations. At least one fraction of the struggle—the owners of the means of production—dismiss that possibility out of hand if it threatens their ownership.

Modern-day socialist societies share some of the contradictions and conflicts of capitalist societies and have their own unique ones as well. Socialism rests on the ideological pillar of economic equality and political decentralization. The ideological bedrock of contemporary socialist societies is that these societies are transitional constructions that are lending toward communism—a utopian vi-

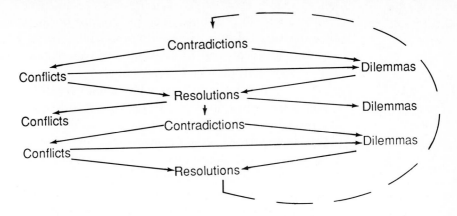

sion in which there are no social classes and no state apparatuses, and people are free to pursue their own creative impulses in conjunction with a universally held belief in the value of working for the betterment of other people. The goal of socialist ideology is for every person to have the same standard of living and an equal voice in political decisions. Socialism also promises rapid industrialization and an increase in the standard of living for everyone. The goal of allowing everyone to participate in decision making and to share equally in the surplus produced contradicts the goal of rapid industrialization and increased standard of living.[4] Without centralized decision making and the reinvestment of surplus, material progress is restrained. The contradiction is whether to centralize authority and concentrate the wealth in the state in order to industrialize rapidly or to permit the redistribution of wealth and the decentralization of decision making.[5] From this contradiction flows many of the conflicts and much of the crime that characterize modern-day socialist societies. For example, the inability of the centralized planning bureaucracy to respond quickly to changes in consumer demands creates a circumstance in which black-market activities can and do flourish.[6] The same contradiction also leads to a demand for social services that institutionalizes the manufacture and distribution of illegal papers for travel and the right to purchase goods and gain access of official offices.[7] Defenders of socialism argue that once the primary task of providing material goods to everyone in the society has been accomplished, then attention can be turned to attaining the goals of humane and cooperative social relations.[8]

An equally important contradiction in socialist societies that leads to widespread criminality is centered in the state's desire to accumulate capital and increase productivity through the exploitation of natural resources. In an economic system that promises full employment but in which some jobs are much less desirable than others, there must be some mechanism created to fill the undesirable jobs. One solution is to provide significantly higher wages to those who will work at the least desirable jobs. In the Soviet Union, this is practiced, and mineworkers are among the highest paid workers in the labor force. This solution, however, reveals other contradictions, particularly that between the ideology of "to each according to their needs from each according to their ability." In other words, in a society committed to economic equality, an incentive system based upon higher wages for some is contradictory. Another solution, also utilized in many of today's socialist societies (especially the Soviet Union), is to rely on the labor of criminals to perform the work others are unwilling to do. The Soviet practice of prison labor camps in Siberia, where work conditions are among the most arduous of anyplace in the world, can be seen as a solution to the dilemma. It is possible, as well, that the Soviet practice of meting out severe penalties for relatively trivial crimes reflects the need to maintain a large labor force of prisoners.[9]

Crime in Capitalist Societies

The capitalist economy depends upon the production and consumption of commodities by large numbers of people. There is, then, at the outset a two-fold problem to be solved: How do we make people work to produce the commodities and how do we create a desire for the commodities on the part of large numbers of people?

Some commodities—food, clothing, and shelter—are essential for survival. If the only means available for obtaining these essentials is to work for someone who owns them, people will generally choose to work rather than starve or freeze to death. But capitalism does not depend upon the production and consumption of necessities alone. It also depends upon the production and consumption of goods and services that have little or nothing to do with survival. For capitalism to develop, people must be motivated to work in order to purchase unessential commodities.

There are many ways that people are taught to want nonessential commodities—advertizing, socialization into a world in which the acquisition of nonessential commodities bestows status and a sense of personal integrity on those who can display them, and the necessity to accumulate property in order to stave off the possibility of falling below the level of consumption necessary for survival.

Creating the desire to consume, though, simultaneously creates the seeds of discontent and the possibility that people will discover ways of being able to increase consumption without working. If—instead of spending 8 hours at a boring, tedious, and sometimes dangerous occupation—a person can obtain the money necessary for purchasing commodities by theft, fraud, trickery, or bribery, then some people will choose that option. In an effort to avoid this possibility, the people who own the means of production and those who manage the state pass laws making such acts illegal. In this way, they try to reduce the attractiveness of alternative routes to consumption.

There are other forces at work that push people to discover alternative ways of accumulating capital. Not all people have an equal opportunity to consume the products they are taught to want. Different kinds of work pay different wages. Some jobs pay only enough for survival. In capitalist economies, there are vast differences in the wages people receive and in the wealth they can accumulate.

How, then, can a set of social relations be sustained that requires the vast majority of people to spend their lives working at tasks they find unsatisfactory in order to be able to have a large enough population of consumers to fuel the engines of capitalist production and consumption? There are many possible solutions to this dilemma, and most of these have been tried at one time or another in the history of capitalism. One solution to this contradiction is to create a class of people who can be forced to work but do not form an essential part of the consuming population. This was the solution tried during the period of capitalism that depended upon slavery. Slaves were not a major part of the consuming population, but they did provide most of the essential labor for a minimum expense. This solution, however, created its own contradictions: "the system could justify slavery only by defining the Black as inhuman—But the system depended on mutual obligations, duties, responsibilities and even rights, that implicity recognized the slave's humanity."[10]

Today, capitalism depends upon wage labor. People must work for wages in order to have the power to consume and must consume in order for the economy to survive. This, too, creates its own contradictions. There is only one source of profit for the capitalist: the difference between the wage that the capitalist pays the worker and the price for which the product of that worker's labor is sold. If the worker is paid the full amount for which the product is sold, then there is no profit, and the economic systems comes to a grinding halt. Without an accumulation of surplus to reinvest, the economy collapses. If, on the other hand, the worker is not paid enough to survive, then the population is decimated, and there is no one to purchase the commodities produced. Thus there is a fundamental *wages, profits, and consumption contradiction* in capitalist economies. Dealing with that contradiction explains a large part of the history of modern capitalism. Workers seek to earn higher wages and owners seek to pay the minimum amount. When workers do not have high enough wages to buy cars, houses, luxury items, and products of new technologies, the economy is sluggish. When workers are paid high wages that cut into the profits of the owners', there is less money to reinvest in new technologies and improved production. Foreign competition then cuts even further into the profits. This contradiction creates different conflicts and attempted resolutions: economists argue over whether it is better to increase profits to encourage investment in new productive capacities or to increase wages to encourage more consumption. Government policy vacillates in an attempt to accommodate these contradictory tendencies.

From the point of view of crime, the conflicts culminate in criminal behavior on the part of both workers and owners. Owners cut corners, violate health and safety regulations, illegally deal in the stock market, and violate securities and exchange regulations; workers steal from employers, supplement their wages by selling illegal drugs, illegally strike and organize, and join illegal political groups. The state sits squarely in the midst of the contradiction: Although generally influenced more by owners than workers, it cannot allow the ongoing conflict to disrupt social, political, and economic relations to the point of destroying the existing economic systems (capitalism) or the existing political system (democracy). It responds by passing laws to keep workers from disrupting production or stealing property and owners from disregarding the health and safety of workers and consumers. It also passes laws prohibiting certain economic activities that undermine the state's own interests (avoiding taxes by laundering money through overseas banks) or give one group of capitalists an advantage over another (insider trading on the stock market, which disenfranchises those who are not privy to secret corporate information or forming monopolies). State and government officials work to block efforts by extranational bodies (such as the United Nations) to establish codes of conduct for multinational corporations in developing nations.[11] Another tactic is to maintain laws that allow the reserve labor force available in less-developed countries to enter the country for temporary jobs (such as in agriculture) where it can be employed at low wages without accruing any benefits from state-supported institutions such as welfare, education, and unemployment.[12]

Under capitalism, there is also a fundamental *wages–labor supply contradiction*. The owners pursuing the logic of capitalist economies will strive to pay as little as possible to the workers. It is not possible, however, to pay nothing, unless there is an overabundance of labor that allows workers to be used up and discarded and then replaced with others flowing in. In advanced industrial societies, such a solution is impossible (as is slave labor) because much of the labor needed requires skills that take time to learn. However, if there is full employment under capitalism, workers have an advantage in the struggle for increased shares of profits with owners. If there is a reserve labor force—that is, a significant proportion of the labor force that is unemployed or underemployed—then, when the demands of labor threaten the profits of the owners, the owners can turn to the reserve army of labor to replace the workers. The reserve army, though, forms an underclass that cannot consume but nonetheless is socialized into a system in which consumption is the necessary condition for happiness. Criminal behavior offers a solution for the underclass: What they cannot earn legitimately they can earn illegitimately.

Goths and Vandals: An illustration

The most basic contradiction of capitalism, as previously noted, is between the public nature of production and the private ownership of the means of production. This builds into the economic system a conflict between workers and owners over who will receive how much of the profit generated by the products produced through the labor of the workers. If the workers and the capitalists both persistently pursue their own interests, then the relationship between workers and capitalists, indeed, the entire system of production, will eventually be destroyed. This contradiction, along with others, produces a wide range of conflicts; that is, antagonistic struggles between the parties. The conflicts, in turn, create dilemmas for state and government officials who must select from among alternative strategies.

The attempt by workers to organize and demand higher wages, better working conditions, tenure of employment, and so forth, is a result of this basic contradiction. The attempt by owners to resist these demands creates conflicts. The dilemma for the owners, the state, and government is how to resolve the conflicts; how to maintain the capitalist system without fermenting a revolution or destroying the capitalists' right to ownership and control of their property.

When capitalism was still in its infancy in Europe, production centered on cottage industries. Families worked together in their own homes producing wool, clothing, and other commodities. Merchants purchased these goods, traveled to the urban centers, and sold them for a profit. With the development of machines, however, this set of social, political, and economic relations was revolutionized. Merchants with some accumulated capital now seized the opportunity to build factories that could produce the same goods at a much lower cost, with the resultant higher profits to the capitalists. The workers were forced to change their lives to accommodate the change. Rather than being independent producers who sold their products, they were now employed as wage earners doing routine pieces of the production process. The work was taken out of their homes, out of their control, and routinized to an extent that made their labor tedious and backbreaking:

> The hours of work were fourteen, fifteen, or even sixteen a day, six days a week throughout the year except for Christmas Day and Good Friday . . . the human animal broke down under the burden; and he squandered his time in palliatives—drink, lechery, bloodsports. Or he revolted, burned down the factory, or broke up the machinery.[13]

During the 1700s and 1800s, "machine smashing" periodically ripped through Europe:

> Attacks on machines took place from the 1760's when Hargreaves' spinning jenny was repeatedly smashed, and mills which used the jenny were turned over. According to traditional accounts, Hargreaves was chased out of the neighborhood and his promotor, the factory owner, 'Parsley' Peel, retreated from North East Lancashire

in disgust, taking his capital to another area where he hoped the work force would be more sensible. Peel's mills near Blackburn and Accrington were completely destroyed, one having been already re-built after attacks by machine-smashers only a few years before.

There were many more attacks on machines. One of the most famous periods of disturbances was during the war in Europe when from 1811 to 1813 various kinds of new machines were attacked . . . the attackers were known as 'Luddites,' . . . in 1830 there was an explosion of popular discontent throughout southern and eastern England when the rural poor attacked the hated threshing machines and set fire to hay ricks. . . . Machine smashing was also employed by workers as a means of obtaining higher wages and better working conditions. . . . Along the coasts, local residents also engaged in the systematic wrecking of ships. In response to demands of the mercantile classes, government put teeth into the laws forbidding the activity. So too did the government intervene against the machine-smashers. Whatever their motivations, they experienced the law as 'the lash or the whip, the threat of transportation, the gallows at Tyburn, and the awesome sight of the bodies of convicts swinging in chains.[14]

This historical process reveals the contradictions and conflicts and their relationship to criminality: The conflicts between owners and workers stemmed from the fundamental contradiction over the private ownership of the means of production and the public nature of the productive process. These conflicts led the workers to smash the owners' property and the state to intervene on the owners' side with criminal laws and sanctions against the workers.

From the vantage point of the 20th century, the legitimacy of capitalism as an economic system is ingrained in our consciousness to such a degree that we automatically accept the logic of the state passing laws to protect the interests of the capitalists. But that apparent simplicity is misleading. When the workers rebelled against the introduction of machines and factories, it was not logically or scientifically determined that the state should pass laws and punish workers for smashing the machines that were turning their work into alienated, inhuman labor. State officials could have sided with the workers. Had the workers controlled the state, this no doubt would have happened. The law could have made it a crime for the capitalists to build factories; it could have forced them to put the machines in the homes of the workers to protect their way of life; or it could have made it a crime to manufacture, transport, or utilize the machines at all. The choice made by those in power in the 17th and 18th centuries was to pass laws forcing and coercing the workers to accept the new way of producing commodities. The choice made by many workers was to rebel and assault the new system in an effort to return to their way of life. The workers ultimately lost the battle, and the industrialization of Europe continued apace.

Phantom Capitalists

Michael Levi's brilliant study of what he calls "Phantom Capitalists" provides another excellent illustration of how structural contradictions induce criminality.[15] In his research into London's white-collar crime, Levi discovered two major types of fraud: "long firm" and "slippery slope." Both types involve the creation of companies that serve as fronts for the purpose of purchasing goods on credit. In the case of "long firm" fraud, an entrepreneur establishes an elaborate network of rented offices, hired secretaries, leased telephones, phony credit ratings, and business letterhead stationery. He then places a large order to a foreign company; for example, an order for 10 thousand shirts made in Taiwan. The company receiving the order checks out the credit references, calls the telephone listed on the stationery, and so forth. Finding the business to be legitimate, the shirts are sent on credit. When the shirts arrive, the fraudster immediately sells them at a substantial discount—say one half their wholesale price—to a person willing to buy merchandise without asking too many questions. The fraudster then pockets the entire purchase price, closes up the office, pays off the secretaries, and disappears. Or, at least changes his or her name and the name of the company and perpetrates the fraud again.

While the "long firm" fraudster enters into the entire transaction from the beginning with the clear idea of obtaining goods by fraud, selling them, and covering his or her tracks, the "slippery slope" fraudster is a legitimate businessperson who gets involved through a series of setbacks that create the need for an infusion of cash. Initially, Levi found, the businessperson intends to buy on credit, sell the goods, and postpone paying the creditors in order to generate more capital. He or she, however, committed fraud at the point when purchasing the goods on credit with no intention of paying the creditors upon sale of the goods. If things go favorably for the businessperson, he or she may be able to recoup the losses after a few quick sales and avoid detection. If, however, things do not go favorably, he or she will be in danger of detection. In either case, from the point of view of the law and criminology, the "slippery slope" fraud is as much a crime as the "long firm" fraud, although the courts may look with more compassion on the "slippery slope" fraudster.

The contradiction in capitalist economies that produces these types of crime is at the very heart of the commodity-exchange process. Manufacturers could of course insist on cash before delivery for all the goods they produce. If they did so, however, someone who was willing to take a chance on retailers and sell them the goods on credit would begin competing with them. The manufacturer giving credit, if he or she chose clients wisely, would thrive, while the one insisting on cash would shrivel. Credit becomes the oil of capitalism's machinery. But with that innovation, comes the possibility and indeed even the certainty that some people will discover and employ ways of turning the credit system to their own advantage, enabling them to accumulate capital without having to produce the capital to begin with.

White-Collar and Corporate Crime

Examples of how contradictions in the economic and political system culminate in white-collar, corporate, and governmental crime are legion. Take, for example, the problem of controlling corporate executives' expenditure of investors' money. If there are no restrictions on how executives can invest and spend the money entrusted to them, it will be difficult to generate the large sums of money needed to compete in today's world of monopolies and conglomerates. On the other hand, if the executive's hands are tied by specific investment restrictions, then the opportunity to take advantage of changes in the marketplace severely restricts the likelihood of success. That dilemma was manifested rather dramatically in the case of the Barton Oil Company.

The owners of the Barton Oil Company sold shares in an oil-exploration company they owned.[16] They took the funds generated by this sale of stock and divided them between the exploration company, an unnumbered Swiss bank account, and investments in subsidiary companies that were not involved in oil exploration. The subsidiary companies were subsequently declared bankrupt. The oil exploration company also failed. The stockholders lost their investment. The Bartons, however, increased their net worth considerably during this period. Exactly how they managed to increase their net worth while losing all the stockholders' money is not entirely clear. The courts, however, were asked to try the owners on criminal charges for misusing stockholder funds that were entrusted to them, the prosecutor said, for the specific purpose of investing in oil exploration. The defense was that the owners were seeking to maximize the stockholders' earnings by investing in what they thought were the best investments at the time. The court recognized the dilemma: If stock investors are not protected by the agreement to invest in the way they are told, they will lose confidence in the system and cease to invest their money. If, the companies hands are tied, though, and they can only invest in what they know are bad investments, the stockholders will also lose confidence as they lose their money. There is no resolution to this contradiction. The law balances on a high wire trying to create legitimacy by giving the impression that it is protecting stockholders while at the same time giving maximum freedom to executives to use stockholders' money as they see fit. The result is that some executives will take advantage of this situation and convert stockholders' investments to their own personal use or misuse them in the course of doing business.

Contradictions of this sort permeate the business world and explain the persistence and widespread character of corporate and white-collar crime. Some people engaged as lawyers, stockbrokers, or business executives of corporations are invariably privy to insider information. For example, if IBM is about to try to take over the Xerox Corporation, it must first consult with lawyers and financial consultants. These meetings will be conducted in the utmost secrecy. Those involved in the meetings, however, must know what is going to transpire. In a large transaction, the number of people involved can easily number in the hundreds. They all know that, when the announcement becomes public, the stock value of the corporations involved is going to change dramatically. It is a criminal act for any of the participants to use this information to buy or sell stocks. This law is designed to make the purchase and sale of stocks appear fair so that investors will not conclude that buying stocks is an insiders' game that can be won only by those in the know. For those in the know, however, the possibility of immense personal wealth is substantial. The risk is minimal, given the difficulty of tracing stock purchases and sales and the small number of federal agents assigned to check on such matters. The consequence is that insider trading on the stock market is rampant.

Federal efforts to curtail insider trading are sporadic and ineffectual. When enforcement is attempted, the revelations of widespread criminality among lawyers, corporate executives, and stockbrokers are considerable. In 1986, the Securities and Exchange Commission arrested and prosecuted dozens of lawyers, stockbrokers, and investors for insider trading, which accounted for tens of millions of dollars of criminally acquired funds by people in the leading law firms and brokerages in the country.[17]

One final example will suffice to give a sense of how the theory of structural contradictions applies to the prevalence and distribution of white-collar and corporate criminality. In the 1980s, many of the major banks of the United States were found guilty of criminally transferring funds to overseas banks. Many of these funds were the profits of organized crime. The banks indicted included leading banks in New York, Chicago, Boston, and Philadelphia. In June of 1986, to cite just one example, the brokerage house of Shearson and Lehman Brothers, Inc., the former manager of its Philadelphia office, and six other men—including the son-in-law of former chief of police and Mayor Frank Rizzo—were charged with conspiracy in the operation of an illegal sports-gambling enterprise and the laundering of $1.2 million for an organized-crime gambling syndicate.[18] Other banks and brokerage houses were indicted in 1986 for laundering money from organized-crime syndicates. The laundered money consisted of profits that depended upon the distribution of drugs, illegal gambling, and skimming profits from legitimate businesses to avoid paying taxes. Given the nature of organized crime in America, these profits must also be seen as profits gained from murder, intimidation, threats, and exploitation.[19]

Why would the major banks and some of the major brokerage houses in America engage in such criminal activities in complicity with organized crime? The answer lies in the immense profits to be had from transferring money. Federal law limits the amount of money a bank can transfer without filing a report to the government to $10,000. If a bank insists on filing such a report, depositors will take their money elsewhere. The banks want the profits, the criminals want the transfers, and the government wants for the most part to overlook the requirement, so business is conducted as usual.

Public Corruption

The corruption of public officials in capitalist societies is as much a part of the landscape as the air we breathe. Politicians from local alderman to Presidents and Congresspeople are exposed throughout the capitalist world as having accepted bribes, payoffs, and illegal campaign contributions. In Puerto Rico in 1968, the FBI indicted a former San Juan police lieutenant colonel and three detectives (one of whom was a lawyer) with the murder of seven people and the theft of over a million dollars in jewelry and gems. In New York City during the same period, a borough president committed suicide when it was revealed that he was taking bribes from companies seeking contracts with the government. Dozens of other New York City politicians and government officials were indicted in the same probe—including a former deputy director of New York City's Parking Violations Bureau and an assistant to the mayor in charge of letting hospital and health-care contracts. The companies themselves were indicted and fined $600,000. At the federal level, every administration since George Washington's has experienced a rash of resignations and criminal indictments of high-level officials, a pattern that some thought reached its peak when Vice-President Agnew was indicted and pleaded "no contest" to a charge of soliciting and accepting bribes for giving contracts and President Nixon was threatened with impeachment for criminal acts. Under the administration of Ronald Reagan, over *200* high-level appointees were forced to resign either because they were indicted or suspected of criminal acts.

The widespread corruption of public officials suggests that choosing between administrations in terms of a propensity for corruption may be as difficult as choosing the healthiest stalk in a stack of rotten hay.

Electoral politics demands that candidates for office spend huge sums of money on political campaigns—for the presidency, over $100 million; for a seat in Congress, between $500,000 and $3 million. Governor Rockefeller of West Virginia spent over $10 million in a re-election campaign in which he was unopposed in the Democratic primary and his Republican opponent was given no chance whatsoever to win.[20] Electoral politics combined with a capitalist economy create a seed-bed for corruption. Politicians must amass huge amounts of money to compete successfully for elected office. People with the money to contribute do so in order to gain favorable treatment in dealing with the government, whether it be in legislative decisions or in obtaining contracts, licenses, and franchises. If contributions to political campaigns are allowed, the possibility and probability of corruption is omnipresent.[21] If campaign contributions are not allowed, the electorate may not have maximum exposure to the candidates. Resolving that dilemma in the United States led to a system of campaign financing that guarantees corruption.[22]

America is not alone in generating political corruption as a result of financing campaign contributions. Helmut Kohl, the chancellor of West Germany, admitted that, while he was chairman of the Christian Democratic Union (1974–1980), he accepted illegal political contributions from the Friedrich Flick Industrieverwaltung. To make matters worse, Chancellor Kohl apparently lied about his knowledge of the illegal campaign contributions before a parliamentary committee. The Bonn public prosecutor's office investigated the allegations that Kohl perjured himself and the possibility of pursuing criminal charges against him.[23] Some capitalist countries limit the funds for campaigning to those that are supplied by state taxation. That system, however, produces its own contradictions and does not solve the problem, as the case of Chancellor Kohl indicates. There may be better or worse ways of encouraging or discouraging corruption in politics, but electoral politics—in which money influences success or failure—is bound to breed varying degrees of corruption.

In a similar vein, the corruption of the police is institutionalized in capitalist countries. Basically the problem is that, for the police to appear to do their job most efficiently, they must (1) permit some forms of criminality (gambling, drug dealing) to take place in order (2) to manage crime better in the community and keep the citizenry from being aware of what is taking place.

> The law-enforcement system is placed squarely in the middle of two essentially conflicting demands. On the one hand, the job obligates police to enforce the law, albeit with discretion; at the same time, considerable disagreement rages over whether or not some acts should be subject to legal sanction. This conflict is heightened by the fact that some influencial persons in the community insist that all laws be rigorously enforced, while others demand that some laws not be enforced, at least not against them. Faced with such a dilemma and such an ambivalent situation, the law enforcers do what any well-managed bureaucracy would do under similar circumstances. They follow the line of least resistance. Using the discretion inherent in their positions, they resolve the problem by estab-

lishing procedures that minimize organizational strains and that provide the greatest promise of rewards for the organization and the individuals involved. Typically this means that law enforcers adopt a tolerance policy toward the vices, selectively enforcing the laws when it is to their advantage to do so. [By] limiting the visibility of such activity as sexual deviance, gambling, and prostitution they appease those who demand the enforcement of applicable laws. At the same time, since controlling visibility does not eliminate access for persons sufficiently interested to ferret out the tolerated vice areas, those demanding such services are also satisfied.[24]

The contradiction between appearance and reality leads to co-operation between some criminals and the police, which leads in turn to institutionalized corruption.[25]

Street Crime

The forces that lead to street crime are not very different. As we have seen, capitalism produces a large class of people unable to consume the commodities they are taught to want. These people live with a constant dilemma, to accept failure by conventional standards and do without the "good things of life" or even necessities, or discover alternative ways of getting the money to buy the commodities they desire. Alternative ways are available to the lower classes as well as to the white-collar workers, corporate executives, and government officials. But lower-class people cannot engage in insider trading, embezzlement, "long firm" fraud (unless they learn the skills from someone experienced in the trade), or bribery. They can steal from grocery stores, traffick in drugs, pick pockets, run a crap game, or burgle houses. These activities require some skill, but they are not dependent upon having a particular occupation or position. Like the factory owner who commits violence against workers by refusing to adhere to factory safety and health regulations, lower-class crime also may involve violence to avoid detection or to commit the criminal act. Street crimes are less profitable, probably more likely to lead to detection, and certainly, if the criminal is caught, more likely to culminate in criminal sanctions. To protect themselves from being caught and punished, it may be necessary for criminals to engage in violence. The specifics change, but the overall pattern of responding to contradictions in the political, economic, and social relations of our historical moment remain the cause of the criminality. This ap-

Civilian patrols: the
Guardian Angels. *(Jim
Anderson/Woodfin
Camp & Assoc.)*

plies whether it is the criminality of middle-class women who shop-lift, lower-class women who prostitute themselves or sell drugs, street-gangs members who steal and fight, or bankers who laun-der money for organized criminals.

Woman and Crime

The conflicts generated by structural contradictions explain the role of women in crime as both perpetrators and victims. Women are part of the reserve army of labor. Having been defined as in-ferior and unable to compete in the economic sphere, they are rel-egated to a position of dependence upon males for personal protec-tion and economic well-being. The family is conceived of as a necessary part of the social relations and the family in turn is defined as one in which the women stay at home and take care of the children. This leads, as we noted earlier, to a perception of women as property. Property is by definition something to be used and exploited by the owner, whether that property is a factory, an automobile, or a woman. Some of the violence against women is a result of male responses to women who do not permit exploitation or abuse. Other women are economically dependent upon men and tolerate abuse because the alternative is unbearable. We do not, of course, understand all the psychological and sociological reasons for women's tolerance of male abuse, but we can explain structurally how these crimes are generated through the social, political, and economic relations of the society.

There are, however, countervailing forces opposing the wholesale mistreatment of women. In a society in which women are defined as the property of men, if women are allowed to be raped and abused, then the "property" of some men will be mistreated by strangers. Within the home there is greater ambivalence about such matters: The law does not protect wives everywhere from rape and, in practice, does not often protect them from physical abuse. The law does prohibit people who are not "family" from abusing women because the property of one man must be protected from predators.

Women are not defenseless. They do not stand idly by and allow their own debasement and disenfranchisement politically and interpersonally. The women's movement has been built on the ashes of criminal acts committed by women struggling for hundreds of years to gain political, economic, and social equality. In the face of opposition to women demanding equality, the law has responded by defining such activities as criminal. For centuries, women have gone to prison to stop discrimination. Women also rebel on a personal level and fight back—even to the point of killing their boyfriends and spouses—against the mistreatment.[26]

Other women engage in crime for the same reasons that most men do—shoplifters to increase their ability to consume; prostitutes to earn more money selling sex than they can working at other jobs; drug pushers to avoid being tied down to a house, husband, and children. Women join groups that supplement the criminality of male gangs as an independent way of being part of a group that defies conventionality and provides an alternative to housework or demeaning labor.[27]

Given the sexist nature of discrimination, however, it is to be expected that crimes against and criminality of, women will be less apparent and less frequent than the crimes against, and criminality of men. Lower-class women socialized into believing that they should accept a more-passive, dependent role will be less likely to commit economic crimes—their status and success are measured not by their own ability to generate money but by their ability to attract men who do. Women are forced to accept their lower-class status through a legal system that reinforces the dominence of men. The common occurrence of "date rape" on college campuses testifies to the degree to which men assume a right to sexual favors from women they date and the degree to which the law fails to protect women from such abuse. Because of their position as a reserve labor force kept dependent economically, women are rarely in a position to commit white-collar, political, or corporate crimes. The fact remains, however, that women commit less of all types of crime, including violent and property crimes. The structural pressures on lower-class women to commit crime are as great, as if not greater than, the pressures on lower-class men to do so. Lower-class women are often the sole source of financial support for children and relatives. Why, then, do they not commit property crimes? To some degree, they lack the opportunity for learning how, and this lower incidence of crime partially reflects the fact that women are physically less able to face the potential violence of male victims. While these characteristics of women in Western cultures make sense of their lower crime rates, it must be admitted that we do not have an adequate explanation. To date, the study of women and crime has suffered from the fact that males have dominated the area and have not paid sufficient attention to this question.

From the perspective of structural-contradictions theory, what we do know about the relationship between women as perpetrators and victims of crime is quite consistent with the theory. This contrasts with behavioral or normative theories of crime, for which the criminality of women is a complete anomaly that cannot be explained.

Crime in Socialist Societies _____

With respect to crime, socialist societies tend to be closed. One consequence is that we totally lack reliable information about crime. Most research relies on the reports and impressions of people who have immigrated from socialist countries.[28] These data are, obviously, so suspect as to render them of limited value. Furthermore, the form of political organization in the presently existing socialist societies does not allow for an objective and independent assessment of the types and amount of crime. Most socialist societies are also developing nations where expenditures on keeping statistics must be weighed against using limited funds for feeding hungry populations and developing an industrial base.

Bad as the statistics are in capitalist societies (for reasons discussed in earlier chapters), the official statistics in socialist societies are even worse. We must rely on more-impressionistic accounts of crime in socialist societies for our data.

The theory of structural contradictions predicts that some of the same types of crime that characterize capitalist societies will characterize presently existing socialist societies. More important, the theory suggests that the contradictions of socialist societies will generate their own unique constellation of criminal acts.

It is significant, however, that socialist societies typically place great emphasis on the elimination of some of the most exploitative types of criminality. China, for example, which was accurately described as a "nation of opium addicts" prior to the Chinese Communist Revolution in 1949, virtually eliminated opium production and addiction in the years following the revolution. China also eliminated prostitution, gambling, and black-market crimes, which were rampant under the former regime. Cuba also greatly reduced the amount of drug use, prostitution, and frauds that were institutionalized as part of the economy when Cuba was a capitalist country.

Nonetheless, certain contradictions inherent in the political, economic, and social relations of these societies are parallel with but not identical to, those in capitalist societies. People have not yet created a political and economic system in which the contradiction between the ideology that supports the system corresponds to the reality of the existing social relations. The ideology of socialism is that there will be no social classes; every one is to be treated equally. Yet the reality is that if there is a government at all, then some people will be more powerful than others. Even if everyone were economically equal, social classes would emerge along the lines of power differentials. Where there are power differentials and a surplus of goods to be distributed, some people will be tempted to use their power to increase their privileges, that is, their share of the surplus. That process is exactly what has happened in presently existing socialist societies. The contradiction, then, between the ideology of equality and the reality of inequality leads to conflicts between the social classes. Socialist societies appear to be more effective in controlling much of the street crime than capitalist societies through the utilization of neighborhood policing groups. In China, for example, urban areas are broken down into small neighborhoods where everyone knows his or her neighbors and works with them in community organizations. Because everyone receives basically the same income, an increase in commodity consumption by anyone in the community would immediately bring attention. It is also more difficult under such circumstances to commit criminal acts anonymously.

Brady summed up a central contradiction in his study of crime and criminal justice in China:

> the central struggle is fundamentally a conflict between competing ideas for economic development . . . the Ethic of Social Revolution and the Ethic of Bureaucratic Centralization. The two ethics and their conflicts result from a contradiction between social and economic necessitates . . . [socialist societies] must have a closely coordinated economy to organize labor and marshall scarce material and technological resources for industrial growth. At the same time, the leadership remains committed to decentralized popular participation and ongoing social change.[29]

An alternative to official statistics are the reports of people who were or are in a position to observe criminality in socialist countries. As mentioned, that these people are immigrants who left their country and desire to remain in capitalist countries limits the credibility of their reports. Nevertheless, we may learn something from these accounts. For example, a former Soviet journalist now living in New York published a book titled *Hustling on Gorky Street*.[30] Brokhin describes a cast of thieves operating in the Soviet Union that would make Damon Runyon's mouth water; men with names like Alex the Louse, Nyuma the Con, and Yan (Cross Eyes) Rokotov are described in colorful detail. These men deal in black-market commodities, money exchanges, prostitution, drugs, and stolen property. In short, the underworld of the Soviet Union parallels that of New York or London, including the bribery of public officials:

> 'You need money and I need an apartment,' a woman in Saratov tells a local housing official. Two thousand rubles change hands and the official tells his assistant: 'satisfy the request of our worthy client.'
> In Leningrad a motorist finds his Volga automobile will be repaired a lot faster if he slips 50 rubles to the body shop manager.

Another customer had warned him in advance: 'unless you grease the manager's palm, you won't be going anywhere in your Volga.'

For the right bribe in Soviet Armenia, a clerk at the Industrial Medical Examination Commission certifies pensioners for high disability payments they don't deserve. The total loss to the state by the time the scheme is uncovered: 22,500 rubles, equivalent to $29,700.

Construction officials of the Cheboksaty Tractor Trust were found to have spent the equivalent of $845,000 of state money on a landscaped river retreat for themselves and their friends. The retreat included marble baths and beautiful hostesses who played 'love games' with the guests.[31]

A common crime in the Soviet Union involves the forging of documents. In a country in which a person must have official approval to take a train, purchase consumer goods, or take a trip, the acquiring of forged and phony papers has developed to a fine art. Apparently this practice is so common that it is comparable to the frequency with which Americans violate criminal laws restricting the use of marijuana, juvenile theft, and driving while intoxicated.

In Poland, scandals involving the corruption of public officials are fairly commonplace. A survey of the population disclosed that most of the people believed it necessary to bribe public officials in order to obtain special considerations, including getting housing and commodities in short supply. During 1974, several scandals in major cities disclosed widespread corruption involving, in one case, as many as 400 local government officials. In another, the mayor of a small town was exposed for having accepted kickbacks from contractors building a public waterworks. In both instances, according to knowledgeable people inside the government, these exposures were little more than the external manifestation of internal struggles for control over the government and the special privileges enjoyed by those on the inside.[32]

The data from socialist societies must be taken as merely suggestive. Official statistics are next to useless when comparing crime cross-culturally. The definition of acts as criminal varies substantially, and no research effort has yet begun to control for the effect of this on comparative data. Because crime is a politically charged phenomenon, official statistics are manipulated to serve the ends deemed desirable by the government. What we are left with is impressions supported by observations, but the conclusions drawn must be seen as highly tentative.

Conclusion _____

In this chapter, we have set forth a theory of crime and criminality that attempts to answer why crime exists and why different types of crime are distributed as they are. The theory suggests that every society contains within it ubiquitous contradictions that generate conflicts accounting for the emergence of criminal laws and the propensity of different social classes and groups to violate those laws. We do not pretend to explain why individual A commits crime and individual B does not. The history of criminology, combined with the facts we know about crime, proves the futility of asking that question. To be scientific requires that we ask questions that focus not on the individual but on the social structure and how different social structures generate different types of criminality. Crime in both socialist and capitalist societies reflects the particular contradictions of those societies.

13

State-Organized Crime

State-organized crime consists of acts committed by state or government officials in the pursuit of their job as representatives of the government. In this chapter, we will apply the theory of structural contradictions developed in the last chapter to state-organized crime. Through this application, we hope to demonstrate the utility of the paradigm as well as clarify some of its theoretical implications.

It is paradoxical that state officials commit criminal acts. It is, after all, the people occupying positions in state institutions who define what is criminal and what is not. How then can it happen that state officials will define as criminal acts in which others or they themselves participate? The answer is found in the contradictions that inhere in the formation of centralized states.

In capitalist societies, the state rests uneasily in the crossfire of contradictions between workers, consumers, owners, and producers. One of the central contradictions occurs because of the necessity for the state to create laws and ideologies in which capitalists can earn a profit and keep the profits they earn. If state officials do not make decisions that protect capital investment and encourage the accumulation of capital, then the entire economic system and social relations that are the essence of capitalism will collapse.

There is, however, a contradiction inherent in capitalism that the people whose labor produces the goods do not own the product of their labor. Given this contradiction, the dilemma arises as to how to convince workers and owners that the system is fair and equitable. One resolution found in all capitalist countries is the creation of a legal system that portends to decide conflicts equitably and fairly. The law, in the words of Antonio Gramsci, establishes *legitimacy* for existing political and economic relations.[1] Law makers and law enforcers accomplish this by creating the illusion that the proclamations are universal, that is, that they apply to all citizens.[2] In the process of protecting the interests of the capitalists in their unflagging effort to increase profits and accumulate capital (the very basis of the economic relations under capitalism), it is sometimes expedient for state and government officials to violate the criminal law. Given the cross-currents of contradictory demands, one can safely predict that some government people who are willing and able to violate the criminal laws will come forward. Thus the history of nation-states is also a history of state-organized crime.

In capitalist societies, the state creates laws protecting private property, contractual obligations, interpersonal conflicts, and so forth. In socialist societies, the state protects property by severe penalties against theft, it demands labor by punishing those who do not work or who come to work unable to produce at a satisfactory level, and of course it also protects personal freedoms by imposing sanctions on those who would deprive another of his or her property or well-being. Ineluctably, the state defines as crime acts in which an individual violently interferes with the rights of others or takes property that belongs to another.

Despite the laws, however, officials of the government or the state will often find themselves caught in a contradiction between complying with the law and meeting other obligations, demands, or institutionalized ends.

When the European states of the 16th and 17th centuries were caught in the contradiction between the desire to create legitimacy for the emerging capitalist system and the desire to accumulate capital wholesale violation of their own, laws prohibiting piracy on the high seas was institutionalized. The wealth and security of the European states was severely threatened by the Spanish conquest of the Americas. Prior to the Spanish conquest there were differences in the wealth of European nations, but after gold, silver, and a large supply of slave labor were discovered in the Americas, Spain was able to claim most of the territories for their own. This meant quite simply that in the near future Spain would dominate Europe as Rome had done centuries before. This fact did not go unnoticed by other European nations, especially England, France, and the Netherlands.

Discovering gold, silver, and cheap labor promised to provide Spain with the possibility of recruiting and arming large military forces, which threatened the fundamental interests of most European states. Thus, conflict between the European states was inevitable. The form of the conflict was a dilemma to be resolved. From time to time, the dilemma was resolved by going to war. A less-drastic resolution, however, was discovered when England, France, and other European nations began issuing "letters of mark" to pirates. These letters of mark gave the pirates the right to land at ports controlled by the issuing nation. They also gave instructions to the navies *not* to attack or interfere with the piracy.[3] These letters were issued, naturally, on the condition that the pirates shared the loot with the issuing government. Pirating involved murder, rape, plunder, destruction of cities and towns, and indeed a collection of criminal acts as heinous and premeditated as can be imagined by the most creative fiction writer.[4] Furthermore, these acts, including piracy, were against the laws of every European nation and against every international agreement existing at the time. Nonetheless, the states of Europe issued letters of mark that violated their own criminal laws but licensed criminality on a massive scale.[5]

Gold, silver, spices, and tea were the bedrock of wealth and military power for European nations in the 15th, 16th, and 17th centuries. A storehouse of gold and silver enabled kings and queens to raise armies, hire skilled ship builders and munitions makers, and equip and maintain large and effective navies and armies—in short, to threaten neighbors and dominate vast territories. To protect their new-found wealth and maintain a monopoly, the Spanish and Portuguese refused other nations the right to trade with their colonies. The British, French, and Dutch were late starters in the colonial enterprise and were left with the dregs of the less-developed world, part of North America and Asia. At the time, neither could provide the wealth or labor that South America produced.

But England, France, and Holland were themselves powerful naval nations. Although initially less adventurous than Spain and Portugal, they soon came to realize the danger posed by the Iberian Peninsula. Enterprising sailors soon found ways to interfere with the shipment of goods from the New World back to Spain and Portugal. Although a highly risky business, it was clear that a fast small ship could outrun the larger, laden vessels that were plodding the seas from the Spanish Main (the Caribbean coast of South America) to Bilbao and from Brazil to Lisbon.

To transport the gold, silver, and spices the long distance from the New World to the Old World was no easy feat. A ship laden with gold could not travel fast and was easy prey for marauders, and it was forced by the prevailing winds and currents to travel in a predictable direction. Thus an opportunity for sailors without scruples to exploit the weaknesses of the transporting ships was born. There were many candidates for this task. The vast wealth that could be gained was as tempting as insider trader on the stock market is today.

Heroes and villains emerged during the days of piracy. Often they were the same person. The most successful French pirate was a man called Borgnefesse, who was given that name as a result of a battle in which his left buttock was shot off.[6] Borgnefesse was a plague on the Spanish, Portuguese, and English ships and a destroyer of towns and cities. He was protected by the French government's letter of mark and landed to divide his ill-gotten gains on the French island of Tortuga. There is no estimating how much he alone provided the French treasury. It is clear, however, from documents in historical archives, that he was well-treated by the governors of the French islands and by the government itself. For all of his criminal exploits, Borgnefesse was allowed to retire to a gentlemen's life in a provincial French city with enough money to keep him comfortable.

The French were not alone. England's most famous, but by no means only, pirate was Sir Francis Drake, whose exploits and successes were rewarded by knighthood, wealth, and power, although he also faced a court on charges of piracy at one point in his career and was exiled by the queen as a result of demands made by the Spanish government.[7] His exile, however, was more fiction than fact. During this exile to Ireland, Drake served as the assistant governor. It was also short-lived, as the government called him back to take charge of a pirate ship outfitted by businessmen investing in the enterprise.[8] Francis Drake's success as a pirate was phenomenal. After his journey of 1572–1573, he returned to England with enough gold and silver taken from Spanish ships and towns to support the government and all its expenses for a period of 7 years.[9] During the voyage, Drake and his men attacked the town of Nombre de Dios, which was a storage depot for gold and silver awaiting transport to Spain. He was repulsed in the attack and reduced to attacking small ships and towns along the Spanish Main. He joined forces with some French pirates and ambushed a silver-laden treasure train near Nombre de Dios.

On returning to England, the Spanish complained bitterly to the Queen of Drake's exploits. He was allowed to go into hiding (after sharing his proceeds with the crown) and was not heard of again until 1575, when he surfaced serving in Ireland under the First Earl of Essex.

The American pirate John Paul Jones was treated much as Drake had been.[10] He was alternately condemned by the government and given a commission in the Navy. Two pirate-smugglers of New Orleans, Jean and Pierre LaFitte, were given free run of the city in return for sharing their loot with the authorities. During the War of 1812, they were recruited by both the English and the American navies, and Jean was commissioned an admiral by the United States in return for betraying the British.[11]

Borgnefesse, Sir Francis Drake, Jean and Pierre Lafitte, and John Paul Jones are only a few of the hundreds of pirates who plied their craft with the state's complicity and cooperation between the 15th and 19th centuries. Their crimes were supported by and their proceeds shared with whatever nation-state would offer them protection and supplies. In theory, each nation-state protected only its own pirates. In practice, they all protected any pirates who were willing to share their gains.

Virtually every nation in the years between 1500 and 1800 was complicitous in piracy. Pirates were provided with ships, provisions, men, protection, and, in some cases, commissions in the navy. In America, John Paul Jones' career went from pirate to admiral and back to pirate in the span of a few short years. Spain and Portugal suffered most, as they were the target of most of the piracy. England, France, and Holland gained the most, as they were able to both reduce Spain's wealth and enhance their own. In time of war, nations enlisted pirates to serve as their navy. In times of peace, they shared in the profits.

These examples are illustrative of state-organized crime. They demonstrate how the state becomes complicitous with criminality, institutionalizing it, supporting it, and sharing in its profits. In today's world, there is evidence that some small villages on islands near Indonesia still pursue a policy of supporting pirates and sharing in their profits. But piracy is seldom a major form of state-organized crime; that role now goes to smuggling.

Smuggling

In the annals of crime, everything from sheep to people, wool to wine, gold, drugs, military weapons, banned books and ideas have been prohibited for either export or import. The paradox is that whatever is prohibited is at the expense of one group of people for the benefit of another. Thus, the laws that prohibit the import or export of a commodity inevitably face a built-in resistance. Some part of the population will always want either to possess or to distribute the prohibited goods. At times, the state finds itself in the position of having its own interests served by violating precisely the same laws passed to prohibit the export or import of the goods in question. Inevitably, one state's prohibition runs counter to the interests of another state's economy. Both internally and externally, the prohibition on the export or import of goods is a choice between supporting the interests of one group over another.

Today, smuggling is the most common form of state-organized crime, and it involves principally the smuggling of military weapons and illegal drugs. It must be emphasized that we are speaking of the import and export of drugs and military weapons only when it is organized by state officials in their official role and when such acts are defined by law as criminal.

It is clear that many governments are implicated in the smuggling of drugs, in violation of their own laws. Turkey and Afghanistan produce vast amounts of government-controlled opium, which far exceeds the world-wide demand for legal opium. The most serious violator of its own laws against smuggling, however, is the United States.

During the Vietnam War, the Central Intelligence Agency (CIA) became complicitous in drug trafficking in Southeast Asia.[12] They did so for what was assumed to be higher moral principles than the dirty business of trading in drugs, that is, to stop communism. The war that America inherited from France in Southeast Asia was one that had long been partially financed by opium traffic. Indeed, prior to the American entrance into the war, the French colonial government received about 50 percent of its administrative costs from profits secured from licensing opium dens in Vietnam.[13]

Both France and the United States depended upon the support of hill tribesmen, whose only staple product was opium. To gain their support, the French and U.S. intelligence services cooperated with the production and distribution of opium. Air America, the CIA airline in Vietnam, regularly transported the bundles of opium from air strips in Laos and Burma to Saigon.[14]

Successful smuggling requires a network of people who can be depended upon to not advertise their occupations. It also requires the cooperation of law-enforcement officials and people who can transport goods. Successful smuggling also requires financing that has the ability (1) to provide large amounts of instant cash and (2) to hide (or launder) money transactions. In today's world, these financial qualities are done most efficiently and safely by banks located where their transactions are not carefully supervised.

These characteristics of successful smuggling, interestingly, are qualities also necessary to successful intelligence work. Thus, covert intelligence agents and established smuggling networks enjoy a symbiotic relationship by virtue of their shared needs.

Covert intelligence requires the movement of goods, money, and people quickly, quietly, and secretly. It requires the silence and allegiance of many people who are temporarily employed for particular purposes and the use of force and violence to guarantee their silence if not to insure their allegiance.

In today's world, the intelligence agencies are called upon not only to gather information but also to see that the foreign policy goals of the government are met. People friendly to a nation's government are recruited, trained, and supported. People who are unfriendly are damaged and, in extreme cases, assassinated. To carry out these enterprises requires much money and long-range planning. But, in democratic countries, the funds for such activities must be approved by elected officials. The CIA and other intelligence agencies have discovered that congressional funding is a fickle master. The work of the agency must go on uninterrupted if it is to succeed. For the military-intelligence establishment the problem is how to finance ongoing clandestine operations—such as the terrorists in Nicaragua, Angola, and Mozambique, or the secret campaign contributions to politicians sympathetic to the aims of the CIA abroad and in the United States. A vacillating Congress sometimes unwilling to provide the funds makes it impossible for CIA and Defense Department officials to do the job they see as their sworn duty and obligation. When a president like John Kennedy or Jimmy Carter also shows hesitation in giving full support to the agency's "secret agendas," then the threat to the completion of their mission is especially acute. On the one hand, the agency's effectiveness is judged according to how well it contains the spread of communist and socialist governments; on the other hand, it is hamstrung by funding that is sporadic and often not sufficient for the task. One solution is to develop alternative sources of funds. The CIA has in the past succeeded in doing this by soliciting large contributions from wealthy capitalists who support the CIA goals. Another solution that emerged with the Vietnam War and the CIA's involvement in narcotics trafficking is to continue trafficking in narcotics and spend the profits on covert-intelligence operations.

Symbiosis is born of shared problems whose solution allows two very different species to survive and prosper, despite different objectives. The Egyptian plover eats the leeches from the crocodile's mouth, for which service the crocodile limits his intake of feathered creatures to birds other than the plover.

When the CIA can gain the allegiance of the mountain War Lords and the Laotian military by transporting opium from the Golden Triangle to Saigon, it enters into a relationship with strange bedfellows; feudal lords whose reign of terror and exploitation of peasants provides funds for equipping vast armies of mercenaries who prey on farmers and competitors with merciless warfare. The CIA no doubt knew the price was high, but it was a price they were apparently willing to pay for the survival and prosperity of Western democratic capitalism. With the end of the war in Vietnam, however, the CIA was poised to either get out of the narcotics business or find other partners. The Vietnam War's end coincided with a period of history when the CIA was severely criticized both politically and publicly. Funding was threatened and covert operations were scrutinized by Congressional Committees.

When Jimmy Carter became president, he appointed Admiral

Stansfeld Turner as Director of the CIA. Turner was adamant about reducing the covert intelligence units of the CIA and other intelligence agencies. The CIA was, in short, threatened with a major reversal of its role in international politics and intrigue. Not surprisingly, with the involvement of people in other branches of government (the Defense Department, the Drug Enforcement Administration, the Federal Bureau of Investigation), officials of the CIA decided to maintain their involvement in international narcotics. To accomplish this, they joined in partnerships with professional smugglers and corrupt banking officials. At the same time, the CIA was seeking a way of financing and organizing the smuggling of military weapons to nations—in particular South Africa, Iran, Syria, and Libya—that were officially banned by U.S. law from receiving military equipment.

All these forces came together in setting up the Nugan Hand Bank in Australia, which could handle the necessary money and business transactions to keep the arms, money, and drugs flowing.

Frank Nugan was an Australian businessman who joined in partnership with an American, Michael Hand, to establish the Nugan Hand Bank in 1976[15] Michael Hand was, prior to coming to Australia, a green beret and CIA contact agent in Vietnam. Hand worked closely with Air America, the CIA airline that transported opium from the Golden Triangle to Saigon.[16]

On the board of the bank and managing the world-wide offices were:

- General Edwin F. Black, Commander of U.S. troops in Thailand during the Vietnam war and, after the war, Assistant Army Chief of Staff for the Pacific. General Black became president of Nugan Hand Hawaii.
- Admiral Earl F. Yates, former chief of staff for Strategic Planning of U.S. forces in Asia and the Pacific. Admiral Yates was president of the Nugan Hand Bank.
- Bernie Houghton, U.S. Naval Intelligence undercover agent. Nugan Hand's representative in Saudi Arabia.
- Tom Clines, director of training in CIA's Clandestine Service, London operative for Nugan Hand who helped the takeover of a London-based bank.
- Dale Holmgreen, former flight service manager in Vietnam for Civil Air Transport, which became Air America. He was on the board of directors of Nugan Hand.

- Walt McDonald, an economist and consultant to CIA, specializing in petroleum. He became a consultant to Nugan Hand and served as head of its Annapolis, Maryland, branch.
- George Farris, a green beret and CIA operative in Vietnam, ran the Washington, D.C., Nugan Hand Bank office.
- General Roy Manors, a Vietnam veteran who helped coordinate the aborted attempt to rescue the Iranian hostages, was Nugan Hand's man in Manila.
- The board of directors of the parent company formed by Michael Hand that preceded the Nugan Hand Bank was Grant Walters, Robert Peterson, David M. Houton, and Spencer Smith, all of whom listed their address as c/o Air America, Army Post Office, San Francisco, California.
- Edwin F. Wilson, a CIA agent involved in arms smuggling, used the Nugan Hand Bank for financing arms shipments to the Middle East. His associate, Theodore S. Shackley, was head of the Miami, Florida, CIA station when the plot to assassinate Fidel Castro by using organized crime figures Santo Trafikcante, Jr., John Roselli, and Sam Giancana was planned and attempted. Shackley was later transferred to Laos, where he organized the Meo Tribesmen and assisted their heroin trafficking. In 1973, Shackley replaced William Colby as head of covert operations for the Far East when Colby became director of CIA [17]

In 1980, the bank came unraveled. The Australian member of the Nugan Hand team, Frank Nugan, was found in his Mercedes on a remote road, dead from gunshot wounds. In his pants pocket was the business card of Nugan Hand's lawyer, William Colby, former director of the CIA. On the back of the card was Colby's itinerary during his visit to Australia. Next to Nugan was a Bible with a meat-pie wrapper marking a page; on the wrapper was the name of Bob Wilson, the California Congressman who was then the ranking Republican member of the House Armed Services Committee.

Auditors called in to investigate the bank opened a veritable Pandora's box of crime and intrigue. Millions of dollars were missing. Many of the principal depositors of the bank were known to be connected with the international narcotics traffic in Asia and the Middle East. The CIA was using Nugan Hand to finance gun smuggling and a vast array of other clandestine operations. Among other things revealed by the auditors was the fact that the CIA secretly and illegally spent millions of dollars in a disinformation campaign against Australian Prime Minister Whitham, falsely accusing him of all kinds of immoral and illegal activities. Although Whitham was later exonerated, he was nonetheless forced to resign as prime minister. The CIA then funneled millions of dollars through the bank into the campaign of a politician more to their liking.

Arms Smuggling

The most prevalent crime of Western capitalist states today is the illegal smuggling of military weapons. It needs to be reiterated that we are considering only those acts that are crimes in the laws of the particular nation-state considered. If it is legal to export arms to Libya it is not state-organized crime if the CIA ships arms to that country. State-organized crime occurs when the laws of a country prohibit the shipment of arms or munitions to a particular nation but a branch of the government still engages in such acts.

The U.S. Congress passed legislation prohibiting the CIA from shipping arms or otherwise supporting the Contra terrorists in Nicaragua (the Boland Amendment). The CIA and Defense Department opposed this legislation and saw it as inimical to the interests of the United States and incompatible with President Reagan's policy of providing military support to groups opposing communism and socialism. In addition, a presidential order prohibited the sale of arms to Iran. These laws undermined long-range plans of the Department of Defense and the CIA to combat communism by supporting terrorist groups. There were, of course, several alternatives open to the officials responsible for running the anticommunist programs. They could comply with the law and wait for a change in law; to do so, however, meant losing what they perceived to be irretrievable ground. They could appeal to private citizens for money to support the antiterrorist groups and they could devise illegal ways of continuing support.

The dilemma was resolved by institutionalizing criminal behavior in the organization. Arms were illegally shipped to Iran. The profits from these arms sales were placed in a CIA-controlled Swiss bank account. The funds were then used to buy arms that were shipped illegally to the Contras, a group of guerrillas fighting against the government of Nicaragua. At the time of these arms shipments, the U.S. Congress had passed legislation forbidding any

HOW A SECRET IRAN ARMS DEAL WORKED

Transaction #5, May-August 1986, summarized in the Tower Commission report

1 **Financing the deal**

Iranian-born intermediary Ghorbanifar gives three post-dated checks totalling $18 million to Saudi businessman Khashoggi, who deposits $15 million in Swiss account of Lake Resources, a company controlled by Secord, a retired USAF general. Secord transfers $6.5 million to a CIA Swiss bank account.

2 **Shipping the arms**

Dept. of Defense signs over TOW and HAWK missile supplies to CIA; they are shipped via CIA-connected Southern Air Transport to Israel. TOWs are "replenishment," to replace Israeli stocks earlier sold to Iran. One batch of HAWK supplies accompanies ex-National Security Adviser Robert McFarlane on flight to Iran; second planeload is turned back to Israel when no hostages are released. More HAWK supplies are shipped to Iran several months later.

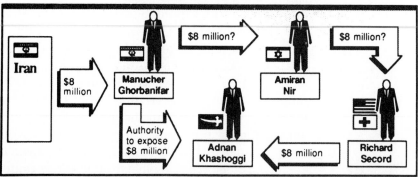

3 **Making the payoff**

Iran transfers $8 million to Ghorbanifar in payment for HAWK supplies received. Ghorbanifar transfers funds, perhaps $8 million, to an Israeli account controlled by Nir, an adviser to the Israeli government; Nir forwards funds to Lake Resources. Ghorbanifar authorizes Khashoggi to expose $8 million against checks held; Secord pays Khashoggi $8 million from Lake Resources account.

Crimes of the State. *(AP/Pat Lyons)*

"I take the Iran-Contra defense—I wouldn't have had to break any laws if your stupid laws had fit in with what I wanted to do." *(copyright 1987 by Herblock in The Washington Post)*

government agency from supplying arms or money to the Contras. The sale of the arms to Iran and the disbursement of the profits to the Contras were criminal acts involving people in the highest offices of the CIA, the Department of Defense, the National Security Council, and the presidential office. There is even suspicion that the violation of criminal laws by officials in the Defense Department and the CIA included illegally contributing some of the profits from the arms sales to the campaigns of U.S. political candidates who supported intervention in Nicaragua.

A political system in which power is divided between a legislative and an executive branch creates inherent contradictions that in the long run have potential for undermining the existing structure. Where conflicts emerge over ideological or strategic differences between the executive and the legislative branches of government, the state bureaucracy responsible for implementing policy is faced with dilemmas that cannot be resolved without violating some of the obligations and goals for which the bureaucracy stands. In most cases, these dilemmas are resolved by acquiescing to the demands of existing laws and regulations. In the case of military, intelligence, and law-enforcement bureaucracies, however, the officials' perception of the importance of their own work often over-rides their commitment to legality. The end result is that these agencies end by committing a host of crimes in the name of protecting freedom, democracy, and capitalism.

Iran and Nicaragua are not the only countries to which the CIA and the Department of Defense have shipped arms illegally in recent years. There are legal restrictions on the shipment of arms and military technology to South Africa as well. A 1963 United Nations embargo reinforced by an act of 1978, prohibits the shipment of military or police equipment to the government of South Africa. Despite these laws, in 1983, $28.6 million of U.S. goods on the State Department's munitions list were shipped to South Africa and an additional $88 million were exported in the first three months of 1984.[18]

The CIA also admits to supporting the rebels in Angola and Mozambique, whose military equipment is used jointly by the South African army and rebel forces.

State-Organized Assassinations _____

The assassination of political leaders whose programs run counter to the interests of a nation has become almost common-place in international politics. It is one of the most sinister of modern-day state-organized crime.

It is well established that the French Intelligence Agency hired a man named Christian David (who also has connection with Robert Vesco and the U.S. Drug Enforcement Agency) to assassinate the Moroccan leftist leader, Ben Barka.[19]

In early 1956, the CIA hired a team of assassins to kill Shiek Fadlallah in Lebanon. Sheik Fadlallah is the leader of a Shiite religious group fighting for control of the Lebanese government. The CIA suspected him of planning the attack on a U.S. Marine barracks. The assassination team planted a car bomb that subsequently exploded, killing 80 people. Sheik Fadlallah was not one of them. Nowhere in the laws of the United States is the CIA or any other government agency given the legal right to plan the assassination of citizens or political leaders of other countries, except in time of war.

There is a good deal of evidence that the U.S. government planned the assassinations of President Diem in Vietnam, Patrice Lumumba in the Congo, and Rafael Trujillo in the Dominican Republic.[20]

While these assassinations cannot be unequivocally laid at the door of the U.S. government, the conspiracy to assassinate Fidel Castro most certainly can. Testimony before Congress revealed that the CIA engaged the services of Chicago's organized-crime patron Sam Giancana, California's John Roselli, and Florida's Santo Traficante, Jr., in a plot to assassinate Fidel Castro.[21]

Other assassination plots have been planned by the Drug Enforcement Agency (DEA) in an attempt to control international drug smuggling.[22] Faced with the difficult task of prosecuting major financiers—many of whom are high-level officials of foreign governments, intelligence agents, and industrialists—the DEA conspired to commit murder. Lou Conein, also known as "Black Luigi," left a position in the White House in 1972 to organize a Special Operations Group (SOG) within the DEA. He brought with him 12 CIA paramilitary specialists on loan to the DEA. George Crile quoted a DEA official: "When you get down to it, Conein was organizing an assassination program. He was frustrated by the big-time operators who were just too insulated to get to. . . . Meetings were held to decide whom to target and what method of assassination to employ."[23]

In 1978, the investigative journalist Jim Hougan wrote: "My own sources tend to confirm Crile's. The scenario they describe is one which some members of the Dirty Dozen (the 12 CIA paramilitarists assigned to Conein and the DEA) would assist their boss in selecting targets for assassination. Once those targets were approved, booby traps obtained from the B.R. for company would be issued and—there is no other word—contracts put out."[24]

The actual assassinations were to be carried out by hired killers, usually nationals of the country of the targeted victim. The hired assassins were to be provided with advice and the necessary "anti-personnel devices." As far as is known, none of the planned assassinations took place. The crime of conspiracy to commit murder, nonetheless, took place many times. And this is but one of numerous cases of state-organized murder conspiracies in recent times. For example, a CIA-produced handbook, distributed in Nicaragua, encouraged indiscriminate assassination of political leaders and citizens known to be sympathetic to the Sandinistas. The pamphlet also provided blueprints for illegal terrorist acts.

The U.S. CIA trained and advised the Chilean Secret Service (DINA) prior to and after the election of Salvadore Allende as President of Chile in 1970. DINA plotted the overthrow of Allende and the murders of General Renee Schneider and President Allende. Later, after General Pinochet became President of Chile, he issued orders to DINA to establish "Operation Condor." FBI agent Robert Scherer sent a top-secret message to Washington in which he stated: "A third and more secret phase of Operation Condor involves the formation of special teams from member countries to travel anywhere in the world to non-member countries to carry out sanctions including assassinations."[25]

The Chilean government institutionalized murder and terrorism as European nations had institutionalized piracy 300 years before: "In early 1974 the Junta sent Julio Duran to deliver a keynote speech before the [Cuban] exile community in Miami. Duran, Chile's delegate to the United Nations General Assembly . . . promised the exiles that henceforth Chile would support their cause.[26]

Duran assured the gathering of political exiles from Cuba that "Chile . . . was dedicated to the overthrow of Castro; Chile, not the United States, was now the hemisphere's leader in the struggle against international communism; Chile, not the United States, was willing to use terror as a routine tool of policy."[27]

Pursuant to the policy, three agents from Chile's Secret Service DINA entered the United States and, on September 21, 1976, planted a bomb in a car in which Orlando Letellier was riding. Letellier was an exile from the Pinochet government. He was the Chilean Ambassador to the United States under Allende and, for a time, Allende's Minister of Defense. As the car in which Letellier was riding with two American friends approached Embassy Row in Washington, D.C., the driver of a gray sedan that was following the Letellier car "pressed one key on the instrument plugged into the cigarette lighter, then pressed another. Michael Moffit a passenger in the car heard a hissing sound, 'like a hot wire placed in water.' He saw a flash of light over his wife's head. Then a deafening, crushing sound."[28]

Moffit's wife and Letellier were both killed by the explosion. But Michael Moffit lived to tell about it. After an extensive investigation, the three DINA agents were arrested and tried for murder. The investigation was hampered by interference from the CIA and by the refusal of the CIA and the FBI to release relevant documents and information.[29]

This was not the only time the CIA and the FBI covered up murders by people associated with them. A Cuban exile, Ricardo (Monkey) Morales, immigrated to Miami in 1960. He was employed by the CIA and the FBI. While in the FBI's employ, Morales went to Venezuela, where he joined the Venezuelan secret police as head of security at Caracas International Airport. In court testimony and published interviews, Morales admitted that he planted a bomb on an Air Cubana flight from Caracas that killed 73 passengers. He and the Miami police both testified in court that this was a CIA job and he was acting under their instructions. He was unrepentant: "If I had to, I would do it over again."[30]

Morales was arrested in Miami overseeing the shipment of 10 tons of marijuana. Because of his status as an undercover agent for the FBI and the CIA, he was never convicted. He openly admits to bombings, murder, and assassination attempts, yet he has never served a day in prison. In 1968, while he was a contract agent for the CIA, he admitted to murdering an anti-Castro activist and trying to execute another. While employed by the FBI, he murdered another Cuban exile, Eladio Ruiz, in broad daylight in downtown Miami. The execution was "reportedly carried out as a warning to Castro sympathizers."[31]

Morales' protection from prosecution for murder, terrorism, and drug dealing only ended when he himself was shot in a Miami bar in 1982.

The most recent example of the U.S. government's involvement in murder and assassination plots in the plan approved by President Reagan for the CIA to "destablize' the Libyan government of Colonel Muammar Qadaffi. The *Washington Post* reported that the plan included an effort to "lure [Qaddafi] into some foreign adventure or terrorist exploit that would give a growing number of Qaddafi opponents in the Libyan military a chance to seize power, or such a foreign adventure might give one of Qaddafi's neighbors, such as Algeria or Egypt, a justification for responding to Qaddafi militarily."[32] A CIA report in 1985 argued that the United States should "stimulate" Qaddafi's fall by encouraging disaffected elements in the Libyan army who could be spurred to assassination attempts."[33]

One of the more highly publicized recent cases of state-organized homicide involves the French government. The French Secret Service was given the job of blowing up the flagship of the Greenpeace environmental organization. Greenpeace is an ecology-environmental group committed to various ecological and environmental issues, including the stopping of atomic testing where it is harmful to the ecology. As such, Greenpeace is often at odds with, and a thorn in the sides of, governments. In the Fall of 1985, the French government planned a series of atomic tests in the South Pacific. The Greenpeace flagship went to Australia to prepare to go to the site of the testing and interfere with it. The French government sent Secret Service agents to Australia to damage the ship so that it could not interrupt the tests. The agent planted explosive devices that crippled the ship and killed one of the crew members.

Conspiracies

American law defines a criminal conspiracy as comprising four elements: (1) an agreement, (2) to achieve an illegal goal, (3) knowing that there is a plan to commit the illegal act and an intention of participating in the conspiracy, and (4) an overt act in furtherance of the illegal goal. The actual act need not be carried out; it is sufficient to have made an agreement to plan the act and take some overt step toward the completion of the act.[34] The courts have defined conspiracy and the necessary conditions very broadly; for example, the overt act need not itself be criminal (sending documents or contacting other people may suffice) and the conspirator(s) may well know that the actual execution of the act will require additional personnel. Because the courts have liberally interpreted conspiracy laws, it is frequently charged in criminal cases, even when the act itself has been committed, because it is easier to gain a conspiracy conviction than a conviction for the criminal act itself. The punishments are usually the same.

Agents and officials of the CIA, the FBI, and the Drug Enforcement Agency are known conspirators in criminal acts ranging from murder to gun smuggling, breaking and entering, illegal wiretapping, illegal bugging, illegal use of violence to coerce compliance, blackmail, fraud, and myriad other criminal offenses committed in the course of routine investigations or crisis situations in which extreme measures are deemed necessary and justifiable.

Other Illegal Activities

By law, the CIA is prohibited from overt intelligence activities in the United States. To engage in such activities is a criminal offense against the people who are the target of the investigation. From 1960 to 1975, (and perhaps beyond that date), the CIA engaged in overt intelligence activities designed to reveal the political attitudes and activities of hundreds of American citizens.[35]

The CIA also carried out a letter-opening campaign against U.S. citizens without court approval and in violation of state and federal laws. This campaign lasted for at least 12 years.[36]

The CIA organized a group of prostitutes and provided them with lavishly decorated apartments, to which they could bring clients. The clients were then given drugs and their responses were recorded by CIA observers (including medical doctors) hidden behind one-way mirrors and paintings. The drugs were tested to see if they would (1) induce amnesia, (2) render a subject suggestible, (3) alter sexual patterns, (4) induce aberrant behavior, (5) get the subject to reveal information he otherwise would not, or (6) create dependency in the subject. At least one of the subjects died as a result of the experience.[37] There is, needless to say, nothing in the American law that gives government officials the right to commit such criminal acts. The rationalization that the clients deserved such treatment for engaging in prostitution would hardly stand up in court as a reasonable defense if any of the perpetrators were ever brought to trial.

The FBI and the CIA engaged in criminal slander designed to disrupt, harass, and discredit legally constituted political parties and political movements in the United States. From 1960–1970, the FBI organized a top-secret illegal campaign against civil rights and antiwar movements called COINTELPRO. The program included planting false documents, threatening people's lives, breaking and entering private offices and homes, stealing documents, and illegal (criminal) surveillance. The extent of such programs in the United States may never be known, but the revelations that have come out from documents secured under the Freedom of Information Act suggest widespread and long-term criminal activities suppressing political parties and ideologies that are unpopular with government officials.[38]

Conclusion _____

There is a strange paradox in the fact that governments pass laws, yet find themselves violating their own dictates. Were the governments all-powerful, it would be a simple thing for them to change the laws to reflect their interests. Such whimsical restructuring of laws would, however, have a price that few governments can afford to pay.

France, England, and Holland dared not declare war against

Spain and Portugal in the early 17th century, in part because France and England were themselves on the brink of war. Yet none of these nations was willing to sit idly by and watch the Iberian countries amass a political and economic power center. A solution was forged in the licensing and equipping of pirate ships to prey on the Spanish. Indeed, it was even possible, when convenient, to try for piracy the same people who had only a short time before been knighted and given a license to plunder. In this way, the state organized criminality for its own ends without having to admit to the world what they were about.

Smuggling goods into a foreign country where those goods are banned and being complicitous with smugglers to export contraband are other solutions to dilemmas posed by attempting to live with the appearance of legality in the face of demands for political and economic advantage unattainable by legitimate means.

In today's world, the United States is often desirous of proving its friendship with one nation (Israel) by passing laws that embargo the shipment of goods to another (Arab states). But the mission of the CIA often conflicts with these political decisions. To stop the "spread of communism" in the Middle East, it may be perceived as necessary to arm factions of the Arab states that oppose other factions. To do this violates the law. Yet the law cannot readily be changed to reflect the subtleties of a conflict in which today it is the Lebanese we wish to arm and tomorrow it is the Syrians. The solution is to institutionalize state crime.

When the interests of one nation are threatened by political changes in another, it is possible to sit idly by and watch economic and political investments disappear into the wind. Few nations, if they have the power, are willing to be so benevolent. Yet the laws of most nations prohibit the kind of intervention (assassination, murder, and disinformation campaigns) that is necessary to change the tide. Covert intelligence operations are a solution, although an illegal one.

The contradictions do not end here. Within each nation's own political reality, there is rarely such hegemony that the intelligence agencies can operate without risk of discovery and the possibility that their autonomy will be threatened. Factions of the U.S. Congress, public-interest groups, "watchdogs," and a host of journalists are constantly on the alert to expose criminality on the part of the intelligence agencies. To avoid these dangers but still carry out their mission, a solution is found in complicity with criminal groups that are specialists in the kinds of operations deemed necessary—murder, assassination, blackmail, kidnapping, smuggling, and money laundering. State-organized crime and organized crime then become intertwined. This circumstance has arisen time and again in the history of the United States. During World War II, the Office of Naval Intelligence called on two leading organized crime figures in the United States—Meyer Lansky and Lucky Luciano—to help them in counteracting the influence of Harry Bridges, a communist labor leader. In return, Lucky Luciano was released from prison and Meyer Lansky was able to take control of a gigantic segment of illegal business profits in the United States.

In Vietnam, as shown, the CIA aided the opium traffic, and today they are implicated with organized crime in assassination attempts as well as in smuggling, money laundering, and, perhaps, international narcotics.

These are the bare outlines of the potential study of state-organized crime. Entrapment, police brutality, violation of civil rights, and a host of other crimes from time to time become institutionalized in government practices. These are the legitimate subjects for analysis by sociologists of crime and criminal law. They represent one set of facts any theory of crime must fit.

In his ground-breaking work on white-collar crime, Edwin Sutherland stated that his concern was to redress an imbalance in sociological analyses of crime that ignored the criminality of the middle- and upper-class businessperson. He argued that theories of criminal behavior focusing on biological or physical characteristics of individuals could not account for the criminality of General Motors or bank embezzlers. Research on state-organized crime reinforces Sutherland's observation. It is patently absurd to attribute the criminality of the queens and kings of Europe from the 16th to the 18th centuries or the presidents of the United States from Dwight Eisenhower to Ronald Reagan—as well as the criminality of state organizations (the English Admiralty and the CIA, among others)—to biological, physical, psychological, or personality characteristics of the criminals. State organized crime is an even more-telling criticism of these theories in that it is an example of criminality that involves the use of violence and the illegal granting of licenses to steal, murder, plunder, and rape on a scale rarely paralleled in the annals of conventional criminal exploits.

Indeed, this foray into the crimes of state—alongside the abundance of evidence presented in this book about the widespread criminality of people in all social classes, races, historical periods, and personal circumstances—can lead to only one conclusion: Crime must be analyzed and explained by seeing how it relates to social structure.

14

Conclusion*

Sir Francis Bacon pointed out long ago that the questions we ask shape our knowledge far more than the theories we propose. Traditionally, criminology asked, Why is it that some people commit crime while others do not? In the face of civil-rights demonstrations, anti-war protests, civil disobedience, the invasion of middle-class leisure by marijuana and cocaine, and blatant criminality by political leaders and giant corporations, criminologists in the 1960s began to wonder if that question was sufficient for an understanding of crime.

As a consequence a "paradigm revolution" came about in criminology. New questions began to dominate criminological inquiry. Now people asked:

- Why are some acts defined by law as criminal while others are not?
- Why, given the definition of certain acts as criminal, are some people arrested, prosecuted, convicted, and sentenced while others are not?
- Why is crime distributed as it is by social class, race, and gender?

These new questions forced a reappraisal. Studies of the law-making process discovered that many acts come to be defined as criminal because of the interplay of power and political struggles reflecting economic conditions. Other studies showed that those arrested, prosecuted, sentenced, and confined are not always the most serious violators but almost always the poorest. Finally, it was noted that official and public definitions of crime ignored white-collar, corporate, state, and organized crime and distorted the actual danger of criminality to people, the seriousness of even major

*This is a revision of a chapter published in David Kairys, *The Politics of Justice,* (New York: Pantheon, 1985).

offenses, and the degree to which we were in fact experiencing a "crime wave" and "soaring crime rates."

These revelations were not particularly new, but they were nonetheless sufficient to create what the philosopher of science T. S. Kuhn refers to as a "paradigm revolution."[1] Until this revolution, criminologists proposed a panoply of social-psychological theories to account for why some people commit crime and others do not: Cultural-transmission theories argued that criminality was normal for some people because they learned crime from their peers, parents, or subculture; psychoanalytic theories proposed the explanation that family relations that were either overly strict or overly permissive were at the root of criminal behavior; personality theories argued that criminals were different from noncriminals in their possession of psychopathic or sociopathic traits; biological explanations argued that genes led some to crime and others away from it; collective behavior was seen as the cause whereby juveniles and, in later years adults, created delinquency out of the pressures and prospects of a particular moment. For a while in the 1950s, almost everyone was arguing that it was "differential opportunity" to achieve status, wealth, and power that led those with few opportunities for success to commit crime. Labeling theory argued that everyone commits crime (primary deviance they called initial acts of crime) but that some are labeled by their peers, the community or themselves and that this leads them to continue in their criminality as their self-image changes to reflect the labels attached to them.

The social-psychological theories seemed plausible in the affluent society of the 1950s. They fared well until their logical structure and empirical foundation was subjected to close scrutiny by radical criminology. Seen in the light shining from the cultural, political, and economic revolutions of the 1960s, it was clear how these theories fell head first into the logical traps Karl Popper warned against relying on auxiliary hypotheses (for example, _all_ people labeled criminal become criminal and _some_ are criminal without the label) and tautologies (for example, sociopathic people are those who show antisocial attitudes by committing criminal acts and crime is a result of sociopathic personalities). Studies of criminal law in action revealed systematic biases in the criminal-law process that tainted the value of research data gathered on institutionalized juveniles.

Moreover, when Martin Luther King, Jr., was jailed for protesting discrimination on buses, lunchrooms, and schools; when black children were murdered and the murderers were not punished; when war protestors were arrested, prosecuted, and shot (for example, Kent State and Greensborough); when Vice President Spiro Agnew was indicted and found guilty (he pleaded *nolo contendre*) to accepting and soliciting bribes and kickbacks and when the CIA, with the approval of the president, plotted the assassination of political leaders of foreign countries—it became impossible to explain violations of the criminal law in terms of sociopathic personalities, IQ, differential association, labeling, or lower-class culture.

Before pleading *nolo contendre,* Spiro Agnew helped fuel the flames of the incipient paradigm revolution with his diatribes favoring a campaign of "law and order" that went even further in its myopic vision of criminality than the criminological establishment:

> When I talk about troublemakers, I'm talking about muggers and criminals in the streets, assassins of political leaders, draft evaders, and flag burners, campus militants, hecklers and demonstrators against candidates for public office and looters and burners of cities.[2]

Agnew was putting the sons and daughters of criminologists and business people in a category with "muggers" and "criminals." That made some realize what the acceptance of the view of crime generated by the government and police really implied.

Problems with the narrowness and limitations of the traditional view were further exacerbated by the rediscovery of widespread criminality by the powerful. Edwin Sutherland had pointed the way to bringing white-collar crime (which is now called corporate crime) under the purview of social science, but in the early 1950s his observations were not well synthesized into the field. When the assassination of President Kennedy and his brother Robert were alleged to be linked to political struggles; when Penn Central executives were found blatantly tapping the till for millions of dollars and still the federal government bailed the corporation out of bankruptcy; when President Nixon was forced to resign for criminal acts against his political and business competitors, when the most powerful multinational corporations of the world hired private detectives to intimidate competitors and critics and when those same corporations engaged in wholesale bribery of foreign governments and local politicians; when, to end with only one of an endless array of possible examples, organized crime was discovered to be not a Mafia but a network of apparently law-abiding businessmen, politicians and law-enforcement officers welded together by their desire for gain and power; then criminological research and theory *had* to change or become an anachronism.

Sociolegal studies of the social, political, and economic forces that led to the definition of some acts as criminal and others not raised serious questions about theoretical paradigms that took the definition of behavior by the state as a given. Vagrancy, drug use, homosexuality, public intoxication, drunkenness, and disorderly conduct were discovered to be the offenses for which 75 to 80 percent of all the arrests were made in cities. Historical analyses revealed the political and economic forces behind the creation of criminal law. Research revealed that the law of theft arose to protect the interests and property of mercantilists against the interests and property of workers; vagrancy laws reflected the tensions in pre-capitalist England between feudal landlords, peasants, and the emergent capitalist class in the cities; "machine smashing" in rural England was a rational response of workers seeking to defy the trend towards boring, monotonous industrial production, but the state came down on the side of the capitalist class and criminalized such acts; hunting, fishing, and wood gathering were transferred from the rights of rural village dwellers to criminality punishable by death as a result of the state's intervention on the side of the landed gentry in opposition to the customs, values, and interests of the majority of the rural population; indeed, even murder came to be defined as an act against the state (that is, as a crime) as a result of political and economic struggles in which the majority of the people were simply powerless to have their views represented at law while the minority wielded their power.

Even laws that were acknowledged by everyone as serious violations of personal freedom and security—laws prohibiting murder, rape, vandalism, and theft—were found, on closer scrutiny, to be based on contradictory values and to have emerged as a result of political and economic forces.

Knowledge reflects its historical context, whether it is knowledge about the sun's movement relative to the earth or about the causes of crime. In the late 1960s, when blacks were protesting against oppression, exploitation, official violence and racism, it was quite predictable that someone would suggest that all criminality of the lower classes was merely a manifestation of a rational response to class oppression; even rape was accounted for as an attack on property held by others. The blatant manipulation of the law by the rich and powerful to protect themselves and the obviousness with which the criminal law was employed to suppress political dissent also predictably led to theories claiming that "all law" was merely a tool for protecting the interests of the ruling (capitalist) class.

Those theories were shortlived even on the fringes of the left. The saving grace of science is that theories must eventually come face to face with facts. "Facts kick," as Dewey put it. The fact is that much criminality simply cannot reasonably be attributed to class oppression—even the criminality of the oppressed; this we know from studies of persons in prison, many of whom clearly articulate the pecuniary or expressive nature of their criminal acts. The problem cannot be solved by taking refuge in the broad brush of argument that it was oppression that created the pecuniary motive or the impulsive action in the first place—that refuge is as tautological as the social psychologists attempt to explain criminal behavior by people's "association" or by their "marginality" when the definition of whether or not the association with criminality is "intense" enough is "proven" by whether or not the person committed a crime, or whether or not a person is "marginal" is evidenced mainly by the fact that the person committed a crime which is, by definition, a "marginal" act.

Nor did the ruling-class theory of law fare much better. Doubtless, much law derives directly from ruling-class participation in and influence over the law-making process. Even when not the direct result of ruling-class intervention, criminal laws often support ruling-class interests at the expense of everyone else. Unfortunately for ruling-class theory, however, many laws have a history that clearly contradicts the ruling-class hypothesis: factory health and safety legislation criminalizes an owner's refusal to comply with official orders to rectify unsafe conditions at work; laws against bringing public officials (at home or abroad); laws against interfering in the political struggles of other nations; even Karl Marx's early study of the laws limiting the length of the working day contradicts ruling class theory. Furthermore, it is also abundantly clear that many laws emerge out of a divided ruling class.[3]

Ruling-class theory, like any theory, can be defended against these empirical exceptions by creating a tautology: laws that derive from interclass conflict or that are not apparently in the interests of the ruling class are, in fact, in their interest "in the long run" because the system is protected from revolutionary change. Absent a revolution this move is a clever tautology because so long as the system survives (and it even took feudalism 800 years to destroy itself) then the laws must, logically, be in the interest of the ruling class. This is a nice way of making a polemical point, but it hardly suffices as an adequate logical structure for a scientific theory.

Early shots at developing an alternative to criminological *theory* were thus wanting. Note, however, that the expansion of empirical studies of criminal law creation and the law in action; a conscious and consistent awareness of the criminality of the rich and powerful; a sensitivity to the political economy of crime—all these and many other changes from the social-psychological approaches of the 1950s are profound and important in the working paradigm of the criminology of the 1970s and 1980s. They represent a shift in focus, perspective, and conceptualization.

Conflict criminology, emerging in the 1960s and 1970s, was first and foremost a reaction *against* the dominant paradigm of the 1950s. It sought a wider area for research and a broader conceptualization of the problem. The study of criminal-law creation and implementation became a cornerstone of criminological inquiry. The broader socio-historical role of political and economic forces were scrutinized as a potential source of explanations of crime and delinquency. Social class was reconceptualized as a social relation characteristic of a particular economic form within a historically determined political organization rather than, as had earlier been the case, translated from a social-psychological experience. Criminology came, as Ralf Dahrendorf had advised it should, "out of Utopia" and down to earth with a more realistic view of the widespread nature of serious criminality and the impossibility of explaining it with simplistic theories.

Critics of conflict criminology often ignore its effect on the dominant assumptions of the discipline and focus almost exclusively on its failure to "explain" crime adequately. As with all social science, the value of the endeavor is more clearly found in the perspective it provides than in its ability to generate empirically valid generalizations. Judged by the standard of producing valid generalizations that meet even minimal scientific requirements, all social science is a failure. Judged by the standard of forcing us to own up to our biases and myopic visions, conflict criminology has succeeded despite the fact that critics grossly distort and misunderstand what is being said.

Conflict criminology's failure to come up with a palatable explanation leads some to seek a return to the social psychology of the past. That is the worst possible alternative, not because it is ideologically conservative, which it invariably is, but because it asks the wrong question.

We cannot find an answer to why some people commit crime while others do not in a world in which almost everyone does. We cannot reasonably assume that there is a discoverable difference between those who commit crime and those who do not. We cannot, we should not, ignore the problem of street crime. But we cannot hope to increase our knowledge by stepping back into the trap of thinking that these acts can be understood without also understanding how the Ford Motor Company can calculate the cost of law suits if someone is killed by faulty engineering and decide, on the basis of cost-effective calculations, to go ahead and produce a dangerous automobile; how employers refuse to spend the money necessary to reduce work hazards; how government officials reward Green Berets for murder; how the CIA hired organized-crime figures to assassinate another nation's president; or how the FBI committed violence against political dissidents. Recognizing the need to reaffirm the importance and prevalence of violent offenses may be a necessary reminder to a criminology focusing on corporate crime, organized crime and political misfeasance and malfeasance, but to forget the character of criminality in all social classes; or to ignore or relegate to a mere curiosity the historical roots of criminal law is to take a giant step backward. The theoretical perspective that follows from asking why some people commit crime and others do not leads one to ignore the political and economic structure. It was precisely the dead end of this too narrow social-psychological question focused on a very minute segment of crime and criminality that gave rise to conflict criminology, the most important shift in theoretical perspectives on crime in the last 50 years.

The challenge for criminology is to link the study of crime with political and economic forces shaping our institutions and our social relations. The most promising paradigm employs the methodology of the dialectic and the theory of contradictions as a starting point for an integrated theoretical criminology. Briefly, this position argues that in every political and economic system there are fundamental contradictions. People acting consciously—albeit with a substantial handicap of inherited traditions, beliefs, and institutions—attempt to deal with these contradictions. The range of reactions is finite but diverse. How one responds to and deals with the contradictions—and, more importantly, how classes of people respond to and deal with the contradictions inherent in their historical moment—determines the shape and contours of the world at that time. Capitalism is thus not a predetermined system and lower-class criminality is not a predetermined response to capitalism—rather, both are solutions to certain structural contradictions of the political economy that generate conflicts, dilemmas, and attempts at resolution. There is a fundamental contradiction in capitalist societies between maximization of profits (which leads capitalists to want to pay low wages) and the necessity for a large class of consumers (who must have money from wages to buy the products). Capitalists fight to keep wages down; workers fight to raise them. Criminal law enters into the resultant conflict stemming from this contradiction by trying to force people to work at jobs not of their choosing and to make it a crime to expropriate the property of others. The law-enforcement establishment selectively enforces laws in a manner that reduces conflicts for their agencies with those who have the power to cause them strain, while workers and the unemployed seek to resolve the problems created for them by these laws through criminal acts from illegal strikes to theft and violence. The process, in a word, is dialectical. It is a process of people writing their own history out of the conflicts and dilemmas generated by structural contradictions written on the slate they inherited as their birthright.

We must reject the plea that if the people (whose vision of crime is unfailingly determined by law-enforcement and media distortions) view crime fearfully and apprehensively, then criminology must study, explain, and try to solve the problem and not quibble over its accuracy. One way to counteract the public apprehension is to provide a more-accurate description of precisely how dangerous the streets really are. For example, the likelihood is very low that a person living in a middle-class neighborhood will be victimized even in the societies with the highest crime rates. Furthermore, it is revealing that a comparison of assaults as evidenced by victim surveys show the rate of assault in Oslo, Norway, New York, and Atlanta to be just about the same.[4] Murder is also greatly overestimated in official statistics—as witnessed by the comparison of murder rates from victim surveys and the murder rates reported by police to the FBI—rates that it is obviously in the interest of the police and the media to exaggerate in order to enhance the standing and position of the former and the sales of the latter. To justify perpetuating and not qualifying the official, self-interested view of crime thrust at the public by the law-enforcement and media establishment is to fail in one of our principal obligations as criminologists. Should we have studied the communist threat in the 1950s because Richard Nixon and Joseph McCarthy were confusing the public with scare stories about the danger to life, limb, security, and safety posed by the "Red Menace"?

Not only criminology but also all criminological and legal scholarship should be committed to correcting the law-enforcement and media definition of crime. A scientific criminology, whether Marxist or behaviorist, must commit itself to understanding the full range of criminality and not accept blindly the pictures given by the *Uniform Crime Reports* or *Time Magazine*. Explanations of crime must be broadly brushed, not narrowly pursuing social-psychological theories to answer the impossible question of why some people commit crime while others do not. Criminology must, as conflict criminology has unquestionably demonstrated, understand, and explain the entire range of phenomena called crime. We must understand the political economic and social forces leading to differences in crime rates in different historical periods, as well as differences between countries in the same period. We must explore the differences between crime in capitalist and socialist societies. We must look carefully at the historical roots of criminal laws and the legislative and appellate court processes that define acts as criminal to understand the larger issues and enlighten the public as to exactly what crime is and what kind of a threat it poses to their well-being. We must continue to examine the legal process to discover why some laws are enforced and others are not and why some people are arrested, prosecuted, and sentenced while others are not.

In the preface to this book it was noted that when a sculptor creates a figure or an artisan working in glass or clay creates a pot, it sometimes happens that a flaw in the work that is hidden from sight in time will manifest itself and the piece of art will fall apart. In the 1960s and 1970s the criminology that was built around psychological, social-psychological, and biological theories of criminal behavior fell apart. It has been possible, however, to restore criminology. By shifting the focus and recognizing the importance of facts previously overlooked, a new criminology emerged from the broken pieces. In this book we have explored the causes and consequences of the revolution in criminological and sociological thinking that followed. We have inquired into the logical and empirical utility of theories of criminal behavior and we have offered an alternative approach and paradigm. We end not with a conclusion but with a challenge: to question, build on, and work for the construction of better theories, and to obtain more reliable facts and, in the end, knowledge that can be put to practice to create a better world.

References

Chapter 1

1. For the first three paragraphs I am indebted to Herbert L. Costner, who—years ago—began writing a textbook on juvenile delinquency with me. Unfortunately, that project floundered on the rocks of unchartered seas.
2. Thomas B. Cottle, "Matthew Washington Who Had Death in His Eyes" (unpublished manuscript, 1970).
3. John R. Coleman, "Who Will Tell the Public 'You've Been Had' on Crime?" *Augustus* 1x, 35 (1986):10–11.
4. William J. Chambliss, "The Saints and the Roughnecks," *Society* 11 (Nov.–Dec. 1973):24–31.
5. Daniel Glaser and Kent Rice, "Crime, Age and Employment," *American Sociological Review* (1959):679–686.
6. Harry King and William J. Chambliss, *Harry King: A Professional Thief's Journey* (New York: Macmillan, 1982), 84–111.
7. Ibid., 85.
8. Paul Hoffman, "Paintings Stolen from Gallery in Milan," *International Herald Tribune* (Paris, 1975):1.
9. Associated Press, "A Trick Costs Christie's Jewels Worth $585,600," *International Herald Tribune*, (Paris, March 21, 1975):1.
10. Nils Christie, *The Definition of Violent Behavior* (Oslo, Norway: Institute of Criminology, 1975).
11. *The Opium Trail* (Boston: New England Free Press, 1960), 13.
12. Ibid., 17.
13. Tamar Lewin, "Reporter's Trial Begins: Insider's Issue is Argued," *New York Times* (Jan. 22, 1985):D1–2.
14. Richard J. H. Johnston, "Mercy Killer Acquitted on Insanity Plea," *New York Times* (November 6, 1973).
15. Judith Valente, "No Jail in Slaying of Despondent Son," *Washington Post,* (May 12, 1984):A1, 12.

16. Associated Press, "Abortionist Given Probation Appeals, Is Offered Job Back," *International Herald Tribune* (Paris: February 19, 1975):3.

17. Associated Press, "Two U.S. Airlines Indicted in Texas," *International Herald Tribune* (Paris: February 15–16, 1975):2.

18. United Press International, January 10, 1969.

19. "No 3: Stans," *Time* (March 24, 1975):28.

20. Ibid.

21. Whitman Knapp, Chairman, commission to investigate allegations of police corruption in New York City (1972).

22. "Police Quell Riot in Capital Slum," *New York Times* (November 3, 1968):46.

23. James Spradley, *You Owe Yourself a Drunk* (Boston: Little Brown), 20.

24. William J. Chambliss, field notes: "A Visit to Atascadero State Hospital for the Sexually Deviant and Criminally Insane" (Report to the California Department of Mental Health, June, 1966).

25. Joey, *Killer* (Chicago: Playboy Publications, 1979), 17.

Chapter 2

1. Chief Justice Warren Burger's address to the American Bar Association (Houston, TX, 1981).

2. Edwin H. Sutherland and Donald R. Cressey, *Principles of Criminology* (Philadelphia: J. B. Lippincott, 1978), 82.

3. National Commission, "The Wickersham Commission" (1931):12–13.

4. David Seidman and Michael Couzens, "Getting the Crime Rate Down: Political Pressure and Crime Reporting," *Law and Society Review* 8 (1974):457–493.

5. Federal Bureau of Investigation, *Uniform Crime Reports Handbook* (Washington, D.C.: Department of Justice, 1981).

6. Ibid.

7. William Selke and Harold Pepinsky, "The Politics of Police Reporting in Indianapolis, 1948–78," *Law and Human Behavior* 6, Nos. 3/4. Reprinted in William J. Chambliss, *Criminal Law in Action* (New York: John Wiley, 1984):178–190.

8. Seidman and Couzens, "Getting the Crime Rate Down," 469.

9. R. Mcleary, B. C. Nienstedt, and J. M. Erven, "Uniform Crime Reports as Organizational Outcomes: Three Times Series Quasi-Experiments," *Social Problems* 29 (1982):361–372.
   Marvin Wolfgang, "Criminality and the Criminologist," *Journal of Criminal Law, Criminology and Police Science* 54:115–162.

10. Selke and Pepinsky, "The Politics of Police Reporting," 190.

11. Bureau of Justice Statistics, *Criminal Victimization 1984* (U.S. Department of Justice, 1984), 1.

12. Herbert L. Costner, "On Methodology in the Sociology of Crime" (pa-

per presented at the meetings of the Pacific Sociological Association, 1967).

13. Patrick A. Langan and Christopher A. Innes, *Trends in Victimization: 1978–1982* (U.S. Department of Justice, 1985), 1.

14. Bureau of Justice Statistics, *Criminal Victimization 1985* (U.S. Department of Justice, 1985), 1.

15. James Q. Wilson, *Thinking About Crime* (New York: Basic Books, 1975).
   —— and Richard Herrnstein, *Crime and Human Nature* (New York: Simon and Schuster, 1985).

16. Roland J. Chilton, "Race, Age, Gender and Changes in Urban Arrest Rates" (paper presented at the meetings of the American Sociological Association, Detroit, 1985).
   M. J. Hindelang, "Race Involvement in Common Law Personal Crimes," *American Sociological Review* 43 (1978):93–109.

17. Hindelang, "Race Involvement," 100.

18. Chilton, "Urban Arrest Rates."

19. James Jacobs, "Race Relations and the Prison Subculture," in *Crime and Justice* Vol. 1, ed. Norval Morris and Michael Tonry (Chicago: University of Chicago Press, 1979).
   Colin Loftin, Ronald C. Kestler, and David Greenberg, "Social Inequality and Crime Control" (unpublished manuscript, 1984).

20. Chambliss and Seidman, *Law, Order, and Power,* 285–301.
   Harold Garfinkel, "Conditions of Successful Degradation Ceremonies," *American Journal of Sociology* 61 (1956):420–424.
   Jerome Skolnick, *Justice Without Trial: Law Enforcement in Democratic Society* (New York: John Wiley and Sons, 1975).

21. William J. Chambliss, *Criminal Law in Action* (New York: Macmillan, 1984), 167–177.
   Janet Schmidt, "The Creation of Parole Guidelines: From Rehabilitation to Retribution," *Contemporary Crises* 3:419.

22. William J. Chambliss, "The Saints and the Roughnecks," *Society* 11:24–31.
   John P. McIver, "The Impact of Race on Patrol Officer Behavior" (Paper presented at the annual meetings of the American Society of Criminology, San Diego, 1986).
   Marjorie Zatz, "The Changing Forms of Racial/Ethnic Biases in Sentencing," *Journal of Research in Crime and Delinquency* Vol. 24, No. 1 (1987):69–92.

23. Michael Hindelang, Travis Hirschi, and Joseph Weis, "Correlates of Delinquency: The Illusion of Discrepancy Between Self-Report and Official Measures," *American Sociological Review* 44 (December 1979):995–1014.

24. National Crime Surveys (Washington, D.C.: U.S. Department of Justice, 1973–1985).

25. William J. Chambliss, "The Saints and the Roughnecks."

26. Department of Justice, *Criminal Victimization in the United States* (Washington, D.C.: U.S. Department of Justice, 1967).

27. Margaret Zahn and Marc Reidel, *The Nature and Pattern of American Homicide* (Washington, D.C.: U.S. Department of Justice, 1985).

28. Bureau of Justice Statistics, *National Crime Survey* (Washington, D.C.: U.S. Department of Justice, 1974), 3.

29. Andrew Hacker, "Getting Used to Mugging," *The New York Review of Books* (April 19, 1973). Reprinted in William J. Chambliss and Milton Mankoff, *Whose Law, What Order?* (New York: John Wiley and Sons, 1976), 215–224.

30. Austin Porterfield, *Youth in Trouble* (Fort Worth, TX: Lex Potisham Foundation, 1946).

31. James S. Wallerstein and Clement J. Wylie, "Our Law-Abiding Law-Breakers," *Probation* 25 (1947):107–112.

32. Delbert S. Elliot and David Huiznga, "Social Class and Delinquent Behavior in a National Youth Panel," *Criminology* 21, No. 2 (May 1983):149–177.

33. Charles Tittle, Wayne J. Villamez, and Douglas A. Smith, "The Myth of Social Class and Criminality: An Empirical Assessment of the Empirical Evidence," *American Sociological Review* 43 (1979):643–656.

34. Marjorie Zatz, "Biases in Sentencing."

35. Donald Gibbons, *Delinquent Behavior* (Englewood Cliffs, NJ: Prentice Hall, 1978).

36. Raymond J. Michalowski, *Order, Law, and Crime* (New York: Random House, 1984), 302.

37. Eugene Kanin, "Reference Groups and Sex Conduct Norm Violation," *Sociological Quarterly* 8 (1967):495–502.
    Clifford Kirkpatrick and Eugene Kanin, "Male Sex Aggression on a University Campus," *American Sociological Review* 36 (1957):461–474.

38. Thomas J. Meyer, "Date Rape: A Serious Problem That Few Think About," *Chronicle of Higher Education* (Dec. 5, 1984):17–24.

39. Edmund F. McGarrell and Timonthy J. Glanagan, *The Sourcebook of Criminal Justice Statistics* (Washington, D.C.: U.S. Department of Justice, 1985).

40. "Where Are the Children?" *Augustus* (Jan. 1986):36–37.

41. James A. Inciardi, "Little Girls and Sex: A Glimpse at the World of the 'Baby Pro,'" *Deviant Behavior* 5 (1984):71–78.

42. Edwin M. Schur and H. A. Bedau, *Victimless Crimes: Two Sides of a Controversy* (Englewood Cliffs, NJ: Prentice-Hall, 1974).

43. McGarrell and Glanagan, *The Sourcebook* op. cit.

44. Laurel Richardson, *New Other Woman* (Chicago: University of Chicago Press, 1986).

45. *Hardwick vs. Georgia,* U.S. Supreme Court (1986).

46. Alfred C. Kinsey, W. B. Pomeroy, and W. C. Martin, *Sexual Behavior in the Human Male* (Philadelphia: Saunders, 1948).

47. Frances T. Cullen, *Rethinking Crime and Deviance Theory: The Emergence of a Structuring Tradition* (Totowa, NJ: Rowman and Allanheld, 1984), 3.

48. Eleanor Miller, *Street Woman* (Philadelphia: Temple University Press, 1985).

49. Dane Archer and Rosemary Gartner, *Violence and Crime in Cross-National Perspective* (New Haven, CT: Yale University, 1984), 27.

50. William J. Chambliss, *Crime Rates, Crime Myths and Official Smokescreens* (Oslo, Norway: Institute of Criminology, 1979).

51. British Home Office, *Victims of Crime in Britain* (London: Her Majesty's Printing Office, 1984).
    National Council for Crime Prevention, *Crime in Sweden* (Stockholm, Sweden: Brottsförebyggende rädet, 1985).

52. Michalowski, *Order, Law, and Crime.*

53. Harold Pepinsky and Paul Jasilow, *Myths That Cause Crime* (Cabin John, MD: Seven Locks Press, 1984).

Chapter 3

1. Sanford Kadish, "The Crisis of Overcriminalization," *Annals of the American Academy of Political and Social Science* 374 (1967):157–170.

2. Alan A. Block, *East Side, West Side* (New Brunswick, NJ: Transaction, 1984).
    —— and William J. Chambliss, *Organizing Crime* (New York: Elsevier Publishers, 1981).
    —— and Frank R. Scarpitti, *Poisoning for Profit: The Mafia and Toxic Waste in America* (New York: William Morrow and Co., 1985).
    William J. Chambliss, *On the Take* (Bloomington, IN: Indiana University Press, 1978).
    Philip Jenkins and Gary W. Potter, "Before the Krays: Organized Crime in London: 1920–1960," (unpublished manuscript, Department of Criminal Justice, Pennsylvania State University, August, 1987:1–35.

3. Lincoln Steffens, *The Shame of the Cities* (New York: Harcourt Brace and World, 1931).

4. 28 U.S.C. §591 et. seq.

5. Robert Winter-Berger, *Washington Payoff* (New York: Dell, 1972).

6. Block and Scarpitti, *Poisoning for Profit.*

7. Marshall B. Clinard and Peter C. Yeager, *Corporate Crime* (New York: The Free Press, 1980), 3.

8. Edwin H. Sutherland, "White-Collar Criminality," *American Sociological Review* V (1940):1–12.

9. Edwin H. Sutherland, *White-Collar Crime* (New York: Dryden Press, 1949).

10. Clinard and Yeager, *Corporate Crime.*
11. Congressional Record (1974).
12. D. Walsh, "Mafia-Teamster Tie Reported But Kleindienst Ends Bugging," *International Herald Tribune* (April 30, 1973):1–2.
13. J. Thomas, "Kleindienst and Fitzimmons Linked to Teamster Inquiry," *New York Times* (April 28, 1978):A-13.
14. Nancy Frank, *Crimes Against Health and Safety* (New York: Harrow and Heston, 1985), 21–25.
15. James P. Brady, "Arson, Fiscal Crisis, and Community Action: Dialectics of an Urban Crime and Popular Response," *Crime and Delinquency* 28 (1982):247–270.

    ———, "Arson, Urban Economy and Organized Crime: The Case of Boston," *Social Problems* 31 (1985):1–27.
16. Brady, "Arson, Urban Economy and Organized Crime," 253.
17. Jim Handy, *Gift of the Devil: A History of Guatemala.* (Boston: South End Press, 1984).
18. Clinard and Yeager, *Corporate Crime,* 11–50.
19. Ralph Nader, "Uncollected Taxes," *The New Republic* (Oct. 6, 1973):10–11.
20. Ibid., 10.
21. Robert Criles, "A Tax Assessor Has Many Friends," *The Nation* (Feb. 1974):13–24.
22. Rudy Platiel, "Record of Safety in Workplace Near Genocide, Professor Says," *Toronto: Globe and Mail* (April 6, 1984).
23. Patrick Donnelly, "OSHA: The Sociology of Worker Health and Safety" (Ph.D. dissertation, University of Delaware, 1980), 4.

    Daniel Borman, *Death on the Job* (New York: Monthly Review Press, 1978).

    Kitty Calavita, "The Demise of the 'Occupational Safety and Health Administration': A Case Study in Symbolic Action," *Social Problems* 30 (1983):437–448.

    Sidney Lens, "Dead on the Job," *The Progressive* (Nov. 1979):50–52.

    J. Page and M. W. O'Brien, *Bitter Wages* (New York: Grossman, 1972).

    Charles Reasons, M. C. Paterson, and L. Ross, *Assault on the Worker* (Toronto: Butterworth, 1981).

    R. Scott, *Muscle and Blood* (New York: E. P. Dutton, 1974).

    L. Reeve Stearns, "Fact and Fiction of a Model Enforcement Bureaucracy: The Labor Inspectorate of Sweden," *British Journal of Law and Society* 6 (1979):1–23.

    J. Swartz, "Silent Killers at Work," *Crime and Social Justice* 3 (1975):15–20.

    L. Tataryn, *Dying for a Living* (Toronto: Deneau and Greenberg, 1979).
24. Ronald C. Cramer, "Corporate Crime: An Organizational Perspective," in *White-Collar and Economic Crime,* ed. P. Wickman and T. Dailey (Lexington, MA: Lexington Books, 1982), 75–94.
25. Daniel Curran, "Dead Laws for Dead Men: The Case of Federal Coal

Mine Health and Safety Legislation" (Ph.D. dissertation, University of Delaware, 1980).

26. Jeffrey H. Reiman, *The Rich Get Richer and the Poor Get Prison: Ideology, Class and Criminal Justice* (New York: John Wiley and Sons, 1979).

27. Jonathan A. Bennett, "Kerr-McGee Death Was No 'Accident,'" *The Guardian* (Jan. 22, 1986).

28. Ibid., 1.

29. Donnelly, "OSHA," 12.

30. Curran, "Dead Laws for Dead Men," 109.

31. Ibid, 110.

32. John Braithwaite, *Corporate Crime in the Pharmaceutical Industry* (London: Routledge and Kegal Paul, 1984).
Michael Levi, "De Maximis non Curat Lex: Combatting the Other Drug Problem," *Modern Law Review* (1985).

33. David Ermann and Richard J. Liundman, *Corporate and Governmental Deviance: Problems of Organizational Behavior in Contemporary Society* (New York: Oxford University Press, 1982).

34. M. Dowie, "The Corporate Crime of the Century," *Mother Jones* (Nov. 1979):23–25.
Jerome Skolnick and Elliott Currie, "Pinto Madness," *Crisis in American Institutions* (Boston: Little, Brown, 1979), 23–40.

35. Dowie, "The Corporate Crime," 23–25.
Stanley Eitzen and Douglas Timmer, *Criminology* (New York: John Wiley and Sons, 1985), 307–308.

36. Leslie Maitland Werner, "GM Is Sued by U.S. on X-Car Defects Involving Breaks," *New York Times* (Aug. 4, 1983):A-1.

37. Block and Scarpitti, *Poisoning for Profit*.

38. Ibid.

39. Friends Service Committee, *Report on Migratory Child Labor in the U.S.* (Washington, D.C.: U.S. Department of Labor, 1972).
———, *Child Labor in the U.S.* (Washington, D.C.: U.S. Government Printing Office, 1970).

40. New York Times, Jan.–March, 1981.

41. International Herald Tribune, March 15, 1983.

42. Friends Service Committee, *Migratory Child Labor in the U.S.* (Philadelphia: Friends Service Committee, 1972).

43. Clinard and Yeager, *Corporate Crime*, 8.

44. Ibid., 9.

45. Bureau of Justice Statistics, *Special Report: Robbery Victims* (Washington, D.C.: U.S. Department of Justice, 1987), 1.

46. Gilbert Geis, "Deterring Corporate Crime," in *Corporate Crime in America,* ed. Ralph Nader and Mark Green (New York: Grossman, 1973), 12.

47. William J. Chambliss, "State-Organized Crime" (paper presented at the American Society of Criminology, San Diego, CA, November 1985).

48. The Pike Committee, *CIA: The Pike Report* (New York: Spokesman Press, 1977).

49. John Dinges and Saul Landau, *Assassination on Embassy Row* (New York: McGraw-Hill, 1980).

50. T. B. Barry, B. Wood, and D. Preusch, *Dollars and Dictators: A Guide to Central America* (New York: Grove Press, 1983), 3.

51. Noam Chomsky, *Turning the Tide* (Boston: South End Press, 1985). Jim Handy, *Gift of the Devil: A History of Guatemala* (Boston: South End Press, 1984).

52. Chomsky, *Turning the Tide,* 14.

53. Alfred McCoy, *The Politics of Heroin in Southeast Asia* (New York: Harper and Row, 1972).

54. Richard Hofstadter and Michael Wallace, *Violence: A Documentary History* (New York: Alfred A. Knopf, 1970). Richard Rubenstein, *Rebels in Eden: Mass Political Violence in the United States* (Boston: Little, Brown, 1970).

55. C. Vann Woodward, *The Strange Career of Jim Crow* (New York: Oxford University Press, 1958).

56. Joseph L. Albini, *The American Mafia: Genesis of a Legend* (New York: Appleton-Century Crofts, 1971). William J. Chambliss, *On the Take.* Donald R. Cressey, *Theft of the Nation* (New York: Harper and Row, 1969). Michael Levi, *The Phantom Capitalists: The Organization and Control of Long Firm Fraud* (London: Heinemann, 1981). Peter Reuter, *Disorganized Crime: The Economics of the Visible Hand* (Cambridge, MA: MIT Press, 1983).

57. Government Accounting Office, *Attorney General's Task Force on Organized Crime* (Washington, D.C.: U.S. Government Printing Office, 1985).

58. Chambliss, *On the Take.*

59. Daniel Bell, "Crime as an American Way of Life: A Queer Ladder of Social Mobility," in *The End of Ideology: On the Exhaustion of Political Ideas in the Fifties,* rev. ed. (New York: Free Press, 1962), 127–150.

60. William J. Chambliss, "Markets, Profits, Labor and Smack," *Contemporary Crises* 1 (1977):53–76.

61. Bruce Jackson, *A Thief's Primer* (New York: Macmillan, 1969). Harry King and William J. Chambliss, *Harry King: A Professional Thief's Journey* (New York: John Wiley and Sons, 1982). Edwin H. Sutherland, *The Professional Thief* (Chicago: University of Chicago Press, 1953).

62. King and Chambliss, *A Professional Thief's Journey,* 1–30.

63. Marvin G. Wolfgang, Robert Figlio, Simon Singer, and Paul Tracy, *National Survey of Crime Severity* (Washington, D.C.: Bureau of Justice Statistics, 1985).

Chapter 4

1. H. L. A. Hart, *The Morality of Criminal Law* (Jerusalem, Israel: The Magnes Press, 1964), 1.

2. It was thought for a time that incest was the one universal prohibition among all peoples. It is clear, however, that even incest is not prohibited everywhere; what is defined as incest in one culture is defined as appropriate in another.

3. John F. Galliher and John R. Cross, *Morals Legislation Without Morality: The Case of Nevada* (New Brunswick, NJ: Rutgers University Press, 1983).

   ———, "Symbolic Severity in the Land of Easy Virtue: Nevada's High Marijuana Penalty," *Social Problems* 29 (1982):380–387.

   John F. Galliher, James L. McCartney, and Barbara Baum, "Nebraska's Marijuana Law: A Case of Unexpected Legislative Innovation," *Law and Society Review* 8 (1974):441–456.

   John F. Galliher and Linda Vasilick, "Utah's Liberal Drug Laws: Structural Foundations and Triggering Events," *Social Problems* 26 (1979):284–293.

   John F. Galliher and Alyn Walker, "The Puzzle of the Marijuana Tax Act of 1937," *Social Problems* 24 (1977):367–376.

4. Jerome Skolnick, *House of Cards: The Legalization and Control of Casino Gambling* (Boston: Little, Brown, 1977).

5. James Graham, "Amphetamine Politics on Capitol Hill," *Transaction* 9 (1972):145–146.

6. Ivan Fallon and James Srodes, *Dreammaker: The Rise and Fall of John DeLorean* (New York: G. P. Putnam and Sons, 1983).

7. Jerome Hall, *Law, Social Science and Criminal Theory* (Littleton, MO: Fred B. Rothman & Co., 1982).

   ———, *Principles of Criminal Law* (Chicago: Bobbs-Merrill, 1972).

8. Arie Freiberg and Pat O'Malley, "State Intervention and the Civil Offense," *Law and Society Review* 18 (1984):380.

9. Steve Blum-West and Timothy J. Carter, "Bringing White-Collar Crime Back In: An Examination of Crimes and Torts," *Social Problems* 30 (1983):545–554.

10. Nancy Frank, "From Criminal to Civil Penalties in the History of Health and Safety Laws," *Social Problems* 30 (1983):532–545.

11. Emile Durkheim, *The Division of Labor in Society* (New York: The Free Press, 1933), 73, 77, 79–81. For an excellent critique, see Heinz Steinert, "The Function of Criminal Law," *Contemporary Crises* 2 (1978):167; and Emilio Lamo de Espinosa, "Social and Legal Order in Sociological Functionalism," *Contemporary Crises* 4 (1980):43.

12. A. L. Morton, *A People's History of England* (London: Lawrencle-Wisehart, 1938) 70.

13. Morton, *A People's History,* ibid:90.

14. C. Ray Jeffrey, "The Development of Crime in Early English Soci-

ety," *Journal of Criminal Law, Criminology and Police Science* 47 (1957):666.

15. Jerome Hall, *Theft, Law, and Society* 2d. ed. (Indianapolis: Bobbs-Merrill, 1952):4.

16. Ibid., 34–35.

17. Ibid., 63–66.

18. Ibid., 66.

19. Karl Marx, *The Process of Capitalist Production* Vol. 1, taken from the third German ed. by Samuel Moore and Edward Aveling, ed. Frederick Engels (New York: Humboldt Publishing Co., 1890), 715.

20. Edward P. Thompson, *Whigs and Hunters: The Origin of the Black Act* (New York: Pantheon Books, 1976).

21. Sir Leon Radzinowicz, *History of English Criminal Law and Its Administration from 1750,* 4 vols. (London: Stevens, 1948–1968).

22. Douglas Hay, "Property, Authority and Criminal Law," in D. Hay, P. Linebough, J. Rule, E. P. Thompson, and C. Winslow, *Albion's Fatal Free: Crime and Society in Eighteenth-Century England* (London: 1 Allen Lane, Penguin Books, 1975), 27.

23. Hay, "Property, Authority and Criminal Law," 28. For an excellent parallel study of the postbellum South, see Steven Hahn, "Hunting, Fishing and Foraging: Common Rights and Class Relations in the Postbellum South," *Radical History Review* Vol. 26 (1982):37–62.

24. 23 Ed. 3 (1348).

25. 25 Ed. 3 (1351).

26. Caleb Foote, "Vagrancy-Type Law and Its Administration," *University of Pennsylvania Law Review* 104 (1956):615.

27. Frank Bradshaw, *A Social History of England* (London: University of London Press, 1915), 54.

28. 1 Edw. 6.C.3 (1547).

29. William J. Chambliss, "A Sociological Analysis of the Law of Vagrancy," *Social Problems* 12 (1964):45–69.

30. Christopher R. Adamson, "Punishment After Slavery: Southern State Penal Systems, 1865–1890," *Social Problems* 30 (1983):556–569.

31. Chambliss, "A Sociological Analysis," op. cit.

32. *Edwards vs. California,* 314 U.S.:160 (1941).

33. *Papachristou vs. City of Jacksonville,* 405 U.S.:156 (1972).

34. Ibid.

35. Jerome Skolnick, *The Politics of Protest* (New York: Simon and Schuster, 1969), 4.

36. Karl F. Shumann, "Crime as a Reflection of Universal Norms" (paper presented at the meeting of the European Group for the Study of Deviance, Amsterdam, 1975).

37. William J. Chambliss, "State-Organized Crime" (paper presented at the annual meetings of the American Society of Criminology, San Diego, CA, November 1986).

38. Irving Louis Horowitz and M. Liebowitz, "Social Deviance and Polit-

ical Marginality: Towards a Redefinition of the Relationship Between Sociology and Politics," *Social Problems* 15 (1968):108–123.

39. Stanley Cohen, "Protest, Unrest and Delinquency: Convergences in Labels and Behavior," in *The Sociology of Crime and Delinquency: The New Criminologists,* ed. Paul Wiles (London: Barnes and Noble, 1976), 108–123.

40. Hall, *Theft, Law and Society,* 4.

41. William J. Chambliss and Edward Sbarbaro, "Public Opinion and Legislation" (unpublished manuscript, 1986).

42. Craig M. Bradley, "Racketeering and the Federalization of Crime," *American Criminal Law Review* 22 (1984–1985):214–272.

43. Hans H. Gerth and C. Wright Mills, *From Max Weber: Essays in Sociology* (Glencoe, IL: The Free Press, 1946):66.

44. Marx, *The Process of Capitalist Production.*
Karl Marx, "Capital Punishment," *New York Daily Tribune* (1853). Reprinted in *Karl Marx; Selected Writings in Sociology and Social Philosophy,* ed. T. B. Boltomure and M. Rubel (London: Tavistock, 1968).

45. Gabriel Kolko, *The Triumph of Conservatism* (New York: The Free Press, 1963).

46. John Braithwaite, *Corporate Crime in the Pharmaceutical Industry* (London: Routledge and Kegan Paul, 1984), 276.

47. W. G. O. Carson, "Symbolic and Instrumental Dimensions of Early Factory Legislation," in *Crime, Criminology and Public Policy,* ed. R. Hood (London: Heinemann, 1974).

48. Richard O. Boyer and Herbert M. Morais, *Labor's Untold Story* (New York: United Electrical, Radio and Machine Workers of America, 1955).
Sidney Harring, "Class Conflict and the Suppression of Tramps in Buffalo, 1982–1984," *Law and Society Review* 11 (1977):873–911.

49. Karl Klare, "Judicial Deradicalization of the Wagner Act and the Origins of Modern Legal Consciousness, 1937–1941," *Minnesota Law Review* 62 (1978):265–266.

50. Ibid., 266.

51. Kolko, *The Triumph of Conservatism.*

52. Alan Hunt, "Perspectives in the Sociology of Law," in *The Sociology of Law,* ed. P. Carlen (Staffordshire, England: University of Keele Press, 1976), 33–43.

53. Kolko, *The Triumph of Conservatism.*

54. Kitty Calavita, *"A Sociological Analysis of U.S. Immigration Law"* (Ph.D. dissertation, Department of Sociology, University of Delaware, 1980).

55. J. Anderson, Editorial, *Philadelphia Evening Bulletin* (Oct. 5, 1977), 72.

56. James M. Graham, "Amphetamine Politics on Capitol Hill," *Society* Vol. 9, No. 3, (Jan. 1974):14–23.

57. Kolko, *The Triumph of Conservatism.*

58. Lawrence Friedman, *Law and Society: An Introduction* (Englewood Cliffs, NJ: Prentice-Hall, 1977), 99. *See also* John Hagan and Jeffrey Leon, "Rediscovering Delinquency: Social History, Political Ideology and the Sociology of Law," *American Sociological Review* 42 (1977):587–598.

59. Thorsten Sellin, *Culture, Conflict and Crime* (New York: Social Science Research Council, 1938), 7.

60. Hubert M. Blalock, *Toward a Theory of Minority Group Relations* (New York: McGraw-Hill, 1970).

61. William J. Chambliss, "On Lawmaking," *British Journal of Law and Society* (1977):149–171. *See also* William J. Chambliss and Robert B. Seidman, *Law, Order, and Power* rev. ed. (Reading, MA: Addison-Wesley, 1982).

62. Chambliss and Seidman, *Law, Order, and Power,* Chap. 4.

63. Calavita, "A Sociological Analysis," 131.

64. Geoffrey Pearson, "Goths and Vandals: Crime in History," *Contemporary Crises* 2 (1978):119–139.

65. Karl Klare, "Judicial Deradicalization."

66. Boyer and Morais, "Early Factory Legislation."

67. Eugene D. Genovese, *Roll Jordan Roll: The World the Slave Made* (New York: Pantheon, 1974).

68. A. M. Garfinkle, C. Lefcourt, and D. B. Schulder, "Women's Servitude Under Law," in *Law Against the People,* ed. R. Lefcourt (New York: Random House, 1971), 105–123.

69. Ibid.

70. Albie Sachs and Joan Hoff Wilson, *Sexism and Law* (London: Martin Roberson, 1978).

71. Susan Griffin, "Rape. The All American Crime," in *Criminal Law in Action,* ed. William J. Chambliss (New York: Macmillan, 1975), 187.

72. Robert Lefcourt, *Law Against the People* (New York: Random House, 1971), 105–123.

73. A. David Freeman, "Legitimizing Racial Discrimination through Anti-Discrimination Law: A Critical Review of Supreme Court Doctrine," *Minnesota Law Review* 62 (1978):1049–1119.

74. *Roe vs. Wade,* 410 U.S.:113 (1973).

75. Susan Carangella-Macdonald, "Marxian Theory and Legal Change in Rape: Michigan's Model Rape Reform Legislation" (Paper presented at the meeting of the American Society of Criminology, Cincinnati, OH, November 1984).

Chapter 5

1. Norwood Russell Hanson, *Patterns of Discovery* (London: Cambridge University Press, 1968).

Imre Lakatos and Alan Musgrove, *Criticism and the Growth of Knowledge* (London: Cambridge University Press, 1970).

Karl Popper, *The Logic of Scientific Discovery* (New York: Basic Books, 1959).

2. Karl Popper, *Conjectures and Refutations: The Growth of Scientific Knowledge* (New York: Basic Books, 1963).

3. Michael Scriven, "Explanation and Prediction in Evolutionary Theory," *Science* 130 (1959):477–482.

4. L. Poincare, *The Foundations of Science: Science and Hypothesis, The Value of Science* (Lancaster, PA: The Science Press, 1946).

5. Thomas S. Kuhn, "Logic of Discovery or Psychology of Research?" in Lakatos and Musgrove, *Criticism and the Growth of Knowledge* (London: Cambridge University Press, 1970) 1–2.

6. Susan Langer, *Philosophy in a New Key: A Study in the Symbolism of Reason, Life, and Art* (Cambridge, MA: Harvard University Press, 1951).

7. Pierre van den Berghe, "Dialectic and Functionalism: Toward a Theoretical Synthesis," *American Sociological Review* (1963):695–705.

8. This comment was made in personal correspondence from Marjorie Zatz in commenting on this manuscript.

9. Popper, *Conjectures and Refutations,* 6.

10. Canon Graham, *The Evolution of Living Things* (Manchester, England: Manchester University Press, 1958).

11. Hanson, *Patterns of Discovery.*

12. Ibid.

13. Albert K. Cohen, "Multiple Factor Approaches," in Marvin Wolfgang, Leonard Savitz, and Harry Johnson, *The Sociology of Crime and Delinquency* (New York: John Wiley and Sons, 1970), 123–127.

14. Hanson, *Patterns of Discovery,* 64.

Chapter 6

1. Karl Popper, *The Logic of Scientific Discovery* (New York: Basic Books, 1939), 59.

2. Thomas S. Kuhn, *The Structure of Scientific Revolution* (Chicago: University of Chicago Press, 1962).

3. Sawyer F. Sylvester, "The History of Criminological Theory and Its Prospects for the 1990's" (paper delivered at the annual meetings of the American Association for the Advancement of Science, San Francisco, February 1974).

4. This observation was made in personal correspondence to an earlier version of this chapter, which Professor Roland Chilton reviewed.

5. Phillip Jenkins, "Varieties of Enlightenment Criminology," *British Journal of Criminology* 24 (1984):112–130.

6. Sylvester, "Criminological Theory."

7. William Godwin, *Enquiry Concerning Political Justice,* ed. Issac Krantnica (London: Pelican Books, 1976).

8. Jenkins, "Enlightenment Criminology," 16.

9. Ibid., 17.

10. Ibid., 18–19.

11. Emile Durkheim, *Suicide* (Glencoe, IL: The Free Press, 1951).

12. Ibid.

13. William J. Chambliss, "Functional and Conflict Theories," *Whose Law, What Order?* (New York: John Wiley and Sons, 1976).

14. William J. Chambliss, *Crime and the Legal Process* (New York: McGraw-Hill, 1969).
    Tony Platt, *The Triumph of Benevolence* (Chicago: University of Chicago Press, 1975).
    Richard Quinney, *The Social Reality of Crime* (Boston: Little, Brown, 1970).
    Ian Taylor, Paul Walton, and Jock Young, *The New Criminology* (London: Routledge and Kegan Paul, 1973).
    Austin Turk, *Criminality and Legal Order* (Chicago: Rand McNally, 1969).

15. Frank Tannenbaum, *Crime and the Community* (Boston: Ginn and Co., 1938), 25.

16. E. R. Hawkins and W. W. Waller, "Critical Notes on the Cost of Crime," *Journal of Criminal Law, Criminology and Police Science* 26 (1936):136–149.

17. Sellin Thorsten, *Culture Conflict and Crime* (New York: Social Science Research Council, 1938).

18. Robert K. Merton, *Social Theory and Social Structure* (New York: The Free Press, 1968), 134.

19. Karl F. Schuessler, *Edwin Sutherland on Analyzing Crime* (Chicago: University of Chicago Press, 1973).
    Edwin H. Sutherland, *White-Collar Crime: The Uncut Version,* Introduction by Gilbert Geis and Colin Goff (New Haven: Yale University Press, 1983).

20. James F. Short, Jr., and F. Ivan Nye, "The Extent of Unrecorded Delinquency: Tentative Conclusions," *Journal of Criminal Law, Criminology and Police Science* 49 (1958):296–302.

21. Eldridge Cleaver, *Soul on Ice* (New York: McGraw-Hill, 1968).

22. Harry King and William J. Chambliss, *Harry King: A Professional Thief's Journey* (New York: Macmillan, 1982).

23. William J. Chambliss, "On Lawmaking," *British Journal of Law and Society* 6 (1979):149–171.

24. Karl Marx, *Capital* vol. 1, (New York: International Publishers, 1967), 282–326.

25. Alfred R. Lindesmith, *Opiate Addiction* (Bloomington, IN: Principia Press, 1947).

26. Alfred R. Lindesmith, *The Addict and the Law* (Bloomington, IN: Indiana University Press, 1967).

27. William J. Chambliss, "Markets, Profits, Labor and Smack," *Contemporary Crises* 1 (1977):53–76.
28. Lindesmith, *The Addict and the Law.*
29. Kai T. Erikson, *Wayward Puritans: A Study in the Sociology of Deviance* (New York: John Wiley and Sons, 1966).
30. William J. Chambliss, "Functional and Conflict Theories," 12.

Chapter 7

1. Leonard Savitz, Stanley Turner, and Toby Dickman, "The Origin of Scientific Criminology: Franz Joseph Gall as the First Criminologist," in *Theory in Criminology: Contemporary Views,* ed. Robert Meier (Beverly Hills, CA: Sage Publications, 1977).
2. Cesare Lombroso, *L'Umo Delinquente* (Torino, Italy: Bocca, 1896–1897).
3. Charles Goring, *The English Convict: A Statistical Study* (Montclair, NJ: Patterson Smith, 1913; reprinted 1972).
4. Raffaele Garofalo, *Criminology* (Boston: Little, Brown and Co., 1914).
5. Stephen Jay Gould, *The Mismeasure of Man* (New York: W. W. Norton and Co., 1981).
6. William Sheldon, *Varieties of Delinquent Youth* (New York: Harper and Bros., 1949).
7. Sheldon Glueck and Eleanor Glueck, *Unraveling Juvenile Delinquency* (New York: Commonwealth Fund, 1950).
———, *Physique and Delinquency* (New York: Harper and Row, 1956).
8. Juan B. Cortes and Florence M. Gatti, *Delinquency and Crime: A Bio-Psycho-Sound Approach* (New York: Seminar Press, 1972).
9. Thomas J. Meyer, "Date Rape: A Serious Problem That Few Talk About," *Chronicle of Higher Education* (Dec. 1984):5.
10. Sheldon, *Varieties of Delinquent Youth.*
11. Leon J. Kamin, "Is Crime in the Genes? The Answer May Depend on Who Chooses What Evidence," *Scientific American* (Feb. 1986):22–27.
12. Janet Katz and Charles Abel, "The Medicalization of Repression," *Contemporary Crises* 8 (1984):227–241.
13. Richard Dugdale, *The Jukes* (New York: Putnam, 1877; reprinted: Arno Press, 1970).
14. Henry H. Goddard, *The Kallikak Family* (New York: Macmillan, 1923).
15. Gould, *The Mismeasure of Man.*
16. Mark Haller, *Eugenics* (New Brunswick, NJ: Rutgers University Press, 1963).
17. *Relf vs. Weinberger* 1974 U.S. District Court:1199.
18. Rosalind Petchecky, "Reproduction, Ethics and Public Policy," *Hastings Center Report* 9 (Oct. 1979):29–41.
19. For a review of the genetic research, *see* Lee Ellis, "Genetics and Criminal Behavior," *Criminology* 20/1 (May 1982):43–66.
20. Johannes Lange, *Crime as Destiny* (New York: Charles Boni, 1930).

21. Karl Christiansen, "A Preliminary Study of Criminality Among Twins," *Biosocial Bases of Criminal Behavior,* ed. Sarnoff Mednick and Karl O. Christiansen (New York: Gardner Press, 1977).

22. Barry Hutchings and Sarnoff A. Mednick, "Criminality in Adoptees and Their Adoptive and Biological Parents: A Pilot Study," *Biosocial Bases of Criminal Behavior,* ed. Sarnoff Mednick and Karl O. Christiansen (New York: Gardner Press, 1977).

23. Sarnoff A. Mednick, "Bioscial Factors and Primary Prevention of Antisocial Behavior," *New Paths in Criminology,* ed. Sarnoff Mednick and S. Gloria Shaham (Lexington, MA: D. C. Heath, 1979).

24. Hans Eysenck, *Crime and Personality* (Boston: Houghton Mifflin, 1964).

25. George Vold, *Theoretical Criminology,* 2d. ed. (New York: Oxford University Press, 1979), 119–122.

26. Ian Taylor, Paul Walton, and Jock Young, *The New Criminology* (New York: Harper and Row, 1973), 57–66.

27. Patricia Jacobs et al., "Aggressive Behavior, Mental Subnormality and the XYY Male," *Nature* 208 (1965):1351–1352.

28. H. A. Witkin et al., "XYY and XXY Men: Criminality and Aggression," *Science* 193 (1976):547–555.

29. Richard Fox, "The XYY Offender: A Modern Myth," *Journal of Criminal Law, Criminology and Policy Science* 62 (1971):59–73.
Reed Pyeritz et al., "The XYY Male: The Making of a Myth," *Biology as a Social Weapon* (Minneapolis, MN: Burgess Publishing Co., 1977).
T. R. Sarbin and J. E. Miller, "Demonism Revisited: The XYY Chromosomal Abnormality," *Issues in Criminology* 5/2 (1971).

30. Katherina Dalton, "Menstruation and Crime," *British Medical Journal* 2 (1961):1752–1753.

31. Julie Horney, "Menstrual Cycles and Criminal Responsibility," *Law and Human Behavior* 2/1 (1978):25–36.

32. Lee Bowker, "Menstruation and Female Criminality; a New Look at the Data" (paper presented at the meeting of the American Society of Criminology, Dallas, November 1978).

33. Sarnoff Mednick and Jan Volavka, "Biology and Crime," *Crime and Justice,* ed. Norval Morris and Michael Tonry (Chicago: University of Chicago Press, 1980).
Saleem Shah and Loren Roth, 'Biological and Psychophysiological Factors in Criminality," *Handbook of Criminology,* ed. Daniel Glaser (Chicago: Rand McNally, 1974), 101–174.

34. Dianne Hales and Robert E. Hales, "The Bonding Hormone," *American Health Magazine* (Nov.–Dec. 1982):1–14.

35. Katherine Blick Hoyenga and Kermit T. Hoyenga, *The Question of Sex Differences* (Boston: Little, Brown and Co., 1979), 129–140.

36. Leonard Hippchen (ed.), *Ecologic-Biochemical Approaches to Treatment of Delinquents and Criminals* (New York: Von Nostrand Reinhold, 1978).

37. Alexander Schauss and C. Simonson, "A Critical Analysis of the Diets

of Chronic Juvenile Offenders," Part I, *Journal of Orthomolecular Psychiatry* 8 (1979):1949–1957; Part II, *Journal of Orthomolecular Psychiatry* 8 (1979):222–226.

38. Shah and Roth, "Factors in Criminology."
J. A. Yaryura-Tobias and F. Neziroglu, "Violent Behavior Brain Dysrhythmia and Glucose Dysfunction and New Syndrome," *Journal of Orthopsychiatry* 4 (1975):182–188.

39. Graeme Neuman, *Understanding Violence* (New York: J. B. Lippincott, 1979).
Ray Wunderlick, "Neuroallergy as a Contributing Factor to Social Misfits: Diagnosis and Treatment," *Ecologi-Biochemical Approaches to Treatment of Delinquents and Criminals,* ed. Leonard Hippchen (New York: Von Nostrand Reinhold, 1978), 229–253.

40. Gould, *The Mismeasure of Man.*

41. Ibid., 150.

42. Ibid., 156.

43. Michael J. Hindelang and Travis Hirschi, "Intelligence and Delinquency," *American Sociological Review* (August, 1977):571–587.

44. Edward O. Wilson, "What Is Sociobiology?" *Sociobiology and Human Nature,* ed. Michael Gregory, Anita Silvers, and Diane Sutch (San Francisco: Jossey Bass, 1978), 1–12.

45. C. R. Jeffery, "Criminology as an Interdisciplinary Behavioral Science," *Criminology* 16 (1978):157.

46. Ibid., 162.

47. Ibid., 164.

48. James Q. Wilson and Richard J. Herrnstein, *Crime and Human Nature* (New York: Simon and Schuster, 1985).

49. Kamin, "Is Crime in the Genes?"

50. Kamin, "Is Crime in the Genes?" 27.

51. Wilson and Herrnstein, *Crime and Human Nature,* 70.

52. The concept of deferred gratification, as applied to crime, was first suggested by Albert K. Cohen. Cohen's use of this concept was, however, very different from the way Wilson and Herrnstein chose to use it. *See* Albert K. Cohen, *Delinquent Boys* (Glencoe, IL: The Free Press, 1958).

53. Kamin, "Is Crime in the Genes?" 22.

54. Ibid., 22.

55. David Gordon, "Class and the Economics of Crime," *The Review of Radical Political Economics* 3 (1971):51–72.

56. Jeffery, "Criminology," 166.

57. C. Ray Jeffery, *Crime Prevention Through Environmental Design* (Beverly Hills, CA: 1971) 231. As cited in Tony Platt and Paul Takagi, "Biosocial Criminology: A Critique," *Crime and Social Justice* 11 (1979):5–13.

58. Geoffrey Pearson, "Goths and Vandals—Crime in History," *Contemporary Crises* 2 (1978):119–139.

59. Mark Vernon, W. Sweet, and Frank Ervin, "Role of Brain Disease in Riots and Urban Violence," *Journal of the American Medical Association* 201 (1967):895.
60. Gould, *The Mismeasure of Man,* 115.
61. Kamin, "Is Crime in the Genes?" 24.
62. Ibid., 26.
63. Newman, *Understanding Violence.*
64. Ashley Montague, *Sociobiology Examined* (London: Oxford University Press, 1980).
65. Stephen Jay Gould, "Biological Potential vs. Biological Determinism," *Natural History Magazine* (May 1976).
66. For a discussion of reductionism and sociobiology, see R. C. Lewontin, Steven Rose, and Leon J. Kamin, *Not in Our Genes* (New York: Pantheon Books, 1984).

Chapter 8

1. Sigmund Freud, "Some Charactertypes Met Within Psychoanalytic Work," *Collected Papers* Vol. IV (London: Hogarth Press, 1925).
2. K. R. Eissler, "Some Problems of Delinquency," in *Searchlights on Delinquency,* ed. K. R. Eissler (New York: International Universities Press, 1949), 3–25.

   Kate Friedlander, "Latent Delinquency and Ego Development," in *Searchlights on Delinquency,* 205–215.

   Jeanne Lampl-De Groot, "Neurotics, Delinquents and Ideal-Formation," in *Searchlights on Delinquency,* 246–255.
3. Eissler, "Problems of Delinquency," 9.
4. Ibid., 10.
5. Ibid., 24.
6. Friedlander, "Latent Delinquency," 208.
7. See Eissler, "Problems of Delinquency," 17*ff;* Aichhorn's position is clearly indicated in the statement dictated to Margaret Fries, as follows:

> The treatment of neurotics we have learned from Freud. However, there appear in growing children attempts to solve situations arising from inner conflicts which do not express themselves in the form of neuroses but which appear as *Schwer Erziehbarkeit* [behavior problems] and *Verwahrlosung* [waywardness]. There is no method of direct treatment for this type of disorder. If a treatment is successful in making it impossible for the child to express his inner conflict in this form, he will then have to resort to expressing it in a neurosis. The resulting

> neurosis can then be treated by psychoanalysis and in this way the problem of treating upward children is solved.

Quoted in Margaret Fries, "Some Points in the Transformation of a Neurotic Child," *Searchlights on Delinquency,* 216.

8. Kate Friedlander, *The Psychoanalytical Approach to Juvenile Delinquency* (New York: International Universities Press, 1947).
9. Anna Freud, "Certain Types and Stages of Social Maladjustment," in *Searchlights on Delinquency,* 193.
10. August Aichborn, *Wayward Youth* (New York: The Viking Press, 1935), 189.
11. Aichborn, *Wayward Youth,* 162.
12. Ibid., 173.
13. Ibid., 193.
14. Ibid., 195.
15. Ibid., 196.
16. Ibid., 164.
17. Ibid., 164.
18. Ibid., 197.
19. Ibid., 164.
20. Ibid., 148.
21. Ibid., 200.
22. Friedlander, "Latent Delinquency," 206.
23. *See* Aichhorn, *Wayward Youth,* 122, 235.
24. Ibid., 235.
25. Ibid., 235.
26. Ibid., 39–41.
27. Ibid., 40.
28. Ibid., 167.
29. Ibid., 40.
30. Ibid., 9.
31. Ibid., 938.
32. Ibid., 361.
33. Ibid., 89.
34. Robert G. Andry, *Delinquency and Parental Pathology* (London: Methune and Co. Ltd., 1960).
35. Adelaide M. Johnson, "Sanction for Superego Lacunae of Adolescents," in *Searchlights on Delinquency,* 225–245.
36. Fritz Redl and David Wineman, *The Aggressive Child* (Glencoe, IL: The Free Press, 1957), 76–140.
37. Ibid., 123.
38. *See* the following:
Leonard Berkowitz, *Aggression: A Social Psychological Analysis* (New York: McGraw-Hill, 1962).
J. Dollard, L. Doob, N. Miller, O. Mowrer, and R. Sears, *Frustration*

and Aggression (New Haven, CT: Yale University Press, 1939). Although it is guided by Freudian conceptions, this volume also has a distinctly behavioristic emphasis.

Norman R. F. Maier, *Frustration: The Study of Behavior Without a Goal* (Ann Arbor: University of Michigan Press, 1961; original copyright, 1949).

39. Maier, *Frustration,* 164.

40. W. Healy and Augusta F. Bronner, *New Light on Delinquency and Its Treatment* (New Haven, CT: Yale University Press, 1936).

41. Berkowitz, *Aggression,* 308.

42. Ibid., 313.

43. Ibid., 308.

44. Ibid., 311.

45. Ibid., 308.

46. Ibid., 312.

47. Ibid., 309–310.

48. *See* the subsequent sections of this chapter.

49. Berkowitz, *Aggression,* 176–178.

50. Ibid., 99.

51. Ibid., 189–192, *passim.*

52. Ibid., 191.

53. David Abrahamsen, *The Psychology of Crime* (New York: Holt, Rinehart & Winston, 1960).

———, *The Murdering Mind* (New York: Harper and Row, 1973).

———, *Who Are the Guilty: A Stury of Education and Crime* (New York: Holt, Rinehart & Winston, 1952).

54. S. Yochelson and S. E. Samenow, *The Criminal Personality,* Vols. 1–2 (New York: Jason Avonson, 1976).

55. Ibid., 35.

56. Ibid., 30, Chaps. 4–6.

57. Donald R. Cressey, *Studies in Institutional Organization and Change* (New York: Holt, Rinehart & Winston, 1959).

Irving Goffman, *Asylums* (Chicago: Aldone-Atherton, 1961).

Gresham M. Sykes, *The Society of Captives: A Study of a Maximum Security Prison* (Princeton, NJ: Princeton University Press, 1958).

58. Karl F. Schuessler and Donald R. Cressey, "Personality Characteristics of Criminals," *American Journal of Sociobiology* 55 (1950):476–484.

59. Malin Akerttrom, *Crooks and Squares* (New Brunswick, NJ: Transaction Books, 1985).

60. Jerome Miller, "The Search for the Criminal Man: Part II," *Augustus* (Aug. 1985):16.

61. Michael Hakeem, "A Critique of the Psychiatric Approach to Crime and Correction," *Law and Contemporary Problems* 23 (1958):650–682.

F. Alexander and William Healy, *Roots of Crime: Psychoanalytic*

Studies (New York: Alfred A. Knopf, 1948). Cited in Robert W. White, *The Abnormal Personality* (New York: The Ronald Press, 1948), 396.

Chapter 9

1. Herman Schwendinger and Julia R. Siegel Schwendinger, *Adolescent Subculture and Delinquency* (New York: Praeger, 1985).
2. Ibid., xi.
3. Freda Adler, *Sisters in Crime* (New York: McGraw-Hill, 1975). Rita Simon, *Women and Crime* (Lexington, MA: Lexington Books, 1975).
4. Ann Campell, *The Girls in the Gang* (New Brunswick, NJ: Rutgers University Press, 1984).
5. Caryn B. Horowitz, "Factors Influencing Shoplifting Activity Among Adult Women" (Unpublished Ph.D. dissertation, University of Delaware, 1986).
6. William J. Chambliss, "State Organized Crime" (paper presented at the annual meetings of the American Society of Criminology, San-Diego, CA, November 1986).
7. Edwin H. Sutherland, *White-Collar Crime* (New York: Dryden, 1949).
8. Edwin H. Sutherland and Donald R. Cressey, *Principles of Criminology* (Philadelphia: J. B. Lippincott, 1974), 76.
9. James F. Short, Jr., "Differential Association and Delinquency," *Social Problems* 4 (1965):233–239.
10. Gary A. Jensen, "Parents, Peers and Delinquent Action: A Test of Differential Association Perspective," *American Journal of Sociology* 78 (1972):572–575.
11. Travis Hirschi, *Causes of Delinquency* (Berkeley: University of California Press, 1969).
12. Richard L. Matsueda, "Testing Control Theory and Differential Association: A Causal Modeling Approach," *American Sociological Review* 47 (1982):489–504.
13. Ibid., 504.
14. James S. Coleman, *The Methods of Sociology: Scope, Objectives, and Methods* (Philadelphia: American Academy of Political and Social Science, 1969), 109. *See also* Aaron Cicourel, *Method and Measurement in Sociology* (New York: The Free Press, 1964); D. L. Phillips and K. J. Clancy, "Some Effects of Social Desirability in Survey Studies," *American Journal of Sociology* 27 (1972):922–935.
15. David Greenberg, *Mathematical Criminology* (New Brunswick: Rutgers University Press, 1979), Chaps. 2–3.
16. William J. Chambliss, "The Roughnecks and the Saints," *Society* 11 (Nov.–Dec. 1973):24–31.
17. Schwendinger and Schwendinger, *Adolescent Subculture*.

18. Alfred R. Lindesmith, *Opiate Addiction* (Bloomington, IN: Principia Press, 1947). Recent research fails to confirm Lindesmith's theory that, once a person is "hooked" on opiates, he or she will never break the habit.

19. Lindesmith, *Opiate Addiction.*

20. Donald R. Cressey, *Other People's Money: A Study of the Social Psychology of Embezzlement* (Belmont, CA: Wadsworth, 1971). Recent studies suggest some serious limitations on Cressey's theory. *See* Gwynne Nettler, "Embezzlement Without Problems," *British Journal of Criminology* 14 (1974):70–77.

21. T. R. Young, *Criminological Theories as Science* (Collins, CO: The Red Feather Institute, 1982).

22. Mary Beth Cameron, *The Booster and the Snitch: Department Store Shoplifting* (Glencoe, IL: The Free Press, 1964).

23. Amatai Etzioni, *Capital Corruption: The Attack on American Democracy* (New York: Harcourt, Brace and Jovanovich, 1984).

24. William J. Chambliss, *On the Take* (Bloomington: Indiana University Press, 1978).

25. Edward Greer, *Big Steel: Black Politics and Corporate Power in Gary, Indiana* (New York: Monthly Review Press, 1979).
    Alan A. Block and Frank R. Scarpitti, *Poisoning for Profit: The Mafia and Toxic Waste in America* (New York: William Morrow and Co., 1985).
    George Crile, "Tax Assessor Has Many Friends," *Harpers Magazine* 245 #1470 (1972):103.

26. Truman Capote, *In Cold Blood* (New York: Random House, 1965).

27. *New York Times* (November 6, 1973).

28. Stuart Palmer, *A Study of Murder* (New York: Cromwell, 1960).

29. Judith Cummings, "The F.B.I.'s Most Unwanted Spy Case," *Time* (Feb. 10, 1985):37.

30. Harry King and William J. Chambliss, *Harry King: A Professional Thief's Journey* (New York: John Wiley and Sons, 1982).

31. Daniel Glaser, "Criminal Theories and Behavior Images," *American Journal of Sociology* 61 (1956):433–444.

32. C. Ray Jeffrey, "An Integrated Theory of Criminal Behavior," *Journal of Criminal Law, Criminology and Police Science* 49 (1959):533–552.

33. Ronald Akers, *Deviant Behavior: A Social Learning Approach* (Belmont, CA: Wadsworth, 1977). *See also* Robert L. Burgess and Ronald Akers, "A Differential Association-Reinforcement Theory of Criminal Behavior," *Social Problems* 14 (1966):128–147.

34. Hirschi, *Causes of Delinquency.*

35. Michael Wiatrowski, Stephen Hansell, Charles Massey, and David Wilson, "Curriculum Tracking and Delinquency," *American Sociological Review* 46 (1982):151–160.

36. Ross Matsueda, "Testing Control and Differential Association The-

ory: A Causal Modeling Approach," *American Sociological Review* (August 1982):489–504.

37. Sheldon Glueck and Eleanor Glueck, *500 Criminal Careers* (New York: Alfred A. Knopf, 1982).
——————, *Unraveling Juvenile Delinquency* (Cambridge, MA: Howard, 1950).
38. Hanan Selvin and Travis Hirschi, *Principals of Survey Analysis* (New York: Free Press, 1973).
39. Ivan F. Nye, *Family Relationships and Delinquent Behavior* (New York: John Wiley and Sons, 1958).
40. Chambliss, "The Roughnecks and the Saints."
41. James F. Short, Jr., and Fred Strotdbeck, *Group Process and Gang Delinquency* (Chicago: University of Chicago Press, 1965).
42. David Matza, *Delinquency and Drift* (New York: John Wiley and Sons, 1964).
43. Gresham Sykes and David Matza, "Techniques of Neutralization: A Theory of Delinquency," *American Sociological Review* 2 (1957):664–670.
44. Albert K. Cohen, *Delinquent Boys: The Culture of the Gang* (New York: Free Press, 1955).

Chapter 10

1. James Q. Wilson and Richard J. Herrnstein, *Crime and Human Nature* (New York: Simon and Schuster, 1978).
2. Edward Sbarbaro and William J. Chambliss, "Crime, Public Opinion, and Criminal Law" (Washington, D.C.: Department of Sociology, The George Washington University), 1987.
3. Ibid.
4. Ibid.
5. Marvin Wolfgang, Robert Figlio, Simon Singer, and Paul Tracy. *National Survey of Crime Severity* (Washington, D.C.: Bureau of Justice Statistics, 1985).
6. Kitty Calavita, "The Demise of the Occupational Safety and Health Administration: A Case Study in Symbolic Action," *Social Problems* 30 (1983):437–448.
7. John Gallaher and John Cross, *Morals Legislation Without Morality* (New Brunswick, NJ: Rutgers University Press, 1983).
8. Albert K. Cohen, "The Study of Social Disorganization and Deviant Behavior," in *Sociology Today,* ed. Robert K. Merton, Leonard Broom, and Leonard Cottrell (New York: Basic Books, 1959), 452.
9. Robert K. Merton, "Social Structure and Anomie," *American Sociological Review* 3 (1938):672–682.
10. Albert K. Cohen, *Delinquent Boys: The Culture of the Gang* (Glencoe, IL: Free Press, 1958).

11. William Graham Sumner, *Folkways* (New York: Mentor, 1960).
12. Emile Durkheim, *Suicide,* trans. John A. Spaulding and George Simpson (Glencoe, IL: The Free Press, 1897).
13. Jack Douglas, *The Social Meanings of Suicide* (Princeton, NJ: Princeton University Press, 1967).
14. Merton, "Social Structure and Anomie," 672.
15. John Braithwaite, "Merton's Theory of Crime and Differential Class Symbols of Success," *Crime and Social Justice* 7/8 (1979–1980):90–94.

    Ian Taylor, Paul Walton, and Jock Young, *The New Criminology* (London: Routledge and Kegan Paul, 1973).
16. Richard A. Cloward and Lloyd Ohlin, *Delinquency and Opportunity: A Theory of Delinquent Gangs* (New York: Free Press, 1960).
17. William J. Chambliss, "The Roughnecks and the Saints," *Society* 11 (Nov.–Dec. 1973):24–31.
18. Clifford R. Shaw and H. McKay, *Social Factors in Juvenile Delinquency* (Washington, D.C.: National Commission of Law Observance and Enforcement, 1931).

    Florian Znaniencki, *The Polish Peasant in America* (Urbana: University of Illinois Press, 1984).
19. Thorsten Selling, *Culture Conflict and Crime* (New York: Social Science Research Council, 1938).
20. Elise Boulding, "Women and Social Violence," *International Social Science Journal* 30 (1978):801–815.

    Susan Brownmiller, *Against Our Will* (New York: Simon and Schuster, 1975).

    Lorenne Clark and Debra Lewis, *Rape: The Price of Coercive Sexuality* (Toronto, Canada: The Women's Press, 1977).

    Angela Davis, "Racism and the Contemporary Literature on Rape," *Freedomways* 16 (1976):25–33.

    Susan Griffin, "Rape: The All American Crime," *Ramparts* 10 (1971):26–35.

    Renee Kassinsky, "Rape: A Normal Act?" *Canadian Forum* (Sept. 1975):18–22.

    Julia Schwendinger and Herman Schwendinger, "Rape Myths; The Legal, Theoretical and Everyday Practice," *Crime and Social Justice* 1 (1972):18–27.
21. Diana Scully and Joseph Marollo, "Riding the Bull at Gilleys': Convicted Rapists Describe the Rewards of Rape," *Social Problems* 32 (1985):246–251.
22. Ibid., 248.
23. Margaret Andersen, *Thinking About Women* (New York: Macmillan, 1985).
24. Allan Griswold Johnson, "On the Prevalence of Rape in the United States," *Signs* 6 (1980):136–146.

25. Thomas J. Meyer, "Date Rape: A Serious Problem That Few Talk About," *Chronicle of Higher Education* (Dec. 5, 1984).

26. Neil Malamuth, Maggie Heim, and Seymour Feshback, "Sexual Responsiveness of College Students to Rape Depictions," *Social Psychology* 38 (1980):399–408.

27. Gwen Broude and Sarah Greene, "Cross-Cultural Codes on Twenty Sexual Attitudes and Practices," *Ethnology* 15 (1976):409–428.
    Peggy Reeves Sanaday, *The Socio-Cultural Context of Rape* (Washington, D.C.: U.S. Department of Commerce, National Technical Information Service, 1979).

28. Marvin Wolfgang, *Patterns in Criminal Homicide* (Philadelphia: University of Pennsylvania Press, 1958).
    ———— and Franco Ferracuti, *The Subculture of Violence* (London: Tavistock, 1967).

29. Roland Chilton, "Continuity in Delinquency Area Research: A Comparison of Studies for Baltimore, Detroit and Indianapolis," *American Sociological Review* 5 (1964):205–224.
    Marc Reidel and Marjorie Zahn, *The Nature and Pattern of American Homicide* (Washington, D.C.: National Institute of Justice, 1985).

30. John Hagan, *Modern Criminology* (New York: McGraw-Hill, 1985).

31. Michael Hindelang, "Race and Involvement in Crime," *American Sociological Review* 43 (1978):93–109.

32. Hindelang, "Race and Involvement in Crime," 107.

33. Margaret Anderson, "Review Essay: Rape Theories, Myths, and Social Change," *Contemporary Crises* 5 (1983):237.

34. Peter Rossi, Emily Waite, Christine Bose, and Richard Berk, "The Seriousness of Crimes: Normative Structure and Individual Differences," *American Sociological Review* 39(1974):224–237.

35. Howard Erlanger, "The Empirical Status of the Subculture of Violence Thesis," *Social Problems* 22 (1974):280–292.

36. Sandra J. Ball and Michael Rokeach, "Values and Violence: A Test of the Subculture of Violence Thesis," *American Sociological Review* 38 (1973):736–749.

37. Charles F. Cannell and Floyd J. Fowler, "Comparison of a Self-Enumerative Procedure and Personal Interview: A Validity Study," *Public Opinion Quarterly* 27 (1963):250–264.
    Derek L. Phillips and Kevin L. Clancy, "Social Desirability in Survey Studies," *American Journal of Sociology* 77 (1972):922.

38. William J. Chambliss, "State-Organized Crime" (Paper presented at the annual meetings of the American Society of Criminology, San Diego, CA, November 1986).

39. Tom Hadden, *Political Crimes in South Africa* (New York: Amnesty International, 1986).

40. Herbert L. Gans, *The Urban Villagers* (New York: Free Press, 1962).

41. Ann Campbell, *The Girls in the Gang* (New Brunswick, NJ: Rutgers University Press, 1984).
    Chambliss, "The Roughnecks and the Saints."
    Ruth Horowitz, *Honor and the American Dream: Culture and Identity in a Chicago Community* (New Brunswick, NJ: Rutgers University Press, 1983).
    Eleanor Miller, *Street Woman* (Philadelphia: Temple University Press, 1986).

42. Eileen Leonard, *Women, Crime and Society: A Critique of Criminology Theory* (New York: Columbia University Press, 1982).

43. Leonard, *Women, Crime and Society,* 182. *See also* Jim Messerschmidt, *Capitalism, Patriarchy, and Crime: Toward a Socialist Feminist Criminology* (New York: Rowman and Littlefield, 1986).
    44. a Adler, *Sisters in Crime: The Rise of the New Female Criminal* (New York: McGraw-Hill, 1975).
    Rita James Simon, *Women and Crime* (Lexington, MA: Lexington Books, 1975).

45. Brownmiller, *Against Our Will.*

46. Kai Erikson's study of the Puritan community in New England applies the logic of functionalism to explain three different "crime waves." This theory was discussed in detail in Chapter 4.

47. Kingsley Davis, "Prostitution," in *Contemporary Social Problems,* ed. Robert K. Merton and Robert Nisbet (New York: Houghton Mifflin, 1971).

48. Richard L. Rubenstein, *The Cunning of History* (New York: Harper and Row, 1975), 10.

49. Immanuel Wallerstein, *The Modern World System* (New York: Academic Press, 1974).

Chapter 11

1. Edwin Lemert, *Social Pathology* (New York: McGraw-Hill, 1951).
   Alfred R. Lindesmith, *Opiate Addiction* (Bloomington, IN: Principia Press, 1947).
   Frank Tannenbaum, *Crime and the Community* (New York: Columbia University Press, 1938).

2. Howard Becker, *The Outsiders* (Glencoe, IL: The Free Press, 1963).

3. Clarence Schrag, *Crime and Justice: American Style* (Rockville, MD: National Institutes of Mental Health, 1971), 90–92.

4. William J. Chambliss, *Crime and the Legal Process* (New York: McGraw-Hill, 1969).
   Austin Turk, *Criminality and the Legal Order* (New York: Rand-McNally, 1968).

Richard Quinney, *Crime and Justice in America* (New York: Little, Brown and Co., 1970).

5. Ralf Dahrendorf, "Out of Utopia: Toward a Re-Orientation of Sociological Theory," *American Journal of Sociology* (1958).

6. C. Wright Mills, *The Power Elite* (New York: Oxford University Press, 1956).

———, *The Sociological Imagination* (New York: Oxford University Press, 1959).

7. Raymond J. Michalowski, "Radical Criminology in the United States: The Evolution of Marxist Perspectives on Law, Crime and the State" (Paper presented at the University of North Carolina, 1986). The discussion of conflict paradigms in this text is a restatement of the insightful analysis presented by Michalowski in his paper.

8. Michalowski, "Radical Criminology," 10.

9. George Vold, *Theoretical Criminology* (New York: Oxford University Press, 1958), 204.

10. Turk, *Criminality and the Legal Order,* xii.

11. Ibid., 31–32.

12. Ibid., 9–10.

13. Thorsten Sellin, *Culture, Conflict and Crime* (New York: Social Science Research Council, 1938).

14. William J. Chambliss, "A Sociological Analysis of the Law of Vagrancy," *Social Problems* 12 (1964):45–69.
Jerome Hall, *Theft, Law and Society* (Indianapolis, IN: Bobbs-Merrill, 1952).

15. Ian Taylor, Raul Walton, and Jock Young, *The New Criminology* (London: Routledge and Kegan Paul, 1973).

16. Malin Akerstrom, *Crooks and Squares* (New Brunswick, NJ: Transaction Books, 1986).

17. Harry King and William J. Chambliss, *Harry King: A Professional Thief's Journey* (New York: John Wiley and Sons, 1982).

18. Edwin H. Sutherland, *The Professional Thief* (Chicago: University of Chicago Press, 1937).

19. Fred Block, "Beyond Corporate Liberalism," *Social Problems* 24 (1977):360.

20. Karl Marx, "The So-Called Primitive Accumulation," *Capital* vol. 1 part III: 713–744. *See also* Raymond J. Michalowski, *Order, Law and Crime* (New York: Random House, 1985), 26.

21. G. Esping-Anderson, Richard Friedland, and Eric Ohlin Wright, "Modes of Class Struggle and the Capitalist State," *Kapitalistate* 4 (1976):89

22. Ibid., 89.

23. John Dugard, *Human Rights and the South African Legal Order* (Princeton, NJ: Princeton University Press, 1978).

24. Piers Beirne and Richard Quinney, *Marxism and Law* (New York:

John Wiley and Sons, 1982), 16. *See also* Michalowski, *Order, Law and Crime.*

25. William Bonger, *Criminality and Economic Conditions,* trans. Henry P. Horton (Boston: Little, Brown and Co., 1916).

26. Ibid., 268.

27. Ibid., 278.

28. Ibid., 383–384.

29. Ibid., 386–387.

30. Ibid., 263.

31. Ibid., 266.

32. Michalowski, "Radical Criminology."

33. Leon J. Kamin, "Is Crime in the Genes? The Answer May Depend on Who Chooses What Evidence," *Scientific American* (Feb. 1986):22–27.

34. Judith Blau and Peter Blau, *Inequality and Heterogeneity: A Primitive Theory of Social Structure* (New York: The Free Press, 1977).

35. D. Wallace and Drew Humphries, "Urban Crime and Capital Accumulation: 1950–1971," in *Crime and Capitalism,* ed. David Greenberg (Palo Alto, CA: Mayfield, 1981), 140–156.

36. John Braithwaite, *Corporate Crime in the Pharmaceutical Industry* (London: Routledge and Kegan Paul, 1984).

37. Julia Schwendinger and Herman Schwendinger, *Rape and Inequality* (New York: Praeger, 1983).

38. Ibid., 179.

39. James Messerschmidt, *Capitalism, Patriarchy and Crime: Toward a Socialist Feminist Criminology* (New York: Rowman and Allenhend, 1986).

40. Freda Adler, *Sisters in Crime* (New York: McGraw-Hill, 1975). Rita James Simon, *Women and Crime* (Lexington, MA: Lexington Books, 1975).

41. Eleanor Miller, *Street Woman* (Philadelphia; Temple University Press, 1986), 172, 175.

42. Michalowski, *Order, Law and Crime,* 26.

43. Herman Schwendinger and Julia Seigel Schwendinger, *Adolescent Subcultures and Delinquency* (New York: Praeger, 1985), xii.

44. Ibid., 34–35.

45. David Greenberg, "Delinquency and the Age Structure of Society," *Contemporary Crises* 1 (1977):189–223.

46. Mark Colvin and John Pauly, "A Critique of Criminology: Toward an Integrated Structural-Marxist Theory of Delinquency Production," *American Journal of Sociobiology* 89 (1983):513–551.

47. Colvin and Pauly, "A Critique of Criminology," 514.

48. Melvin L. Kohn, "Social Class and Parental Values: Another Confirmation of the Relationship," *American Sociological Review* 41 (1976):538–545. *See also* Melvin L. Kohn and Carmi Shoder, "Occupational Experience and Psychological Functioning: An Assessment

of Reciprocal Effects," *American Sociological Review* 38 (1973):97–118; and Melvin L. Kohn, *Class and Conformity* (Chicago: University of Chicago Press, 1977).

49. Colvin and Pauly, "A Critique of Criminology," 514.
50. Ibid., 515.
51. Ibid., 536.

Chapter 12

1. Karl Marx, *The Grundrisse,* trans. David McLellan (New York: Harper and Row, 1971), 95.
2. George Homans, *Social Behavior: Its Elementary Forms,*Q rev. ed. (New York: Harcourt Brace Jovanovich, 1974).
3. Frederick Engels, *Selected Works of Marx and Engels* (Moscow: Progress Press, 1969), 620.
4. Rudolf Bahro, *The Alternative in Eastern Europe* (New York: Shocken Books, 1978).
5. James P. Brady, "The Transformation of Justice: China and Cuba," *The Insurgent Sociologist* X (1981):5–25.
   Maria Lós, "The Double Economic Structure of Communist Societies" (paper presented at the University of Ottowa, Department of Sociology, 1987).
   ———, "The Myth of Popular Justice Under Communism," *Justice Quarterly* 2 (1985):447–471.
   Luis P. Salas, "Juvenile Delinquency in Post-Revolutionary Cuba: Characteristics and Cuban Explanations," *Estudios Cubanos* 9 (1979):43–61.
6. Raymond J. Michalowski and Marjorie S. Zatz, "Black Dollars for Blue Jeans" (paper presented at the International Social Science Conference, Havana, Cuba, 1987).
   Janos Kenedi, *Do It Yourself: Hungary's Hidden Economy* (London: Pluto Press, 1982).
7. "Deviance Among Russian Immigrants" (paper submitted for anonymous review).
8. Bahro, *The Alternative in Eastern Europe.*
9. Maria Lós, "The Double Economic Structure of Communist Societies," *Contemporary Cruises* 11 (1987):25–58.
10. Eugene D. Genovese, *Roll Jordan Roll* (New York: Pantheon Books, 1974).
11. Ronald Kramer and Raymond J. Michalowski, "The Space Between Laws: The Problem of Corporate Crime in a Transnational Context" (unpublished manuscript, 1986).
12. Kitty Calavita, *U.S. Immigration Law and the Control of Labor, 1820–1924* (New York: Academic Press, 1984).

13. Geoffrey Pearson, "Goths and Vandals—Crime in History," *Contemporary Crises* 2 (1978):119–139.
14. Pearson, "Goths and Vandals," 121, 128, 129–130.
15. Michael Levi, *Phantom Capitalists: The Organization and Control of Long Firm Fraud* (London: Heinemann, 1981).
16. Andrew Hopkins, "Crime Without Punishment: The Appin Mine Disaster," *The Australian Quarterly Summer* (1981):455–465.
17. Scandals involving the major companies were reported in *The New York Times* from January 1986 through December 1987.
18. Linsey Gruson, "U.S. Accuses Shearson of Money Laundering," *New York Times* (June 27, 1986):1.18.
19. Alan A. BLock, *East Side, West Side* (Cardiff, Wales: University College Cardiff Press, 1979).
20. Chambliss, *On the Take* (Bloomington: Indiana University Press, 1978).
21. Ibid.
22. Phillip Jenkins and Gary Potter, "The Cabal Model in Europe" (Unpublished manuscript, Department of Criminal Justice, Pennsylvania State University, 1986).
23. Heinz Steinhart and William J. Chambliss, "Der Kommentar," *Kriminologisches* 5 (1983):81–88.
24. William J. Chambliss, *On the Take*, 90–91.
25. Alan A. Block and William J. Chambliss, *Organizing Crime* (New York: Elsevier, 1984).
Amitai Etzioni, *Capitol Corruption: The Attack on American Democracy* (New York: Harcourt Brace Jovanovich, 1984).
26. *See* the television movie "The Burning Bed"—a story about a woman who finally fought back against a brutal and dehumanizing husband and family by setting fire to the bed on which her husband slept, the same bed on which he had raped and beaten her on innumerable occasions.
27. Ann Campbell, *The Girls in the Gang* (New Brunswick, NJ: Rutgers University Press, 1984).
28. Louise Shelley, *Readings in Comparative Criminology* (Carbondale: Southern Illinois University Press, 1981).
29. James P. Brady, *Justice and Politics in People's China* (London: Academic Press, 1982).
30. Yuri Brokhin, *Hustling on Gorky Street* (New York: Random House, 1978).
31. Ibid., 47–50.
32. William J. Chambliss, "Crime in Capitalist and Socialist Societies," *Indian Journal of Criminology and Criminalistics* vol. 1 (1981):13–18.

Chapter 13

1. Antonio Gramsci, *Letters from Prison* (New York: Harper and Row, 1973).

2. It is worthy of note that who is defined as a "citizen" varies in different historical periods. Women in Western democracies were not considered citizens with a right to vote until the 20th century—for example, not until 1921 in the United States. In English Common Law, women were not allowed to run for public office or attend universities because they were not considered "persons." The legal system was, nonetheless, a source of legitimacy because through law the most powerful people in the society came to see gender discrimination as correct. *See* Chapter 4 for a discussion of how these laws changed.

3. Joel Best, "Licensed to Steal: A Sociology of English Piracy, 1550–1750" (Unpublished manuscript, 1981).

4. K. R. Andrews, *English Privateering Voyages to the West Indies, 1598–1695* (London: Hakluyt Society Series 11, CXI, 1959).
   British Museum, *Sir Francis Drake* (London: British Museum Publications Ltd., 1977).
   A. J. Collins, *Jewels and Plate of Queen Elizabeth I* (London: Harley MS 1650 and Stone MS 555, 1955).
   Robert De La Croix, *John Paul Jones* (London: Frederick Muller Ltd., 1962).
   A. O. Exquemling, *De Americanaenshe Zee-Rooves* (London: British Museum, 1670), 301.
   Robert Lane-Poole, *The Barbary Corsairs* (London: T. Fisher Unwin, 1890).
   Louis Le Golif, *The Manuscripts of Louis Le Golif alias Bonhnefesse* (London: British Museum, 1680).

5. William J. Chambliss, "State-Organized Crime" (paper presented at the American Society of Criminology, November 1986).

6. Le Golif, *The Manuscripts of Louis Le Golif.*

7. British Museum, *Sir Francis Drake.*

8. Jessie Peabody Frothingham, *Sea Fighters from Drake to Farragut* (Freeport, NY: Books for Libraries, Inc., 1902).

9. Frothingham, *Sea Fighters.*

10. De La Croix, *John Paul Jones.*

11. Frank Sherry, *Raiders and Rebels* (New York: Hearst Marine Books, 1986), 360–361.

12. William J. Chambliss, "Markets, Profits, Labor and Smack," *Contemporary Crises* 1 (1977):53–57.
    Alfred W. McCoy, *The Politics of Heroin in Southeasst Asia* (New York: Harper and Row, 1973).

13. Ibid., 57.

14. Ibid., 56.

15. The Government of the Commonwealth of Australia, *Royal Commission of Inquiry Into the Nugan Hand Group: Final Report* (Canberra: Australian Government Publishing Service, 1985).

16. *Royal Commission of Inquiry,* vol. 1.

17. *Royal Commission of Inquiry,* vol. 2.

18. NARMIC, *Military Exports to South Africa: A Research Report on the*

Arms Embargo (Philadelphia; American Friends Service Committee, 1984).

19. Jim Hougan, Secret Agenda (New York: Random House, 1984).

———, *Spooks: The Haunting of America—The Private Use of Secret Agents* (New York: William Morrow, 1978).

Henrik Kruger, *The Great Heroin Coup* (Boston: South End Press, 1980).

John Owen, *Sleight of Hand: The 25 Million Nugan Hand Bank Scandal* (Sydney, Australia: Calporteur Press, 1983).

20. The Pike Report, *CIA* (Nottingham, England: Spokesman Books, 1977).

21. Warren Hinckle and William Turner, *The Fish Is Red: The Story of the Secret War Against Castro* (New York: Harper and Row, 1981).

22. Hougan, *Spooks,* 123–138.

23. George Crile, *The Washington Post* (June 13, 1976).

24. Hougan, *Spooks,* 132.

25. John Dinges and Saul Landau, *Assassination on Embassy Row* (New York: McGraw-Hill, 1980), 23.

26. Transnational Institute, *T.N.I.,* (1981).

27. Dinges and Landau, *Assassination on Embassy Row,* 239.

28. John Dinges and Saul Landau, "The C.I.A.'s Link to Chile's Plot," *The Nation* (June 12, 1982):712–713.

29. Dinges and Landau, "The C.I.A.'s Link."

30. Penny Lernoux, "The Miami Connection," *The Nation* (Feb. 18, 1984):186–198.

31. Lernoux, "The Miami Connection," 188.

32. *The Guardian,* January 1985:6.

33. *The Guardian,* 10.

34. *American Criminal Law Review,* vol. 23 (Chicago: American Bar Association, 1984), 524–529.

35. Rockefeller Report, *Report to the President by the Commission on CIA Activities Within the United States* (Washington, D.C.: U.S. Government Printing Office, 1975).

36. Rockefeller Report, *Report to the President,* 101–115.

37. Jack Anderson and Lee Whitten, "The CIA's 'Sex Squad' " *Washington Post* (June 22, 1976):8–13.

John M. Crewdson and Jo Thomas, "Abuses in Testing of Drugs by CIA to be Panel Focus," *New York Times* (Sept, 20, 1977).

John Jacobs, "The Diaries of a CIA Operative," *Washington Post* (Sept. 5, 1977), 1.

38. *COINTELPRO: The FBI's Secret War on Political Freedom* (New York: Monad Press, 1975).

Chapter 14

1. T. S. Kuhn, *The Structure of Scientific Revolutions* (Chicago: University of Chicago Press, 1974).

2. S. T. Agnew, *The Wisdom of Spiro T. Agnew* (New York: Morrow, 1969), 40.

3. Chambliss and Seidman, *Law, Order and Power. See also* Kitty Calavita, "U.S. Immigration Law and the Control of American Labor," *Contemporary Crises* 5 (1981):341–368.

4. William J. Chambliss, *Crime Rates, Crime Myths and Official Smokescreens* (Stockholm: Institute of Criminology, 1976).

Index

A

Abortion, 94
  abortion laws, 128
  as victimless crime, 52
Abrahamsen, David, 226
ABSCAM, 61–62
Adolescent-subculture theory, 292–296
  basis of, 293
  economic factors in, 293–294
  importance of, 294–295
  school influences, 295
Adoption studies, 182–183
Adult criminality
  drug addiction study, 239
  embezzlement study, 239–240
  murderers, studies on, 241–242
  political corruption study, 240–241
  shoplifting study, 240
Advocacy of illegal acts, as state-organized crime, 80
Age factors, victim-survey findings, 37
Aichhorn, August, 211, 212–218
Akers, Ronald, 243
Akerstrom, Malin, 228
Alloplastic disorders, 211
"Altruism" personality type, 287
Altruistic suicide, 257
American wars of independence, 82
Analytic-induction technique, 239
Andrews, Lowell Lee, 241
Annual victim surveys. *See* Victim surveys
Anomic suicide, 257

Anomie theory
  Durkheim's theory, 257, 269
  Merton's theory, 257–260
    adaptations of person, 258–259
    basis of, 258
    goals/means discrepancy, 258
    limitations of, 259–260
    society, role in, 259
    white-collar crime example, 259
Arms smuggling, 337–340
  Contras, 337–339
  example of process, 338
Arson, 67–68
  death related to, 67
  reason for, 67
  statistical information, 67
Assassinations, 340–344
  CIA, 340–341
    Chilean Secret Service (DINA) in, 341–342
    Drug Enforcement Agency in, 341
    Greenpeace ship sabotage, 343–344
    Libyan government scheme, 343
  as state-organized crime, 78
Atavism, theory of, 172–173, 204–205
Attitude towards crime study, 264
Automobile industry, product safety, 73–74
Autonomic nervous system studies, 183–185, 198–199
  fear response, study of, 184
  introverts/extroverts, study of, 184
Autoplastic disorders, 211
Auxiliary hypothesis, as poor scientific theory, 142

B

Barton Oil Company, 313–314
Beccaria, Cesare, theory of criminology, 153–154, 156
Becker, Howard, 159, 276, 277
Behavioral theories, flaws of, 251–255
Bentham, Jeremy, 154
Berkowitz, Leonard, 223–224
Binet, Alfred, 193
Biochemical-factor studies, 190–192
  nutritional factors, 191
  testosterone levels and crime, 190–191
Biological theories
  adoption studies, 182–183
  autonomic nervous system studies, 183–185, 198–199
  biochemical-factor studies, 190–192
  biology/environment approach, 199–202
  early studies, 173–174
  heredity studies, 178–181
  intelligence studies, 192–193
  PMS studies, 188–190
  race/class bias in, 203–205
  shortcomings of, 231–233
  sociobiology, 197–198
  studies of physical characteristics, 173–178
  twin studies, 181–182
  XYY studies, 185–188
  See also specific theories.
Biology/environment approach, 199–202
  Jeffrey's model, 198–199
    model of behavior, 198
    treatment approaches, 199
  Wilson/Herrnstein model, 199–202
    central thesis of, 200
    delay of gratification concept, 200–201
    flaws of, 199, 202, 204
    introversion in, 201
Black Act, 106–107
Blalock, Hubert, 120
Blau, Judith, 290
Blau, Peter, 290
Body type theories
  Cortes and Gatti, 176, 177
  Glueck and Glueck, 176
  Sheldon, 175–176
Bonger, William, 156

Borgnefesse, 330
Bourgeoisie, 286
Brady, James, 67
Braithwaite, John, 72–73, 116, 290
Bribery, 67–68
  source of information, 67, 68
  U.S. corporations to foreign governments, 66–67
Brownmiller, Susan, 270
Brown vs. Board of Education, 127
Burger, Warren, 28

C

Cameron, Mary Beth, 240
Campaign contributions, as corporate crime, 65, 316–317
Capitalism, 303
  influence on early lawmaking, 105, 107
Capitalist societies
  and adolescent-subculture theory, 292–296
  contradictions in, 302, 303, 304
  crime in, 306–321
    and consumption, desire for, 306–307
    corporate crime, 313–315
    historical illustration, 309–312
    owners/workers participation in crime, 308–309
    phantom capitalists, 312–313
    police corruption, 317–318
    political corruption, 316–318
    street crime, 318–319
    wage-labor supply contradiction and, 309
    women and crime, 319–321
  protection by state, 328
  and rape, 290–291
  social classes, 286
Carrier Case, influence on law of theft, 103
Carson, W. G., 116, 117
Carter, Jimmy, 253–254, 334
Catlin, G., 288
Child-labor market, 75–77
  illegal immigrants, 75, 76
  laws related to, 75
  legal requirements, 75–76
  migratory workers, 76
Children, crimes against, 47–49
  child abuse/neglect, 47–48

Children, crimes against (*cont.*)
  child pornography/prostitution, 48–
    49
Chilean Secret Service (DINA), 341–
    342
China, crime in, 322–323
Christiansen, Karl, 181–182
Chromosomal studies. *See* XYY stud-
    ies
CIA
  assassinations/attempts
    Chilean Secret Service (DINA) in,
      341–342
    Drug Enforcement Agency in, 341
    Greenpeace ship sabotage, 343–
      344
    Libyan government scheme, 343
  criminal slander, 345
  funding for, 334
  Operation Success, 79
  overt intelligence activities, prohi-
    bition of, 344–345
  smuggling, 334–340
    reasons for entering, 335
Cities, crime statistics, 42
Civil law
  compensation to victim, 98
  probability of harm, 97
  rules of evidence, 99
Civil Rights Movement, 85–86
Class bias, and study of crime, 203–
    204
Classical School of Criminology, 154
  Beccaria's theory, 153–154, 156
  Bentham's theory, 154
Cloward, Richard, 260
Cohen, Albert, 256, 266
COINTELPRO, 345
Compensation versus punishment,
    criminal versus civil law, 98
Conein, Lou, 341
Conflict-oriented criminology, 159–161
  contributions of, 160–161
  relationship to new criminology,
    162
Conflict perspective, 157–158
  deviant behavior, 152
  historical basis of, 156–157
  illegal drugs illustration, 166–167
Consensus perspective, 100, 112–113,
    156, 157–158
  crime in Puritan New England, 167–
    168
  deviant behavior, 152

errors related to, 112–113
  definitions of crime/deviance, 112–
    113
  historical basis of, 156
  illegal drugs illustration, 156, 157–
    158
Conspiracy, 344
  definition of, 344
Consumer Product Safety Commis-
    sion, 72
Contradictions. *See* Structural con-
    tradictions
Contras, arms shipment to, 337–339
Control theories, 245
  "bonding" of criminal acts, 245
Corporate crime
  bribery
    source of information, 67, 68
    U.S. corporations to foreign gov-
      ernments, 66–67
  campaign contributions as, 65, 316–
    317
  definition of, 63
  examples of, 63, 64, 65–66
  insider trading, 314–315
  investor's money, spending of, 313–
    314
  laundering money, 315
  money transfers overseas, 315
  versus occupational crime, 65
Corruption, 57–62
  indictments, 58–62
    examples of, 58–60
  investigation of, 58
    federal staff, 58
  sources of information about, 58
  U.S. presidents, scandals related to,
    60–62
  See also Police corruptions; Poli-
    tical corruption; White-collar
    crime.
Cressey, Donald, 239–240
Crime
  data about. *See* Data on crime
  definitional difficulty
    changes over time, 94
    lack of norms, 93–94, 96
  irrational and rational acts and, 204
  political nature of, 203
  types of, 11–25
    drugs, 13–14
    mercy killing, 24–25
    murder, organized, 23–24
    police corruption, 20–21

political corruption, 17–18
political crime, 21–22
professional thieves, 11–12
rebellions/riots, 19–20
state-organized crime, 12–13
status, crimes of, 22–23
white-collar crime, 14–17
varieties of, case examples, 6–10
Crime as Destiny (Lange), 181
Crime and Economic Conditions (Bongers), 285
Crime and Human Nature (Herrnstein and Wilson), 199
Crime and Personality (Eysenck), 184
Crime rate, rise in, 28
Criminal law
  crime, criteria for, 97
  enforcement of, 97
  historical view, 101–112
    Black Act, death penalty, 106–107
    capitalist economy, influence of, 105, 107
    Carrier Case, influence of, 103
    English law (early), 101–102
    feudal England, 102–103, 106
    poaching/trespass, 105–108
    16th through 18th centuries, 103–104
    vagrancy laws, 108–112
  legality, principle of, 98
  mens rea, 97
  punishment of offender, 98
  racism in, 124, 127
  rules of evidence, 99
  sexism in, 124–127
    changes versus equality, 126–127
    rights denied, 124–126
    women's movement and, 127, 128–129
  theories of, 99–100
    analysis of theories, 120–121
    consensus theory (Durkheim's theory), 100, 112–113
    pluralist theory, 120
    ruling-class theory, 115–116
    societal-needs theory, 100–101, 113–115
    structural-contradictions theory, 120–124
    See also specific theories.
Criminal mind, 227–228
  characteristics of, 227
  limitation of theory, 227–228

Criminal slander, 345
Criminological theory
  biological theories, 172–206
    adoption studies, 182–183
    atavism, 172–173
    autonomic nervous systems studies, 183–185, 198–199
    biochemical factor studies, 190–192
    biology/environment approach, 199–202
    early studies, 173–174
    heredity studies, 178–181
    intelligence studies, 192–193
    PMS studies, 188–190
    race/class bias in, 203–205
    shortcomings of, 231–233
    sociobiology, 197–198
    studies of physical characteristics, 173–178
    twin studies, 181–182
    XYY studies, 185–188
  capitalist society, crime in, 306–321
  conflict perspective, 157–158
    illegal drugs illustration, 166–167
  consensus perspective, 156, 157–158
    crime in Puritan New England, 167–168
    illegal drugs illustration, 156, 157–158
  historical view, 152–158
    Beccaria's theory, 153–154, 156
    Bentham's classical theory, 154
    de Sade's theory, 155–156
    Godwin's social theory, 154–155
    religious explanations, 153
  modern developments (1950–1988), 158–165
    conflict-oriented criminology, 159–161
    juvenile delinquency, 159, 161, 165
    Marxist social psychology, application of, 163–165
    new criminology, 160, 161–163
  psychiatric models, 210–228
    criminal mind, 227–228
    frustration-instigated behavior, 222–227
    psychoanalytic perspectives, 210–222
    shortcomings of, 231–233
  socialist society, crime in, 321–325

Criminological theory (*continued*)
  social-psychological theories, 231–
    250
    analytic-induction technique, 239
    control theories, 245
    differential-association theory,
      234–245
    family relations and delin-
      quency, 246–248
    questionnaire studies, 235–239
    situational theory, 249–250
  sociological models, 255–271
    differential social organization,
      268–269
    functional theories, 269–271
    normative theories, 256–260, 269
    opportunity theories, 260–261
    subculture theories, 261–268
  structural contradictions, 300–306
  structural theories, 275–296
    adolescent-subculture theory,
      292–296
    functional-conflict theories, 278–
      279
    inequality and crime, 290–292
    labeling perspective, 276–278
    Marxist criminology, 280–296
    power-conflict theories, 279–280
    roots of, 275
    scientific value of, 300
  See also individual theories.
Criminology
  explanation of, 10
  facts/theories, as basis of, 28
  See also Criminological theory
Cross-cultural studies
  findings of, 54
  limitations of, 53
Cullen, Frances, 51

D

Dahrendorf, Ralf, 278
Dalton, Katharina, 189
Darwin, Charles, 142, 145, 172, 205,
  252
Data on crime, 29–54
  bias in crime statistics, 29–32
    and arrest data, 31–32
    "crimes known to police," 29
    Uniform Crime Reports, problem
      areas, 29–31
  cross-cultural studies, 53–54

    findings of, 54
    limitations of, 53
  self-report surveys, 43–52
    interpretation of data, 44
    shortcomings of, 44–45
    types of crimes surveyed, 44
    victimless crimes, 49–52
    violence against children, 47–49
    violence against women, 46–47
  victim-surveys, 32–43
    age factors, 37
    cities, crime statistics, 42
    distribution of victims, 35–37
    findings of, 33–35
    first surveys, 33
    homicide statistics, 40–42
    racial factors, 37–39
Death penalty, history of law, Black
  Act, 106–107
Degeneration theory, 205
Delinquency
  and delayed gratification, 200–201
  working-class delinquency theory,
    266–268
  See also specific criminological the-
    ories.
DeLorean, John, 15, 96
de Sade, Marquis, 155
Deviant behavior
  conflict perspective, 152
  consensus perspective, 152
  definitional difficulties, 113
  formulating theory of, 51–52
  juvenile delinquency, 159–160, 165
  See also Criminological theory.
Dialectical methodology, new criminology as, 164–165
Differential-association theory, 234–
  245
  and adult criminality, 239–243
    drug addiction study, 239
  associations, variables related to,
    235
  basis of, 224–225
  contradictory findings, 241–242
  embezzlement study, 239–240
  as good-scientific theory, 235
  political corruption study, 240–241
  and reinforcement theory, 243–245
    differential identification theory,
      243
    differential reinforcement the-
      ory, 243–244
    limitations of, 244–245

research tests related to, 244
shoplifting study, 240
testing of, 235–237
  questionnaire studies, 235–239
Differential social organization, 268–269
Donovan, Raymond J., 7
Drake, Sir Francis, 330–331
Drug Enforcement Agency, 341
Drugs, 13–14
  addicts, case examples, 13–14
  drug addiction study, 239
  smuggling, 81
  and society
    conflict perspective, 166–167
    consensus perspective, 156, 157–158
Dugdale, Richard, 179
Durkheim, Emile, 100, 113, 156, 257, 269
Durkheim's theory
  anomie theory, 257, 269
  criminal law, theory of, 100–101, 112–113
  functional theory of crime, 269–270
  See also Consensus theory.

E

Economic conditions
  "altruism" personality type, 287
  anthropological studies and, 288–289
  classes in capitalist society, 286
  "egoism" personality type, 287
  See also Capitalist societies, crime in; Socialist societies, crime in.
Ectomorphs, 176
Ego
  development of, 212
  ego weak children, and delinquency, 218–219
  faulty development, 212–214
"Egoism" personality type, 287
Egoistic suicide, 257
Eisenhower, Dwight, 61
Eissler, Karl, 211
Embezzlement study, 239–240
Empirical validity
  bad theory
    auxiliary hypothesis, 142
    tautology, 142–143
    teleological reasoning, 143

  utility of, interrelatedness of criteria, 139–141
Endomorphs, 176
Engels, Frederick, 156
English law
  capitalist economy, influence of, 105
  Carrier Case, influence of, 103
  early, 101–102
  feudal England, 102–103
  poaching/trespass, 105–108
    Black Act, 106–107
  16th through 18th centuries, 103–104
  vagrancy laws, 108–112
    and end of feudalism, 108–109
    as source of cheap labor, 109
Environmental Protection Agency, 74
Erikson, Kai, 167–168
Eskimo society, 288
Ethics in Government Act, 58
Eugenics
  germ-plasm concept, 178–179
  goal of, 179
  weaknesses of, 180
European nations (15th–19th centuries)
  piracy, 329–332
    Borgnefesse, 330
    crimes related to, 329
    Drake, Sir Francis, 330–331
    Jones, John Paul, 331
    Lafitte, Jean and Pierre, 331
    letters of mark, 329
    as state-organized crime, 332
Extroversion, CNS responses, 184
Eysenck, Hans, 184

F

Fadlallah, Shiek, 340
Falsifiability, and scientific theory, 138
Family relations and delinquency
  Gluecks' research, 246
  influencing actions of family, 247–248
  psychoanalytic view, 213–215, 216
  weaknesses of studies, 246–247, 248
Family studies
  Jukes and *Kallikaks* studies, 179
  weaknesses of, 180
Farmers' rebellions, 82–83
Fatalistic suicide, 257
Fear response, study of, 184

Felix, Kenneth P., 14
Female criminality, PMS studies, 188–190
Ferri, Enrico, 173
Feudal England, criminal law, 102–103, 106
Foreign Corrupt Practices Act (1978), 67
Fraud, types of, 312–313
Freud, Sigmund, 210–211, 212
Freudian theory, 210–211
    See also Psychoanalytic perspective.
Friedlander, Kate, 211
Frustration-instigated behavior, 222–227
    displacement of aggression, 221–222
    ego controls, lack of, 224
    frustration-instigated delinquency, versus non-frustration instigated delinquency, 225–226
    motivated delinquent, 225
    multiple-factor approach, 226–227
    of rejected child, 223–224
    responses to frustration, nonspecificity of, 222–223
Functional-conflict theories, 278–279
    applied to criminology, 279
    basic ideas in, 278–279
    flaws of, 279
Functional theories, 269–271
    classic approach, 270
    Durkheim's theory, 269–270
    of prostitution, 270–271
    rape, 270

G

Gall, Franz Joseph, 172
Galton, Francis, 178, 195
Garofalo, Raffaele, natural crimes, theory of, 173–174, 203
Generality, and scientific theory, 138
Germ-plasm concept, heredity studies, 178–179
Glaser, Daniel, 243
Glueck, Eleanor, 176, 246
Glueck, Sheldon, 176, 246
Goddard, Henry H., 179
Godwin, William, 154–155
Goring, Charles, 173, 192
Gould, Stephen, 194–195
Governmental crime. *See* State-organized crime

Government overthrow, as state-organized crime, 78–79
Gramsci, Antonio, 156, 328
Greenberg, David, 294
Greenpeace ship sabotage, 343–344
Griffin, Susan, 262
Griffith, Charles, 242
Gurney, Edward J., 19

H

Hacker, Andrew, 42
Hall, Jerome, 96, 104–105, 113–114
Hand, Michael, 335–336
Harding, Warren G., 60
Hart, H. L. A., 94
Hate reaction, of delinquent, 214
Hay, Douglas, 105, 107
Heredity studies, 178–181
    adoption studies, 182–183
    eugenics
        germ-plasm concept, 178–179
        goal of, 179
        weaknesses of, 180
    family studies
        Jukes and *Kallikaks* studies, 179
        weaknesses of, 180
    twin studies, 181–182
Herrnstein, Richard, 199–202
Hindelang, Michael J., 196
Hippchen, Leonard, 191
Hirschi, Travis, 196, 236–237, 245
Homeless, arresting of, 22–23
Homicide, statistical information, 40–42
Hooten, Ernest, biological theory of criminology, 174–175
Hormonal factors
    PMS studies, 188–190
    testosterone levels and crime, 190–191
Horney, Julie, 189

I

Id, 212
Immigrants, criminal behavior, views of, 261–262
Incest, 47
Incidence of crime, victim-survey findings, 35–37
Inequality and crime, 290–292
    mode of production and, 292

rape studies, 290
women and crime, 291–292
Infanticide, 47
Insider trading, as corporate crime, 14, 314–315
Intelligence activities, 344–345
covert intelligence, 333
funding for, 334–335
See also CIA.
Intelligence studies, 192–193
early studies, 193
groups studied, 192
low intelligence and criminality, 195–197
delinquency, 196–197
groups studied, 195
Intelligence tests, 193–194
Binet's IQ tests, 193
misconceptions related to, 194–195
inheritability equals inevitability, 194
within versus between group variation, 195
race and, 195
and socioeconomic status, 194
Stanford-Binet test, 193, 196
Introversion, CNS responses, 184, 201

J

Jacobs, Patricia, 186
Jeffrey, C. Ray, 198–199, 203–204, 243
Jensen, Arthur, 195
Jensen, Gary, 236, 245
Johnson, Allan Griswold, 262
Jones, John Paul, 331
Jukes, The (Dugdale), 179
Juvenile delinquency, 159–160, 161, 165
and intelligence, 196–197
and nutrition, 191
research interest in, 159–160, 165
scope of issue, 160
See also Criminological theory and specific theories.

K

Kallikaks, The (Goddard), 179
Kleindienst, Richard G., 65
Klinefelter's Syndrome, 187, 188
Knapp Commission Report, 20–21
Kohl, Helmut, 317

Kolko, Gabriel, 116, 118
Kuhn, T. S., 350

L

Labeling perspective, 276–278
basic propositions, 276–277
Becker's work, 276
Lafitte, Jean and Pierre, 331
Lange, Johannes, 181
Latent delinquency concept, Aichorn's theory, 217–218
Laundering money, 68–69, 315
Law
criminal versus civil law, 97
compensation versus punishment, 98
legality (retroactivity), 98
mens rea, 97
probability versus reasonable doubt, 97–98
rules of evidence, 99
See also Criminal law.
Legality (retroactivity), criminal versus civil law, 98
Letters of Mark, 329
Levi, Michael, 312
Libyan government scheme, 343
Lindesmith, Alfred R., 166, 239
Lombroso, Cesare, 156
atavism, theory of, 172–173, 204–205

M

Maier, Norman, 222, 224–225
Mail, as state-organized crime, 80–81
Male versus female aggression, 185–186, 187–188
See also Women and crime.
Martin, John Bartlow, 159
Marx, Karl, 156
Marxist based criminology, 163–164, 280–290
adolescent-subculture theory, 292–296
basis of, 293
economic factors in, 293–294
importance of, 294–295
school influences, 295
Bonger's theory, 285–290
criminological theorists associated with, 281, 282

Marxist based criminology (*cont.*)
  economic conditions and, 285–290
    "altruism" personality type, 287
    anthropological studies and, 288–
      289
    classes in capitalist society, 286
    "egoism" personality type, 287
  inequality and crime
    mode of production and, 292
    rape studies, 290
    women and crime, 291–292
  and new criminology, 280–281
Marxist theory, 281–285
  basis of, 283–285
  criticism of, 281–282
  dialectic in, 281
Mednick, Sarnoff, 183–184
Mens rea, criminal versus civil law,
  97
Mercy killing, 24–25
  case examples, 24–25
Merton, Robert, 161, 257
Mesomorphs, 176, 177, 178
Messerschmidt, James, 291
Miller, Eleanor, 52, 291–292
Miller, Richard, 242
Miller, Walter, 265
Miller, Warren, 159
Mills, C. Wright, 278
Money laundering, 68–69, 315
  examples of, 68–69, 315
  laws for prevention of, 68
Montague, Ashley, 206
Morgan, Lewis H., 289
Murder, 23–24
  homicide statistics, 40–42
  organized, hit man, 23–24
Murderers, 241–242

N

National Labor Relations Act (1933),
  117–118, 123
Native American rebellions, 82
Natural crimes, theory of, 173–174,
  203
New criminology, 160, 161–164
  basis of, 161–162, 164
  conflict criminology, role in, 162
  criminal behavior, explanation of,
    162–163
  as dialectical methodology, 164–165
New Criminology, The (Taylor, Walton, and Young), 160, 280

Newmen, Graeme, 206
Nixon, Richard M., 18, 60, 65
Norman Conquest, and lawmaking,
  101–102
Normative theories, 256–260, 269
  anomie theory
    Durkheim's theory, 257, 269
    Merton's theory, 257–260
  sociological models
    "facts fitting theories" concept,
      256
    See also specific theories.
  women in, 269
Norms, scope/meaning of, 256–257
North American Indian society, 288–
  289
Nugan, Frank, 335–336
Nutrition, and deviant behavior, 191
Nye, F. Ivan, 247

O

Occupational crime, 63
  definition of, 63
  versus corporate crime, 65
Of Crimes and Punishments (Beccaria), 153
Office of Safety and Health Administration (OSHA), 70
Ohlin, Lloyd, 260
Operation Success, 79
Opportunity theories, 260–261
  society/class role in, 260
Organized crime, 86–89
  definition of, 86
  murder, organized, 23–24
  Organized Crime Control Act
    (1970), 88
  scope of, 87
    measurement criteria, 87–88
    volume of business generated, 88–
      89
    widespread nature of, 88
  types of crimes, 86–87
Organized Crime Control Act (1970),
  88, 115, 120

P

Palmer, Stuart, 242
Paradigms

conflict paradigm, 152
consensus paradigm, 152
Parsimony, and scientific theory, 138, 140
Phantom capitalists, fraud, types of, 312–313
Pharmaceutical industry, product safety, 72–73
Phrenology, 172
Piracy
  Borgnefesse, 330
  crimes related to, 329
  Drake, Sir Francis, 330–331
  Jones, John Paul, 331
  Lafitte, Jean and Pierre, 331
  letters of Mark, 329
  as state-organized crime, 332
Pity, 173
Pleasure principle, versus reality principle, and delinquency, 213–214
Pluralist theory, 120
  limitations of, 120
PMS studies, 188–190
  major studies, 189
  popularity of theory versus empirical evidence, 190
Poaching/trespass
  English law, 105–108
    Black Act, 106–107
Poland, crime in, 324
Police corruption, 20–21, 317–318
  conflicting demands of job and, 317–318
  Knapp Commission Report, 20–21
Political corruption, 17–18, 316–318
  at state/local level, 62
  campaign contributions, 65, 316–317
  indictments, 58–62
  scope of, 316
  study of, 240–241
  U.S. presidents, scandals related to, 60–62
  Watergate, 18–19
  in West German government, 317
Political crime, 21–22, 81–86
  definition of, 81
  goal of, 81
  historical view, 82–86
    American wars of independence, 82
    civil rights movement, 85–86

farmers' rebellions, 82–83
    Native American rebellions, 82
    slave uprisings, 84–85
    student revolts (1960's), 86
    workers' rebellions, 83–84
Popper, Karl, 132
Pornography, child, 48–49
Porterfield, Austin, 43
Power-conflict theories, 279–280
  basics of, 279
  influence of, 280
Presidents of U.S., scandals related to, 60–62
Probability versus reasonable doubt, criminal versus civil law, 97–98
Probity, 173
Product safety, 72–74
  examples of, 72–74
  manufacturing by-products, 72
  statistical information, 72
Professional thieves, 11–12
  case examples, 11, 89–91
  connections with law, the "fix," 11, 90
  hierarchy of profession, 89
  team approach, 90
  types of thievery, 11–12, 89
Prostitution
  child, 48
  functional theory of, 270–271
  as victimless crime, 52
Proletariat, 286
Psychiatric models, 210–228
  criminal mind, 227–228
  frustration-instigated behavior, 222–227
  psychoanalytic perspectives, 210–222
  shortcomings of, 231–233
  See also specific models.
Psychoanalytic perspective, 210–222
  Aichorn's theory, 212–218
    early family experiences in, 213–215, 216
    hate reactions concept, 214
    influence of, 218
    latent delinquency concept, 217–218
    pleasure principle versus reality principle, 213–214
    rehabilitation of delinquents, 216
  alloplastic disorders, 211
  autoplastic disorders, 211

Psychoanalytic perspective (*cont.*)
  criminality versus neuroticism, 211–212
  ego weak children, 218–220
    characteristics of, 218–219
    "unsocialized aggressive" category of delinquency, 220
  Freud's view, criminal behavior, 211
Psychoticism, characteristics of, 202
Puritans, crime study of, 167–168

Q

Questionnaire studies, 235–239
  differential-association theory, testing of, 235–239
  high correlations found, 236
  limitations of, 237–239
Quinney, Richard, 278

R

Racial bias
  in criminal law, 124–127
  and study of crime, 204–205
Racial factors, race and arrest, statistical information, 37–39
Rape
  and capitalism, 290–291
  functional theory of, 270
  myths about, 262
  statistical information, 46
  subcultural theories of, 262–263
Reagan, Ronald, 61, 112, 254
Rebellions/riots, 19–20
  See also Political crime.
Redl, Fritz, 218–220
Rehabilitation of delinquents, Aichorn's theory, 216
Religious explanations, of criminology, 153
Richmond Youth Study, 236, 237
Roe v. Wade, 52, 94, 128
Rules of evidence, criminal versus civil law, 99
Ruling-class theory, 115–116
  limitations of, 117–118, 123
    historical examples, 117–119
  Marx and, 116
  research support for, 116–117
  ruling-class intervention, examples of, 119

Weber and, 116
See also Marxist based criminology.

S

Schrag, Clarence, 276
Schur, Edwin, 49
Schwendinger, Herman, 290, 291, 292–294
Schwendinger, Julia, 290, 291, 292–294
Scientific theory, 131–148
  compared to social sciences, 134–135
  Enlightenment, emergence of, 153, 156, 171
  explanation/description relationship, 144–148
    bias and, 144–145
    correlations, limitations of, 146–147, 148
    importance of, 147
    pure description, 145
  explanation of events in, 136–139
    "commonsense" explanations, 137
    questions to be answered, 137
  misconceptions about, 132
  utility of
    criteria for determining, 133, 138–139
    empirical validity and, 138, 139, 140, 141–142
    falsifiability and, 138
    generality and, 138
    implications for change and, 138–139
    parsimony and, 138, 140
Self-report studies. *See* Questionnaire studies
Self-report surveys
  interpretation of data, 44
  shortcomings of, 44–45
  types of crimes surveyed, 44
  victimless crimes, 49–52
  violence against children, 47–49
  violence against women, 46–47
Sellin, Thorsten, 160
Sexism
  changes versus equality, 126–127
  rights denied, 124–126
  women as property of men, 127, 319–320

Sheldon, William
  body type theory, 175–176
    ectomorphs, 176
    endomorphs, 176
    mesomorphs, 176, 177, 178
Shockley, William, 195
Shoplifting study, 240
Short, James F., Jr., 236
Situational theory, and delinquency, 249–250
Slaves, freedom of
  slave uprisings, 84–85
  and vagrancy laws, 110
Smuggling
  arms smuggling, 337–340
    arms shipment to Contras, 337–339
    example of process, 338
  CIA, 334–340
    Nugan-Hand Bank, 335–336
    reasons for entering, 335
  during Vietnam War, 332–333, 335
  factors for success, 333
  relationship to intelligence work, 333
  as state-organized crime, 81
  as tax evasion, 69
Social classes
  attitude towards crime study, 264
  capitalist society
    bourgeoisie, 286
    lower proletariat, 286
    petty bourgeoisie, 286
    proletariat, 286
Social complex, 135
Socialism, 303
Socialist societies
  contradictions in, 303, 304–306
  crime in, 321–324
    China, 322–323
    closed nature of, 321
    Poland, 324
    protection by state, 328
    Soviet Union, 323–324
    statistical deficiencies, 322
    structural contradictions in, 322, 323, 334
Social-psychological theories
  analytic-induction technique, 239
  control theories, 245
  differential-association theory, 234–245
  family relations and delinquency, 246–248

questionnaire studies, 235–239
  situational theory, 249–250
  See also specific theories.
Social sciences
  characteristics of, 134–135
  compared to scientific theory, 134–135
"Social Structure and Anomie," (Merton), 257
Social theory
  of criminology, 156
    de Sade's theory, 155–156
    Godwin's theory, 154–155
Societal-needs theory, 100–101, 113–115
  and early history of law, 114
  legal change, order of, 113–114
  organized crime example, 115
  society in, 114
Sociobiology, 197–198
Sociobiology (Wilson), 197
Sociological models
  attitude towards crime study, 264
  differential social organization, 268–269
  functional theories, 269–271
  normative theories, 256–260, 269
  opportunity theories, 260–261
  subculture theories, 261–268
Sodomy, 94, 96
  definition of, 51
  and states, differences in law, 51, 94, 96
Soviet Union, crime in, 323–324
Speck, Richard, 186
Spencer, Herbert, 156
Stanford-Binet test, 193, 196
Stans, Maurice, 18, 60
State-organized crime, 12–13, 78–81, 327–348
  advocacy of illegal acts, 80
  assassination, 78, 340–344
  case examples, 12
  conspiracy, 344
  criminal slander, 345
  definition of, 78
  government overthrow, 78–79
  intelligence activities, 344–345
  mail, interception of, 80–81
  piracy
    Borgnefesse, 330
    crimes related to, 329
    Drake, Sir Francis, 330–331
    Jones, John Paul, 331

State-organized crime (*continued*)
  Lafitte, Jean and Pierre, 331
  letters of Mark, 329
  as state-organized crime, 332
  smuggling, 81, 332–340
    arms smuggling, 337–340
  statistical information, lack of, 78
  See also specific crimes.
Statistics on crime. *See* Data on crime
Status, 22–23
Stellin, Thorsten, 279–280
Street crime, 318–319
  and capitalism, 318
  motivations related to, 318
Structural contradictions, 300–306
  of capitalist societies, 302, 303, 304
    public production-private owner-
      ship contradiction, 302, 309
    wage labor and, 307–308
    wages-labor supply contradic-
      tion, 309
  conflicts
    basis of, 301
    and organization of a society, 301
  contradiction, creation of, 300
  and criminal behavior, 301
  people as less than human, 302–303
  of socialist societies, 303, 304–306
    crime and, 322, 323, 324
  theory of, 120–124
    basics of, 121
    issues related to, 128–129
    structural-contradictions, types of,
      122
  See also Capitalist societies, crime
    in.
Structural theories
  adolescent-subculture theory, 292–
    296
  functional-conflict theories, 278–279
  inequality and crime, 290–292
  labeling perspective, 276–278
  Marxist criminology, 280–296
  power-conflict theories, 279–280
  roots of, 275
  scientific value of, 300
  See also specific theories.
Student revolts (1960's), 86
Subcultural theories, 261–268
  delinquency, 266–268
    working-class delinquency the-
      ory, 266–268
  failure of, 264–265
  rape, theories of, 262–263

violence, study of, 263–264
Suicide
  Durkheim's theory, 257
  types of, 257
Superego, faulty development, 212–
  214
Sutherland, Edwin H., 64, 161, 203,
  234, 276, 351

T

Tannebaum, Frank, 160
Tautology, as poor scientific theory,
  142–143
Tax evasion, 69
  smuggling as, 69
  undervaluation of corporate prop-
    erty, 69
Teapot Dome Scandal, 60
Teleological reasoning, as poor sci-
  entific theory, 143
Terman, Lewis, 193
Theft in history of law
  Carrier Case, 103
  societal-needs theory, 114
Thompson, E. P., 105, 106, 252
Tort law. *See* Civil law
Toxic waste
  illegal dumping, 62, 74–75
    statistical information, 74
Turk, Austin, 278, 279
Turner, Admiral, 334–335
Twin studies, 181–182
  findings, major similarities, 182
  first study, 181

U

Uniform Crime Reports
  problem areas, 29–31, 34
    crime categories, 29–30
    crime clock gimmick, 31
    data deficiencies, 31–32
    political influences, 30
United Fruit Company, 79

V

Vagrancy laws
  English law, 108–112
    and end of feudalism, 108–109

as source of cheap labor, 109
in United States, 109–112
   and ex-slaves, 110
   vagueness of, 111–112
Varieties of Delinquent Youth (Sheldon), 175
Victimless crime
   abortion issue, 52
   and concept of deviant behavior, 51–52
   prostitution, 52
   statistical information, measurement difficulty, 50–51
   types of, 49
Victim surveys
   age factors, 37
   cities, 42
   distribution of victims, 35–37
   findings of, 33–35
   first surveys, 33
   homicide statistics, 40–42
   racial factors, 37–39
Violence
   definitional difficulties, 112–113
   government related, 265
   subculture of violence theory, 263–264
Violence (Newmen), 206
Vold, George, 278, 279

W

Wagner Act (1933), 117–118, 123
Washington, George, 60
Watergate, 60
Wayward Puritans (Erikson), 167–168
Wayward Youth (Aichhorn), 213
Weber, Max, 156, 279, 283
White-collar crime, 14–17, 62–78
   arson, 67–68
      death related to, 67
      reason for, 67
      statistical information, 67
   bribery, 67–68
      source of information, 67, 68
      U.S. corporations to foreign governments, 66–67
   case examples, 14–17
   child-labor market, 75–77
      illegal immigrants, 75, 76
      laws related to, 75
      legal requirements, 75–76
      migratory workers, 76

corporate crime
   campaign contributions, relationship to, 65
   definition of, 63
   examples of, 63, 64, 65–66
   as normal corporate decision-making, 72
   versus occupational crime, 65
   legal scope of, 62–63
   losses/costs related to, 77–78
   money laundering, 68–69
      examples of, 68–69
      laws for prevention of, 68
   occupational crime, 63
      definition of, 63
   product safety, 72–74
      automobile industry, 73–74
      examples of, 72–74
      pharmaceutical industry, 72–73
      statistical information, 72
   research studies
      first study, 64
      scope of corporate crime, 64–65
   tax evasion, 69
      smuggling as, 69
      undervaluation of corporate property, 69
   toxic wastes, 74–75
      statistical information, 74
   work place hazards, 69–71
      documentation problems, 71
      examples of, 70–71
      manufacturing by-products, 72
      OSHA and law enforcement, 70
      statistical information, 69–70, 71
Wickensham Commission, 29
Williams, Roy, 14
Wilson, E. O., 197
Wilson, James Q., 199–202
Winans, R. F., 14
Wineman, David, 218–220
Women
   crimes against
      common factors, 46
      incest, 47
      statistical information, 46–47
   and normative theories, 269
   as property, 127, 319–320
   theory of crime and, 269
Women and crime
   bias in theories of criminality, 233–234
   capitalism and, 290–291
   crime for freedom, 320

Women and crime (*continued*)
  lower-class women, 291–292, 320–321
  perpetrator/victim, dual role, 319
  property/white-collar crime, 321
  studies, deficiencies of, 321
  women as property position, 127, 319–320
Women's movement, 127, 128–129
  influence on law, 128–129
  abortion laws, 128
Workers' rebellions, 83–84
  ruling-class theory, contradiction to, 117
Working-class delinquency theory, 266–268
Work place hazards, 69–71
  documentation problems, 71
  examples of, 70–71
  OSHA and law enforcement, 70
  statistical information, 69–70, 71

X

XYY studies, 185–188
  groups studied, 185
  impact of, 187
  major studies, 186
  male versus female aggression, 185–186, 187–188
  other variables for consideration, 188
  traits of XYY men, 187